U.S. ARMY PSYOP

BOOK 3
EXECUTING PSYCHOLOGICAL OPERATIONS

TACTICAL PSYCHOLOGICAL OPERATIONS TACTICS, TECHNIQUES AND PROCEDURES

FULL-SIZE 8.5"X11" EDITION

FM 3-05.302
(MCRP 3-40.6B)

Headquarters, Department of the Army

U.S. Army PSYOP Book 3 - Executing Psychological Operations

Tactical Psychological Operations Tactics, Techniques and Procedures - Full-Size 8.5"x11" Edition - FM 3-05.302 (MCRP 3-40.6B)

U.S. Army

This edition first published 2019 by Carlile Military Library. "Carlile Military Library" and its associated logos and devices are trademarks. Carlile Military Library is an imprint of Carlile Media. The appearance of U.S. Department of Defense (DoD) visual information does not imply or constitute DoD endorsement.

New material copyright © 2019 Carlile Media. **All rights reserved.**

Published in the United States of America.

ISBN-13: 978-1-949117-10-3
ISBN-10: 1949117103

WWW.CARLILE.MEDIA

PUBLISHER'S NOTE

This is book 3 of 3 in the C.M.L. U.S. Army PSYOP series (ISBN: 978-1-949117-10-3, FM 3-05.302) which is written for an audience of PSYOP personnel, providing guidance on executing effective PSYOP activities at the tactical level.

• PSYOP Book 1: Psychological Operations Handbook (ISBN: 978-1-949117-08-0, FM 3-05.30) covers the fundamentals of military psychological operations in support of the national interest and is the Army's keystone publication for PSYOP principles and activities. It is written not exclusively for PSYOP personnel but for a wide military audience in order to provide a general understanding of and appreciation for PSYOP potential and value.

• PSYOP Book 2: Implementing Psychological Operations - Psychological Operations Tactics, Techniques and Procedures (ISBN: 978-1-949117-09-7, FM 3-05.301) builds on the previous publication to provide PSYOP commanders and planners with the information required to implement PSYOP activities at the operational level.

FM 3-05.302
MCRP 3-40.6B

Field Manual
No. 3-05.302

Headquarters
Department of the Army
Washington, DC, 28 October 2005

Tactical Psychological Operations Tactics, Techniques, and Procedures

Contents

		Page
	PREFACE	vi
Chapter 1	INTRODUCTION TO TACTICAL PSYCHOLOGICAL OPERATIONS	1-1
	PSYOP Core Tasks and Roles	1-1
	PSYOP in Full-Spectrum Operations	1-2
	Elements of Combat Power	1-2
	Battlespace	1-3
	Battlefield Organization	1-3
	Command Authority	1-3
	PSYOP Approval Authority	1-4
	Themes and PSYOP Objectives	1-4
	PSYOP at the Tactical Level	1-4
	Summary	1-4
Chapter 2	CAPABILITIES AND ORGANIZATION	2-1
	Tactical Psychological Operations Battalion	2-1
	Tactical Psychological Operations Company	2-2
	Tactical Psychological Operations Development Detachment	2-3
	Tactical Psychological Operations Detachment	2-4
	Tactical Psychological Operations Team	2-6
	Summary	2-8

Marine Corps distribution: PCN 14400015800

Contents

Chapter 3	COMMAND RELATIONSHIPS	3-1
	Joint Force Command	3-1
	PSYOP Coordination	3-4
	Supported Unit Command Relationships	3-6
	Summary	3-6
Chapter 4	MISSION PLANNING	4-1
	Military Operations and Mission Planning	4-1
	Military Decision-Making Process	4-2
	Decision Making in a Time-Constrained Environment	4-8
	Troop-Leading Procedures and the Military Decision-Making Process	4-12
	Summary	4-20
Chapter 5	EMPLOYMENT	5-1
	Tactical Psychological Operations Battalion	5-1
	Headquarters Support Company	5-2
	Tactical Psychological Operations Company	5-3
	PSYOP Support Element	5-4
	Tactical Psychological Operations Detachment	5-8
	Tactical Psychological Operations Team	5-9
	Summary	5-10
Chapter 6	SEVEN-PHASE PSYOP PROCESS	6-1
	Planning (Phase I)	6-1
	Target Audience Analysis (Phase II)	6-4
	Series Development (Phase III)	6-11
	Product Development and Design (Phase IV)	6-18
	Approval (Phase V)	6-33
	Production, Distribution, and Dissemination (Phase VI)	6-37
	Evaluation (Phase VII)	6-43
	Summary	6-47
Chapter 7	TACTICAL PSYCHOLOGICAL OPERATIONS TEAM OPERATIONS	7-1
	Introduction	7-1
	Integration With Supported Unit	7-1
	Employment	7-4
	Loudspeaker Operations	7-7
	Printed Product Dissemination	7-11
	Face-to-Face Communication	7-13
	Pretesting and Posttesting	7-18
	Civil Disturbance	7-19
	Summary	7-21
Chapter 8	INTELLIGENCE SUPPORT	8-1
	Intelligence Preparation of the Battlefield	8-1
	Information Management Categories	8-3
	Integrating Into Supported Unit's Intelligence Process	8-4
	Determining Where to Send Requests for Information	8-4
	Tactical PSYOP Considerations During IPB METT–TC	8-4
	Gathering PSYOP-Relevant Information	8-6
	Evaluation Methods	8-7

	PSYOP Situation Reports	8-8
	Summary	8-8
Chapter 9	**SUPPORT AND SUSTAINMENT**	**9-1**
	Maintenance Categories and Responsibilities	9-1
	Garrison Maintenance Requirements	9-1
	Deployment Maintenance Requirements	9-2
	Special Maintenance Considerations	9-4
	Recovery	9-4
	Summary	9-6
Appendix A	**COORDINATION AND LIAISON**	**A-1**
Appendix B	**ASSESSMENTS**	**B-1**
Appendix C	**SUPPORT TO INTERNMENT/RESETTLEMENT OPERATIONS**	**C-1**
Appendix D	**PROPAGANDA ASSESSMENT**	**D-1**
Appendix E	**SAMPLE PSYOP APPENDIX**	**E-1**
Appendix F	**CAPABILITIES BRIEF**	**F-1**
Appendix G	**TACTICAL PSYOP REPORT AND REQUEST FORMATS**	**G-1**
Appendix H	**LEAFLET OPERATIONS**	**H-1**
Appendix I	**TACTICAL PSYCHOLOGICAL OPERATIONS TEAM BATTLEFIELD SURVIVAL TECHNIQUES**	**I-1**
Appendix J	**USE OF INTERPRETERS**	**J-1**
Appendix K	**RULES OF ENGAGEMENT**	**K-1**
	GLOSSARY	Glossary-1
	REFERENCES	References-1
	INDEX	Index-1

Figures

Figure 1-1. Full-spectrum operations	1-2
Figure 1-2. Battlespace components	1-3
Figure 2-1. Tactical Psychological Operations battalion	2-2
Figure 2-2. Tactical Psychological Operations company	2-3
Figure 2-3. Tactical Psychological Operations development detachment	2-4
Figure 2-4. TPD meeting with local sheikh in Iraq	2-5
Figure 2-5. Tactical Psychological Operations detachment	2-6
Figure 3-1. JPOTF in joint force organization	3-4
Figure 3-2. JPOTF and the PSYOP coordination chain	3-5
Figure 4-1. Seven steps of military decision-making process	4-3
Figure 4-2. Timesaving techniques and procedures	4-8
Figure 4-3. Parallel sequence of the MDMP and TLP	4-12
Figure 5-1. TPC task organization	5-3

Contents

Figure 5-2. Deployable Print Production Center 5-4
Figure 5-3. PSYOP process 5-5
Figure 5-4. On-camera interview 5-7
Figure 6-1. Example of PO and SPO linkage 6-2
Figure 6-2. Example format of an initial PSYOP plan 6-3
Figure 6-3. Example format of PSYOP plan with MOEs determined 6-4
Figure 6-4. Example TAAW 6-8
Figure 6-5. PSYOP SCW example 6-12
Figure 6-6. PSYOP SDW example 6-15
Figure 6-7. Example PSYOP SEM 6-19
Figure 6-8. Example of a PAW for a handbill 6-21
Figure 6-9. Example of a PAW for face-to-face communication 6-22
Figure 6-10. PSYOP soldiers conducting a survey at a university in Iraq 6-24
Figure 6-11. FFEO format 6-27
Figure 6-12. Example FFEO 6-28
Figure 6-13. Example pretest questionnaire 6-30
Figure 6-14. Example posttest questionnaire 6-31
Figure 6-15. Conducting an internal product review board 6-32
Figure 6-16. Example of a change to the appendix 6-34
Figure 6-17 Example of a PSYOP transmission matrix 6-35
Figure 6-18 Example of a series executive summary 6-36
Figure 6-19. Tab C (PAW Index) to Change 1 to Appendix 2 (PSYOP) 6-36
Figure 6-20. Phase VI of the PSYOP process 6-37
Figure 6-21. Members of the Iraqi National Guard assisting in a pretest 6-39
Figure 6-22. Example for evaluating PSYOP 6-45
Figure 6-23. Series evaluation grid example 6-46
Figure 7-1. TPT assisting supported unit during cordon and search in Iraq 7-2
Figure 7-2. TPTs conducting loudspeaker operations in Iraq 7-8
Figure 7-3. Environmental conditions 7-9
Figure 7-4. TPT member disseminating handbills in Iraq 7-12
Figure 7-5. Rewards for justice matchbooks 7-12
Figure 7-6. TPT conducting face-to-face communication with Iraqi locals 7-14
Figure 7-7. PSYOP Soldier interfacing with members of a target audience 7-15
Figure 9-1. POMR plan 9-6
Figure A-1. Sample outline of a liaison officer handbook A-4
Figure A-2. Liaison checklist, before departing the sending unit A-6
Figure A-3. Liaison duties during the liaison tour A-7
Figure B-1. PSYOP geographic assessment (deliberate) B-1
Figure B-2. Rapid local assessment format sample B-8
Figure B-3. Sample media assessment format B-10
Figure C-1. Example of task organization to meet mission requirements C-2
Figure C-2. TPD organization supporting internment/resettlement C-2

Figure C-3. Typical I/R facility layout C-3
Figure D-1. Example of electronic media propaganda D-1
Figure D-2. Example of propaganda inconsistencies D-3
Figure D-3. Example of questionable propaganda audience D-4
Figure D-4. Example of television propaganda D-5
Figure D-5. Sample SCAME format D-6
Figure E-1. Sample PSYOP appendix E-1
Figure G-1. Sample SITREP format G-1
Figure G-2. MEDEVAC request G-2
Figure H-1. Oblong pattern of leaflets on the ground H-2
Figure H-2. Example of leaflet calculation work sheet H-3
Figure H-3. Path of the leaflet cloud H-7
Figure H-4. Pattern in which 90 percent of the leaflets will land H-8
Figure H-5. Static-line box employment H-10
Figure H-6. Steps in the assembly of the static-line box H-10
Figure I-1. Fuel estimation formula I-2
Figure I-2. Water estimation formula I-2

Tables

Table 3-1. Joint command relationships and inherent responsibilities 3-1
Table 3-2. Joint support categories 3-2
Table 3-3. Army command and support relationships and inherent responsibilities 3-3
Table 6-1. Source documents for the PAW 6-20
Table 9-1. Classes of supply 9-2
Table H-1. Standard leaflet rates of descent and spread factor H-4
Table H-2. Standard leaflets per pound H-5
Table H-3. Autorotating leaflet descent time factors H-5
Table H-4. Non-autorotating leaflet descent time factors H-6
Table H-5. Example of leaflet drifts H-6
Table H-6. Example of major axis determination H-7
Table H-7. Example of minor axis determination H-8
Table I-1. Movement techniques and characteristics I-4

Preface

Field Manual (FM) 3-05.302 presents tactics, techniques, and procedures for implementing United States (U.S.) Army tactical Psychological Operations (PSYOP) doctrine in FM 3-05.30, *Psychological Operations*. FM 3-05.302, along with FM 3-05.301, *Psychological Operations Tactics, Techniques, and Procedures*, provides general guidance for commanders, planners, and PSYOP personnel who must plan and conduct effective PSYOP across the full spectrum of operations. This manual, along with FM 3-05.301, provides guidance for tactical PSYOP personnel to accomplish a broad range of missions successfully, using the latest organizational structure, terminology, and capabilities.

FM 3-05.302 is a guide, not a regulation. As such, the tactics, techniques, and procedures it presents should not limit creativity or imagination, provided that they adhere to Army doctrine, U.S. national policy, and the commander's intent. The targeted user of this manual is primarily the tactical PSYOP community. Written to give standardized PSYOP doctrine to PSYOP officers, noncommissioned officers (NCOs), enlisted Soldiers, and civilians, FM 3-05.302 is a comprehensive how-to manual, focusing on critical tactical PSYOP tasks, duties, and responsibilities.

This manual describes procedures and provides templates for conducting tactical PSYOP missions in a systematic, chronological fashion. Its organization generally follows the PSYOP development process, from planning through execution.

This manual contains numerous acronyms, abbreviations, and terms. Users should refer to the Glossary at the back of this manual for their meanings or definitions.

The proponent of this manual is the United States Army Training and Doctrine Command (TRADOC).

Submit comments and recommended changes to Commander, USAJFKSWCS, ATTN: AOJK-DTD-PO, Fort Bragg, NC 28310-5000.

Unless stated otherwise, the term *Psychological Operations task force* (POTF) is used in lieu of combined Psychological Operations task force (CPOTF), combined joint Psychological Operations task force (CJPOTF), or joint Psychological Operations task force (JPOTF).

Unless this publication states otherwise, masculine nouns and pronouns do not refer exclusively to men.

This manual does not implement any international standardization agreements (STANAGs).

Chapter 1

Introduction to Tactical Psychological Operations

The mission of PSYOP is the same mission at all operational levels—to influence the behavior of foreign target audiences (TAs) to support U.S. national objectives. Tactical PSYOP forces provide supported commanders a nonlethal fires capability to change the behavior of a local populace or adversary force in any environment. PSYOP support encompasses the planning, analysis, development, design, approval, production, distribution, dissemination, and evaluation of PSYOP series across the operational spectrum.

At the tactical level, PSYOP forces are the supported commander's most effective capability for communicating with foreign TAs. Whether providing information during foreign humanitarian assistance (FHA) operations or broadcasting surrender instructions while supporting combat operations, tactical PSYOP forces provide a powerful capability to the supported commander.

PSYOP CORE TASKS AND ROLES

1-1. To accomplish the PSYOP mission, PSYOP Soldiers perform six core tasks:

- *Develop.* Development involves the selection of Psychological Operations objectives (POs) and supporting Psychological Operations objectives (SPOs), measures of effectiveness (MOEs), target audience analysis (TAA), series development, individual product development, and approval. The analysis of propaganda and the development of counterpropaganda begin during development but are embedded throughout the other core tasks.
- *Design.* Design is the technical aspect of taking what was conceptualized in the development stage and creating an audio, visual, or audiovisual prototype. This task demands technical expertise in many communication fields.
- *Produce.* Production is the transformation of approved PSYOP product prototypes into various media forms that are compatible with the way foreign populations are accustomed to receiving information. Some production requirements may be contracted to private industry, while other requirements may be performed by units attached or under the tactical control (TACON) or operational control (OPCON) of PSYOP forces.
- *Distribute.* Distribution is the movement of completed products from the production source to the point of dissemination. This task may include the temporary physical or electronic storage of PSYOP products at intermediate locations. The task can be complicated by classification requirements, as products are often classified before dissemination.
- *Disseminate.* Dissemination involves the delivery of PSYOP products directly to the desired TA. PSYOP forces must leverage as many different media and dissemination means as possible to ensure access to the targeted foreign population.
- *Evaluate.* Evaluation is the most resource intensive of all PSYOP tasks. This task requires PSYOP Soldiers to integrate into the intelligence and targeting process. Evaluation includes analysis of MOEs, impact indicators, surveys, interviews, pretesting, and posttesting to determine the degree to which PSYOP objectives are achieved.

Chapter 1

1-2. PSYOP Soldiers also perform the following five roles (not to be confused with capabilities, described in Chapter 2) to meet the intent of the supported commander:
- Advise the commander.
- Influence foreign populations.
- Provide public information.
- Serve as the supported commander's voice to foreign TAs.
- Counter enemy propaganda, misinformation, disinformation, and opposing information.

1-3. Tactical Psychological Operations detachments (TPDs) and tactical Psychological Operations teams (TPTs) focus primarily on Phases VI and VII of the PSYOP process (described in Chapter 6) using the capability to conduct face-to-face communication. The tactical Psychological Operations development detachment (TPDD) has the ability to conduct Phases I through V of the PSYOP process and a limited ability to conduct Phase VI.

PSYOP IN FULL-SPECTRUM OPERATIONS

1-4. Doctrine addresses the range of Army operations across the spectrum of conflict. Commanders at all echelons may combine different types of operations simultaneously and sequentially to accomplish missions in war and military operations other than war (MOOTW). For each mission, commanders determine the emphasis forces place on each type of operation (offense, defense, stability and reconstruction, and civil support) (Figure 1-1). Likewise, PSYOP are conducted throughout the range of full-spectrum operations and are key to achieving U.S. objectives. PSYOP are inherently joint and frequently combined operations that include conventional forces and special operations forces (SOF).

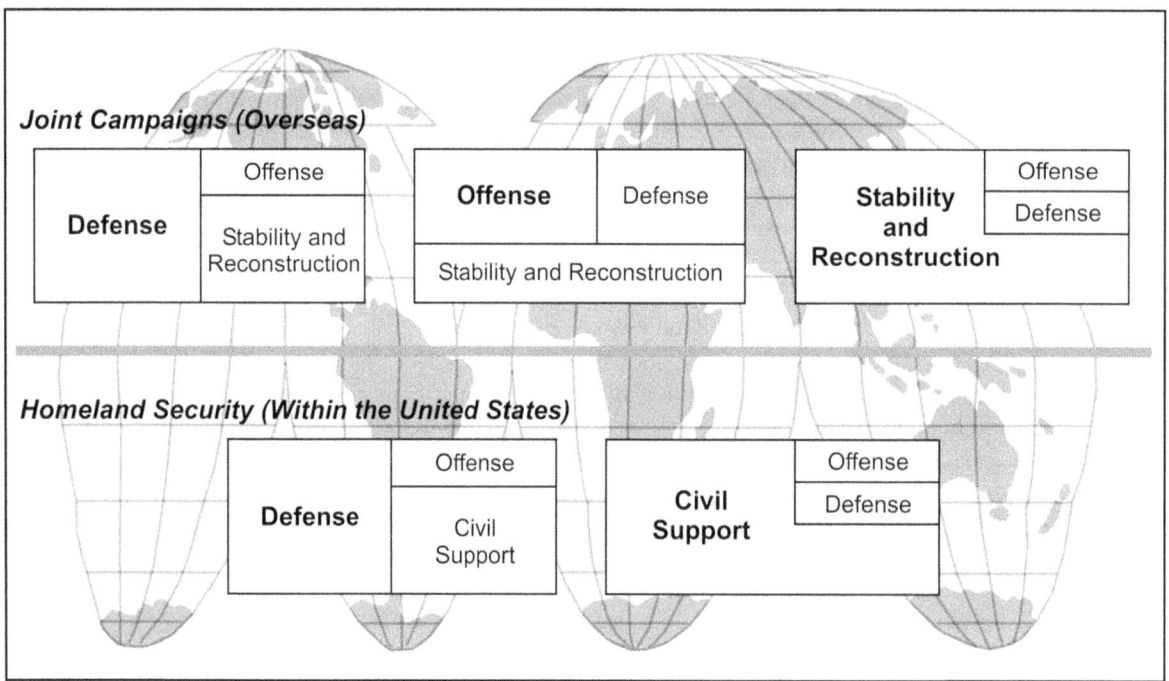

Figure 1-1. Full-spectrum operations

ELEMENTS OF COMBAT POWER

1-5. The elements of combat power are building blocks that underlie the generation of combat power. In land operations, commanders combine and apply the elements of combat power—maneuver, firepower, leadership, protection, and information—to meet constantly changing requirements, to produce overwhelming effects, and to defeat the enemy. Of the five elements of combat power, PSYOP are considered both an element of information and an element of firepower. By definition, PSYOP fall under the element of information because they are normally within the context of offensive information operations (IO); however, PSYOP are also considered an element of firepower because they are a means of nonlethal fires.

BATTLESPACE

1-6. To envision the part of the information environment within their battlespace, commanders determine the information activities that affect their operation and the capabilities of their own and opposing command and control (C2) and information systems. They must understand conceptually how the area of interest (AOI) and area of influence lie within the information environment (Figure 1-2). Operationally, PSYOP take place within the information environment.

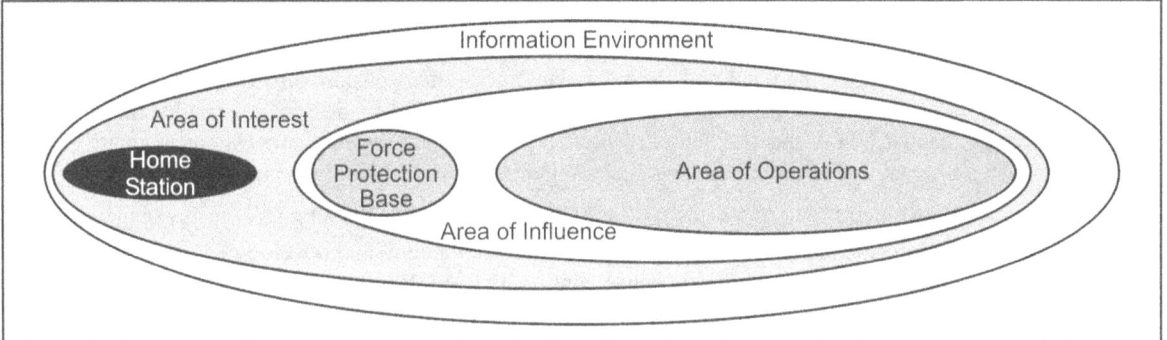

Figure 1-2. Battlespace components

BATTLEFIELD ORGANIZATION

1-7. The battlefield organization is the allocation of forces in the area of operations (AO) by purpose. It consists of three all-encompassing categories of operations—decisive, shaping, and sustaining. Purpose unifies all elements of the battlefield organization by providing the common focus for all actions.

1-8. PSYOP are primarily shaping operations. Shaping operations at any echelon create and preserve conditions for the success of the decisive operation. They include lethal and nonlethal activities conducted throughout the AO. Shaping operations support the decisive operation by affecting enemy capabilities and forces or by influencing enemy decisions.

1-9. Within the battlefield organization of decisive, shaping, and sustaining operations, commanders designate and shift the main effort. Thus, PSYOP, as a shaping operation, may be a unit's main effort before the execution of the decisive operation.

COMMAND AUTHORITY

1-10. Tactical PSYOP forces normally support a maneuver commander in an attached relationship. While the centralized planning of PSYOP objectives and the subsequent decentralized execution require constant coordination (Appendix A) along all levels of the tactical PSYOP chain, command authority of PSYOP forces rests with the supported commander. He exercises authority through his Deputy/Assistant Chief of Staff for Operations and Plans (G-3) or his operations staff officer (S-3).

1-11. Tactical PSYOP forces should be attached as early as possible to facilitate planning. While attachment implies combat service support (CSS) is provided by the gaining unit, PSYOP-unique equipment (such as tactical loudspeakers and other specialized equipment) requires continued support from PSYOP support channels present in-theater, normally by the POTF or the special operations theater support element (SOTSE).

Chapter 1

PSYOP APPROVAL AUTHORITY

1-12. The Secretary of Defense (SecDef) normally delegates PSYOP approval authority to the supported geographic combatant commander (GCC) in the Joint Chiefs of Staff (JCS) execution order and in accordance with (IAW) the Joint Strategic Capabilities Plan (JSCP). The GCC retains PSYOP approval authority following the approval of the PSYOP plan from the President or the SecDef. During a crisis, the supported GCC may, in turn, subdelegate PSYOP approval authority to the designated commander, joint task force (CJTF) or subdelegate down to the division level with SecDef approval.

THEMES AND PSYOP OBJECTIVES

1-13. The key to centralized planning and decentralized execution of PSYOP is clarity in the statement of broad themes and measurable PSYOP objectives. Broad themes that originate at policy-maker level set the parameters that PSYOP must operate within. Measurable PSYOP objectives ensure that PSYOP series are behavior-focused and reflect national and theater policy and strategy. Approval of PSYOP objectives and broad themes is reserved by policies and the JSCP at levels (President or SecDef, combatant command, joint force commander [JFC], and U.S. Country Teams) where the interagency process can evaluate PSYOP plans against a broad range of considerations, including other national level information programs.

1-14. For maximum flexibility in the execution of PSYOP below GCC or CJTF level, PSYOP approval can and should be subdelegated to the lowest level where PSYOP planning and development capability provide support. Policy guidance does not preclude subdelegation of PSYOP approval below CJTF level; however, PSYOP oversight—as described in Chairman of the Joint Chiefs of Staff Instruction (CJCSI) 3110.05C, *Joint Psychological Operations Supplement to the Joint Strategic Capabilities Plan FY 2002*—requires that the SecDef approve the subdelegation of PSYOP approval below the GCC or the CJTF. An example of how to request PSYOP approval is included in FM 3-05.301.

PSYOP AT THE TACTICAL LEVEL

1-15. Commanders subordinate to CJTFs can use and modify approved series, within the guidelines issued by the higher headquarters (HQ), to achieve their specific objectives. The parameters for tactical PSYOP forces in developing, designing, producing, and disseminating are articulated in the PSYOP support plan. Typically, tactical units can use any series approved at the combatant command level. They can also develop, design, and produce series on specific areas, such as force protection or civilian noninterference, without the series being approved at joint task force (JTF) level; however, the series must be approved in the initial plan signed by the SecDef. Tactical PSYOP forces can develop series outside the specific parameters, but the series must go through the same approval process used for POTF-level series.

SUMMARY

1-16. Tactical PSYOP provide nonlethal fire support at the lowest level where Army units are typically engaged throughout full-spectrum operations. Tactical PSYOP have the ability to interact with foreign audiences at the point where behavior is most effectively changed and evaluated.

Chapter 2
Capabilities and Organization

Tactical PSYOP units organize, plan, and execute operations in support of SOF and conventional forces. They conduct PSYOP to change the behavior of foreign TAs in support of the PSYOP and supported commander's objectives. This chapter describes the formal organization of the tactical Psychological Operations battalion (tactical POB) and its organic elements and assets. It also focuses on the capabilities of the tactical POB and its current tables of organization and equipment (TOEs).

TACTICAL PSYCHOLOGICAL OPERATIONS BATTALION

2-1. The tactical POB conducts operational- and tactical-level PSYOP at corps and below and can support an Army-level or equivalent Marine forces HQ. During stability and reconstruction operations (S&RO), the tactical POB may support a division-level or equivalent unit. It also supports select special operations (SO) or conventional task forces at Army-level equivalent-sized units. Rarely does an entire tactical battalion deploy, and, in most cases, its components are attached to other units. When the tactical POB deploys in support of a maneuver unit, it is normally task-organized with assets from a Psychological Operations dissemination battalion (PDB). At the battalion level, the tactical POB is generally augmented with a theater support team from the dissemination battalion's signal company, which provides electronic product distribution and C2 support. In addition, the team may be equipped to establish a local area network (LAN) for internal communications within the tactical POB HQ.

2-2. The tactical POB conducts PSYOP in support of tactical and internment/resettlement (I/R) missions. It provides command, staff, and planning support to SOF and conventional forces and collects PSYOP-relevant information, including testing and evaluation data, for a POTF.

CAPABILITIES

2-3. Capabilities of the tactical POB include the following:
- Command and control assigned and attached elements.
- Augment the supported unit PSYOP staff element.
- Establish, when directed, a POTF with regional and dissemination PSYOP asset augmentation.
- Plan, coordinate, and execute PSYOP at the operational and tactical levels.
- Provide PSYOP staff and planning support to the military police I/R command or brigade operations at GCC, JFC, and corps levels.
- Execute PSYOP programs as directed by a POTF.
- Conduct PSYOP assessments (Appendix B).
- Provide support to I/R operations (Appendix C).

ORGANIZATION

2-4. The tactical POB (Figure 2-1, page 2-2) consists of three tactical Psychological Operations companies (TPCs) and a headquarters and support company (HSC). The tactical POB HSC provides functions and capabilities similar to other HSCs. It focuses on support to staff and supporting elements within the company.

Chapter 2

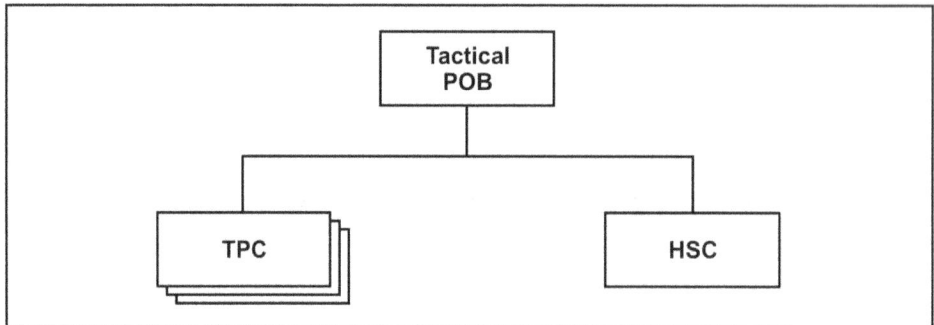

Figure 2-1. Tactical Psychological Operations battalion

TACTICAL PSYCHOLOGICAL OPERATIONS COMPANY

2-5. The TPC is the central element of PSYOP support to ground commanders. During high intensity conflict (HIC), the TPC normally provides PSYOP support at division level and below. During S&RO, the TPC may support a brigade-level or equivalent unit. Supported units include Active Army and Reserve Component (RC) units, as well as Marine, SOF, and air security units. Support elements are tailored to provide PSYOP staff planning and tactical PSYOP support. The TPC has limited organic product development, design, and production capability.

2-6. The TPC is normally task-organized with assets from the print, broadcast, and support companies of the dissemination battalion. Each TPC may be task-organized with a Deployable Print Production Center (DPPC) from the print company of the dissemination battalion. This tactical vehicle-mounted, light print asset provides the forward-deployed TPC with a responsive and mobile digital print capability. The TPC is then able to produce a limited number of products—such as leaflets, handbills, posters, and other printed material—within the guidance assigned by the PSYOP plan. Normally, the support company provides communications teams to augment the TPDs and the TPDD of the TPC. This support may include a Flyaway Broadcast System (FABS) or a Special Operations Media System–Broadcast (SOMS–B) to provide the TPC a direct support (DS) broadcast asset (when the TPC supports a division-level or equivalent maneuver unit). The TPC provides staff planning, conducts the PSYOP process, and coordinates with the next-higher PSYOP element for additional PSYOP support.

CAPABILITIES

2-7. Capabilities of the TPC include the following:
- Provide PSYOP staff support to division or brigade HQ.
- Conduct the PSYOP process (described in Chapter 6).
- Coordinate additional PSYOP support requirements with next-higher PSYOP element.
- Conduct supporting Psychological Operations programs (SPPs).
- Collect, evaluate, and report PSYOP-relevant information obtained from TPDs and TPTs.
- Provide support to I/R operations.

ORGANIZATION

2-8. The TPC (Figure 2-2, page 2-3) consists of a company HQ section, three TPDs, and a TPDD. The company HQ section has a commander; commander's driver and clerk; first sergeant; supply sergeant; and nuclear, biological, and chemical (NBC) specialist.

Capabilities and Organization

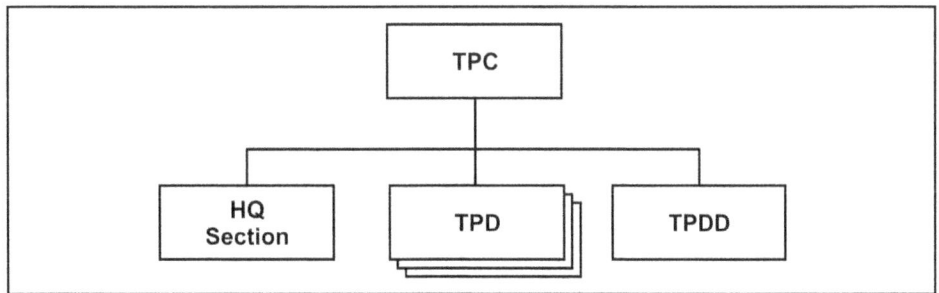

Figure 2-2. Tactical Psychological Operations company

TACTICAL PSYCHOLOGICAL OPERATIONS DEVELOPMENT DETACHMENT

2-9. The TPDD is normally collocated with the TPC and provides the supported commander with responsive PSYOP support. Each TPC has one TPDD that coordinates closely with the supported unit's staff to conduct the PSYOP process.

2-10. The TPDD provides PSYOP staff planning, creates and produces series for SPPs, and manages the execution of SPPs. The TPDD synchronizes and coordinates PSYOP by subordinate or attached elements. The TPDD also provides PSYOP support to the TPDs in support of I/R operations.

CAPABILITIES

2-11. Capabilities of the TPDD include the following:
- Conduct the PSYOP process.
- Provide support to I/R operations.
- Collect, evaluate, and report PSYOP-relevant information obtained from TPDs and TPTs.
- Create and produce series for SPPs and manage the execution of SPPs.
- Coordinate additional PSYOP support requirements with next-higher PSYOP element.

ORGANIZATION

2-12. The TPDD (Figure 2-3, page 2-4) is a 13-man detachment. The TPDD consists of three teams—the plans and programs team (PPT), the target audience analysis team (TAAT), and the Psychological Operations development team (PDT).

Plans and Programs Team

2-13. The PPT is the center for action in the TPDD. It consists of two officers, an operations NCO, a team leader, and an assistant team leader. The PPT conducts Phase I of the PSYOP process (Planning, described in Chapter 6), PSYOP assessments, and the military decision-making process (MDMP). PPT members manage the PSYOP process, manage all SPPs, and maintain contact with the POTF or the Psychological Operations support element (PSE).

Target Audience Analysis Team

2-14. The TAAT executes Phase II of the PSYOP process (TAA, described in Chapter 6). The members also maintain TA files while monitoring intelligence reports to detect any shifts in attitudes, behavior trends, or conditions of all TAs within their area of interest. The TAAT also analyzes propaganda and conducts a comprehensive analysis of the source, content, audience, media, and effects (SCAME) reports (Appendix D) initially conducted by TPT members. The TAAT also looks for propaganda, such as television (TV), Internet, radio, or regional news agencies. The TAAT, in concert with Psychological Operations development center (PDC) assets, then assesses each individual SCAME to determine the opponent propaganda plan. The TAAT manages Phase VII (Evaluation) of the PSYOP process (described in Chapter 6). The TAAT is usually the section that conducts aerial loudspeaker missions.

Chapter 2

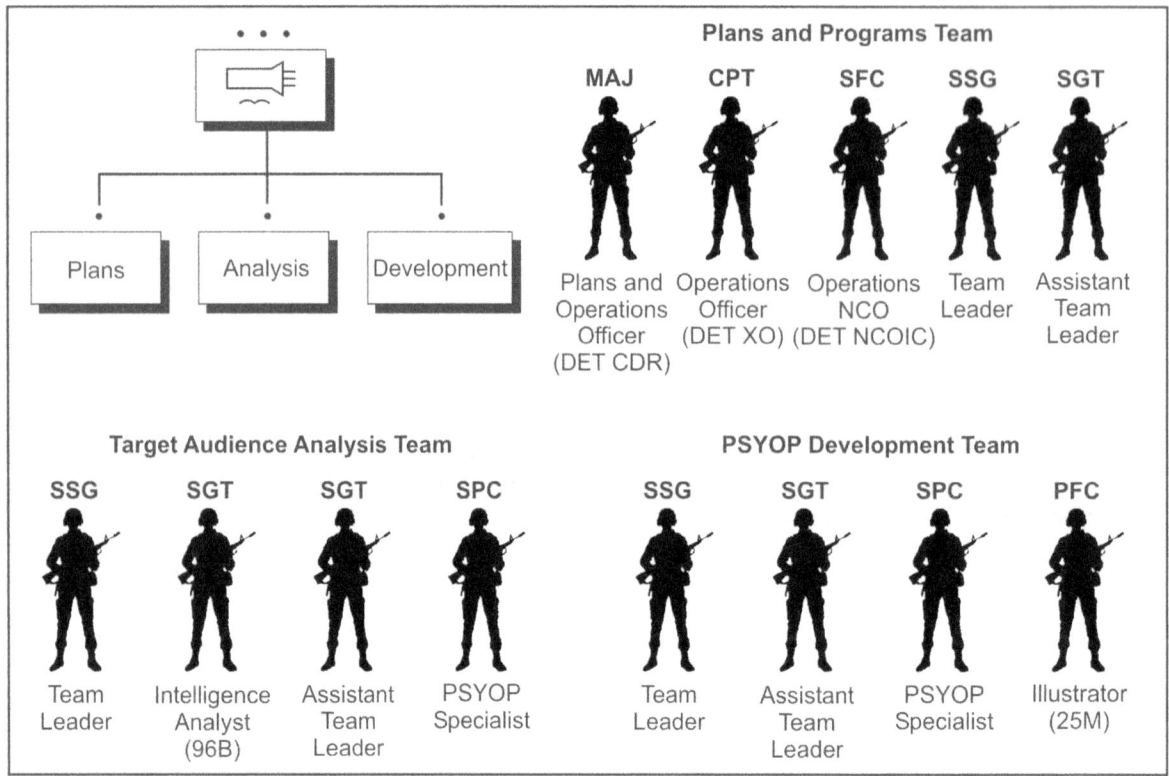

Figure 2-3. Tactical Psychological Operations development detachment

Psychological Operations Development Team

2-15. The PDT conducts Phase IV (Product Development and Design) and the production portion of Phase VI (Production, Distribution, and Dissemination, described in Chapter 6). The PDT has the TPDD's only illustration and graphics capability with the Product Development Workstation (PDW). The PDW enables the PDT to design text and graphic visual products for a series. The PDT also has limited audio design and production capabilities. The PDT may coordinate production through external assets (POTF or indigenous resources). They also manage picture archives and series archives, maintain series books, and manage translation.

TACTICAL PSYCHOLOGICAL OPERATIONS DETACHMENT

2-16. The TPD normally provides PSYOP support to a brigade-sized element or equivalent, such as a Marine expeditionary brigade (MEB), a Special Forces (SF) battalion, a Ranger regiment, a special mission unit, an armored cavalry regiment, a Stryker Brigade, or a separate infantry regiment or brigade. During S&RO, the TPD may support a battalion or equivalent-level unit. The TPD analyzes the next-higher-level unit operation order (OPORD) and the associated PSYOP appendix or tab—Appendix 2 (PSYOP) to Annex P (Information Operations) for Army OPORDs and operation plans (OPLANs), and Tab D (PSYOP) to Appendix 3 (Information Operations) to Annex C (Operations) for Joint OPORDs and OPLANs—to determine specified and implied PSYOP tasks. These tasks are subsequently incorporated into the supported unit's PSYOP plan. They also focus specifically on how they will support the scheme of maneuver (Figure 2-4, page 2-5). Therefore, the TPD commander normally recommends to the operations officer that he retain his organic TPTs under TPD control or allocate them to subordinate units.

Capabilities and Organization

Figure 2-4. TPD meeting with local sheikh in Iraq

2-17. The TPD exercises staff supervision over TPTs allocated to subordinate supported units, monitoring their status and providing assistance in PSYOP planning as needed. Unlike the TPC, however, the TPD does not have any PSYOP product development capability. The focus of TPD planning is on the execution of series to support the maneuver commander. Should the TPD identify a requirement for a series, it would request its development through the TPDD.

CAPABILITIES

2-18. Capabilities of the TPD include the following:
- Provide PSYOP staff support to brigade (battalion in S&RO).
- Execute PSYOP series.
- Provide support to I/R operations.
- Test and evaluate the effectiveness of PSYOP products and Psychological Operations actions (PSYACTs).

ORGANIZATION

2-19. The TPD (Figure 2-5, page 2-6) is a 13-man detachment commanded by a captain with a staff sergeant (sergeant first class in RC units and in future Active Army units) as the noncommissioned officer in charge (NCOIC). The TPD is composed of a four-man detachment HQ and three TPTs consisting of three men each.

EQUIPMENT

2-20. TPD equipment includes—
- 1 x M1114.
- 1 x 1/4-ton trailer.
- 1 x family of loudspeakers (FOL).
- 1 x man-portable loudspeaker (MPLS).
- 2 x AN/PRC 148 Multiband Intra-Team Radio (MBITR).
- 1 x VRC 91.

Chapter 2

- 1 x ISU 90.
- 1 x laptop computer.
- 1 x 3-kilowatt generator.
- 1 x AN/PRC 150.
- 1 x OE 254.

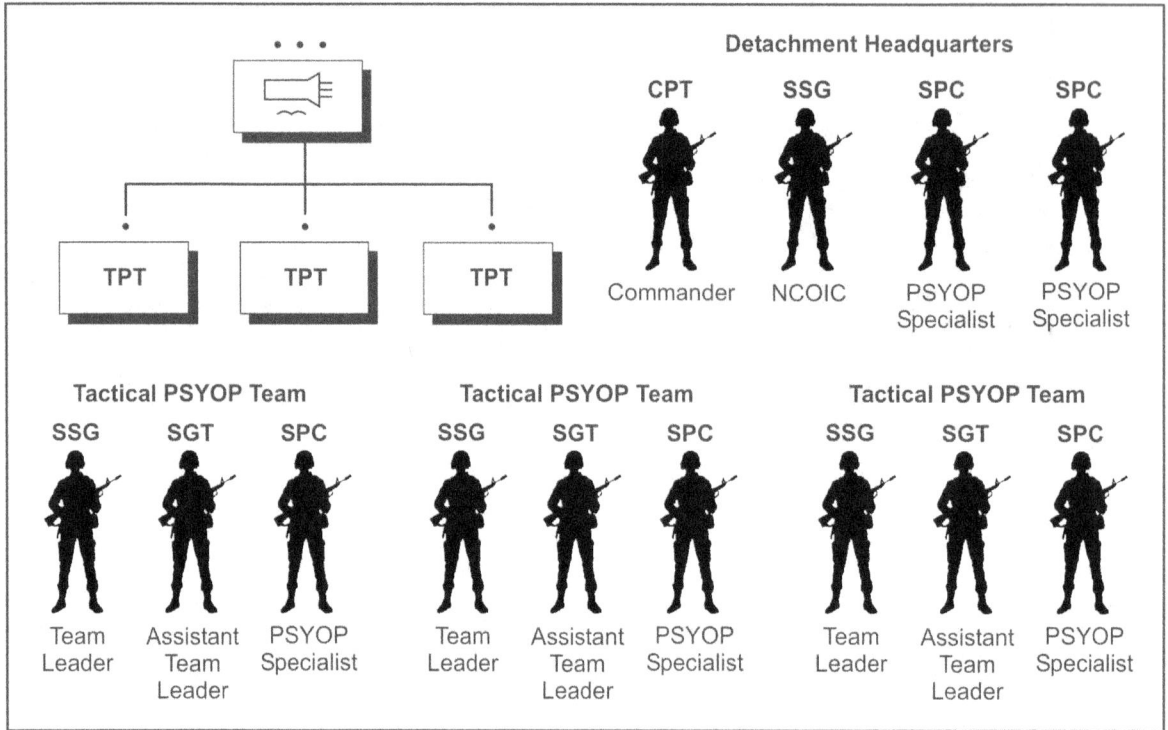

Figure 2-5. Tactical Psychological Operations detachment

TACTICAL PSYCHOLOGICAL OPERATIONS TEAM

2-21. The TPT normally provides PSYOP support at battalion level and below. During S&RO, the TPT may support a company-level or equivalent unit. It can work for the TPDD, the TPD, and a supported unit commander. When attached to a supported unit, the TPT chief acts as the PSYOP staff advisor to the supported commander. The TPT is in many ways the most crucial link to the entire PSYOP process. It is typically in continuous contact with the TA and thus can immediately assess the impact of PSYOP on the TA. The feedback the TPT gives to the TPD and maneuver commander often determines the overall success of PSYOP in any given area of responsibility (AOR), especially in stability operations where PSYOP have a major role.

2-22. The TPT provides staff planning and PSYOP support for operations conducted by the supported unit. It coordinates with the TPD for developing PSYOP series to meet the supported commander's requirements. The TPT is the primary executor of the PSYOP series developed and produced by the TPDD, PSE, or POTF.

CAPABILITIES

2-23. Capabilities of the TPT include the following:
- Provide PSYOP staff support.
- Conduct tactical PSYOP.
- Execute PSYOP series, which can include audio, visual, and audiovisual products.
- Coordinate for the conduct of PSYACTs in support of PSYOP series.

- Coordinate PSYOP support requirements with the TPD.
- Collect and report PSYOP-relevant information obtained.
- Provide support to I/R operations.

ORGANIZATION

2-24. The TPT is organized under the TPD (Figure 2-5, page 2-6). It is a three-man team commanded by a staff sergeant.

EQUIPMENT

2-25. TPT equipment includes—
- 1 x M1114.
- 1 x 1/4-ton trailer.
- 1 x FOL.
- 1 x MPLS.
- 2 x AN/PRC 148 MBITR.
- 1 x VRC 91.
- 1 x ENG kit.
- 1 x laptop computer.
- 1 x AN/PRC 150.
- 1 x Phraselator.
- 1 x OE 254.

INDIVIDUAL FORCE PROTECTION EQUIPMENT

2-26. Individual force protection equipment may include—
- Body armor, standard load-bearing equipment (LBE), and Kevlar helmet.
- AN/PVS 7/14 night-vision device.
- M4/M203/M249/9mm weapons.
- PEQ 2 infrared laser.
- ACOG M68 site.

Note. Other equipment varies, based upon modified table of organization and equipment (MTOE) and Table of Distribution and Allowance (TDA) special authorizations. TPTs currently have no product development or production capability.

FAMILY OF LOUDSPEAKERS

2-27. The FOL consists of several different systems—an MPLS, a vehicle-mounted system, a watercraft-mounted system, and a rotary-wing aircraft-mounted system. In remote broadcast, the FOL can be linked to the single-channel ground and airborne radio system (SINCGARS) radio. Persons at remote locations can broadcast forward to the location of the loudspeaker. The MPLS has a remote radio headset, which allows operators standing within 25 feet of the MPLS to broadcast through the speaker. The MPLS speaker cone can be placed on a 25- or 50-foot remote cable, forward of the operator. When recording sound effects or messages, the FOL can operate off a compact disc (CD) or tape player. PSYOP Soldiers can record sounds in the field and make recordings of voice or sound effects for use on the spot.

2-28. The FOL require contractor support for maintenance and repair. Supported commanders of the units to which the TPTs are attached must understand loudspeaker capabilities, security, and integration. One of the principal tasks of the TPT leader is to acquaint supported leaders with the variety of missions loudspeakers can support.

Chapter 2

Vehicle-Mounted Loudspeaker System

2-29. The mobility of vehicle-mounted loudspeakers enables the TPT to move rapidly to wherever a TA may be found. Though presenting a vulnerable target, this method permits greater mobility. General data for mounted operations are as follows:

- Maximum range: 1,800 meters.
- Effective range and limitations: Broadcasts are limited by terrain, vegetation, high winds, and other noises on the battlefield. TPTs should use radio communications with other Soldiers and units to determine if the volume used is sufficient during broadcast.
- Weight of speaker and low-frequency modules (LFMs):
  - Two-man-lift speaker: 46 pounds.
  - LFM: 123 pounds.
  - Amplifier: 30 pounds.
  - Amplifier base: 18 pounds.
- Power source: Vehicle power.

Manpack Loudspeaker System

2-30. Loudspeakers are an extension of face-to-face communication. Ordinarily denied or restricted areas become accessible when the speakers are hand-carried within hearing range of the TA. General data for dismounted operations are as follows:

- Maximum range: 700 to 1,000 meters.
- Effective range and limitations: Broadcasts are limited by terrain, vegetation, high winds, and other noises on the battlefield. TPTs should use radio communications with other Soldiers and units to determine if the volume used is sufficient during broadcast.
- Weight: 55 pounds.
- Power source: Three BA-5590 batteries.

Aerial Loudspeaker System

2-31. Airborne loudspeaker-equipped rotary-wing aircraft are especially useful because they broaden the areas of loudspeaker accessibility and increase mobility. Important information about the aerial loudspeaker system (ALS) is as follows:

- Maximum range: 2,500 meters (varies, based on the altitude of flight and climatic conditions).
- Power source: Helicopter-powered.
- Other: Requires airworthiness release memorandum.

Note. The ALS is a legacy system that is limited in its employment to only low-threat or permissive environment. Aircraft must operate low enough (depending on terrain features, weather, and, especially, wind velocity) to make the announcer's message audible to the intended TA; however, low altitude puts both the personnel and the aircraft within the range of small-arms fire.

SUMMARY

2-32. The tactical POB conducts operational- and tactical-level PSYOP at corps level and below, and can support an Army-level or equivalent Marine force HQ. The tactical POB staff and elements of the companies conduct planning and operations at the operational and tactical level for the Army, corps, or division. Rarely does an entire tactical battalion deploy, and, in most cases, its components are attached to other units. The TPC is the central element of PSYOP support to maneuver commanders.

Chapter 3
Command Relationships

Army forces at the theater level and operating outside the continental United States (OCONUS) are assigned under a JFC, as discussed in Joint Publication (JP) 0-2, *Unified Action Armed Forces (UNAAF)*; JP 3-0, *Doctrine for Joint Operations*; and FM 100-7, *Decisive Force: The Army in Theater Operations*. A JFC is a combatant commander, a subunified commander, or a JTF commander authorized to exercise combatant command (COCOM) or OPCON over a joint force. Combatant commanders provide strategic direction and operational focus to forces by developing strategy, planning theater campaigns, organizing the theater, and establishing command relationships.

JOINT FORCE COMMAND

3-1. JFCs plan, conduct, and support campaigns in the theater of war, subordinate theater campaigns, major operations, and battles. The four joint command relationships are COCOM, OPCON, TACON, and support. Table 3-1 shows the inherent responsibilities associated with COCOM, OPCON, and TACON. Table 3-2, page 3-2, shows the four categories of support and the definitions for each category.

Table 3-1. Joint command relationships and inherent responsibilities

Inherent Responsibilities Are:	If Relationship Is:		
	COCOM	OPCON	TACON
Has command relationship with:	Gaining combatant commander; gaining Service component commander	Gaining command	Gaining command
May be task-organized by:	Gaining combatant commander; gaining Service component commander	Gaining command	Parent unit
Receives logistics support from:	Gaining Service component commander	Service component command; parent unit	Parent unit
Assigned position or AO by:	Gaining component commander	Gaining command	Gaining command
Provides liaison to:	As required by gaining component commander	As required by gaining command	As required by gaining command
Establishes and maintains communications with:	As required by gaining component commander	As required by gaining command	As required by gaining command and parent units
Has priorities established by:	Gaining component commander	Gaining command	Gaining command
Gaining unit can impose further command relationship/authority of:	OPCON; TACON; direct support; mutual support; general support; close support	OPCON; TACON; direct support; mutual support; general support; close support	Direct support; mutual support; general support; close support

Chapter 3

Table 3-2. Joint support categories

Category	Definition
General Support	The action given to the supported force as a whole, rather than to a particular subdivision thereof.
Mutual Support	The action units render each other against an enemy because of their assigned tasks, their position relative to each other and to the enemy, and their inherent capabilities.
Direct Support	A mission requiring a force to support another specific force and authorizing it to answer directly to the supported force's request for assistance.
Close Support	The action of the supporting force against targets or objectives that are sufficiently near the supported force as to require detailed integration or coordination of the supporting action with fire, movement, or other actions of the supported force.

COMBATANT COMMAND (COMMAND AUTHORITY)

3-2. COCOM is a nontransferable command authority exercised only by combatant commanders unless the SecDef directs otherwise. Combatant commanders exercise COCOM over assigned forces. COCOM provides full authority to organize and employ commands and forces to accomplish missions. Combatant commanders exercise COCOM through subordinate commands—including subunified commands, Service component commands, functional component commands, and JTFs.

OPERATIONAL CONTROL

3-3. OPCON is inherent in COCOM. It is the authority to perform the functions of command that involve organizing and employing commands and forces, assigning tasks, designating objectives, and giving authoritative direction necessary to accomplish the mission. OPCON may be exercised at any echelon at or below the level of the COCOM. It can be delegated or transferred. Army commanders use it routinely to task-organize forces. The SecDef must approve transferring OPCON of units between combatant commanders. OPCON does not in-and-of-itself include authoritative direction for logistics or matters of administration, discipline, internal organization, or unit training.

TACTICAL CONTROL

3-4. TACON is authority normally limited to the detailed and specified local direction of movement and maneuver of forces to accomplish a task. It allows commanders below COCOM level to apply force and to direct the tactical use of CSS assets, but it does not provide authority to change organizational structure or to direct administrative or logistics support. The commander of the parent unit continues to exercise those responsibilities unless otherwise specified in the establishing directive. Combatant commanders use TACON to delegate limited authority to direct the tactical use of combat forces. TACON is often the command relationship established between forces of different nations in a multinational force. It may be appropriate when tactical-level Army units are placed under another Service HQ. The COCOM may exercise TACON or delegate it to any level of his subordinate command.

SUPPORT

3-5. Joint doctrine establishes support as a command authority. Commanders establish it between subordinate commanders when one organization must aid, protect, or sustain another. Under joint doctrine, there are four categories of support (Table 3-2). General support (GS) and DS describe the supporting command's focus. Mutual support and close support are forms of activity based on proximity and combat actions. Army doctrine establishes four support relationships: direct, reinforcing, general, and general support reinforcing.

3-6. These relationships are important to tactical PSYOP forces, as they describe command relationships after deploying OCONUS on official deployment instructions. Normally, United States Special Operations Command (USSOCOM) directs deployment of tactical PSYOP forces that fall under the COCOM of a GCC. The GCC further gives OPCON of the unit to a subordinate joint force command or Service component command—such as the Army Service component command (ASCC). The PSYOP unit is then further assigned or attached to its gaining unit as apportioned in the original deployment order (DEPORD), OPLAN, OPORD, or fragmentary order (FRAGO).

3-7. The command relationships are also important because they describe who has responsibilities for logistical support for the deployed tactical PSYOP unit and whether the gaining unit has the authority to task-organize that unit. This understanding is critical because tactical PSYOP forces are normally attached to a maneuver force (Table 3-3). While attached, tactical PSYOP forces receive logistical support from the supported unit. Logistical support for PSYOP-specific equipment, such as loudspeaker replacement parts, is provided through the PSYOP coordination chain.

Table 3-3. Army command and support relationships and inherent responsibilities

	IF RELATIONSHIP IS:	Has Command Relationship With:	May Be Task-Organized By:	Receives CSS From:	Assigned Position or AO By:	Provides Liaison To:	Establishes/ Maintains Communications With:	Has Priorities Established By:	Gaining Unit Can Impose Further Command or Support Relationship Of:
COMMAND	Attached	Gaining unit	Gaining unit	Gaining unit	Gaining unit	As required by gaining unit	Unit to which attached	Gaining unit	Attached; OPCON; TACON; GS; GSR; R; DS
	OPCON	Gaining unit	Parent unit and gaining unit; may pass OPCON to lower HQ NOTE 1	Parent unit	Gaining unit	As required by gaining unit	As required by gaining unit and parent unit	Gaining unit	OPCON; TACON; GS; GSR; R; DS
	TACON	Gaining unit	Parent unit	Parent unit	Gaining unit	As required by gaining unit	As required by gaining unit and parent unit	Gaining unit	GS; GSR; R; DS
	Assigned	Parent unit	Parent unit	Parent unit	Gaining unit	As required by parent unit	As required by parent unit	Parent unit	Not applicable
SUPPORT	Direct Support (DS)	Parent unit	Parent unit	Parent unit	Supported unit	Supported unit	Parent unit; supported unit	Supported unit	NOTE 2
	Reinforcing (R)	Parent unit	Parent unit	Parent unit	Reinforced unit	Reinforced unit	Parent unit; reinforced unit	Reinforced unit; then parent unit	Not applicable
	General Support Reinforcing (GSR)	Parent unit	Parent unit	Parent unit	Parent unit	Reinforced unit and as required by parent unit	Reinforced unit and as required by parent unit	Parent unit; then reinforced unit	Not applicable
	General Support (GS)	Parent unit	Parent unit	Parent unit	Parent unit	As required by parent unit	As required by parent unit	Parent unit	Not applicable

NOTE 1: In North Atlantic Treaty Organization (NATO), the gaining unit may not task-organize a multinational unit (see TACON).
NOTE 2: Commanders of units in DS may further assign support relationships between their subordinate units and elements of the supported unit after coordination with the supported commander.
SPECIAL NOTE: Coordinating Authority—A commander or individual assigned responsibility for coordinating specific functions or activities involving forces of two or more military departments, two or more joint force components, or two or more forces of the same Service. The commander or individual has the authority to require consultation between the agencies involved, but does not have the authority to compel agreement. In the event that essential agreement cannot be obtained, the matter shall be referred to the appointing authority. Coordinating authority is a consultation relationship, not an authority through which command may be exercised. Coordinating authority is more applicable to planning and similar activities than to operations.

Chapter 3

PSYOP COORDINATION

3-8. PSYOP forces are habitually attached; therefore, coordinating authority between PSYOP elements is critical to synchronize and coordinate the PSYOP effort throughout all echelons. In the absence of coordination, contradictory PSYOP may occur, potentially compromising the effectiveness of the information operations effort. The following paragraphs describe coordinating authority and how coordinating chains complement chains of command.

COORDINATING AUTHORITY

3-9. Coordinating authority is the authority to coordinate specific functions and activities involving two or more forces. The establishing directive specifies the common task to be coordinated without disturbing other organizational relationships of the forces. The commander or individual exercising coordinating authority can require consultation between the agencies involved but cannot compel agreement. Coordinating authority applies more to planning than to operations.

3-10. Tactical PSYOP forces are normally attached to maneuver units of a JTF or component command of a geographic combatant command (Figure 3-1). The POTF, however, usually retains coordinating authority over these tactical units as described either in the OPLAN, OPORD, or FRAGO or in the establishing directive sending tactical units to maneuver HQ. Maintaining coordinating authority of tactical PSYOP forces allows the POTF to direct and coordinate theater-level PSYOP programs and activities and to delineate approval authority for series execution. In this way, the POTF plan becomes coordinated and synchronized.

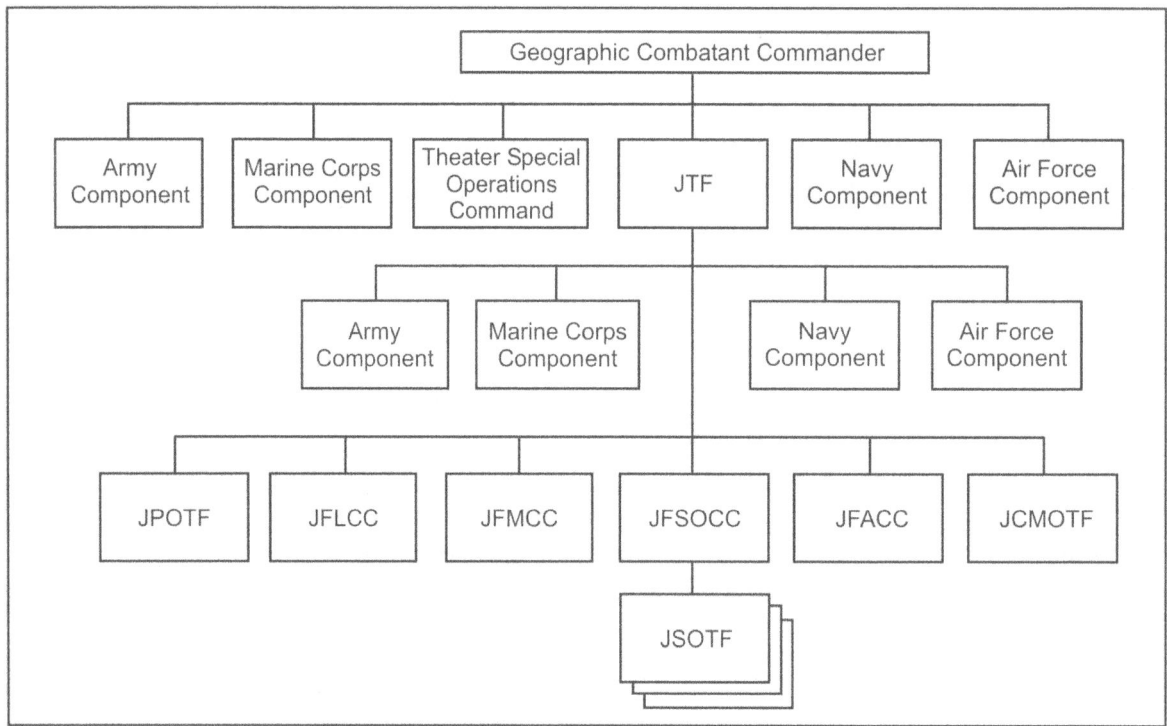

Figure 3-1. JPOTF in joint force organization

COORDINATION CHAIN

3-11. Using the example in Figure 3-1, the JPOTF is a component command of a JTF established by a GCC. Normally, tactical PSYOP forces are attached directly from the GCC to the JTF or the ASCC commander, who further attaches the tactical PSYOP unit to a functional component like the joint force land component commander (JFLCC) or the joint special operations task force (JSOTF). The solid lines represent direct chain of command. Typically, no command authority exists between the deployed tactical

Command Relationships

PSYOP forces and the POTF. However, the coordination chain exists as it appears in Figure 3-2. The adjacent operational commanders, such as the JFLCC or JSOTF, have attached tactical PSYOP forces that retain this coordination authority with the POTF. The Army- or corps-level PSEs must conduct this type of routine, direct coordination with the POTF to conduct effective, synchronized PSYOP.

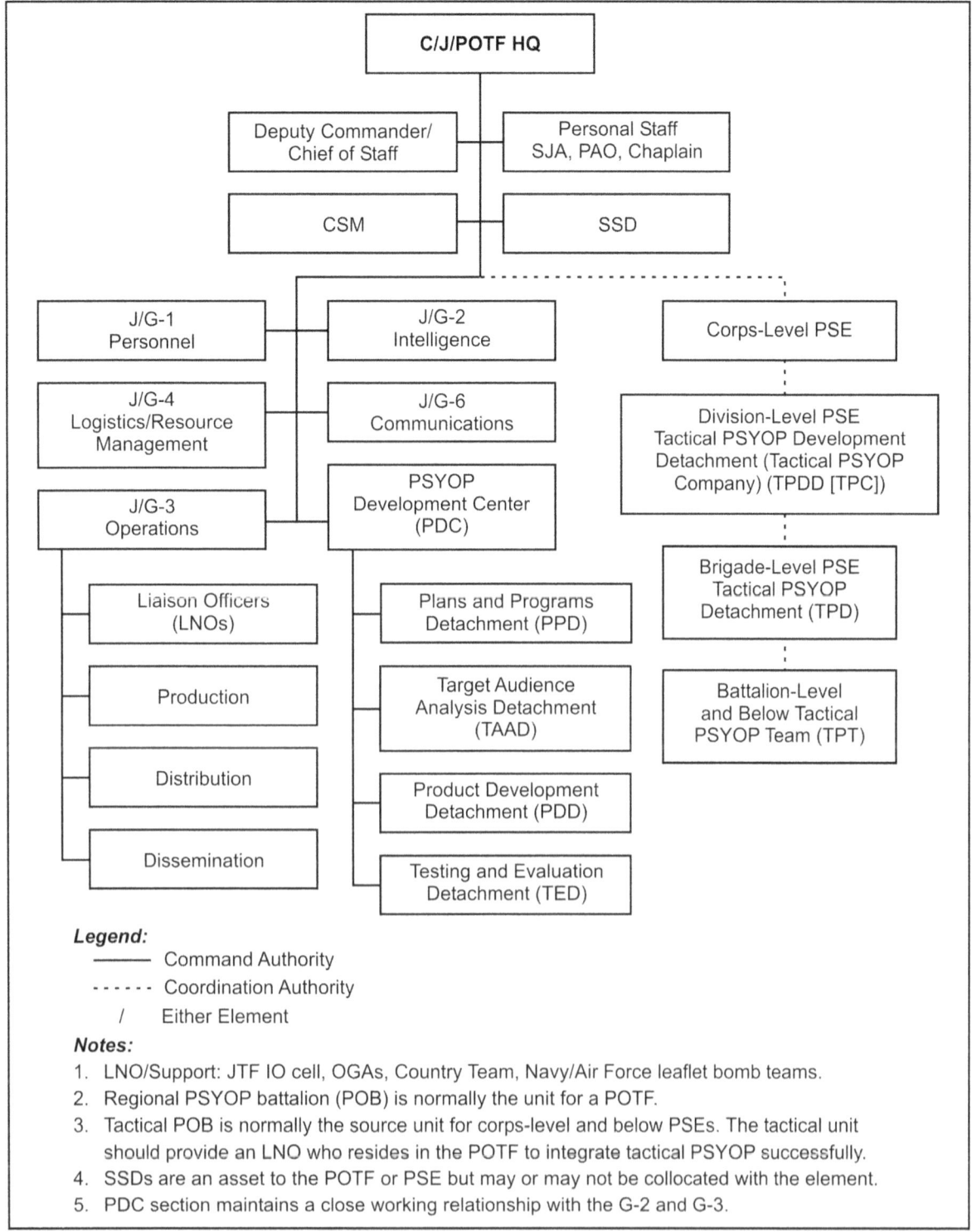

Figure 3-2. JPOTF and the PSYOP coordination chain

SUPPORTED UNIT COMMAND RELATIONSHIPS

3-12. Upon attachment to a maneuver command, the commander of the supporting tactical PSYOP unit becomes the PSYOP staff planner for the supported unit. The attached tactical PSYOP unit plans and executes PSYOP for the supported commander under the staff supervision of the G-3 or S-3, and coordinates and synchronizes PSYOP with IO through the Deputy/Assistant Chief of Staff for Information Operations (G-7) at corps and division, or the information operations staff officer (S-7) at brigade level.

3-13. At the Army corps and division levels, the G-7 (IO) coordinates and synchronizes the five core elements of IO. At the unified command level and other-than-Army Service component level, IO and its elements are coordinated in the IO cell within the staff supervision of the J-3 or G-3.

3-14. The U.S. Army established a G-7 and S-7 coordinating staff officer at the corps, division, and brigade levels, as described in FM 6-0, *Mission Command: Command and Control of Army Forces*. The PSYOP staff officer located in the division or corps G-3 moved from the staff supervision of the G-3 to the G-7 with this change in doctrine. The PSYOP officer in G-7 performs functions similar to those of a liaison officer (LNO), in that he does not plan PSYOP but coordinates and integrates PSYOP with IO. In the absence of a Psychological Operations assessment team (POAT), PSE, or POTF, the PSYOP officer may be required to write the PSYOP appendix to the IO annex to plans and orders. The attached TPC supporting the division or Service equivalent (brigade in S&RO) or tactical POB supporting the corps or Service equivalent (division in S&RO) plans and executes PSYOP for the supported commander under the staff supervision of the G-3. The PSYOP staff officer in the supported division or corps G-7 must maintain a close relationship with the supporting TPC or tactical POB to coordinate planned PSYOP with IO.

3-15. The G-7 does not command any IO-capable units. He integrates their respective capabilities to ensure synergism. Placing the PSYOP staff officer under the staff supervision of the G-7 does not change any of the PSYOP command relationships or put at risk the ability of PSYOP to support the commander effectively.

SUMMARY

3-16. Because PSYOP elements are not inherent within maneuver units, but attached for operational missions, the command relationships are exceedingly important. A tactical PSYOP element not only supports the maneuver commander but also is a crucial link to the success of the POTF mission. The PSYOP coordination chain between tactical PSYOP and the POTF must be maintained to ensure that PSYOP efforts at all levels are synchronized. In this respect, the tactical PSYOP element plays a dual role and thus must clearly understand how it relates to the POTF and the maneuver commander.

Chapter 4
Mission Planning

Operational planning and tactical planning are complementary, but they differ in the execution. While operational planning focuses on developing plans for campaigns and major operations, tactical planning revolves around battles and engagements conducted to accomplish specific military objectives. PSYOP planners, whether assigned as a member of a division or brigade staff or as a leader of a TPD or TPT, should understand how to plan PSYOP effectively at the tactical level. This chapter covers the factors involved with PSYOP mission planning in support of tactical operations.

MILITARY OPERATIONS AND MISSION PLANNING

4-1. Given the unpredictable nature of military operations, mission planning must be flexible enough to adapt to an ever-changing environment. PSYOP mission planning at brigade level and below requires the planner to be skilled not only with MDMP, but also to be intuitive and able to make decisions based upon assessments, rather than a comparison of multiple courses of action (COAs), if necessary. The purpose of planning is not to eliminate uncertainty, but to develop a framework for action in the midst of uncertainty.

NATURE OF PLANNING

4-2. Plans forecast, but they cannot predict the outcome of operations. A good PSYOP plan is one that acts as a guide through each phase of an operation, while remaining flexible to facilitate effective action in the face of unforeseen events. An effective planning process is structured, but it also allows for the planner's creativity, insight, and initiative. When planning for PSYOP, it is difficult to foresee how a particular TA will react to military operations. The two planning processes—MDMP and troop-leading procedures (TLP)—assist in choosing the most appropriate COA.

4-3. The MDMP is more appropriate for use in units with coordinating staff elements. It provides a sequence of decisions and interactions between the commander and the staff for developing effective plans. Tactical PSYOP units typically use the MDMP while planning at corps, division, brigade, and battalion levels.

SCIENCE AND ART OF PLANNING

4-4. Several aspects of military operations are quantifiable—specifically, fuel consumption, movement rates, and weapons effects. These aspects are part of the science of planning. Other aspects—such as choosing tactics and understanding relationships between friendly forces, adversaries, and the environment—constitute the art of planning.

4-5. The science of planning includes the physical capabilities of friendly and enemy organizations and systems, as well as an understanding of the time frame for initiating certain actions. It also includes the techniques, procedures, and control measures used in planning. While not always easy, the science of planning is straightforward. PSYOP planners should understand the physical and procedural constraints under which their supported units operate. However, because military operations are a human activity, planning cannot be reduced to a simple formula. Therefore, understanding the factors involved in the art of planning is necessary.

4-6. Planning for military operations is a complex process. Planning for PSYOP in support of operations adds to that complexity. Whether planning for corps, division, brigade, or battalion operations, PSYOP planning involves developing SPPs within the supported commander's intent. For the PSYOP Soldier at the

Chapter 4

tactical level, planning requires creative application of the PSYOP process, tactics, techniques, procedures, and available resources. An understanding of these factors defines a starting point from which planners create solutions to particular tactical problems.

4-7. The factors of mission, enemy, terrain and weather, troops and support available, time available, civil considerations (METT-TC) form a set of circumstances. Another factor to consider in the planning process includes knowing the effects of operations on Soldiers. This understanding assists PSYOP planners in developing simple, flexible plans for a variety of situations.

SUPPORTED UNIT PLANNING

4-8. To incorporate PSYOP properly into the planning process, tactical PSYOP units must be integrated with their supported unit as early as possible. Failure to do so may result in the PSYOP effort not supporting the accomplishment of the maneuver commander's objective.

4-9. Tactical PSYOP support is a nonlethal fire asset. At all levels, the PSYOP planner should work closely with the S-3, PSE, and other members of the staff. When the supported unit has an IO section or staff, the PSYOP planner should participate in the coordination and synchronization of the IO effort.

MILITARY DECISION-MAKING PROCESS

4-10. MDMP is a single, established, and proven analytical process. Although described in more detail in FM 3-05.301, this chapter covers the process as it applies to decision making for tactical PSEs.

4-11. The PSYOP planner's effort during planning focuses on helping the supported commander make decisions and on developing effective plans and orders. The desired outcome of this effort is accomplished by integrating information with sound doctrine and technical competence. During planning, initial efforts focus on mission analysis. Mission analysis develops information to help the commander understand the situation and the mission.

4-12. During COA development and COA comparison, PSYOP planners provide tactically sound recommendations to the commander supporting the selection of a COA. After the commander makes a decision, the PSYOP planner assists the staff in preparing the plan and in coordinating all necessary details.

CRITICAL TASKS DURING PLANNING

4-13. Critical tasks performed during planning include—
- Identifying specified and implied tasks.
- Identifying constraints.
- Identifying key facts and assumptions.
- Performing intelligence preparation of the battlefield (IPB).
- Formulating the concept of operations (CONOPS) and support that are consistent with the commander's intent.
- Developing the scheme of maneuver supporting the COA.
- Preparing, authenticating, and distributing portions of the plan, annexes, estimates, appendixes, and supporting plans (see Appendix E).
- Determining SPOs, potential target audiences (PTAs), and MOEs.

RECOMMENDATIONS THROUGHOUT PLANNING

4-14. Throughout planning, PSYOP planners prepare recommendations regarding—
- Units and PSYOP-unique capabilities, limitations, and employment.
- Risk identification and mitigation.
- Resource allocation and employment synchronization of organic and supporting assets (including those of other Services).
- General locations and movements of PSYOP units.

Mission Planning

SEVEN STEPS OF MILITARY DECISION-MAKING PROCESS

4-15. The MDMP has seven steps (Figure 4-1). Each step begins with inputs that build upon the previous step. Each step, in turn, has output that drives subsequent steps. Errors committed early in the process impact on later steps.

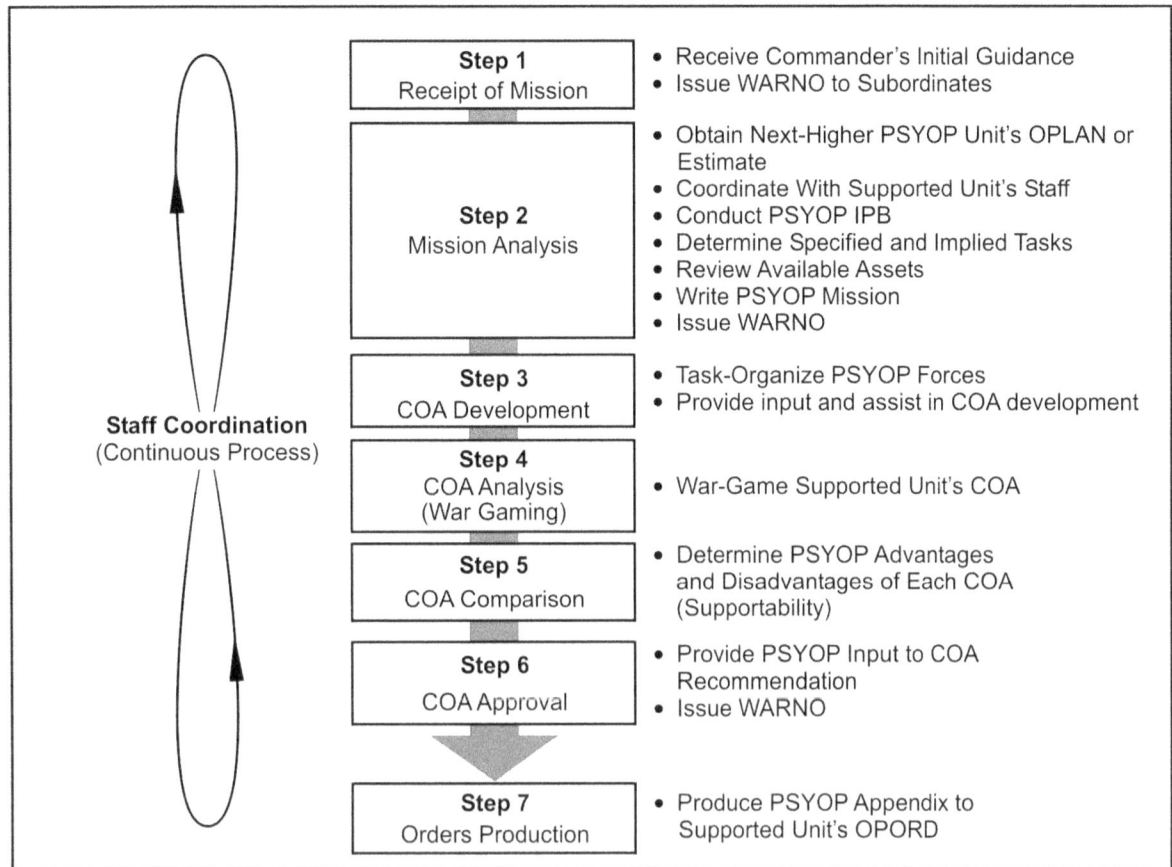

Figure 4-1. Seven steps of military decision-making process

Step 1: Receipt of Mission

4-16. The decision-making process begins with the receipt or anticipation of a new mission. The mission can come from an order issued by higher HQ or be derived from an ongoing operation. When a mission is received, the PSYOP HQ issues a warning order (WARNO) to subordinates, alerting them of the pending planning process. PSYOP HQ should obtain copies of the supported unit standing operating procedure (SOP). Unit SOPs identify who are to attend, who the alternates are, and where attendees should assemble. The SOPs ensure that individuals understand what is expected of them during the process.

4-17. Upon receipt of the mission, planners additionally consider—

- Conducting an initial assessment—what the mission is and the support PSYOP can provide.
- Determining the time available from receipt of the mission to execution—time available to plan, prepare, and execute the mission for own and subordinate units.
- Developing an initial list of the commander's objectives—what the commander must do to achieve mission success.

Step 2: Mission Analysis

4-18. Mission analysis begins immediately upon receipt of a WARNO. PSYOP planners prepare for mission analysis by gathering needed tools, including—

- Higher HQ's order or plan, with graphics, as well as a copy of the POTF's or PSYOP HQ's OPORD or appendix.
- Maps of the AO.
- Own, supported unit's, and higher HQ's SOPs.
- Appropriate FMs.
- Existing staff estimates.

4-19. Mission analysis is crucial to the MDMP. It defines the tactical problem and begins the process of determining feasible solutions. Mission analysis consists of the following 17 tasks and results in a staff briefing to the commander:

- *Task 1: Analyze the higher supported HQ's or POTF order.*
    - CONOPS and scheme of maneuver.
    - Tasks to subordinate units.
    - Coordinating instructions.
    - PSYOP appendix.
    - Intelligence annex.
    - IO annex.
    - Civil Affairs (CA) annex.
    - Public affairs annex.
- *Task 2: Conduct initial IPB.*
    - Identify PTAs.
    - Use PSYOP references and supported unit intelligence staff officer (S-2).
    - Identify PSYOP information requirements (IRs).
- *Task 3: Determine specified, implied, and essential tasks.*
    - PSYOP objectives (objectives obtained via SecDef approval).
    - Additional PSYOP supporting objectives for each objective.
    - PTAs for each PSYOP supporting objective.
    - PSYOP enabling actions.
- *Task 4: Review available assets.*
    - Current capabilities and limitations.
    - PSYOP assets.
    - Supported unit assets.
    - Other PSYOP assets.
    - Local nationals (LN) assets.
- *Task 5: Determine constraints.* Supported unit and higher PSYOP unit imposed.
- *Task 6: Identify critical facts and assumptions.* PSYOP-specific information.
- *Task 7: Conduct risk assessment.*
    - Threats to the PSYOP force.
    - Inherent risks in PSYOP and control measures.
- *Task 8: Determine initial commander's critical information requirements (CCIR).* What are the critical intelligence gaps that affect PSYOP?
- *Task 9: Determine the initial reconnaissance requirements.*
    - Town or area assessment by PSYOP units.
    - Nomination for inclusion in supported unit's reconnaissance and surveillance collection plan.
    - Request for information to higher PSYOP HQ.

- *Task 10: Plan the use of available time.*
- *Task 11: Write the restated mission.*
- *Task 12: Conduct a mission analysis briefing.*
- *Task 13: Approve the restated mission.*
- *Task 14: Develop the commander's intent for the PSYOP appendix.*
  - PSYOP purpose.
  - Key tasks.
  - End state.
- *Task 15: Issue the commander's guidance.*
- *Task 16: Issue a WARNO.*
  - Situation.
  - Mission.
  - General instructions.
  - Special instructions.
- *Task 17: Review facts and assumptions.*

Step 3: Course of Action Development

4-20. After receiving the restated mission, commander's intent, and commander's planning guidance, PSYOP planners assist in developing COAs for the commander's approval. The commander's direct involvement in COA development can greatly aid in producing comprehensive and flexible COAs within the available time.

Criteria

4-21. COAs should meet the criteria of—
- *Feasibility.* Do PSYOP units have the required resources? Do they have time to pull the resources together? Does the TAA support the assumption that the PTAs are effective at achieving the SPOs?
- *Acceptability.* Do advantages outweigh cost (resources, impact on other SPPs and on PSYOP credibility)?
- *Suitability.* Do the COAs accomplish the mission and fall within the POs?
- *Distinguishability.* Is the proposed series or SPP different from existing or proposed series or SPP?
- *Completeness.* Proposed PSYOP series or SPPs support unit COAs.

4-22. A good COA prepares PSYOP forces for future operations, provides flexibility to handle unforeseen events during execution, and falls within a PO. It also provides the maximum latitude for initiative by subordinates.

Steps

4-23. COA development involves six steps:
- *Step 1: Analyze relative combat power.*
  - What series or SPPs are conducted to achieve supported unit and POs?
  - What series or SPPs are conducted to counter enemy actions?
- *Step 2: Generate options.* How are PSYOP employed to support the COA, rules of engagement (ROE), or rules of interaction (ROI) restrictions for PSYOP units?
- *Step 3: Array initial forces.*
  - PSYOP forces needed to accomplish each task.
  - Other units tasked with PSYACTs or PSYOP enabling actions.
  - Force protection restrictions for PSYOP units.

- *Step 4: Develop the concept of operations.* How will the execution of series or SPPs accomplish the commander's intent for PSYOP?
- *Step 5: Assign HQ.* Task-organize PSYOP forces.
- *Step 6: Prepare COA statements and sketches.* Series execution matrix (SEM).

4-24. Upon completion of COA development, the staff prepares to brief the COAs to the commander. PSYOP planners should be able to expand upon the PSYOP supportability of each supported COA.

4-25. After the briefing, the commander gives additional guidance. If he rejects all COAs, the staff must start over with the COA development process. If one or more of the COAs are accepted, staff members begin COA analysis. The commander may create a new COA by incorporating elements of one or more COAs developed by the staff. The staff then prepares to war-game the new COA.

Step 4: Course of Action Analysis

4-26. COA analysis, or war gaming, is a disciplined process that visualizes the flow of battle. The process considers friendly dispositions, strengths, and weaknesses; enemy assets and probable COAs; and characteristics of the AO. The critical tool for the PSYOP planner is the SEM. The staff's attention focuses on each phase of the operation in a logical sequence during the war-gaming process. It is an iterative process of action, reaction, and counteraction.

4-27. War gaming stimulates ideas and provides insights that otherwise may not be discovered. It highlights critical PSYOP tasks and provides familiarity with tactical possibilities otherwise difficult to achieve. War gaming is the most valuable task during COA analysis and comparison and should be allocated more time than any other task. During the war game, the staff takes a COA and begins to develop a detailed plan, while determining the strengths or weaknesses of each COA. War gaming tests a COA or improves a developed COA. The commander and his staff may change an existing COA, combine COAs, or develop a new COA after identifying unforeseen critical events, tasks, requirements, or problems.

4-28. PSYOP planners help the coordinating staff by analyzing the PSYOP series or SPP that could best support the COA. Every staff member must determine the force requirements for external support, the risks, and the strengths and weaknesses of each COA.

Steps

4-29. The war-gaming process involves eight steps:
- *Step 1: Gather the tools.* Maps, mission analysis products, intelligence updates, and other needed materials.
- *Step 2: List all friendly forces.* Assigned, attached, and supporting PSYOP forces.
- *Step 3: List assumptions.* From TAA resources.
- *Step 4: List known critical events and decision points (DPs) that have an impact on PSYOP.*
- *Step 5: Determine evaluation criteria.* How are COAs compared?
- *Step 6: Select the war-gaming method.* Supported unit's method.
- *Step 7: Select a method to record and display results.* Supported unit.
- *Step 8: War-game the battle and assess the results.* Supported unit's method.

Results

4-30. The COA analysis will have many results, including refining and modifying the COA. Some results will specifically affect PSYOP forces. Strengths and weaknesses of the COA are identified, analyzed, and evaluated. After the completion of the war game, tactical PSYOP units or elements should be task-organized to execute the series or SPP. PSYOP requirements for supporting deception and surprise are identified. PSYOP integrate into the targeting process, including identifying or confirming high-payoff targets.

Step 5: Course of Action Comparison

4-31. The COA comparison starts with the supported unit staff and PSYOP planner analyzing and evaluating the advantages and disadvantages of each COA. Each staff member presents his findings for the other's consideration. Using the evaluation criteria developed earlier, the staff then outlines each COA. Comparing the strengths and weaknesses of the COAs identifies their advantages and disadvantages with respect to each other. Comparing feasible COAs identifies the COA with the highest probability of success against the most likely enemy COA and the most dangerous enemy COA.

Key Questions

4-32. The actual comparison of COAs is critical. Key questions to keep in mind during COA comparison are—

- Which COA can PSYOP best support?
- Which COA best supports accomplishing the POs?
- Which COA poses the minimum risk to Soldiers and equipment?
- Which COA best positions the unit for future operations?
- Which COA provides the best flexibility to meet "unknowns" during execution?

4-33. The staff assists the commander in making the best decision. The most common tool is the decision matrix—illustrated in FM 5-0, *Army Planning and Orders Production*. The decision matrix uses evaluation criteria to assess the effectiveness and efficiency of each COA. Decision matrixes alone cannot provide decision solutions. The matrix should use the evaluation criteria developed earlier. However, planners must avoid portraying opinions as being factual.

Step 6: Course of Action Approval

4-34. After the decision briefing, the commander decides on the COA he believes is the most advantageous. If he rejects all developed COAs, the staff must start the process over again. If the commander modifies a proposed COA or gives the staff an entirely different one, the staff must war-game the revised or new COA to derive the products that result from the war-gaming process. Once the commander has selected a COA, he may refine his intent statement to support the selected COA. He then issues any additional guidance on priorities for combat support (CS) or CSS activities, orders preparation, rehearsals, and preparation for mission execution. When the commander approves a COA, the PSYOP unit or element provides input to the PSYOP portion of the support unit's WARNO.

Commander's Decision Briefing

4-35. The XO or S-3 normally conducts the commander's decision briefing. PSYOP planners should be prepared to brief PSYOP points personally or to provide PSYOP input to the S-3 or XO for his brief. The decision-briefing format includes—

- Intent of higher commanders one and two levels up.
- Updated IPB.
- Restated mission.
- Status of own forces.
- Own COAs, including—
  - Assumptions used in planning.
  - Results of staff estimates.
  - Advantages and disadvantages (including risks) with decision matrix showing COA comparison.
- Recommended COA.

Chapter 4

Step 7: Orders Production

4-36. Based on the commander's decision and final guidance, the staff refines the COA, completes the plan, and prepares to issue the order. As part of this process, PSYOP planners—
- Refine the PSYOP portion of the COA.
- Develop the PSYOP appendix—
  - Detailing the supporting PSYOP plans (time- or event-phased and synchronized).
  - Remembering that the PSYOP appendix is the supported unit's plan for PSYOP.
- Make sure the commander reviews and approves the PSYOP appendix.
- Make sure the PSYOP appendix is issued as part of the supported unit's OPORD.

DECISION MAKING IN A TIME-CONSTRAINED ENVIRONMENT

4-37. The focus of any planning process should be to develop a flexible, tactically sound, and fully integrated and synchronized plan quickly—one that increases the likelihood of mission success with the fewest casualties possible. However, any operation may be overcome by events unforeseen in the initial plan. Fleeting opportunities or unexpected enemy actions may require a quick decision to implement a new or modified plan. Before a PSYOP planner can conduct decision making in a time-constrained environment, he must master the steps in the full MDMP and the PSYOP process. A planner can only shorten both processes if he fully understands the role of every step of the process, the requirements to produce the necessary results, and the risk associated with compressing these.

4-38. Anticipation, organization, and prior preparation are the keys to success in a time-constrained environment. The commander decides how to shorten the process (Figure 4-2). The following paragraphs discuss suggested techniques and procedures that will save time. These techniques and procedures are not exhaustive or the only ways to save time, but they have proved useful to units in the past. These techniques are not necessarily sequential in nature, nor are all of them useful in all situations. The ones that work for a unit depend on the unit's training and the factors of METT-TC in a given situation. The commander may use these techniques or techniques of his own choosing to abbreviate the process.

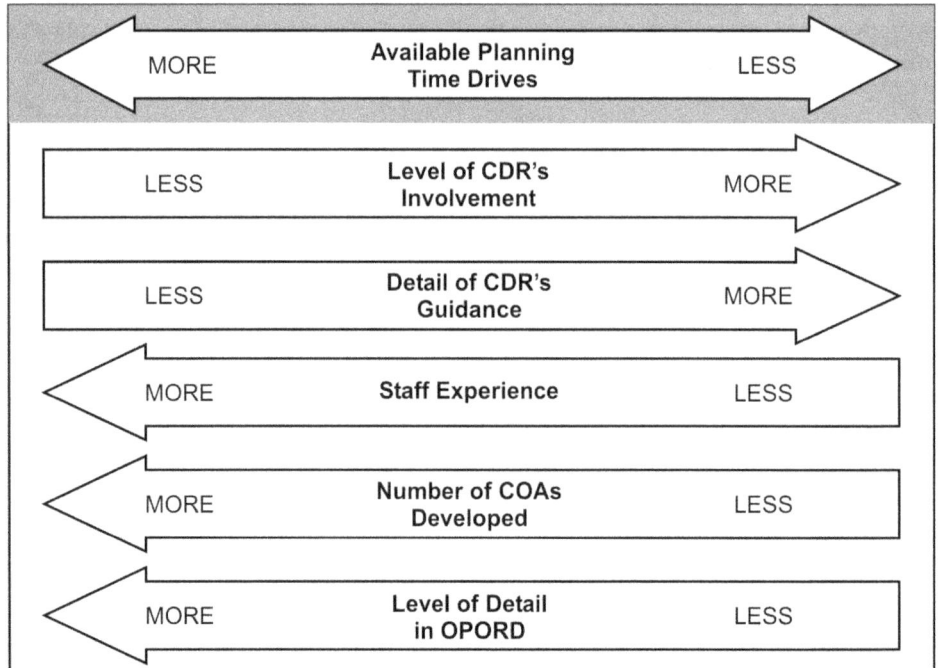

Figure 4-2. Timesaving techniques and procedures

TIME CONSIDERATIONS

4-39. The most significant factor to consider in planning is time. Time is the only nonrenewable resource and is often the most critical one. The planning process may be abbreviated when too little time exists for the thorough and comprehensive application of the process.

Techniques

4-40. There are several techniques to save time, including—

- Maximizing parallel planning. Although parallel planning is the norm, maximizing its use in a time-constrained environment is critical. The importance of WARNOs increases as available time decreases. A verbal WARNO becomes worth more than a written order. The same WARNO used in the full MDMP should be issued when the process is abbreviated. In addition to WARNOs, units must share all available information with subordinates, especially IPB products, as early as possible.
- Increasing the commander's involvement, thus allowing him to make decisions during the process without waiting for detailed briefings after each step.
- Having the commander become more directive in his guidance, thereby limiting options and focusing members on areas the commander feels are most important.
- Limiting the number of COAs developed and war-gamed. This technique is the one that saves the most time. In extreme cases, the commander can direct the development of only one COA. The goal is an acceptable COA that meets mission requirements in the time available, even if the COA is not optimal.

Advantages

4-41. The advantages of abbreviating the MDMP are that the abbreviated process—

- Maximizes the use of available time.
- Allows subordinates more planning time.
- Focuses staff efforts on the commander's guidance.
- Facilitates adapting to a rapidly changing situation.
- Allows the commander to compensate for the lack of a staff or for an inexperienced staff.

Disadvantages

4-42. The disadvantages of abbreviating the MDMP are that the abbreviated process—

- Is more directive and limits staff flexibility and initiative.
- Does not explore all available options when developing friendly COAs.
- May result in only an oral order or a FRAGO.
- Increases the risk of overlooking an essential factor or not uncovering a significantly better option.
- May decrease coordination and synchronization of the plan.
- Increases the risk that PSYOP may be ineffective or counterproductive.

Uses

4-43. The time saved on any MDMP step can be used to—

- Conduct the PSYOP process thoroughly.
- Conduct a more deliberate and detailed war game.
- Consider potential branches and sequels in detail.
- Focus more on rehearsing and preparing the plan.

Chapter 4

ROLE OF COMMANDER, PLANNER, AND STAFF

4-44. The commander decides how to adjust the MDMP, giving specific guidance to the staff to focus the process and save time. Commanders who have access to only a small staff rely even more than normal on their own expertise, intuition, and creativity and on their understanding of the environment. Because of this factor, PSYOP planners should make sure they have had ample time to advise the supported commander on PSYOP capabilities and limitations. They may have to select a COA, mentally war-game it, and confirm their decision to the staff in a relatively short time. If so, the decision is based more on experience than on a formal integrated staff process.

4-45. Commanders normally avoid changing their guidance unless a situation has significantly changed. Frequent minor changes to the guidance can easily result in lost time as the staff makes constant minor adjustments to the plan.

4-46. While executing the MDMP in a time-constrained environment, the PSYOP planner must not allow planning to be done on his behalf. PSYOP planners should be ready to provide accurate, up-to-date assessments quickly and to move directly into COA development. When time is short, the commander and staff use as much of the previously analyzed information and products from earlier decisions as possible.

4-47. Although some products may change significantly, many remain the same or require little change—for example, the IPB, which is continuously updated. The staff must use every opportunity to conduct parallel planning with the unit's higher HQ. Parallel planning can save significant time, but if not carefully managed, it can also waste time. Consequently, tactical PSEs should maintain regular contact with the next-higher PSYOP element. As a rule, the staff must not get ahead of the higher HQ in the planning process.

Receipt of Mission

4-48. This part of the process does not change in a time-constrained environment. However, the commander decides at this step whether the process must be abbreviated and, if so, specifies the particulars.

Mission Analysis

4-49. The commander's involvement is the key to saving time in mission analysis. Supervising and managing the mission analysis process must personally involve the commander. If time is unavailable to conduct a detailed mission analysis, the commander and staff rapidly perform mission analysis together to determine the restated mission.

4-50. As time permits, staff officers conduct a formal mission analysis briefing. However, they may be forced to brief their estimates orally, without the use of charts or other tools, and to cover only information that changed from the last staff estimate. When severely time-constrained, they brief only critical information that directly affects the new mission. If the commander has been directly involved in the mission analysis, he may decide to skip the mission analysis briefing completely.

4-51. A key way to save time is to issue the commander's guidance. The elements of the commander's guidance may be the same as elements in the full MDMP, but the guidance is more detailed and directive. The commander can provide detailed information, outlining what he expects in each COA developed, including tentative task organization and scheme of maneuver. He may also determine which enemy COAs he wants friendly COAs war-gamed against, as well as the branches or sequels he wants incorporated in each COA. Detailed guidance keeps the staff focused by establishing parameters within which to work. Once the guidance is issued, PSYOP planners immediately send a WARNO to subordinate units to begin TAA and series development.

Course of Action Development

4-52. The greatest time saved comes when the commander directs development of only a few COAs, instead of many. Performing a hasty war game at the end of COA development can save time. A hasty war game allows commanders to determine if they favor one or more of the proposed COAs. It develops and matures one or more COAs before the formal war game. If the commander cannot be present during the hasty war game, the staff delivers a COA back brief to the commander afterward. From the hasty war game, the commander refines one or more COAs before the detailed war game. In extreme situations, this may be the only opportunity to conduct a war game.

4-53. Commanders may also use a hasty war game to select a single COA for further development. Such a decision allows the staff and subordinates to focus on one COA, rather than several. It also lets the staff concentrate on synchronizing the COA earlier. The fastest way to develop a plan is for the commander to direct development of one COA with branches against the most likely enemy COA. The technique should be used only when time is severely limited. This choice of COA is often intuitive, relying on the commander's experience and judgment.

Course of Action Analysis

4-54. The commander and staff war-game as many COAs as possible to make sure all elements are fully integrated and synchronized. An early decision to limit the number of COAs war-gamed or to develop only one COA saves the greatest amount of time. It is best to war-game friendly COAs against all feasible enemy COAs. However, war-gaming against a smaller number of enemy COAs can save additional time. At a minimum, the decisive operation is war-gamed against the most likely enemy COA. The commander's involvement can save significant time in COA analysis by focusing the staff on the essential aspects of the war game. The commander can supervise the war game and make decisions, provide guidance, and stop unsatisfactory concepts. If time is available to war-game multiple COAs, the commander may identify the COA he favors.

Course of Action Comparison

4-55. If the commander decides to war-game only one COA or if he chooses one COA during the war game, no COA comparison is necessary. If multiple COAs have been war-gamed and the commander has not made a decision, the staff must perform a COA comparison. Limiting the evaluation criteria is the only significant shortcut in this step.

Course of Action Approval

4-56. If the commander has observed and participated in the planning process, the decision may be rapidly apparent and the commander can make an on-the-spot decision. If the commander has not participated in the process to this point or has not made a decision, a decision briefing is still required.

4-57. Good COA comparison charts and sketches assist the commander in visualizing and distinguishing between each COA. The staff must make sure the COAs are complete with tentative task organization, COA statement, and task and purpose for each subordinate unit.

4-58. Limiting the COA briefing to only the most critical points can also save time. If only one COA was developed, no decision is required, unless the developed COA becomes unsuitable, infeasible, or unacceptable. If this situation occurs, another COA must be developed. Once the decision is made, the staff immediately issues a WARNO.

Orders Production

4-59. In a time-constrained environment, time is important and a verbal FRAGO may be issued immediately after the commander makes a COA decision. The staff follows the verbal FRAGO with a written order as soon as possible. If a verbal order is not issued, the staff immediately sends out a WARNO, followed as quickly as possible by a written order. In all cases, the staff captures all the information in any verbal orders and WARNOs and produces a written order to follow up on any previously issued orders.

TROOP-LEADING PROCEDURES AND THE MILITARY DECISION-MAKING PROCESS

4-60. As a rule, company-level and smaller units do not have formal staffs. Nonetheless, leaders of companies, platoons, squads, and sections all plan for missions. They use key members of their organization to help them plan. For example, TPT leaders conduct planning with an infantry company commander, XO, and first sergeant. TPTs use TLP to assist them in planning and preparing for operations. TLP are a sequence of activities that small unit leaders use to plan and prepare for operations. They enable small unit leaders to maximize available planning time while developing effective plans and adequately preparing their unit for an operation.

SEQUENCE OF ACTIVITIES

4-61. TLP extend the MDMP to small-unit level. Where the MDMP provides a structure for interaction between a commander and staff, TLP prescribe a sequence of activities for planning and preparing for operations. Although the two processes are similar, they are not identical. TLP and the MDMP are linked by information flow. The type, amount, and timeliness of the information passed from higher to lower HQ directly impact the lower unit leader's TLP.

4-62. Figure 4-3 illustrates the parallel sequences of the MDMP and TLP. However, events do not always occur in the order shown. For example, TLP may start with receipt of an OPORD. WARNOs may arrive at any time. TPT leaders should remain flexible. They adapt TLP to fit the situation, rather than try to alter the situation to fit a preconceived idea of how events should flow.

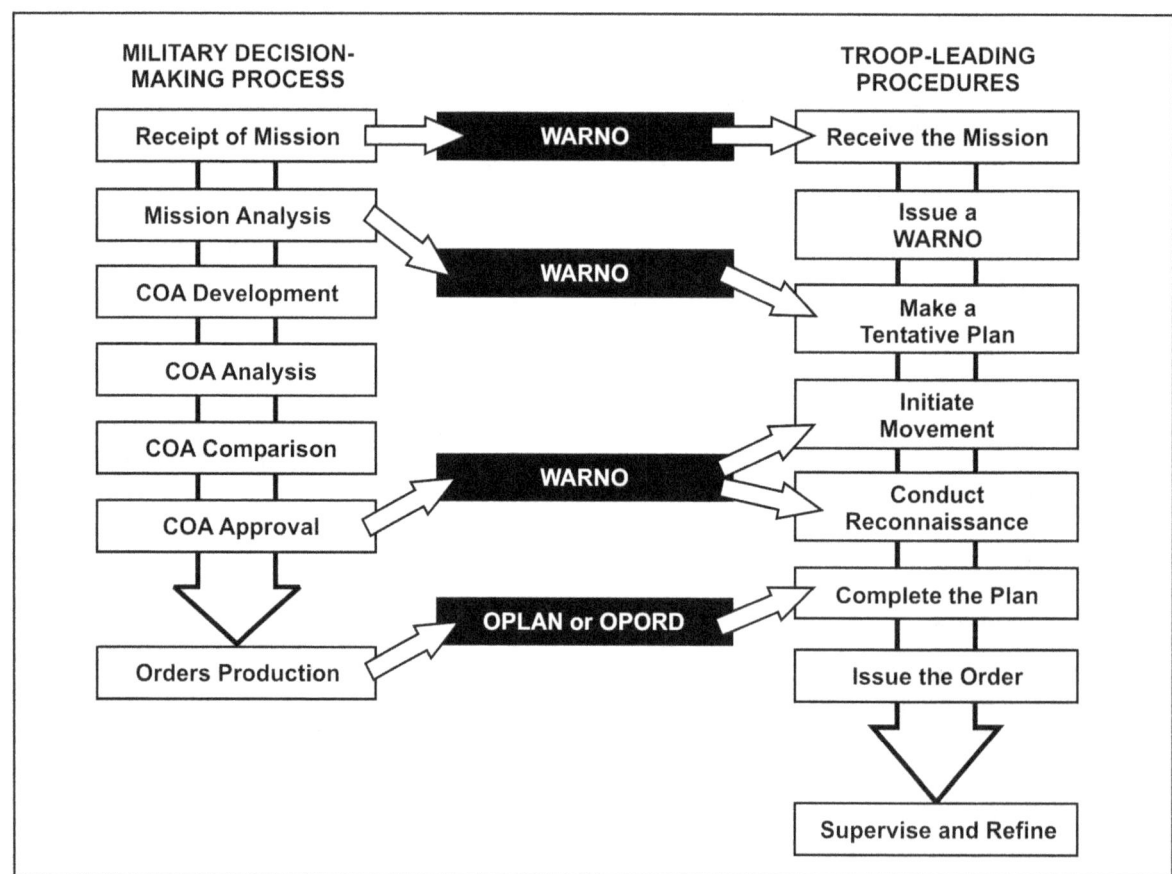

Figure 4-3. Parallel sequence of the MDMP and TLP

Mission Planning

4-63. TPT leaders adapt the TLP steps to the situation, based on their experience and the experience of their subordinates. Normally, the first three steps *(Receive the Mission, Issue a WARNO,* and *Make a Tentative Plan)* occur in order. However, the sequence of subsequent steps is based on the situation. The tasks involved in some steps (for example, *Initiate Movement* and *Conduct Reconnaissance*) may occur several times. The last step, *Supervise and Refine*, occurs throughout. In some situations, time constraints or other factors may prevent TPT leaders from performing each step thoroughly.

4-64. As the TPD performs the MDMP, it normally issues at least three WARNOs—upon receipt of the mission, upon completion of the mission analysis, and when the commander approves a COA. However, the number of WARNOs is not fixed. WARNOs serve a function in planning, similar to that of FRAGOs during execution. Commanders may issue a WARNO whenever they need to disseminate additional planning information or to initiate necessary preparatory action, such as movement or reconnaissance.

4-65. The first WARNO normally contains minimal information. It alerts leaders that a new mission is pending. It normally contains information on the—

- Type of operation.
- General location of the operation.
- Reconnaissance to initiate.
- Movement to initiate.
- Initial timeline.

4-66. The WARNO issued at the end of mission analysis contains essential information for planning and for directives to initiate movements and reconnaissance. Typically, the WARNO includes—

- Terrain analysis and associated products.
- Enemy composition, disposition, and strength.
- Higher HQ's restated mission.
- Commander's intent.
- AO and area of interest (AI).
- CCIR.
- Essential elements of enemy information.
- Risk guidance.
- Reconnaissance to initiate.
- Security measures.
- Mobility and countermobility guidance.
- Priorities.
- Revised timeline.
- Guidance on rehearsals.

4-67. The WARNO issued after COA approval normally contains the—

- Higher HQ's mission.
- CONOPS.
- AO.
- Principal tasks assigned to subordinate units.
- Preparation and rehearsal instructions not included in SOP.
- Final timeline for the operation.

4-68. TPT leaders begin TLP when they receive the initial WARNO or perceive a new mission. As each subsequent order arrives, leaders modify their assessments, update tentative plans, and continue to supervise and assess preparations. In some situations, the higher HQ may not issue the full sequence of WARNOs—security considerations or tempo may make it impractical. Commanders carefully consider decisions to eliminate WARNOs. Subordinate units must have enough information to plan and prepare for the operation. In other cases, TPT leaders may initiate TLP before receiving a WARNO, based upon existing plans and orders (contingency plans or "be-prepared" missions) and an understanding of the situation.

4-69. Parallel planning depends on distributing information as it is received or developed. TPT leaders cannot complete their plans until they receive their unit mission. If each successive WARNO contains enough information, the TPD's final order will confirm what subordinate leaders have already analyzed and put into their tentative plan.

STEPS IN TROOP-LEADING PROCEDURES

4-70. TLP provide small unit leaders the framework for planning and preparing for operations. The paragraphs that follow discuss the eight TLP steps in detail.

Step 1: Receive the Mission

4-71. Receipt of a mission may occur in several ways. It may begin with the initial WARNO or with the TPT leader's receipt of an OPORD. Frequently, leaders receive a mission in a FRAGO over the radio. Ideally, they receive a series of WARNOs, the OPORD, and a briefing from their commander.

4-72. Upon receipt of mission, TPT leaders perform an initial assessment of the situation and allocate the time available for planning and preparation, including rehearsals and movement. This initial assessment and time allocation form the basis of their initial WARNO. Leaders issue the initial WARNO quickly to give subordinates as much time as possible for planning and preparation.

Perform an Initial Assessment

4-73. The initial assessment addresses the factors of METT-TC. The order and detail in which TPT leaders analyze the factors of METT-TC are flexible, depending on the amount of information available and the relative importance of each factor. For example, TPT leaders may concentrate on the mission, enemy, and terrain, leaving weather and civil considerations until they receive more detailed information.

4-74. Often, TPT leaders do not receive their final unit mission until dissemination of the WARNO after COA approval or the OPORD. Effective leaders do not wait until their higher HQ completes planning to begin their planning. Using all information available, TPT leaders develop their unit mission as completely as possible. They focus on the mission, commander's intent, and CONOPS of their higher and next-higher PSYOP unit. They identify the major tasks their team most likely will be assigned and develop a mission statement based on information they have received. At this stage, the mission may be incomplete. For example, an initial mission statement could be, "TPTs 963 and 981 support cordon and search by A/1-61N by disseminating products and coordinating PSYACTs within series IZA03ka." Although not complete, this information allows subordinates to start preparations. During Steps 3 and 6 of TLP, leaders complete a formal mission statement.

Allocate the Available Time

4-75. Based on what they know, Army leaders estimate the time available to plan and prepare for the mission. They begin by identifying the times at which major planning and preparation events, including rehearsals, must be complete. Reverse planning helps in estimating time. TPT leaders identify the critical times specified by higher HQ and work back from them, estimating how much time each event will consume. Critical times might include aircraft loading times, the line of departure (LD) time, or the start point (SP) time for movement. Through reverse planning, leaders arrive at the time available to plan and prepare for the operation. They limit the amount of time they use to one-third and allocate the remaining two-thirds of time for preparing subordinates.

Step 2: Issue a Warning Order

4-76. When the TPT leader completes the initial assessment of the situation and allocates the available time, he issues a WARNO. The WARNO contains as much detail as possible.

Nature of Warning Order

4-77. The WARNO informs subordinates of the unit mission and gives them the leader's timeline. Army leaders may also send other instructions or information they think will help subordinates prepare for the new mission, including information on the enemy, the nature of the higher PSYOP HQ's plan, and specific instructions for preparing their units. The most important consideration is that leaders not delay issuing the initial WARNO. As more information becomes available, leaders can—and should—issue additional WARNOs. By issuing the initial WARNO as quickly as possible, TPT leaders enable their subordinates to begin their own planning and preparation.

Format of Warning Order

4-78. WARNOs follow the five-paragraph OPORD format. Normally, an initial WARNO issued below battalion level includes the—

- Mission or nature of the operation.
- Time and place for issuing the OPORD.
- Units or elements participating in the operation.
- Specific tasks not addressed by unit SOP.
- Timeline for the operation.

Step 3: Make a Tentative Plan

4-79. After TPT leaders have issued the initial WARNO, they develop a tentative plan. This step combines MDMP Steps 2 through 6. At levels below battalion, these steps are less structured than they are for units with staffs. Often, leaders perform the steps mentally, but they may include their principal subordinates—especially during COA development, analysis, and comparison. However, TPT leaders select the COA on which to base the tentative plan. To frame the tentative plan, TPT leaders perform a mission analysis. This mission analysis follows the METT-TC format, continuing the initial assessment performed in TLP Step 1 and leading to COA development, as described in the following paragraphs.

Mission

4-80. TPT leaders analyze the WARNO to determine how their unit contributes to the higher HQ's mission. They examine information affecting their mission, including—

- *TPD or higher HQ's mission and commander's intent.* TPT leaders determine the mission and commander's intent of their higher and next-higher HQ. When these are unavailable, TPT leaders infer them from the information they have. When TPT leaders receive the actual mission and commander's intent, they revise their plan, as necessary.
- *Higher HQ's CONOPS.* TPT leaders examine the CONOPS to determine how their unit mission and tasks contribute to the higher HQ's mission success. They determine details that will affect their operations, such as control measures and execution times.
- *Specified, implied, and essential tasks.* From WARNOs and the OPORD, TPT leaders extract the specified and implied tasks assigned to their unit. To understand how each task fits within the commander's intent and CONOPS, they determine why each task was assigned to their unit. From the specified and implied tasks, leaders identify essential tasks. These tasks must be completed to accomplish the mission. Failure to complete an essential task results in mission failure.
- *Constraints.* TPT leaders also identify constraints placed on their unit. Constraints can take the form of a specified requirement (for example, conduct a loudspeaker broadcast at a specified time) or a prohibition on action (for example, no loudspeaker operations before H-hour).

4-81. The product of this part of the mission analysis is the restated mission. The restated mission is a simple, concise expression of the essential tasks the unit must accomplish and the purpose to be achieved. The mission statement states *who* (the unit), *what* (the task), *when* (either the critical time or on order), *where* (location), and *why* (the purpose of the operation).

Chapter 4

Enemy

4-82. With the restated mission as the focus, TPT leaders continue the analysis of the enemy. For TPT operations, leaders must know the enemy's composition, disposition, strength, recent activities, ability to reinforce, and possible COAs. Much of this information comes from higher HQ. Additional information comes from adjacent units and other leaders. Some information is derived from the leader's experience. TPT leaders determine how available information applies to their operation. They also determine what information they should have, but do not have, on the enemy. They identify these intelligence gaps to their higher HQ or take action (such as participating in reconnaissance patrols) to obtain the necessary information.

Terrain and Weather

4-83. This aspect of mission analysis addresses the military aspects of terrain, known by the memory aid OAKOC—

- **O**bservation and fields of fire.
- **A**venues of approach.
- **K**ey terrain.
- **O**bstacles.
- **C**over and concealment.

4-84. The consideration of weather effects is an important part of mission analysis. TPT leaders review the forecasts and conclusions available from higher HQ and develop their own conclusions on the effects of weather on the mission. The analysis considers the effects on the Soldiers, equipment, and ability to conduct PSYOP. TPT leaders identify the aspects of weather that can affect the mission. They focus on factors with effects they can mitigate. For example, TPT leaders may modify a loudspeaker broadcast position based upon wind direction. TPT leaders include instructions on mitigating weather effects in their tentative plan.

Troops and Support Available

4-85. Perhaps the most important aspect of mission analysis is determining the combat potential of one's own force. TPT leaders know the status of their Soldiers' morale, their experience and training, and the strengths and weaknesses of subordinates. They realistically and unemotionally determine all available resources. The assessment includes knowing the strengths and status of Soldiers and their equipment. It also includes understanding the full array of assets supported by the TPT. Leaders know, for example, what type of security element is available to them and when it will become available. They consider any new limitations based on level of training or recent fighting.

Time Available

4-86. TPT leaders should know how much time is available for preparing, moving, fighting, and sustaining. They should understand the amount of time to prepare for certain tasks—such as orders production, rehearsals, and subordinate preparations.

Civil Considerations

4-87. Civil considerations are how the man-made infrastructure, civilian institutions, and attitudes and activities of the civilian leaders, populations, and organizations within an AO influence the conduct of military operations. Only rarely are military operations conducted in uninhabited areas. Most often, units are surrounded by noncombatants. These noncombatants include residents of the AO, local officials, and government and nongovernmental organizations (NGOs). Based on information from higher HQ and their own knowledge and judgment, TPT leaders identify civil considerations that affect their mission and the mission of the supported unit.

Mission Planning

Course of Action Development

4-88. Mission analysis provides information needed to develop COAs. The purpose of COA development is to determine one or more ways to accomplish the mission. At lower echelons, the mission may be a single task. Most missions and tasks can be accomplished in more than one way. However, in a time-constrained environment, TPT leaders may develop only one COA. Normally, they develop two or more COAs. Leaders do not wait for a complete order before beginning COA development. They develop COAs as soon as they have enough information to do so. To develop a COA, leaders focus on the actions the unit must take at the objective and reverse plan to the starting point. These actions include—

- *Analyzing relative combat power.* During this step, TPT leaders and their supported unit compare the combat power of friendly and enemy forces to determine whether the friendly forces have enough combat power to defeat the enemy forces. Below battalion level, relative combat power comparisons are rough and generally rely on professional judgment.
- *Generating options.* Leaders first identify where and when the unit can conduct PSYOP to achieve specific results (with respect to terrain, enemy, or time) that accomplish the mission. They then determine the requirements for the operation, including the tactical tasks assigned to them. TPT leaders begin with the specified, implied, and essential tasks identified during mission analysis.
- *Arraying forces.* The TPT leader then coordinates with the supported unit to determine what combinations of Soldiers, weapons, and other systems must be at each location to accomplish each task.
- *Developing a CONOPS.* The CONOPS describes how the leader envisions the operation unfolding, from its start to its conclusion or end state. It identifies how accomplishing each task leads to executing the next. It also identifies the best ways to use available terrain and to employ unit strengths against enemy weaknesses. PSYOP support considerations should be included in the CONOPS.
- *Assigning responsibilities.* TPT leaders assign responsibility for each task to a subordinate. Different C2 arrangements may be the distinguishing feature among COAs.
- *Preparing a COA statement and sketch.* TPT leaders base the COA statement on the CONOPS for that COA. The COA statement focuses on all significant actions, from the start of the COA to its finish. Whenever possible, TPT leaders prepare a sketch showing each COA. Another useful technique is to show the time required to achieve each movement and task in the COA sketch. This technique helps gain an appreciation for how much time will pass as each task of the COA is executed. The COA statement states the—
  - Decisive operation and why it is decisive.
  - Form of maneuver or defensive technique to be used.
  - Tasks and purposes of the decisive and shaping operations.
  - Task and purpose of critical battlefield operating system (BOS) elements.
  - Necessary sustaining operations.
  - End state.
- *Analyzing COAs (war-gaming).* For each COA, TPT leaders think through the operation from start to finish. They compare each PSYOP COA with the supported unit's most probable COA, as well as that of the enemy. The leader visualizes a set of actions and reactions—determining what can go wrong and what decision the leader will likely make as a result.
- *Comparing COAs and making a decision.* TPT leaders compare COAs by weighing the advantages, disadvantages, strengths, and weaknesses of each COA noted during the war game. Based upon this comparison and the TPT leaders' professional judgment, TPT leaders advise the supported unit on which PSYOP COA to execute. In comparing COAs, TPT leaders take into account the—
  - Time of the operation.
  - AO.
  - CONOPS.

Chapter 4

- Subordinate unit's tasks and purposes.
- Results from unit reconnaissance.
- Reconnaissance and security operations by higher HQ.

Step 4: Initiate Movement

4-89. TPT leaders initiate movements necessary to continue mission preparation or to position the unit for execution, sometimes before making a tentative plan. They initiate movement as soon as they have enough information, especially when the unit must move to position itself for a task or when time is short. Movements may be to an assembly area, a battle position, a new AO, or a broadcast position. They may include movement of reconnaissance elements, guides, or quartering parties. TPT leaders often initiate movement based upon their supported unit's tentative plan and issue the order to subordinates in the new location.

Step 5: Conduct Reconnaissance

4-90. When time and circumstances allow, TPT leaders personally reconnoiter the AO for the mission. No amount of IPB can substitute for firsthand assessment of METT-TC from within the AO. Unfortunately, many factors can keep leaders from performing a personal reconnaissance. The minimum action necessary is a thorough map reconnaissance, supplemented by imagery and intelligence products. In some cases, subordinates or other elements (such as scouts) may perform the reconnaissance for the leader while the leader completes other TLP steps.

4-91. TPT leaders use the results of the war game to identify information requirements. Reconnaissance operations seek to confirm or deny information that supports the tentative plan. They focus first on information gaps identified during mission analysis. TPT leaders ensure their leader's reconnaissance complements the higher HQ's reconnaissance plan. Reconnaissance may be the only way to develop the information required for planning.

Step 6: Complete the Plan

4-92. During this step, TPT leaders incorporate the result of reconnaissance into their selected COA to complete the order, including preparing overlays, refining the PSYOP target list, coordinating CSS and C2 requirements, and updating the tentative plan as a result of the reconnaissance. At lower levels, this step may entail only confirming or updating information in the tentative plan. If time allows, TPT leaders make final coordination with adjacent units and higher HQ before issuing the order.

4-93. The TPT leader completes his mission statement if it was not provided by the TPD. A complete mission statement may look something like the following: "TPTs 963 and 981 support A/1-61N by disseminating products IZA03kaLS02 and IZA03kaHB02 and by coordinating for the execution of IZA03kaAC01 in the next 24 hours."

Step 7: Issue the Order

4-94. Small unit orders are normally issued orally and supplemented by graphics and other control measures. The order follows the standard five-paragraph OPORD format. Typically, TPT leaders reiterate the intent of their higher and next-higher commander.

4-95. The ideal location for issuing the order is a point in the AO with a view of the objective and other aspects of the terrain. The leader may perform a leader's reconnaissance, complete the order, and then summon subordinates to a specified location to receive it. Sometimes, security or other constraints make it infeasible to issue the order on the terrain. In that case, TPT leaders use a sand table, detailed sketch, maps, and other products to depict the AO and situation.

Step 8: Supervise and Refine

4-96. Throughout TLP, TPT leaders monitor mission preparations, refine the plan, perform coordination with supporting units, and supervise and assess preparations. Normally unit SOPs state individual responsibilities and the sequence of preparation activities. TPT leaders supervise subordinates and inspect their personnel and equipment to make sure the TPT is ready for the mission.

4-97. A crucial component of preparation is the rehearsal. Rehearsals allow TPT leaders to assess their subordinates' preparations. They may identify areas that require more supervision. TPT leaders conduct rehearsals to—

- Practice essential tasks.
- Identify weaknesses or problems in the plan.
- Coordinate subordinate element actions.
- Improve the Soldier's understanding of the CONOPS.
- Foster confidence among Soldiers.

4-98. Company-sized and smaller units use five types of rehearsals:

- *Confirmation brief.* Immediately after receiving the order, subordinate leaders brief their superior on the order they just received. They brief their understanding of the commander's intent, the specific tasks they have been assigned and their purposes, and the relationship of their tasks to those of other elements conducting the operation. They repeat any important coordinating measures specified in the order. The confirmation brief is normally used with other types of rehearsals.
- *Backbrief.* The backbrief differs from the confirmation brief in that subordinate leaders are given time to complete their plan. Backbriefs require the fewest resources and are often the only option under time-constrained conditions. Subordinate leaders explain their actions from start to finish of the mission. Backbriefs are performed sequentially, with all leaders going over their tasks. When time is available, backbriefs can be combined with other types of rehearsals. This way, all element leaders can coordinate their plans before performing more elaborate drills. If possible, backbriefs are performed overlooking subordinates' AOs, after they have developed their own plans.
- *Combined arms rehearsal.* A combined arms rehearsal requires considerable resources; however, it provides the most planning and training benefit. Depending upon circumstances, units may conduct—
    - *Reduced-force rehearsals.* Circumstances may prohibit a rehearsal with all members of the unit. Unit leaders and other key individuals may perform a rehearsal while most of their subordinates continue to prepare for the operation. TPT leaders not only explain their plans, but also walk through their actions. It reinforces the backbrief given by subordinates, since everyone can see the CONOPS and sequence of tasks.
    - *Full-dress rehearsals.* The preferred rehearsal technique is a full-dress rehearsal. TPT leaders rehearse their subordinates on terrain similar to the AO, initially under good light conditions, and then in limited visibility. Small unit actions are repeated until executed to standard. Full-dress rehearsals help Soldiers to understand clearly what is expected of them and to gain confidence in their ability to accomplish the mission. An important benefit is the opportunity to synchronize the operation. The unit may conduct full-dress rehearsals. They also may be conducted and supported by the higher HQ.
- *Support rehearsals.* At any point in TLP, units may rehearse their support for an operation. For small units, this typically involves coordination and procedure drills for PSYOP, aviation, fire, combat service, or engineer support. Support rehearsals and combined arms rehearsals complement preparations for the operation. They may be conducted separately and then combined into full-dress rehearsals.
- *Battle drills or SOP rehearsal.* Throughout preparation, units rehearse battle drills and SOP actions. These rehearsals do not need a completed order from higher HQ. Leaders place priority on the drills or actions they anticipate occurring during the operation.

4-99. TPT leaders refine their plan based on continuing analysis of their mission and updated intelligence. Most important, TPT leaders know that they create plans to ensure the same mission is accomplished within the commander's intent. If required, they can deviate from the plan and execute changes based on battlefield

Chapter 4

conditions and the enemy. TPT leaders oversee preparations for operations. These include inspections and further coordination with the supported unit. The requirement to supervise is continuous; it is as important as issuing orders. Supervision allows TPT leaders to assess their subordinates' understanding of their orders and to determine where additional guidance is needed. It is crucial to effective preparation.

SUMMARY

4-100. The MDMP provides PSYOP planners the means to develop a solid, coherent, and successful complement to the supported unit's plan or order. Understanding the MDMP does not happen overnight. PSYOP leaders, at all levels, must develop a good understanding of the process through practice and real-world application.

Chapter 5
Employment

This chapter outlines the employment of tactical PSYOP elements in a POTF or a PSE. The echelon of employment for tactical PSEs differs for HIC and S&RO. Tactical PSEs conduct operational- and tactical-level PSYOP at corps, Marine expeditionary force (MEF), or JTF HQ and below by establishing a PSYOP PSE. Corps-level PSE operations may be established by the battalion on no-notice tactical missions, such as noncombatant evacuation operations (NEOs), or in response to a terrorist incident or an incident involving hostages or weapons of mass destruction (WMD). PSYOP force packages are custom-tailored to the specific mission.

TACTICAL PSYCHOLOGICAL OPERATIONS BATTALION

5-1. When a tactical POB deploys, it normally deploys with the establishment of a POTF. A PSE may have an entire tactical POB in its organization. Depending upon the mission, a POTF may include multiple corps PSEs in support of a theater commander. This arrangement does not require a task group, as the task group is reserved for commanding multiple POTFs. However, the POTF should contain a tactical representative who ensures coordination of the POTF and tactical units. This representative, within the POTF, maintains constant contact with the corps PSEs.

5-2. Tactical PSYOP forces are normally attached to maneuver units. The POTF retains coordinating authority with these tactical units. A tactical POB should provide personnel to augment the POTF staff to serve as liaisons, as well as personnel to augment the supported corps staff. The PSYOP liaisons within the corps staff then coordinate with the POTF all PSYOP within the corps area to ensure synchronization of PSYOP.

5-3. The battalion staff normally collocates with the Corps, JTF, or MEF HQ. Dissemination battalion assets should be collocated with or attached to the tactical battalion to facilitate the distribution of PSYOP products to tactical assets. Through reach back with systems like the product distribution system (PDS) and Digital Video Distribution System (DVDS), the tactical POB can receive new PSYOP products and rapidly send area assessments, product recommendations, and testing data back to the POTF.

5-4. Early coordination with the supported unit is critical to the successful employment of PSYOP. Because of the varying nature of missions the tactical POB supports, a tremendous amount of importance is placed on the initial meeting between the PSYOP leader and the supported unit, including the battalion commander at the corps level, down to the TPT leader at the battalion level. The meeting sets the tone of the entire relationship and, therefore, must be polished and professional. The initial meeting should include a capabilities brief (Appendix F) tailored for the type of mission and unit supported.

5-5. A TPB commander task-organizes his unit to support the maneuver commander best. The TPD is usually the building block for task-organizing his forces. As multiple TPDs are task-organized for an operation, a TPC may be employed for C2. The employment of a TPC may include the TPDD if PSYOP series development, design, and production are required at the tactical level. The tactical POB HQ may be employed if multiple TPCs are task-organized or if the operation requires its employment.

5-6. Appendix G provides standardized formats for information reporting. PSYOP elements submit situation reports (SITREPs) to their higher HQ on a regular basis (daily or weekly, dependent on unit SOP). During operations, where the companies and TPDs are not collocated with the battalion HQ, company HQ, or TPDD, TPD commanders submit the SITREP to the company commander, who submits it to the battalion or the POTF. When a TPD is deployed, it submits a SITREP daily or weekly to its company HQ and S-3.

5-7. The following officers have additional responsibilities that are unique to PSYOP units:
- *Commander.* The tactical POB commander serves as the PSYOP staff officer for the supported commander. The tactical POB commander oversees PSYOP integration into the supported unit's plan and ensures PSYOP coordination with IO and between the POTF and subordinate PSYOP elements.
- *Executive officer.* The tactical POB XO normally serves as the tactical LNO to the POTF. He may also function as the PSE officer in charge (OIC) when the battalion is required to organize more than one PSE.
- *Personnel officer.* The personnel staff officer (S-1) oversees the replacement of PSYOP personnel.
- *Intelligence officer.* The S-2 manages all intelligence matters. His specific responsibilities include military intelligence (MI) (collecting and disseminating intelligence), counterintelligence, and MI training. The S-2 plans the collection, processing, and disssemination of intelligence required for tactical POB activities. He advises the commander on the use of tactical POB intelligence assets and provides the S-3 with intelligence support for the operations security (OPSEC) program and deception planning.
- *Operations and training officer.* The S-3 may function as a PSE OIC when the battalion is required to organize more than one PSE.
- *Logistics officer.* The logistics staff officer (S-4) manages the maintenance and replacement of PSYOP-specific equipment.

HEADQUARTERS SUPPORT COMPANY

5-8. A tactical POB task-organizes some personnel as a rear detachment to conduct reachback support. The rear detachment commander is designated by the battalion commander and is often from the HSC. This officer should have sufficient experience and maturity to maintain control of all assigned rear detachment personnel and to provide for the proper care and disposition of all unit records, equipment, property, mail, personal property, and dependents. Upon deployment of the unit, the rear detachment commander—
- Establishes communications with the emergency operations center.
- Establishes communications with the POTF and PSE forward.
- Ensures physical security of occupied and unoccupied buildings in the unit area.
- Ensures proper disposition of records, unit funds, officer association funds, unit property, and classified files.
- Assigns a privately owned vehicle (POV) custodian.
- Assumes responsibility for POV storage coordination from battalion S-2.
- Prepares the POV storage area.
- Receives POVs and takes custody of spare keys.
- Appoints a mail handler and redirects any mail belonging to deploying personnel.
- Works closely with the Family Readiness Group to address all dependents' needs.
- Assigns a rear detachment security manager.
- Conducts inventory of residual classified material and automated data processing (ADP) with the deploying company security manager before deployment.
- Ensures adherence to physical security and crime-prevention measures.
- Conducts a 100-percent change-of-responsible-officer inventory before the deployment of the commander, coordinated through the property book officer.
- Assigns a rear detachment information assurance security officer.
- Consolidates sensitive items into one arms room, assigns an armorer, and conducts a change-of-responsible-person inventory between deploying armorers and rear detachment armorer before deployment of the battalion.

5-9. Various force templates for the HSC may be used, depending on whether tactical PSYOP forces are operating under a POTF or a PSE. Generally, a more robust element from HSC deploys forward if the tactical POB deploys as a POTF. When the tactical POB deploys with a POTF, the majority of HSC collocates with the battalion HQ. The tactical POB commander determines where best to locate maintenance assets. Civilian maintenance support is retained at the tactical POB or POTF HQ. TPCs and TPDs require maintenance support from the maneuver unit. When operating as a PSE, HSC personnel—such as supply or maintenance personnel—are attached to the deploying element as necessary.

TACTICAL PSYCHOLOGICAL OPERATIONS COMPANY

5-10. The TPC is the mainstay of PSYOP support to maneuver commanders. It provides the maneuver commander the ability to influence, either directly or indirectly, the behavioral responses of neutral, friendly, and enemy TAs. The TPC develops, produces, and disseminates products within the guidance assigned by the approval authority. The TPC typically supports component commanders at the division level (brigade in S&RO) and falls under the OPCON of the G-3.

5-11. The TPC HQ and the TPDD typically collocate with the support unit tactical operations center (TOC). The TPC HQ may have PSYOP dissemination battalion assets attached or collocated with it—for example, a Deployable Print Production Center (DPPC), a Deployable Audio Production System (DAPS), a Portable Amplitude Module Transmitter (PAMT), a Portable Frequency Module Transmitter (PFMT), or a wind supported aerial delivery system (WSADS) detachment. The TPC HQ plays a limited role operationally, except for the commander, who ensures execution of the commander's intent and advises the supported commander. The TPC HQ accomplishes several critical functions, including—

- Providing all logistics and administrative functions for the company, with the supported unit providing common Army items.
- Being the first point at which PSYOP-specific equipment receives maintenance beyond operator level and the collection point for equipment that needs to be transferred to a higher-level maintenance facility. TPCs may consider deploying with additional maintenance and supply assets to facilitate repairs.
- Facilitating the distribution of products to the TPD.
- Exercising battle tracking of PSYOP personnel.

5-12. A TPC is a highly tailorable PSYOP element that can be task-organized to provide PSYOP support to PSEs. Figure 5-1 illustrates possible task organization templates.

TPC task organization templates:
- Company HQ with—
  - The PDD and one or more TPDs in support of a division-level unit.
  - One or more TPDs.
  - Augmentation of additional TPDs from another company.
- TPDs deployed—
  - In support of a brigade-level unit.
  - Attached to another TPC.
- TPD deployed with—
  - TPD HQ and all three TPTs.
  - TPD HQ and selected TPTs.
  - TPD HQ augmented by additional TPTs from another detachment.
  - TPD HQ and TPTs from another detachment in place of its own TPTs.
  - Detachment commander or NCOIC and one TPT in support of a task force or SO unit.

Figure 5-1. TPC task organization

PSYOP SUPPORT ELEMENT

5-13. The PSE is a tailored element that can provide PSYOP support. Command relationships must be clearly defined, as PSEs do not contain an organic C2 capability. The size, composition, and capability of the PSE are determined by the requirements of the supported commander. Reachback is critical for the PSE, as it does not provide a full range of PSYOP capabilities. A PSE is often established for smaller-scale missions where the requirements do not justify a POTF with its functional component command status. A PSE differs from a POTF in that it is not a separate functional command.

5-14. A PSE is tailored to the given mission. It may consist of combinations of regional, dissemination, and tactical PSYOP battalions or may be made up of personnel from a regional or tactical battalion exclusively. A PSE composed entirely of tactical PSYOP forces may conduct crisis-response missions, such as a NEO or humanitarian relief. A PSE composed of only tactical PSYOP assets may also support a JSOTF in the absence of a JPOTF.

5-15. A PSE deployed for crisis response can be robust and include the tactical POB staff and HQ and all three TPCs. The main difference between employment as a robust PSE rather than a POTF is the lack of component command status and the limitations on production. The PSE in this instance lacks the ability to develop and produce series on a large scale. However, such missions as NEOs or humanitarian relief primarily use loudspeaker operations, face-to-face communication, and limited production by organic equipment within the TPDD or with attached DPPCs (Figure 5-2).

Figure 5-2. Deployable Print Production Center

5-16. The time required to attach and deploy dissemination battalion assets to the PSE or to augment the PSE with more than a limited number of personnel from the relevant regional battalion must be balanced against the limited amount of time and air transport available. If a crisis-response PSE transitions to sustainment or postcrisis operations, assets from a regional PSYOP battalion and a dissemination battalion rotate into the PSE to conduct PSYOP requiring greater product production capability as individual TPCs or TPDs rotate out.

Employment

5-17. PSEs composed of only tactical PSYOP assets may be established during deliberate planning as well. When supporting unconventional warfare (UW), foreign internal defense (FID), or direct action (DA) operations, especially when supporting other SOF, the exclusive deployment of tactical PSYOP is often mandated. In austere environments with rapidly changing operational conditions, the most effective PSYOP series contain products that are produced quickly within the AO of the supported unit. The attempt to produce complex products in austere environments is not only logistically problematic but also untimely.

5-18. A PSE can be task-organized with an attached TPDD to support the mission. An entire TPDD may be employed or, more often, a scaled-down TPDD can be used depending on requirements. The DPPC normally collocates with a TPDD and provides additional production capacity close to the disseminators. DPPCs deploy based on mission requirements. A PSE with several subordinate TPDDs may have multiple DPPCs depending on the mission.

5-19. The TPDD provides the resources to support MDMP and the PSYOP process. The TPDD ensures that the PSYOP process is conducted throughout the lower echelon PSYOP units. Figure 5-3 depicts the seven phases of the process, discussed in detail in Chapter 6 of this publication.

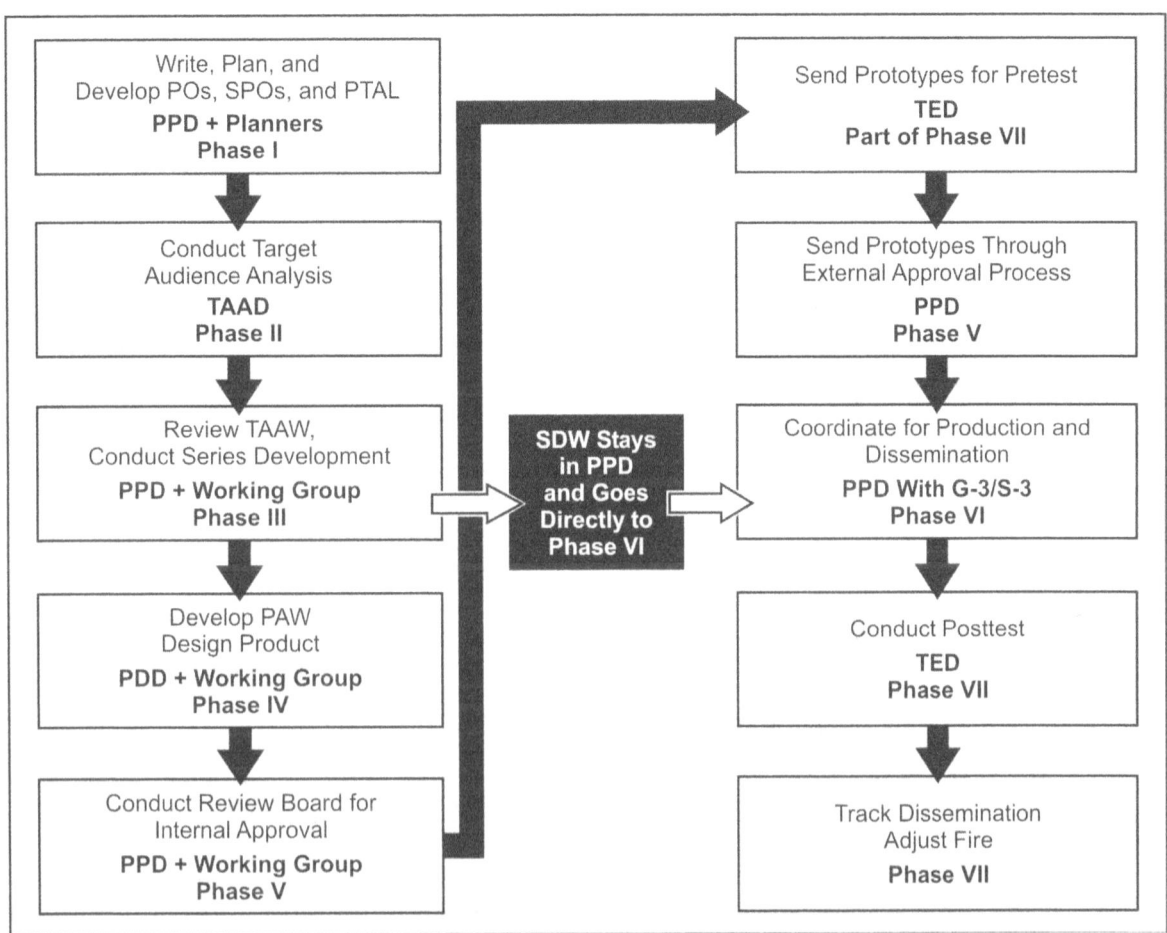

Figure 5-3. PSYOP process

5-20. At the tactical level, the PSYOP process is conducted, even though the TPDD has fewer assets than a PDC. The TPDD takes some information directly from the POTF and generates other information itself. The three teams of a TPDD—the PPT, the TAAT, and the PDT—perform the functions discussed in the following paragraphs.

Chapter 5

PLANS AND PROGRAMS TEAM

5-21. The PPT conducts mission analysis, manages SPOs, manages SPPs, manages the PSYOP process, and may conduct PSYOP assessments. The team integrates into the supported unit's MDMP. The PPT maintains contact with the POTF or the PSE. The PPT advises the commander and supported G-3 on the execution of SPPs.

5-22. PPT personnel and their primary responsibilities include the following:

- *Officer in charge.* The OIC ensures that PSYOP are fully integrated into all aspects of the supported unit's mission. He analyzes the supported unit's mission and provides input into how PSYOP can support the unit's COA. The OIC participates in the supported unit's targeting meetings and identifies PSYOP priorities. He identifies POs, as well as themes and symbols to be stressed or avoided (only done if the supported unit is the highest element in the mission; otherwise, these will be received from higher HQ). The OIC assists the Operations Directorate (J-3) or S-3 in preparing the PSYOP estimate, appendix, or plan to the OPORD, as needed.
- *Operations officer.* The operations officer oversees and manages all operations within the TPDD. Additionally, the TPDD operations officer integrates with the S-2 analysis and control element to monitor all PSYOP IRs and priority intelligence requirements (PIR), and archives all information related to the TA. The TPDD operations officer serves as the primary link with other PSYOP elements. He also reviews the TAA of the TAAT. The operations officer assists the OIC and executes the duties as the Psychological Operations development detachment (PDD) OIC in his absence.
- *Noncommissioned officer in charge.* The NCOIC assists the OIC in analyzing the supported unit mission and in PSYOP planning. The NCOIC monitors and coordinates with subordinate elements to determine product development priorities and oversee the product development process and assign each product a tracking number. The NCOIC develops and supervises the TPDD training program. He also conducts liaison with higher-level PSYOP elements, ensuring mutually supportive PSYOP activities.
- *Team leader.* The team leader assists the NCOIC in monitoring subordinate units. He develops the SPOs and identifies PTAs and available forms of media. The team leader coordinates air operations for movement, leaflet drops (Appendix H), aerial loudspeaker operations, and product support to the TPDs.
- *Assistant team leader.* The assistant team leader assists the PPT chief with his responsibilities and oversees the battle tracking of all friendly and enemy PSYOP-relevant information in the supported unit's area of influence. The assistant team leader determines the viability of leaflet operations by calculating and mapping leaflet drop patterns. He is also responsible for the setup of the PPT and the establishment of communications to all PSYOP elements.

TARGET AUDIENCE ANALYSIS TEAM

5-23. The TAAT reviews and finalizes the potential target audience list (PTAL) received from the PPT. The TAAT then analyzes each TA for its conditions, attitudes, beliefs, vulnerabilities, and susceptibilities. The TAAT combines efforts with the TAAD of the PDC to complete detailed TAA. It also maintains TA files, while monitoring intelligence reports to detect any shifts in attitudes, behavior trends, or conditions of the TA. The TAAT looks for vulnerabilities arising from these conditions that can be exploited by a series of PSYOP products or actions. The TAAT also analyzes opponent propaganda and conducts a comprehensive analysis of SCAME reports (Appendix D) initially conducted by the TPT. The TAAT also looks for propaganda disseminated via TV, Internet, radio, or regional news agencies. The TAAT, in concert with PDC assets, then assesses each SCAME to determine the propaganda plan. The TAAT also develops lines of persuasions (LOPs) and symbols for each TA and establishes credibility of each media type. The TAAT, in TPDDs, also fills the role of the TED of a PDC. Therefore, it writes surveys, manages pretesting and posttesting, and tracks MOEs. These testing responsibilities should be completed with coordination and assistance of the TED whenever possible.

5-24. TAAT personnel and their primary responsibilities include the following:
- *Team leader.* The team leader works closely with the TPDD operations officer. He also assists the TPDD NCOIC with the TPDD training program. The team leader supervises the conduct of aerial loudspeaker operations and advises the TPDD OIC on TA information needed for PSYOP planning. The team leader supervises the development of pretests, posttests, and surveys. He also reviews TPD SITREPs to make sure the TPDD incorporates their requests and observations into all TPDD activities.
- *Intelligence analyst.* The intelligence analyst reviews intelligence reports prepared by outside agencies for PSYOP-relevant information. He compiles all PIR and IRs from the detachment and submits them to the TPDD operations officer for review. The intelligence analyst is responsible for compiling the various conditions that affect each TA.
- *Assistant team leader.* The assistant team leader assists the team leader with his responsibilities, assists in refining TAs, supervises the TAA process, and coordinates for aerial loudspeaker operations. The assistant team leader also develops pretests and posttests to make sure PSYOP products, LOPs, and symbols have their intended effect. He is also responsible for tracking impact indicators to the MOEs.
- *PSYOP specialist.* The PSYOP specialist conducts TAA and may help conduct aerial loudspeaker operations. The PSYOP specialist assists the intelligence sergeant in collecting information on TAs.

PSYOP DEVELOPMENT TEAM

5-25. The PDT develops and produces products to support achievement of the supported commander's objectives. The PDT has the TPDD's only illustration and graphics capability with the PDW. The PDW enables the PDT to produce text and graphic visual products to support the commander's maneuver plan. The PDT also has limited audio and audiovisual production capabilities. Figure 5-4, for example, shows a tactical PSYOP Soldier conducting an on-camera interview near Kandahar, Afghanistan.

Figure 5-4. On-camera interview

5-26. The PDT develops products called for by series development. PDT prepares and executes the production of products or coordinates their production through external assets (POTF or indigenous resources). The PDT also manages picture and product archives, maintains product books, and manages TPDD translators and all product translations. Production assets and personnel are often attached to the PDT.

5-27. PDT personnel and their primary responsibilities include the following:
- *Team leader.* The team leader supervises the PDT during product development and production while assisting the PDD NCOIC with the training programs. The team leader monitors the maintenance of all equipment and coordinates any necessary 20-level maintenance. The team leader coordinates translator support and ensures the appropriate product is translated at the appropriate time into the correct language. The team leader also oversees quality control of all TPDD products.
- *Assistant team leader.* The assistant team leader assists the team leader with his duties and supervises the product development and production process. He maintains the product archive and product books.
- *PSYOP specialist.* The PSYOP specialist oversees the development and organic production of products. He also oversees weekly system maintenance on computers and production equipment.
- *Illustrator.* The illustrator provides assistance to the PSYOP development process by providing graphics and illustrations for products. The illustrator assists during the development process on product layouts and product production with organic assets. He also maintains the picture archive.

5-28. The TPDD operates in a fashion similar to a PDC on a smaller scale. The support the TPDD gives a division is crucial for supporting maneuver commanders; however, many products do not reach the TA without the TPD.

TACTICAL PSYCHOLOGICAL OPERATIONS DETACHMENT

5-29. The TPD provides tactical PSYOP support to brigade-sized units or battalions. The TPD commander recommends the best location for his three TPTs to support the maneuver commander. The TPD commander may maintain control of a TPT to exploit PSYOP-specific targets of opportunity. A TPD can be augmented with one or, less frequently, two additional TPTs for some missions.

5-30. The detachment HQ conducts staff integration with the supported unit HQ and assists in mission analysis and COA development. It maintains communications and conducts command, control, communications, computers, and intelligence (C4I) activities of all its TPTs. The TPD maintains constant communications with the TPDD, the POTF, or the PSE, forwarding information the TPTs obtain during operations. The TPD has no product development capability and therefore receives its products from higher HQ. The HQ section of the TPD compiles all TPT SITREPs and sends a detachment SITREP to the next-higher PSYOP HQ.

5-31. TPD personnel and their primary responsibilities include the following:
- *Detachment commander.* The detachment commander performs duties in the supported command's operations center. He provides functional expertise in PSYOP capabilities and doctrine. The detachment commander integrates directly with the supported unit's staff and ensures inclusion and integration of supporting PSYOP programs in the MDMP. Other typical duties may include the following:
    - Serves, when directed, as the advanced echelon (ADVON) for follow-on PSYOP forces.
    - Applies SO imperatives in PSYOP mission planning and execution.
    - Assists and makes recommendations to the commander and staff on PSYOP matters and requirements.
    - Conducts mission analysis and the PSYOP portion of the IPB.
    - Recommends the types and sizes of PSYOP forces to deploy and determines support requirements.
    - Writes PSYOP supporting plans, PSYOP estimate of the situation, and other documents, as required.
    - Coordinates with supporting PSYOP units.
    - Maintains communication with the POTF HQ or PSE.
    - Oversees and coordinates execution of SPPs.

- *Detachment NCOIC.* The detachment NCOIC assists the TPD OIC in all aspects of his duties. He also ensures that all TPTs receive necessary logistical and product support. Other typical duties may include the following:
    - Assists in coordination with supporting PSYOP units.
    - Establishes and administers the force-protection plan.
    - Coordinates movement and distribution of products to dissemination points.
    - Recommends personnel and equipment deployment packages.
    - Coordinates with the command, control, communications, and computer operations (C4 Ops) officer (S-6) to ensure all communication needs are met.
    - Assists in mission analysis.
    - Assists in staff integration, coordination, and planning.
    - Participates in the planning of all operations.

TACTICAL PSYCHOLOGICAL OPERATIONS TEAM

5-32. The TPT is the base element for all deployments, other than planning conferences and liaison duty. A tactical POB deploys nothing smaller than a TPT for tactical PSYOP missions. A TPT provides tactical PSYOP planning and dissemination support. A TPT may also support a Special Forces operational detachment A (SFODA), a Ranger company, or a smaller SOF element, depending on the mission. A small-scale PSE, such as a PSE working for the Country Team at a U.S. Embassy, can have a single TPT to support a medical civic action program (MEDCAP), a Dental Civic Action Project (DENTCAP), or other operations. A single TPT may be employed operationally. A TPT may also be employed as a primary trainer to various-sized elements in the combined environment, such as joint combined exercise for training (JCET) or JCS exercises. A TPT may deploy with its TPD, separately or as an attachment to another TPD.

5-33. Operationally, the TPT's primary purpose is to execute series and provide tactical PSYOP to the supported commander. The TPT must also advise the commander and staff on the psychological effects of their operations on the TA and population in their AO and answer all PSYOP-related questions. The TPT is the primary disseminator of loudspeaker messages and the primary conductor of face-to-face PSYOP.

5-34. TPT personnel and their primary responsibilities include the following:
- *Team leader.* The TPT leader must be able to assume the same duties and responsibilities of the detachment commander and NCOIC for his team and the supported unit. He must integrate SPPs into the supported unit's plans. Other duties may include the following:
    - Provides cultural expertise and language capability.
    - Conducts team preparation for movement.
    - Determines and coordinates all communication requirements for the team.
    - Serves as the PSYOP planner for the supported commander.
    - Participates in the MDMP.
    - Coordinates with supporting PSYOP units.
    - Administers the force-protection plan.
    - Determines types and quantities of products as required.
    - Executes PSYOP series.
    - Supervises supply and maintenance issues.
    - Submits SITREPs.
    - Identifies PTAs and provides higher PSYOP elements with information through passive collection and by conducting assessments.
    - Conducts staff integration and coordination.
    - Develops PSYOP portion of the supported commander's plan.
    - Coordinates for ammunition issue.
    - Prepares and issues capabilities brief for supported unit.

- *Assistant team leader and PSYOP specialist.* Initiative of the assistant team leader is key. It provides the ability to prepare men and equipment for upcoming missions in a timely manner. The planning process of the supported unit and the coordination with the TPD or PSE can easily monopolize the team leader's time. Equipment rigging and PSYOP-specific tasks may have to be accomplished in a time-constrained environment, with the team leader being occupied with planning. Typical duties performed by the assistant team leader and the PSYOP specialist may include the following:
    - Supervise the interpreter.
    - Supervise vehicle maintenance and preparations.
    - Manage products.
    - Record messages.
    - Update the product book.
    - Execute the maintenance plan.
    - Act as recorder during the mission.
    - Observe and record impact indicators.
    - Use the media kit.
    - Implement force-protection measures.
    - Perform duties as driver.

SUMMARY

5-35. Like all other PSYOP units, tactical PSYOP forces can be employed in several standard elements or in mission-configured, task-organized teams. Tactical PSYOP units are extremely flexible, mainly because of the ability of TPTs to operate effectively in a highly decentralized environment. Tactical PSYOP units have a robust capability to employ organic and attached assets to produce and disseminate products at the local level.

5-36. The TPT provides PSYOP planning and series execution in support of battalion-sized units (company-sized units in S&RO). The primary purpose of the TPT is to integrate and execute tactical PSYOP into the supported battalion commander's maneuver plan. The TPT must also advise the battalion commander and staff on the psychological effects of its operations on the TA in its AO and answer all PSYOP-related questions. The TPT conducts loudspeaker operations, face-to-face communication, and dissemination of approved audio, audiovisual, and printed materials. It is instrumental in gathering PSYOP-relevant information, conducting town or area assessments, observing impact indicators, and gathering pretesting and posttesting data. The TPT also conducts interviews with the TA. It takes pictures and documents cultural behavior for later use in products. The TPT often plays a role in establishing rapport with foreign audiences and in identifying key communicators to use in achieving U.S. national objectives.

Chapter 6
Seven-Phase PSYOP Process

PSYOP forces conduct the PSYOP process in support of operations approved by the President or the SecDef, combatant commanders, U.S. Country Teams, other government agencies (OGAs), and multinational forces across the range of military operations, from peace through conflict to war. Like all Army special operations forces (ARSOF), PSYOP units participate in operations that have a variety of profiles and complex requirements. After applying the Army SO imperatives and the MDMP to a particular mission, PSYOP commanders employ all their resources in tailoring the force to meet unique administrative and operational requirements.

PLANNING (PHASE I)

6-1. Military planning is extremely complex and must be integrated, synchronized, and coordinated at many different levels. PSYOP planners must be involved in the supported unit's planning, including the seven phases of MDMP, and must attend endless meetings and briefings. Five PSYOP-specific planning requirements must be completed for PSYOP forces to conduct the PSYOP process. The five planning requirements are—

- Develop POs.
- Develop SPOs.
- Identify PTAs.
- Determine MOEs.
- Write the PSYOP Appendix to the IO Annex (see Appendix E of this publication for a sample format).

6-2. Typically, a tactical-level PSE does not write a PSYOP OPORD. The POTF writes an overall PSYOP OPORD, as it is a functional component command. A PSE is an attachment to a maneuver unit and normally writes only the PSYOP Appendix to the IO Annex. However, the POTF OPORD must be disseminated down to the lowest elements to ensure understanding and continuity of the PSYOP effort.

PSYOP OBJECTIVES

6-3. POs provide the framework around which the overall PSYOP plan is built. However, the PSYOP planner must remember that approval of PSYOP objectives and broad themes is reserved by policy and the JSCP at levels (the President or SecDef, combatant command, JFC, and U.S. Country Teams) where the interagency process can evaluate PSYOP plans against a broad range of considerations, including other national-level information programs.

6-4. A PO is a statement of measurable response that reflects the desired behavioral change of selected foreign TAs as a result of PSYOP. Another way of stating the purpose of a PO is to state what PSYOP will do to help the commander accomplish his mission.

6-5. POs follow a "verb – object" format. The verb describes the direction of the desired change. The object is the overall behavior to be changed. Some action verbs commonly used in PSYOP are "reduce," "decrease," "prevent," "increase," "establish," and "maintain." For example, one task taken from the commander's intent in the OPORD is "Create a safe and secure environment for the people of Pineland." This statement is not a statement of measurable response reflecting a desired behavioral change. Restated as

Chapter 6

"Decrease criminal activity within Pineland," the statement can now be used as a PO because it can be measured and depicts a desired behavioral change.

6-6. Planners usually develop between 4 and 10 POs, depending on the size of the operation. The POs cover all aspects of the operation, from introduction of forces to the exit strategy, and are sometimes referred to as "cradle to grave," meaning that the PSYOP planner must develop objectives from the entry of forces to the exit of forces. The following are examples of possible POs:

- Decrease violence in the AO.
- Increase participation in national democratic institutions.
- Decrease effectiveness of insurgency or opposition force.
- Decrease injuries resulting from mines and UXO.

6-7. POs are developed at the highest level of PSYOP support and do not change when subordinate units work on their plan. There are no specific tactical POs. Soldiers at the POTF, as well as Soldiers on a TPT, use the same POs. For example, the POTF during an air campaign develops, designs, and produces a leaflet that advises enemy soldiers not to radiate air defense artillery (ADA) equipment. This product falls under the PO "Decrease combat effectiveness of enemy forces." Two weeks later, after ground forces have entered the AO, a TPT conducts a loudspeaker broadcast in support of a deception to redirect attention from the main effort. This product helps achieve the PO "Decrease combat effectiveness of enemy forces."

SUPPORTING PSYOP OBJECTIVES

6-8. Once POs are completed, the planner focuses the PSYOP plan by writing SPOs—the specific behavioral responses desired from the TA. A SPO is what PSYOP will do to get the TA to achieve POs. SPOs are unique for each PO, and each PO always has two or more SPOs. If two or more SPOs cannot be developed for a PO, the PO is too narrow in focus and needs to be rewritten. All SPOs must assist in achieving the PO. Figure 6-1 provides an example of PO and SPO linkage.

PO: Decrease Violence in the AO
SPO 1: TA refrains from committing acts of violence directed against the JTF.
SPO 2: TA refrains from committing acts of interethnic violence.
SPO 3: TA refrains from committing acts of criminal violence.

Figure 6-1. Example of PO and SPO linkage

6-9. SPOs follow a "noun – verb – object" format. The noun is always "TA." A specific TA is never written into the SPO, because often several TAs must be targeted to accomplish the desired behavioral change. The "verb – object" combination describes the desired behavioral change in much the same way as the PO. For example, if the PO is "Decrease violence in the AO," the SPO might be "TA refrains from committing acts of interethnic violence." In this example, the SPO directly supports the PO. The following are more examples of SPOs:

- TA eradicates coca crop.
- TA surrenders.
- TA votes.
- TA reports the locations of mines and UXO.
- TA delays taking hostile action.

6-10. Tactical units may need to develop additional SPOs that were not part of the higher unit's initial plan. In this situation, the tactical unit must obtain approval from the higher HQ (POTF or PSE). Upon approval, the SPO is incorporated into the overall PSYOP plan (by FRAGO) to maintain central control.

POTENTIAL TARGET AUDIENCES

6-11. Following the development of POs and SPOs, planners identify PTAs. PTAs are those audiences the planner initially thinks have the ability to accomplish the SPOs. Planners group the PTAs under their applicable SPOs. The initial PTAs are broad, as the planner rarely has the time to complete exhaustive research in this area. The PTAs are refined later in the PSYOP process. Figure 6-2 shows a template of what the plan is at this point.

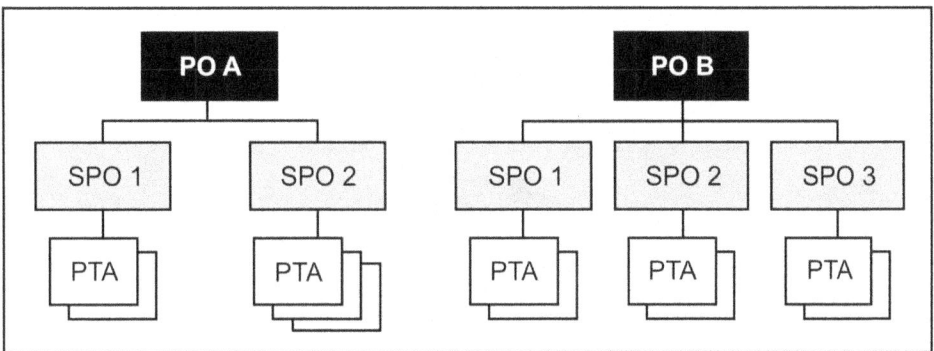

Figure 6-2. Example format of an initial PSYOP plan

MEASURES OF EFFECTIVENESS

6-12. Determining MOEs is the next task for the PSYOP planner. Development of MOEs must occur during the planning process to ensure that organic assets and PSYOP enablers, such as intelligence, are identified to assist in collecting the answers to MOEs (impact indicators) for evaluation by PSYOP. The MOEs are written as questions and tied to a PTA so that PSYOP can evaluate itself at the lowest level. MOEs are submitted as IRs, which are nominated for inclusion in the intelligence, surveillance, and reconnaissance (ISR) plan. This approach allows PSYOP to benefit from other Army or Joint ISR assets to answer some PSYOP MOEs. When MOEs are written as part of the initial PSYOP plan, the PSYOP units know exactly what to look for as they conduct their specific missions. MOEs establish the scale that is key to effective PSYOP evaluation. They focus the collection effort—as it relates to PSYOP—on areas that indicate to what extent objectives are being achieved.

6-13. To assess the overall effectiveness of the PSYOP effort, the PSYOP planner determines questions that must be answered at set points in time. As an example, a SPO is "TA decreases support for insurgents." A potential MOE could be "How much money does the national liberation front give to the insurgency each month?" Another MOE could be "How many recruits joined the insurgency last month?"

6-14. Neither of these measures alone answers whether the SPO "TA decreases support for insurgents" is being achieved. They are, however, specific measured occurrences that must be assessed more than once. Initial answers (impact indicators) to the questions (MOEs) give PSYOP forces the baseline data, while subsequent measures help determine whether the SPO is being achieved. Figure 6-3, page 6-4, shows a template of what the PSYOP plan will look like after MOEs are determined. Once the measurable objectives are clearly stated and PTAs and MOEs are determined, the planner can complete the last of the five PSYOP-specific planning requirements—write the PSYOP appendix.

PSYOP APPENDIX

6-15. At the tactical level, the PSYOP planner writes the PSYOP appendix to the supported unit's plan. The appendix gives PSYOP forces their starting point. The following format articulates some of the essential information that must be present in the appendix for PSYOP forces to be successful. Some of the information present in the appendix is the same as in the higher element's appendix or tab. For example, the POs and the majority of the SPOs, PTAs, and MOEs are the same as those used by the POTF or higher PSE. The Presidential or SecDef themes to stress or avoid are also the same. However, significant portions of the appendix are unique to the supported unit—for example, portions of the execution, service support, and command and signal paragraphs.

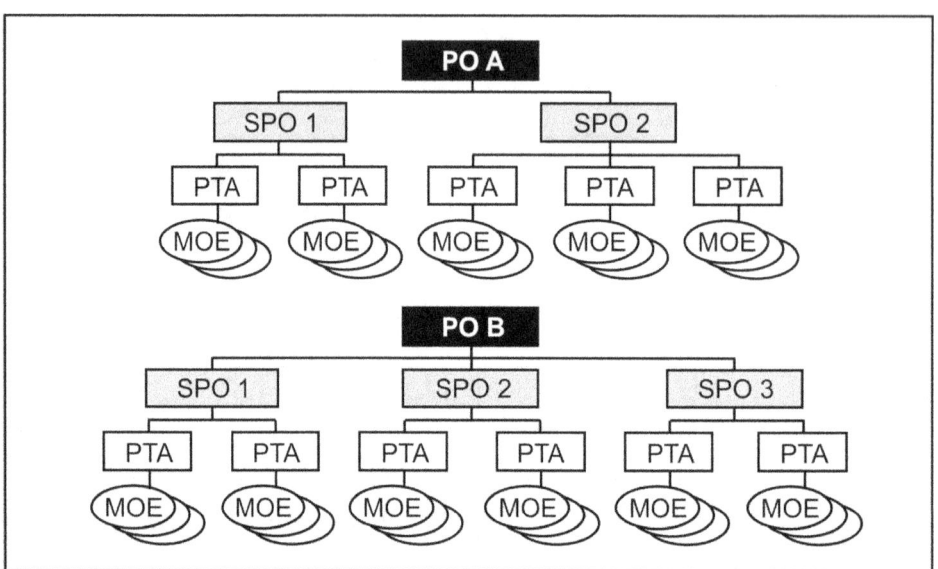

Figure 6-3. Example format of PSYOP plan with MOEs determined

6-16. The PSYOP planner must understand and include the approval process for PSYOP in the initial PSYOP appendix. Normally, the approval process is included in the form of a tab to the PSYOP appendix (see example in Appendix E of this manual). The process should address the following procedures for staffing of PSYOP series:

- *Definition of the approval authority.* Identify and discuss the limits of the approval authority. The PSYOP planner should fully articulate, to the supported commander, that any additions to this approval chain will directly and negatively impact the ability of PSYOP to support his operations.
- *Staffing procedures.* Identify the staff elements that will be included in the PSYOP approval staffing. Specify a time limit for the elements of the staff to respond and state that failing to respond in the given time period implies consent. Articulate that comments from the various staff elements will not result in changes to the series before adjudication of those comments by the approval authority. Also articulate that all PSYOP series must be staffed through the POTF or PSE for comment and approval of product numbers. This staffing is critical to ensure that the PSYOP effort remains centrally controlled and that a unity of effort exists among all PSYOP elements.

TARGET AUDIENCE ANALYSIS (PHASE II)

6-17. TAA is the second phase of the PSYOP process. TAA is a detailed, systematic examination of PSYOP-relevant information to select TAs that can accomplish a given SPO. The target audience analysis process (TAAP) is precise and focuses on a single TA under a single SPO.

6-18. The TAAP seeks to answer four basic questions:
- What TAs will be most effective in accomplishing the desired behavioral or attitudinal response?
- What LOPs will influence the TA to achieve the objective?
- What media will effectively carry the chosen LOP?
- What events will indicate success or failure of the PSYOP effort?

6-19. The TAAP is the research and analysis method for developing PSYOP programs, supporting programs, and their respective series. The process has 10 steps, which allow the PSYOP Soldier to answer the 4 basic questions stated above. The target audience analysis work sheet (TAAW) is the primary tool that facilitates the TAAP. The TAAW aids the PSYOP Soldier in determining LOPs, symbols, and media used in the development of a PSYOP series. Because conditions and vulnerabilities within a TA are continually changing, the TAAP is continuous and the TAAW is constantly reviewed, refined, and updated throughout the process.

6-20. The 10 steps of the TAAP are—
- Step 1: Complete the header data.
- Step 2: Select and refine the TA.
- Step 3: Identify the conditions that affect the TA.
- Step 4: Determine the TA's vulnerabilities.
- Step 5: Select LOPs.
- Step 6: Identify symbols.
- Step 7: Determine susceptibility rating.
- Step 8: Determine accessibility.
- Step 9: Determine the TA's effectiveness.
- Step 10: Determine impact indicators.

HEADER DATA

6-21. Header data help form a frame of reference for the analyst. The data include the series number, the date the original analysis started, the analyst's name, the date the analysis was revised, the revising analyst's name, the operation, and the PO, SPO, and PTA. To conduct TAA, the analyst must have a PTA and a SPO, and the entire TAAP must be directly related to that SPO.

TA SELECTION

6-22. The TAAP begins when the TAAT is given a SPO and a PTA. Because a PTA is usually broad or vague, it may need further refinement during the TAAP. Typically, a PTA is redefined several times during the process. The more specifically defined the PTA is, the more accurate the analysis and the more effective the PSYOP effort will be. Once the PTA is completely refined and broken into a homogeneous group of people that share similar conditions, it becomes a TA. A TA must also have the ability to achieve the desired behavioral change. The TAAT must look for the following characteristics before defining a specific TA:
- Members of the TA must experience similar conditions.
- The TA must retain the ability to achieve the SPO.
- The TA must be a homogeneous group.

6-23. The TA, once narrowly defined, is given a two-letter identifier, as determined by the POTF or the PSE. This identifier is a crucial part of all product numbering and ensures the PSYOP plan remains centrally controlled.

CONDITIONS

6-24. Conditions are those existing elements that affect the TA, but over which the TA has limited control. Conditions affecting a particular TA are limitless, and many may be irrelevant to the SPO. During the TAAP, only those conditions that affect the TA and are relevant to the desired behavioral change (SPO) are listed or considered. Conditions have three elements:
- *Stimulus* – An event, issue, or characteristic. For example, three bombings have occurred in public buildings over the last week.
- *Orientation* – The way the TA feels or thinks about a given stimulus. Continuing with the above example, the TA is afraid to enter any public buildings.
- *Behavior* – The outward, observable action or inaction after being exposed to a stimulus and filtering it through one's own orientation. Continuing with the above example, the TA remains at home.

Chapter 6

6-25. Identifying and listing conditions on the TAAW is a four-step process:
- Step 1: Place the condition (stimulus, orientation, or behavior) under a broad category. Some examples include foreign relations, demographics, economic issues, social issues, political issues, and environmental issues.
- Step 2: Number the conditions sequentially, regardless of their category.
- Step 3: Identify the source of each condition so that the PSYOP reviewer can assess its credibility—for example, CIA intelligence report dated, 2 August 2004.
- Step 4: Indicate the security classification of the information contained in each condition.

6-26. Each condition listed on the TAAW must be thoroughly researched using both open and classified sources, and each source used must be documented. This practice allows others who view the TAAW to reference the information.

6-27. Not all conditions present are readily identifiable. In some instances, assumptions must be made. When this situation occurs, the assumption should be italicized on the TAAW and a request for information (RFI) generated. These RFIs will attempt to substantiate assumptions as facts.

VULNERABILITIES

6-28. Vulnerabilities are the needs, wants, or desires that arise from the conditions of a TA. They are what PSYOP will use to influence the TA. The number of conditions that support the vulnerability determines the strength of the vulnerability. The desire of the TA to fulfill, alleviate, or eliminate a vulnerability provides the motivation for the TA to change its behavior. When the vulnerability is listed on the TAAW, it must address any needs conflicts that exist.

6-29. Determining vulnerabilities is a three-step process:
- Step 1: Identify needs based on conditions—for example, TA needs security.
- Step 2: Categorize and prioritize the needs.
- Step 3: Determine which of the following types of needs conflict exist for each of the vulnerabilities:
  - *Approach–approach.* This conflict arises when different positive ways exist to satisfy a need, but the TA has the means to choose only one.
  - *Approach–avoidance.* This conflict arises when satisfaction of one need has consequences that are unpleasant or dangerous.
  - *Avoidance–avoidance.* This conflict exists when the TA is faced with two choices. Neither of these choices is desirable, but one must be chosen.

LINES OF PERSUASION

6-30. A LOP is an argument used to obtain a desired behavioral response by exploiting vulnerabilities of a TA. It is a detailed, thorough, and concise argument that persuades the TA to behave in the desired manner. A LOP is not a slogan or a tag line.

6-31. Developing a LOP involves four steps:
- Step 1: Articulate a main argument.
- Step 2: Identify any necessary supporting arguments (evidence that must be presented for the TA to believe the main argument).
- Step 3: Determine the type of appeal that will be effective on the TA. (See FM 3-05.301 for a detailed discussion of appeals.)
- Step 4: Determine the technique that has the greatest possibility of success. The same technique will apply to all products within the series. Because of the interactive nature of face-to-face communication, the conversation may drift, and other techniques may be used with the technique identified for the series to address the argument. (See FM 3-05.301 for a detailed discussion of techniques.)

6-32. A LOP that addresses more than one vulnerability is usually more effective on the TA than is a LOP with only one vulnerability. Each vulnerability must be addressed by a LOP. At this point, the TAAT need not determine the effectiveness of the LOP—effectiveness will be determined in a later step.

SYMBOLS

6-33. Symbols are a visual (graphic or short textual), audio, or audiovisual means used to convey, reinforce, or enhance a LOP. To be effective, symbols must be recognizable, meaningful, and relevant to the TA. Each LOP will have its own list of symbols. For symbols to be useful, they must meet three criteria:
- Be recognizable by the TA.
- Have meaning for the TA.
- Help convey the LOP.

SUSCEPTIBILITY RATING

6-34. Each LOP is evaluated on its ability to influence the TA to achieve the desired behavior. Susceptibility is the degree to which the LOP will be successful in influencing the TA to respond in the desired manner or the extent to which a vulnerability can be exploited.

6-35. Susceptibility ratings identify the LOP that will have the greatest influence on the TA and why. Susceptibilities are rated on a scale of 1 to 10—the stronger the vulnerability, the higher the rating. Each rating must be justified and explained on the TAAW. A typical example of susceptibility examines both the advantages and disadvantages of the LOP—specifically, whether the needs conflict of the vulnerability has been addressed. Susceptibility ratings must be kept up-to-date as conditions of the TA change.

ACCESSIBILITY

6-36. Accessibility is defined as the availability of an audience for targeting by PSYOP. It determines which media can reach the TA and to what degree the TA can be influenced by each media type. Media analysis is an eight-step process that allows PSYOP Soldiers to evaluate each form of media. The first seven steps are discussed in FM 3-05.301. The eighth step, which is not addressed in FM 3-05.301, is the technical aspect of each broadcast agency and must be articulated as part of media analysis. The physical location, frequency, and power of the transmitter are crucial to the completion of the PSYOP transmission matrix, which is completed in Phase V.

6-37. The eight steps of the media analysis process are—
- Step 1: Evaluate how the TA currently receives its information.
- Step 2: Determine the TA's current media patterns by assessing the reach and frequency.
- Step 3: Analyze the TA's use for each medium.
- Step 4: Determine if the TA's contact with each medium is active or passive.
- Step 5: Analyze the dynamics of the TA when accessing each particular medium.
- Step 6: Determine any new media that may be effective on the TA.
- Step 7: List each medium on the TAAW in the proper format, which includes the medium's format, advantages, disadvantages, and a 1-to-10 rating. Each rating must be explained on the TAAW.
- Step 8: Articulate the technical aspect of each broadcast agency.

EFFECTIVENESS

6-38. Effectiveness is the ability of the TA to carry out the desired behavioral change. By determining effectiveness, PSYOP can accurately target the audiences that have the greatest probability of achieving the SPO.

6-39. For a TA to be effective, it must have some type of power, control, or authority. In other words, it has some degree of control over its environment, has the authority to act, and has the power to accomplish the

Chapter 6

SPO. However, no TA is all-powerful, and all TAs have some restrictions on their effectiveness. Some restrictions, such as sociological or psychological, may be mitigated by PSYOP. PSYOP may have little legal, economic, or physical control over others.

6-40. Effectiveness is listed on the TAAW by first determining an effectiveness rating on a scale of 1 to 10. Then, a concise explanation describing any restrictions the TA must overcome to achieve the SPO is provided. The needs conflict faced by the TA is also a major factor to be considered. The effectiveness rating is higher when restrictions are successfully mitigated.

IMPACT INDICATORS

6-41. Impact indicators are the events that PSYOP Soldiers look for after a series has been disseminated. They are answers to the MOEs that indicate the effectiveness of a PSYOP series. Impact indicators refine the MOEs developed during Phase I. Figure 6-4, pages 6-8 through 6-11, is an example TAAW.

Tab D (Target Audience Analysis Work Sheet) to Change 1 to (Series XXA02ka) to Appendix 2 (Psychological Operations) to Annex P (Information Operations) to XX Operation Order Number X

Target Audience Analysis

1. Header Data:
    a. Date and analyst's name: Joe Smith, 12 August 2004.
    b. Operation: XX FREEDOM.
    c. PO: Reduce effectiveness of insurgency.
    d. SPO: TA increases insurgent activities reported.
    e. PTA: XX parents.

2. Target Audience: Parents of young children in XX (ka).

3. Conditions:
    a. Source: Intelligence Report from DIA (021300ZAUG04).
        (1) Stimulus: Three bombings within the XX city limits within the last 7 days.
        (2) Orientation: TA has significant feeling of fear.
        (3) Behavior: TA is staying inside and is withdrawing from civic activity.
    b. Source: G-2 Morning Intelligence Update TF 7 (030800ZAUG04).
        (1) Stimulus: Insurgent-recruiting posters found on buildings in XX.
        (2) Orientation: TA has minimal interest, as its children are too young to be recruited.
        (3) Behavior: TA is not doing anything, because of the age of its children.
    c. Source: Intelligence Report from JAC Molesworth (011700ZAUG04).
        (1) Stimulus: Insurgent leader meeting held on 31 July in XX.
        (2) Orientation: TA's fear increasing due to declining faith in coalition.
        (3) Behavior: TA is not actively engaging with Soldiers when they enter the town.
    d. Source: Assumption RFI-PSY-041230ZAUG04.
        (1) Stimulus: No arrests by XX Security Forces of insurgents.
        (2) Orientation: TA feels insecure due to the ineffectiveness of the XX Security Forces.
        (3) Behavior: TA does not report insurgents to XX Security Forces.

4. Vulnerabilities:
    a. Vulnerability: TA needs security (1, 2, 3).

Figure 6-4. Example TAAW

b. Needs Conflict: Approach-Avoidance.

   (1) Approach: TA desires security, which means it wants to report insurgent activity in order to remove insurgents from its neighborhood.

   (2) Avoidance: TA is very concerned about reprisals by insurgents if it is identified as reporting activities.

5. Lines of Persuasion:

   a. LOP 1 Main Argument: Reporting insurgent activity will increase security.

   b. Supporting Argument 1: XX Security forces will arrest identified insurgents.

   c. Supporting Argument 2: Reporting can be done anonymously.

   d. Supporting Argument 3: Reporting insurgent activity is the most direct way parents can protect their children.

   e. Appeal: Self-preservation. Appealing to the TA's desire for security and offering it the ability to participate in its own protection.

   f. Technique: Compare and contrast—for example, emphasize the positives (peaceful neighborhoods) if reporting happens; emphasize the negatives (children being killed, maimed) if nobody reports insurgent activity.

6. Symbols (by line of persuasion):

   For LOP 1: XX Security Force shield – It is important that the TA associates its security to the XX Security Forces. TA is familiar with this symbol.

7. Susceptibility (by line of persuasion):

   This LOP addresses the need of the TA and offers a solution to its needs conflict. The difficulty of this LOP is establishing confidence and trust in the TA that the XX security forces are not corrupted and will indeed arrest insurgents. The TA may also be concerned with what happens to the insurgents after they are arrested. Is the judicial system functional?

8. Accessibility:

   a. Radio: XX has three radio stations that operate: IKJF, IABC, and ILVM. IKJF broadcasts at 91.5MHz from a 10kW transmitter located at BD23679754. IABC broadcasts at 880KHz from a 5kW transmitter located at BD23729688. ILVM broadcasts at 98.5MHz from a 15kW transmitter located at BD25049563. The three radio stations operate from 0600 in the morning until 2200 at night. Approximately 85 percent of the adult population listens to at least 2 hours of programming per day that is commonly a mix of morning hour and evening hour entertainment. The most common programming is entertainment. This entertainment is almost exclusively music consisting of both regional and modern western formats. All three stations are known to be pro-XX government.

   (1) Advantages: High percentage of TA has access to and receives information from radio broadcasts.

   (2) Disadvantage: TA listens mostly for entertainment; therefore, lengthy advertisements or other announcements may cause the TA to change the station or turn off its radios.

   b. Newspapers: Two newspapers are currently produced and in circulation within XX.

   (1) The XX Times is a coalition supportive publication that is semiweekly. Circulation for *The XX Times* is estimated at 10,000 copies per edition. It is generally disseminated throughout the day near marketplaces and public buildings and areas by hand (such as the street corner paperboy of the early 1900s in the United States). This publication is almost exclusively black and white. When color is used, it is only to add importance and to draw the attention of the reader. Pages one and two of the paper are local news articles that are of major interest, and the TA is actively engaged in this portion of the paper, especially letters to the editors.

Figure 6-4. Example TAAW (continued)

(2) The *XX Voice* is an anticoalition publication that is biweekly. This publication is almost exclusively black and white. When color is used, it is only to add importance and to draw the attention of the reader. Circulation for The XX Voice is estimated at 3,500 copies per edition. The publication is generally disseminated within specific neighborhoods known to be supportive of insurgent activities. When and how dissemination is conducted are unknown.

    (a) Advantages: Both papers are widely read beyond actual distribution numbers. Both papers have relatively low cost advertising rates.

    (b) Disadvantages: Neither paper is capable of full color. *Iraqi Voice* is unlikely to publish anything procoalition regardless of proposed monetary compensation. *The XX Times*, although procoalition, is regarded as slightly suspect credibility wise with TA.

c. TV: ICBS is the only TV station available in XX. It leans toward the progovernment side. It airs from 0700 to 2200 daily. News programming dominates the time slots from 0700 to 1000 and from 1800 to 2000. All other time slots are entertainment based, carrying multiple shows via satellite from other countries. Men who are employed generally view the TV between 0700 and 0800, and from 1800 to 2000 for the news. Those who are unemployed generally watch the TV off and on throughout the day. Commercials are shorter than the common blocks found in U.S. programming.

Each commercial is generally 20 seconds long, with a total commercial block of 1 minute. The government is currently using commercials to disseminate civic-action program information. The TA does not turn to the TV for editorial-type programming. It seems to be more concerned with gathering information that will improve quality of life.

(1) Advantages: There is a large viewership, during the evening hours. ICBS is generally eager to air any information that is helpful to the citizens.

(2) Disadvantages: Credibility is still questioned by the TA. Under the previous regime, information was routinely censored and manipulated. Any information disseminated via TV must be true and accurate. Anything offered or promised that is not exact will exacerbate the lack of trust.

d. Handbills: TA is used to seeing handbills in the range of 5 inches by 7 inches, up to 7 inches by 9 inches. They are normally used by religious leaders to provide information about celebrations or ceremonies and commonly disseminated at locations such as the marketplace. The literacy rate in adults (age 16 and over) is 75 percent (82 percent males, 68 percent females). Complex thoughts, words and sentence structures are frequently used. Most of the handbills the TA has seen are of "Xerox" quality. Most are strictly black and white with only a few religious symbols on them. Color is not used as a general rule because of a lack of color copiers. A prototype may be printed in color; however, mass production is usually done through a copy machine.

(1) Advantages: Handbills are long term. There is a sense of permanency because they are easy to store and keep. This may allow for the TA to be exposed to the same LOP several times by the same product, thus reinforcing the LOP. The TA generally trusts the handbills as a source of accurate information, especially when the TA receives the handbills from a respected religious leader or representative.

(2) Disadvantages: The relatively small size does not allow for much explanation of the LOP. Product text must be short and to the point. There is a risk of reprisals if the TA is caught having them on their person.

e. Face-to-Face Communication: Face-to-face communication is a common method for the TA to convey opinions and other types of information. Whether it is through loudspeakers or public address systems (common means of dissemination used at marketplaces or public gatherings) or through speeches, debates or general conversation, the TA seems to enjoy engaging others.

Figure 6-4. Example TAAW (continued)

Seven-Phase PSYOP Process

> Religious leaders and representatives are highly regarded and often address groups of people. The TA's culture lends itself to face-to-face communication, as it feels it can see through the words and truly judge the message by the appearance of the communicator.
>
> (1) Advantages: TA will readily engage in conversation when it does not feel threatened. This method of dissemination allows for questions and further explanation. This in turn allows for the TA to obtain more information that can be tailored individually in order to convey the idea presented.
>
> (2) Disadvantages: The TA may be leery of engaging U.S. or coalition forces, due to the fear of reprisals. Use of translators without rehearsals can also lead to confusion in the conversation. This method also can allow the TA to dwell on a single thought, which can become a roadblock to moving the conversation toward a goal.
>
> 9. Effectiveness:
>
> The TA has the ability to use the anonymous telephone line (cell phones, which are extremely common) and standard landline telephone networks. Members of the TA may have limited exposure to insurgent activities, specifically planning and coordinating. If the TA is unaware of insurgent activities prior to their being conducted, the TA will be unable to report them in time to save lives. The key will be the TA's awareness of what represents an insurgent activity.
>
> 10. Refined MOEs:
>   a. Initial MOE: How many insurgent activities reported each week?
>   b. Refined MOEs:
>   (1) How many insurgent activities were reported to XX by phone each week in XX?
>   (2) How many insurgent activities were reported to XX in person each week in XX?
>   (3) Of those who reported insurgent activities each week, how many indicated they were within this TA?

Figure 6-4. Example TAAW (continued)

SERIES DEVELOPMENT (PHASE III)

6-42. Series development is a complex, creative, and collaborative process that, when done effectively, creates multiple products and actions that change the behavior of one TA and assist in accomplishing one SPO. Historically, few examples have shown that a single product has changed the behavior of a TA. Marketing research has shown that a TA is best influenced by a series of multiple products and actions that incorporate a good mix of media. Additionally, the products and actions must be consistent and coordinated. The size of the series is determined by the complexity of what is required to bring a TA from its current behavior to the desired behavior. The TAAW is the source document for a series. By conducting series development, many of the problems PSYOP encounter by creating one product at a time will be mitigated. Four steps are involved in series development:

- Step 1: Complete a series concept work sheet (SCW).
- Step 2: Complete a series dissemination work sheet (SDW).
- Step 3: Complete a SEM.
- Step 4: Conduct an internal series review board.

SERIES CONCEPT WORK SHEET

6-43. The SCW is the tool used to begin the development of the series to change a single behavior of one TA. Series development is enhanced when conducted as a group effort, where many ideas can come together into a comprehensive plan. The group examines the TAAW and discusses the path the TA must be led down to arrive at the desired conclusion. Although the TAAW recommends LOPs and media, series concept development actually selects the LOP and the types of media to use. The question is, "How does

Chapter 6

the TA proceed from its current behavior to the desired one?" Using the TAAW as the source document, the group determines the types of products and actions necessary to change the targeted behavior of the TA. The group determines any tag line or slogan (textual symbol) required for all products in the series. Input from media experts is considered to ensure that the agreed-upon concepts are feasible with the proposed media types. The exchange of ideas, exhaustive research and analysis reflected in the TAAW, and creativity are all key to successful series development. The steps discussed in the following paragraphs will assist the working group in efficiently developing a series concept. The five steps are—

- *Step 1: Select a LOP from the TAAW.* The LOP selected is based upon the susceptibility ratings. The chosen LOP is the one determined to be most effective in achieving the SPO.
- *Step 2: Determine media types to be employed.* Media are selected based upon the accessibility ratings from the TAAW, not upon availability of dissemination assets. In addition, the working group must consider the media type that will best convey the arguments contained in the LOP. It is critical to select types of media that ensure a good mix and sufficient coverage. A good media mix allows the TA to see the same argument through various media forms, with each subsequent exposure reinforcing the LOP.
- *Step 3: Determine the number of each media type.* The LOP has a large impact on the number of products required within each media type. The following considerations determine the appropriate number of products:
  - Complexity of the LOP.
  - Number of arguments from the LOP that each media type can convey on one product.
  - Arguments from the LOP that are best suited for the specific media type.
  - Duration of the series, which may require more products to maintain the TA's interest over time.
- *Step 4: Determine the arguments from the LOP that will be used in each product or action.* The following must be considered:
  - Sequence of the arguments.
  - Needs conflicts.
  - Arguments from the LOP that are best suited for the specific media type.
  - Number of arguments from the LOP that the media type can convey on one product.
  - Reinforcement of the arguments through media mix.
- *Step 5: Determine how the series is to be staged.* A LOP may have several supporting arguments that build on one another, and each supporting argument may be a distinct stage. In that situation, supporting argument 2 (stage 2) products, for example, should not be disseminated if the TA has rejected supporting argument 1 (stage 1). Therefore, at a DP, after the products in one stage have been disseminated, PSYOP forces determine if the TA is ready for the products in the next stage. The stages must be articulated in the SCW.

Note. Once these five steps have been completed, a SCW is produced, similar to the example provided in Figure 6-5, pages 6-12 through 6-14.

Tab E (Series Concept Work Sheet) to Change 1 (Series XXA02ka) to Appendix 2 (PSYOP) to Annex P (Information Operations) to XX Operation Order Number XX

Series Concept Work Sheet

Series Number: XXA02ka.

PO: Reduce effectiveness of insurgency.

SPO: TA increases insurgent activities reported.

Figure 6-5. PSYOP SCW example

TA: Parents of young XX children in XX City.

Date: 15 August 2004.

LOP: Main Argument: Reporting insurgent activity will increase security.

Supporting Argument 1: XX security forces will arrest identified insurgents.

Supporting Argument 2: Reporting can be done anonymously.

Supporting Argument 3: Reporting insurgent activity is the most direct way parents can protect their children.

Appeal: Self-preservation. Appealing to the TA's desire for security and offering them the ability to participate in their own protection.

Technique: Compare and Contrast. Emphasize the positives if reporting happens—for example, peaceful neighborhoods. Emphasize the negatives if nobody reports insurgent activity—for example, children being killed or maimed.

Symbols to Use: XX Security Force shield. It is important that the TA associates their security to the XX security forces.

Stages: Stage I: All the products and actions that stress supporting argument 1; Stage II: All the products and actions that stress supporting argument 2; Stage III: All the products and actions that stress supporting argument 3.

Media Type 1: 8.5-inch by 5.5-inch two-sided handbill.

Number of Media Type 1: Three.

Products:

XXA02kaHB01 – Emphasize main argument and supporting argument 1.

XXA02kaHB02 – Emphasize main argument and supporting argument 2.

XXA02kaHB03 – Emphasize main argument and supporting argument 3.

Media Type 2: Radio Script

Number of Media Type 2: Three.

Products:

XXA02kaRD01 – This script must be no longer than 30 seconds; however, hit upon entire argument must focus on supporting argument 1.

XXA02kaRD02 – This script must be no longer than 30 seconds; however, hit upon entire argument must focus on supporting argument 2.

XXA02kaRD03 – This script must be no longer than 30 seconds; however, hit upon entire argument must focus on supporting argument 3.

Media Type 3: TV

Number of Media Type 3: Three.

Products:

XXA02kaLS01 – Emphasize main argument and supporting argument 1.

XXA02kaLS02 – Emphasize main argument and supporting argument 2.

XXA02kaLS03 – Emphasize main argument and supporting argument 3.

Media Type 4: One-page newspaper insert.

Number of Media Type 4: Two.

Products:

XXA02kaNP01 – Letter to the editor focusing on entire LOP.

XXA02kaNP02 – Informational in nature stressing argument 2.

Figure 6-5. PSYOP SCW example (continued)

Chapter 6

> Media Type 5: Face-to-face communication.
>
> Number of Media Type 5: Three.
>
> Products:
>
> XXA02kaFF01 – Will be disseminated with HB01 and should stress the same arguments.
>
> XXA02kaFF02 – Will be disseminated with HB02 and should stress the same arguments.
>
> XXA02kaFF03 – Will be disseminated with HB03 and should stress the same arguments.
>
> Media Type 6: PSYACT.
>
> Number of Media Type 6: One.
>
> Product:
>
> IZA02kaAC01 – Raid by Iraqi police on insurgent safe house. This will legitimize supporting argument 1 in the eyes of the TA.

Figure 6-5. PSYOP SCW example (continued)

SERIES DISSEMINATION WORK SHEET

6-44. The SDW sequences and synchronizes the dissemination of all products and actions within the series as reflected on the SCW. There are several considerations in completing the SDW.

6-45. PSYOP personnel begin the SDW by determining the overall series duration, which includes the start and end dates. The duration can begin and end based on date, phase of OPLAN or OPORD, or events. The key to completing the SDW is sequencing. The arguments contained in the LOP must be presented in the proper order. Since each product often focuses on a specific part of the LOP, the sequencing of those products is extremely important. PSYOP Soldiers must avoid oversaturating the TA with too many products at any one time but ensure sufficient coverage to change the behavior of the TA.

6-46. The SDW determines the location and time that each product will be disseminated. Information obtained through SITREPs and answers to IRs provided by the TPTs may be necessary to complete and update the SDW accurately. Six criteria for product dissemination must be considered—

- *Duration* is the start and end date for a particular product. If a product is staged, the stage must be identified here. Like series duration, a calendar date or a specific event can be the determining factor in product duration. Duration reflects the amount of time the product must be accessible by the TA to ensure sufficient exposure to the argument.
- *Timing* is the time of the day, week, month, or year that the product is to be disseminated.
- *Frequency* is the number of times during the duration period that the product will be disseminated.
- *Location* is the geographic area where the product is to be disseminated. The area is dictated by the location of the TA. For mass media, the location is the broadcast agent.
- *Placement* is the physical placement of the product within the geographic location—for example, on telephone poles, in shop windows, in schools, or at local markets. For products going out through mass media, placement is the type of outlet (radio, TV, or newspaper) and the portion of programming or section of the periodical the product should be inserted into.
- *Quantity* refers to the number of copies that need to be produced. Quantity is determined by the type of media; for example, face-to-face products will require one copy per disseminating unit, and radio will require one per disseminating station. Printed products will usually require, at most, one for each member of the TA. The one notable exception is when targeting a small TA located in a denied area. In this case, to ensure at least minimal coverage, the number of leaflets should exceed the number of TA members. Saturation of the TA and the dissemination means will also help determine the number of leaflets needed for a particular TA.

Seven-Phase PSYOP Process

6-47. Once all these factors have been determined for each product, the SDW can be completed. Figure 6-6, pages 6-15 through 6-17, provides an example of the SDW.

Tab F (Series Dissemination Work Sheet) to Change 1 (Series XXA02ka) to Appendix 2 (PSYOP) to Annex P (Information Operations) to XX Operations Order Number XX

Series Dissemination Work Sheet (SDW)

Series Number: XXA02ka.

PSYOP Objective: Reduce effectiveness of insurgency.

Supporting PSYOP Objective: TA increases insurgent activities reported.

Target Audience: Parents of young XX children in XX City.

Date: 15 August 2004.

Series Duration: 4 September 2004 through 1 October 2004.

Product Number: XXA02kaHB01.

Duration: Stage I product. Disseminated on 12 September 2004, with XXA02kaFF01 and XXA02kaLS01.

Timing: At the public market between 1100 and 1300 local.

Frequency: Once.

Location: Public market in XX City.

Placement: Given to TA attending the marketplace.

Quantity: 500.

Product Number: XXA02kaHB02.

Duration: Stage II product. Disseminated on 19 September 2004, with XXA02kaFF02 and XXA02kaLS02.

Timing: At the public market between 1100 and 1300 local.

Frequency: Once.

Location: Public market in XX City.

Placement: Given to TA attending the marketplace.

Quantity: 500.

Product Number: XXA02kaHB03.

Duration: Stage III product. Disseminated on 26 September 2004, with XXA02kaFF03 and XXA02kaLS03.

Timing: At the public market between 1100 and 1300 local.

Frequency: Once.

Location: Public market in XX City.

Placement: Given to TA attending the marketplace.

Quantity: 500.

Product Number: XXA02kaRD01.

Duration: Stage I product. 12 September through 15 September 2004.

Timing: Between the hours of 0700 and 1000 and between 1900 and 2200 local.

Frequency: Three times during morning block and three more times during evening block.

Location: XX City – Three different stations.

Placement: IKJF, IABC, and ILVM.

Quantity: Three.

Figure 6-6. PSYOP SDW example

Chapter 6

> Product Number: XXA02kaRD02.
>
> Duration: Stage II product. 19 September through 23 September 2004.
>
> Timing: Between the hours of 0700 and 1000 and between 1900 and 2200 local.
>
> Frequency: Three times during morning block and three more times during evening block.
>
> Location: XX City – Three different stations.
>
> Placement: IKJF, IABC, and ILVM.
>
> Quantity: Three.
>
> Product Number: XXA02kaRD03.
>
> Duration: Stage III product. 26 September through 29 September 2004.
>
> Timing: Between the hours of 0700 and 1000 and between 1900 and 2200 local.
>
> Frequency: Three times during morning block and three more times during evening block.
>
> Location: XX City – Three different stations.
>
> Placement: IKJF, IABC, and ILVM.
>
> Quantity: Three.
>
> Product Number: XXA02kaLS01.
>
> Duration: Stage I product. Disseminated on 12 September 2004, with XXA02kaFF01 and XXA02kaHB01.
>
> Timing: At the public market between 1100 and 1300 local.
>
> Frequency: Once.
>
> Location: Public market in XX City.
>
> Placement: Broadcast to TA attending the marketplace.
>
> Quantity: One.
>
> Product Number: XXA02kaLS02.
>
> Duration: Stage II product. Disseminated on 19 September 2004, with XXA02kaFF02 and XXA02kaHB02.
>
> Timing: At the public market between 1100 and 1300 local.
>
> Frequency: Once.
>
> Location: Public market in XX City.
>
> Placement: Broadcast to TA attending the marketplace.
>
> Quantity: One.
>
> Product Number: XXA02kaLS03.
>
> Duration: Stage III product. Disseminated on 26 September 2004, with XXA02KAFF03 and XXA02kaHB03.
>
> Timing: At the public market between 1100 and 1300 local.
>
> Frequency: Once.
>
> Location: Public market in XX City.
>
> Placement: Broadcast to TA attending the marketplace.
>
> Quantity: One.
>
> Product Number: XXA02kaNP01.
>
> Duration: 19 September and 26 September 2004.
>
> Timing: Throughout the day.
>
> Frequency: Each Sunday edition.
>
> Location: XX City.
>
> Placement: Full page in *The XX City Times* on page 2.
>
> Quantity: One.

Figure 6-6. PSYOP SDW example (continued)

> Product Number: XXA02kaNP02.
>
> Duration: 22 September and 29 September 2004.
>
> Timing: Throughout the day.
>
> Frequency: Each Sunday edition.
>
> Location: XX City.
>
> Placement: Full page in *The XX City Times*.
>
> Quantity: One.
>
> Product Number: XXA02kaAC01.
>
> Duration: Stage I product. 10 September 2004.
>
> Timing: 1100-1300.
>
> Frequency: Once.
>
> Location: XX City.
>
> Placement: Near the marketplace in XX City.
>
> Quantity: One.
>
> Product Number: XXA02kaFF01.
>
> Duration: Stage I product. Disseminated on 12 September 2004, with XXA02kaHB01 and XXA02kaLS01.
>
> Timing: At the public market between 1100 and 1300 local.
>
> Frequency: Once.
>
> Location: Public market in XX City.
>
> Placement: Given to TA attending the marketplace.
>
> Quantity: One
>
> Product Number: XXA02kaFF02.
>
> Duration: Stage II product. Disseminated on 19 September 2004, with XXA02kaHB02 and XXA02kaLS02.
>
> Timing: At the public market between 1100 and 1300 local.
>
> Frequency: Once.
>
> Location: Public market in XX City.
>
> Placement: Given to TA attending the marketplace.
>
> Quantity: One.
>
> Product Number: XXA02kaFF03.
>
> Duration: Stage III product. Disseminated on 26 September 2004, with XXA02kaHB03 and XXA02kaLS03.
>
> Timing: At the public market between 1100 and 1300 local.
>
> Frequency: Once. Location: Public market in XX City.
>
> Placement: Given to TA attending the marketplace.
>
> Quantity: One.

Figure 6-6. PSYOP SDW example (continued)

SERIES EXECUTION MATRIX

6-48. The SDW is the source document for the SEM. The SEM graphically depicts the execution of a series and is used to—

- Confirm that each product and action is coordinated and synchronized.
- Allow the TPDD to deconflict the execution of multiple series easily.
- Allow the supported commander and staff to visualize how and when a series will be executed.

Chapter 6

- Ensure that the supported unit capabilities are maximized.
- Determine the suspense dates for all product prototypes—either cardinal dates (for example, 1 September) or operational dates (for example, D+1).
- Establish the timelines for translation, pretesting, production, distribution, dissemination, and posttesting.
- Identify stages (if present) of series by placing stage number in dissemination blocks.
- Demonstrate timing of DPs for the execution of the stages.

6-49. The SEM allows the TPDD to time, synchronize, and deconflict the translation, testing, production, distribution, and dissemination of all products within a series. The SEM, when complete, allows the TPDD to determine who receives specific tasks to execute the series. These responsibilities assigned in the Change to the Appendix, which is written in Phase V. DPs control the execution of stages within the series. DPs are indicated on the SEM by the presence of a five-pointed star with a number inside. The information that a DP is based on is usually obtained through posttesting; however, impact indicators, political or operational considerations, and spontaneous events could also support the DP. A determination must be on whether the TA has accepted the arguments presented in the previous stage before executing the next stage. A DP may be placed before the first dissemination in a series. DPs are crucial to ensuring that time and resources are not wasted.

6-50. The SEM also establishes the product prototype suspense date for all products and actions in the series. The product prototype suspense date is critical to Phase V (Approval) of the PSYOP process. It is the date when all product prototypes, or their appropriate substitutes, must be completed so that the internal series review board can convene before the approval phase. Figure 6-7, page 6-19, is an example SEM.

INTERNAL SERIES REVIEW BOARD

6-51. The purpose of the internal series review board is to bring the members of all elements of the TPDD together to review a series, using the following criteria:
- Ensure that the duration of the series is long enough to achieve the desired behavioral response.
- Ensure that the types and numbers of products determined are indeed sufficient.
- Ensure that the sequencing of each product enhances the overall series.
- Ensure that all portions of the LOP are sufficiently addressed.
- Resolve any conflicts in the execution of the series.
- Ensure that the resources necessary to execute the series are available.

6-52. Once the internal series review board is complete, the TPDD can begin to write the Change to the Appendix, which is explained and completed in Phase V. However, certain members of the TPDD can begin the process once the series concept has been approved. In addition, at this point, the series moves into the development and design phase.

PRODUCT DEVELOPMENT AND DESIGN (PHASE IV)

6-53. Phase IV consists of two distinct parts—development and design. Development is the conceptualization of the product. Design is the technical aspect of turning the product concept into a prototype or substitute (a close graphic approximation of the product) of the product. Development and design of PSYOP product prototypes begin only after Phase III of the PSYOP process (Series Development) has concluded. The documents produced during Phase III—namely the SCW, SDW, and SEM—are absolutely essential, along with the TAAW produced in Phase II, to completing the development and design of a product prototype.

6-54. The conclusion of Phase IV produces a product/action work sheet (PAW) for each product or action in the series, untranslated pretest and posttest questionnaires, and an untranslated product prototype or substitutes. Substitutes are created if producing the actual prototype would be prohibitively costly or inappropriate.

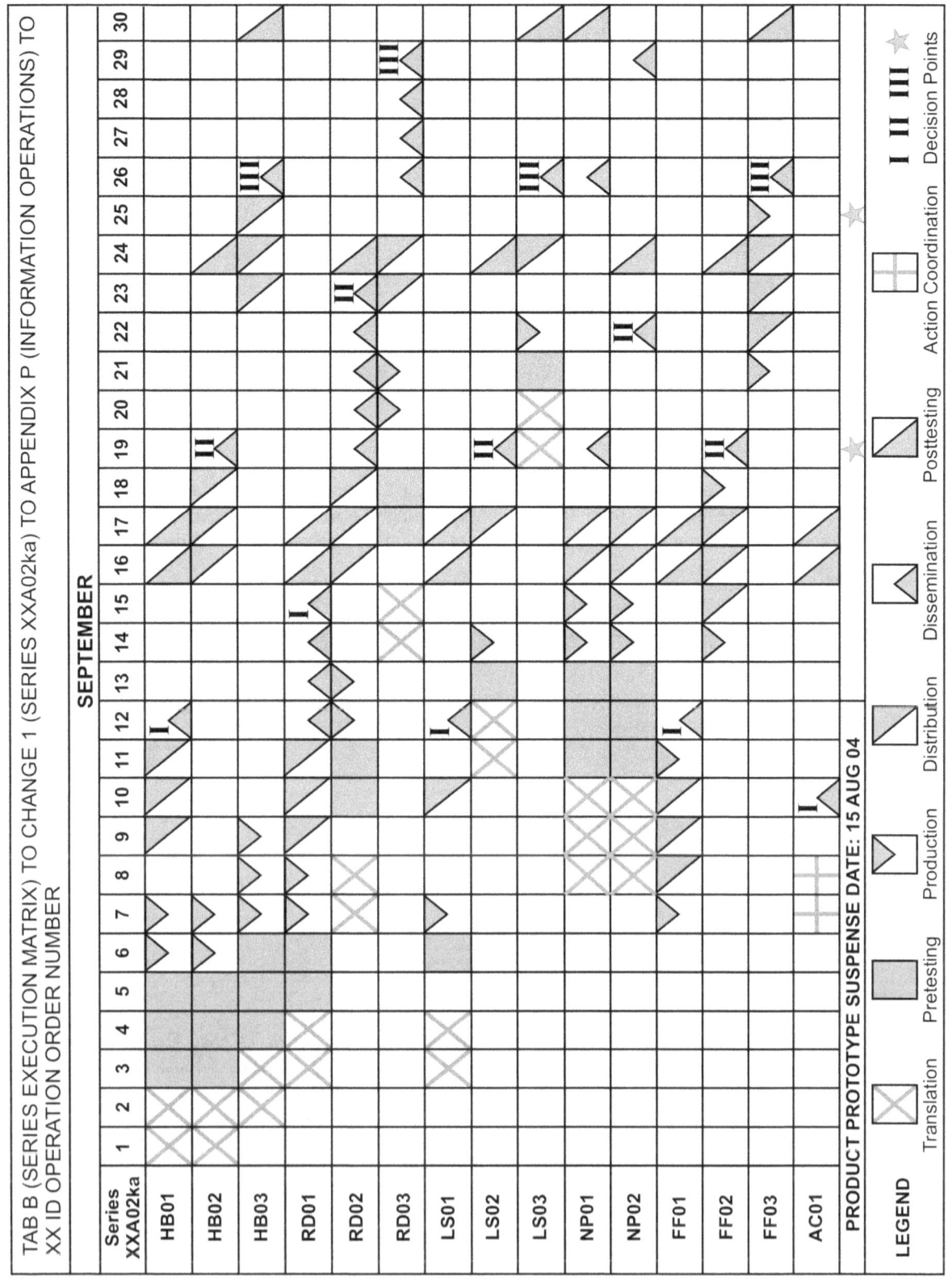

Figure 6-7. Example PSYOP SEM

6-55. Product development and design use the PAW as a source document and conceptual tool for producing prototypes and pretest and posttest questionnaires. The PAW must contain certain information.

Chapter 6

That information can be expressed in line numbers but must be fully articulated, regardless of length. The following information must appear on the PAW:

- Line 1 – Product/action number.
- Line 2 – PO.
- Line 3 – SPO.
- Line 4 – Concurrently disseminated series.
- Line 5 – TA.
- Line 6 – LOPs and symbols.
- Line 7 – Media type.
- Line 8 – Prototype suspense.
- Line 9 – Product/action concept.
- Line 10 – Pretest guidance.
- Line 11 – Posttest guidance.

LINES 1 THROUGH 8

6-56. The first eight lines on a PAW are simply transcribed from other documents. These lines ensure that the team working on this specific product prototype fully understands the series concept and the desired behavioral response being sought from the TA. Lines 9 through 11 are the newly conceptualized part of the PAW, although other documents dictate the parameters of those concepts. Table 6-1 details the source for each item on the PAW.

Table 6-1. Source documents for the PAW

Line	Source
1. Product/Action Number:	SCW, SDW
2. PO:	Appendix, SCW, SDW
3. SPO:	Appendix, SCW, SDW
4. Concurrently Disseminated Series:	All SEMs
5. TA:	TAAW, SCW, SDW
6. LOP and Symbols:	TAAW, SCW
7. Media Type:	SCW, SDW
8. Prototype Suspense:	SEM
9. Product/Action Concept: (Left and Right Limits) TAAW, SCW, SDW, SEM.	None
10. Pretest Guidance: (Left and Right Limits) TAAW, SCW, SDW.	None
11. Posttest Guidance: (Left and Right Limits) TAAW, SCW, SDW.	None

6-57. The first five lines on the PAW are similar to the header data on a TAAW. The PSYOP Soldier working on the PAW should write out these lines to refer back to without having to consult the TAAW and to provide a constant frame of reference during product conceptualization. This way, he can see, at a glance, whom he is addressing (the TA) and what he wants the TA to do (the SPO.) The concurrently disseminated series line should articulate all the series being disseminated during the same timeframe, regardless of the program or supporting program under which they fall. This approach ensures that this particular product will not contradict or mitigate the effects of other series being disseminated concurrently.

6-58. The sixth line on the PAW contains the specific symbols used in this product and the applicable elements of the LOP. If the LOP on the TAAW has three supporting arguments, but this specific product, according to the SCW, only addresses supporting argument 1, then that is the only supporting argument listed on this line. The appeal and technique of a LOP, however, are always listed.

6-59. The seventh line, media, fully describes the media being used, including all the necessary technical aspects for designing the prototype—for example, paper size and weight for visual products or transmission

Seven-Phase PSYOP Process

conventions for TV. Adequately articulating this line should include consultation with technical experts in the production of the media being used. In addition, the PSYOP Soldier may need additional specific technical information not listed on the TAAW. These details need to be obtained through contacting the production source, whether it is organic equipment or a contracted facility.

6-60. The eighth line lists the prototype suspense, which is the same as the suspense listed on the SEM. Each product in the series has the same suspense for prototype production. Individual products, therefore, may have milestones that need to be backward planned from this date.

PRODUCT/ACTION CONCEPT (LINE 9)

6-61. The product/action concept line should be a sufficiently detailed "mind's eye" description that provides enough information so that the designers can produce the prototype. The PSYOP Soldier, however, should avoid scripting out the entire product in the concept line. The concept line should articulate the exact captions of a visual product and simply summarize the key points of a long article. All symbols, graphics, pictures, colors, and textures should be listed, as well as their exact size and location on the product. If specific instances are used, the exact pictures or articles should be cited by date and location. Rudimentary sketches may be included but are unnecessary if an adequate word picture is painted by the text. Figure 6-8, pages 6-21 and 6-22, provides an example of a PAW for a handbill.

Enclosure 1 (XXA02kaHB01) to Tab C (Product/Action Work Sheet Index) to Change 1 (Series XXA02ka) Appendix 2 (Psychological Operations) to Annex P (Information Operations) to XX Operation Order Number XX

Product/Action Work Sheet   DATE: 2 Aug 04

1. Product/Action Number: XXA02kaHB012.

2. PSYOP Objective: Reduce effectiveness of insurgency.

3. Supporting PSYOP Objective: TA increases insurgent activities reported.

4. Concurrently Disseminated Series: XXA02pr, XXA02ma, XXB01ka, XXA01ka, and XXA01pr.

5. Target Audience: Parents of young XX children in XX.

6. LOP and Symbols: Main Argument: Reporting insurgent activity will increase security. Supporting Argument 1: XX security forces will arrest identified insurgents. Appeal: Self-preservation. Appealing to the TA's desire for security and offering them the ability to participate in their own protection. Technique: Compare and contrast (emphasize the positives if reporting happens—for example, peaceful neighborhoods. Emphasize the negatives if nobody reports insurgent activity—for example, children being killed or maimed). Symbols: XX Security Force shield. It is important that the TA associates their security to the XX security forces.

7. Media Type: 8.5-inch by 5.5-inch, two-sided handbill on 20-pound bond paper. The product will be produced by a contracted facility that has four-color capability.

8. Suspense: 15 August 2004.

9. Product/Action Concept: Identical front and back handbill will place XX Security Forces shield in upper right corner of handbill and 33 percent larger XX Security Forces shield in lower left corner of handbill. Picture of XX Security Forces displaying weapons cache in background in semiwatermark with irregular halo effect at outermost edges of picture leaving no useable white space. Picture of child casualty stretching from lower right corner up to 1/3 from bottom of page but not thematically obscuring safe house raid picture. Superimposition of article headline from 11 June 2004 *XX Times* with byline: "Three Sadr militia captured, two killed," with broken-edge bottom on article, as if torn from paper. Top caption reading "The XX Security Forces can stop the insurgents." Caption at top right

Figure 6-8. Example of a PAW for a handbill

Chapter 6

> hand of child casualty photo reading, "Parents, you can prevent this!" Caption at bottom right hand of child casualty photo reading "Report all insurgents."
>
> 10. Pretest Guidance: Methodology: Simple random sample XX citywide. One hundred parents drawn equally from all city schools rosters of home addresses. Rapport questions: Number of children. Ages of children. Extracurricular activities. Personal exposure to harm from insurgents. Survey section questions: Critical elements: Does subject believe insurgents are chief threat to children? Does subject believe XX Security Forces can defeat or destroy the insurgents? Does subject believe XX Security Forces will act upon reports? Bottom line questions: Do you understand what is being said? Will you report insurgents? Will end to insurgency make you safer? Future direction questions: Scaled response: Do you like receiving informational flyers (handbills)? Reporting guidance: Electronic filing of compiled questionnaire statistics will be sent not later than (NLT) 7 September 2004 via Secret Internet Protocol Router Network (SIPRNET) to POTF S-3. Paper copies of questionnaire will be sent to POTF S-3 NLT 9 September 2004.
>
> 11. Posttest Guidance: Posttesting of this product will be with all other Stage I products (XXA02kaFF01, XXA02kaRD01, XXA02kaLS01, and XXA02kaAC01) and must determine if TA has accepted supporting argument one of the LOP to support DP 1. Methodology: Simple random sample XX citywide. One hundred parents drawn equally from all city schools rosters of home addresses. Rapport questions: Pretest questions unchanged. Additionally: Knowledge of AC01 and other arrests. Survey section questions: Same as pretest. Bottom line questions: Same as pretest. Additionally: Have you reported insurgents? Future direction questions: Scaled response: Do you like receiving informational flyers (handbills)? Reporting guidance: Electronic filing of compiled questionnaire statistics will be sent NLT 17 September 2004 via SIPRNET to POTF S-3. Paper copies of questionnaire will be sent to POTF S-3 NLT 20 September 2004.

Figure 6-8. Example of a PAW for a handbill (continued)

6-62. The entire script of an audio or audiovisual product should not be written out—only summarized by key points. The script should include sound effects, formats, and major shots and transitions. With all audiovisual products, except face-to-face, a storyboard must supplement the verbal description of the product conceptualized in Line 9.

6-63. The prototype substitute for face-to-face communication is the face-to-face encounter outline (FFEO). Line 9 of the PAW should articulate the engagement strategy and the types of information that will be included in the actual FFEO. Figure 6-9, pages 6-22 and 6-23, provides an example of a PAW for face-to-face communication.

> Enclosure 12 (XXA02kaFF01) to Tab C (Product/Action Work Sheet Index) to Change 1 (Series XXA02ka) Appendix 2 (Psychological Operations) to Annex P (Information Operations) to XX Operation Order Number X
>
> **Product/Action Work Sheet**   DATE: 2 AUG 04
>
> 1. Product/Action Number: XXA02kaFF01.
> 2. PO: Reduce effectiveness of insurgency.
> 3. SPO: TA increases insurgent activities reported.
> 4. Concurrently Disseminated Series: XXA02pr, XXA02ma, XXB01ka, XXA01ka, and XXA01pr.
> 5. Target Audience: Parents of young XX children in XX.

Figure 6-9. Example of a PAW for face-to-face communication

6. LOP and Symbols: Main Argument: Reporting insurgent activity will increase security. Supporting Argument 1: XX security forces will arrest identified insurgents. Supporting Argument 2 (Not used in this particular product): Reporting can be done anonymously. Supporting Argument 3 (Not used in this particular product): Reporting insurgent activity is the most direct way parents can protect their children. Appeal: Self-preservation. Appealing to the TA's desire for security and offering them the ability to participate in their own protection. Technique: Compare and Contrast (Emphasize the positives if reporting happens, such as peaceful neighborhoods. Emphasize the negatives if nobody reports insurgent activity, such as children being killed or maimed.) Note: Since this is face-to-face, additional techniques may need to be employed due to the fluid nature of face-to-face communication. Symbols (Not used in this particular product): XX Security Force shield. It is important that the TA associates their security to the XX security forces.

7. Media Type: Face-to-face communication.

8. Suspense: 15 August 2004.

9. Product/Action Concept: Develop a flowchart that provides the background information and talking points that will allow the discussion to be successful. This will include documenting statistics on XX security forces arrests, specific instances where security forces conducted successful raids, insurgency reporting success stories, and any related information that bolsters the credibility of XX security forces. The flowchart will include possible contingencies dependent upon the reaction of the TA. NOTE: The flowchart should be developed as close to the suspense date as possible to take advantage of any additional related events or information that may affect the discussion.

10. Pretest Guidance: Methodology: Panel of experts or representative. During rehearsals ensure that the TA would not be offended or react negatively to proposed arguments. Reporting guidance: Report any problems identified back to the TPDD in order to incorporate into future face-to-face.

11. Posttest Guidance: Methodology: Will be conducted concurrently with dissemination. Reporting guidance: The effectiveness of the face-to-face encounter and the arguments contained within will be reported as part of the disseminator's SITREP.

Figure 6-9. Example of a PAW for face-to-face communication (continued)

PRETEST (LINE 10) AND POSTTEST (LINE 11)

6-64. Pretest and posttest guidance cannot be finished until prototype design is complete. The methodology and preliminary test questions, however, may be developed concurrently with the prototype. Pretest guidance should articulate sufficient information so that the pretest questionnaire can be written. The exact questions are not written out in this line; rather, several points are laid out that will be transformed into fully articulated questions on a pretest questionnaire. This line should articulate the methodology to be used in the conduct of the pretest and determines the critical elements that need to be known. These critical elements may be transformed into basic question form.

6-65. The methodology for pretesting and posttesting PSYOP products falls into two categories: survey sampling and focus groups. Survey sampling can be divided into probability and nonprobability samples. Nonprobability samples are simple quota samples that are man-on-the-street, "accidental" surveys. Probability samples consist of simple random, stratified random, and cluster surveys (Figure 6-10, page 6-24). (For a complete description of sample methodology, consult FM 3-05.301.)

6-66. Focus groups consist of either a small cross section of actual TA members, former TA members, or individuals outside the TA who have an in-depth knowledge of the TA. The three types of focus groups are the panel of TA members, the panel of representatives, and the panel of experts. The panel of TA members consists of actual members of the TA and is impossible to convene if the TA is in a denied area. A panel of representatives consists of former members of the TA. Although members of this panel were members of the TA at one time, they are considered representatives because their current conditions differ from the conditions listed for the TA in the TAAW. A panel of experts consists of nonmembers of the TA who have detailed academic or experiential knowledge of the TA.

Figure 6-10. PSYOP soldiers conducting a survey at a university in Iraq

6-67. Focus groups can employ three approaches in the conduct of pretests or posttest—group consultations, individual interviews (written or oral), or a combination of both. Group consultations can be dominated by a few or even a single dominant personality. Conversely, individual interviews lack the group dynamics that may produce a different composite picture of opinion on the product being tested. Combining the two approaches can counterbalance any sway to an extreme that may happen with the use of just one method.

6-68. Posttest guidance on the PAW also articulates methodology and the critical elements, which must be known to be articulated as questions. Posttest questions may be similar or identical to those on the pretest and some additional questions dealing with how the media was received. Posttest guidance may not include a questionnaire; instead, this section may contain the specific indicators the PSYOP Soldier will look for to gauge success. Specific indicators may be listed, along with questionnaire methodology and question guidance. Posttesting must focus on whether the TA accepted the argument presented.

DEVELOPMENT CONSIDERATIONS

6-69. All PSYOP products fall into three basic categories or types: visual, audio, and audiovisual. Each type of product has specific considerations that must be addressed during development. Knowing the basic principles of layout, formats, and writing is essential to conceptualizing effective products.

Visual Products

6-70. All visual products have elements and principles that apply to them to differing degrees. Although a soccer ball or key chain may only have a few words of text on it, the elements of layout and other principles should be applied to its development.

6-71. Eight elements of layout must be considered when developing visual products. They are format, display lines, headlines, subheadlines, captions, illustrations, copy text, and white space. In addition, there are two overriding principles of layout: eye direction and balance. Eye direction is the way the eye is guided from the optical center of the product through the body of text and graphics. Eye direction is accomplished by three methods: suggestive, sequential, and mechanical. (For a complete description of the elements of layout and eye direction, consult FM 3-05.301.)

6-72. Balance is how the weight or volume of text or graphics is distributed around the optical center of the visual product. Optical center is the natural first point of fall for the human eye on any visual product and cannot be changed. The human eye always falls first at this point. The optical center of all noncircular visual products is very similar. It is always on the central axis bisecting the product evenly and usually falls one-third of the way from the top. Most forms of balance are referenced by their relationship to this axis, as opposed to a fixed point. Optical center is different from focal point. The focal point of any visual product is the directed last point of fall for the human eye and is accomplished by design elements.

6-73. All balance is either symmetrical or asymmetrical. Balance is one of five forms. The two symmetrical forms are formal and radial balance. The asymmetrical forms of balance are informal, informal diagonal, and grouping. Grouping is simply the use of any two or more forms of balance on one product. Formal balance equally distributes text and graphics around the optical center axis of the product. Radial balance equally distributes text or graphics around a central point in a circular pattern. Informal balance arranges text or graphics unequally around the optical center axis of the product. Informal diagonal balance arranges text and graphics on opposite sides of a diagonal line running from either corner and is therefore asymmetrical. (For a further discussion of some forms of balance, consult FM 3-05.301.)

6-74. The use of graphic elements can either greatly enhance the effectiveness of a PSYOP product or create a visual break that confuses the TA and detracts from product impact. The graphic portion of any visual product has six major elements that can greatly affect the focal point of a product. The six elements are color, shape, line, mass, texture, and direction.

Color

6-75. The colors used on a product can highlight or play down subsections of the product. In general, primary colors evoke stronger emotions and responses than do pastel colors. Pastel colors can have a calming effect and may also carry the connotation that the subsection they are used in is less important than one done in a primary color. This effect may be enhanced through use of a primary color and a pastel derivative of that color. Using colors that are complimentary of each other, such as red and green, may enhance dissimilarity, derisiveness, or comparison and contrast. The PSYOP Soldier must keep in mind that colors can have overt meaning in a culture, just by their use—for example, in many Western cultures, pink denotes a girl, and light pastel blue, a boy.

Shape

6-76. In general, angular shapes denote more emotion or contention and are suggestive of action and movement. Circular shapes or curves generally evoke tranquility and ideas of harmony and completeness. In addition, shapes can have inherent meaning in a culture. A six-pointed star is sometimes just a star motif. For much of the world, however, it is immediately associated with the Jewish faith. For much of the world, any octagon is synonymous with the idea of a stop sign, regardless of the text or color applied to it. Shapes can have suggestive meaning as well. For instance, two parallel curves with equal indents toward the middle axis running between the two may have no meaning for some cultures; however, this hourglass shape, even without being filled in, is instantly associated with feminine beauty in most Western cultures.

Line

6-77. Lines have characteristics that can highlight or downplay. The weight (width) of a line can suggest varying degrees of separation or connection. The consistency of a line may have suggestive meaning as well—for example, solid lines between objects may be suggestive of direct connections, and dashed lines suggestive of subtle or secondary connections between objects and ideas. Straight lines may suggest direction and movement and curves or wavy lines a static position.

Chapter 6

Mass

6-78. The relative size of subcomponents or sections of a graphic is mass. Generally, objects or graphics of larger mass denote more importance, and smaller masses denote less importance or even irrelevance. Juxtaposition of masses—such as two objects of roughly equal real size placed side by side and one deliberately shrunk to denote smaller significance or potential—can be useful in comparing and contrasting two persons, organizations, or ideas.

Texture

6-79. Textures can be very useful to the PSYOP Soldier to call out ideas or objects and suggestively prioritize subsections of the visual product in the TA's mind. Grainy, watermarked, obscured, or unfocused pictures or graphics may denote something unimportant or less important or less threatening than a sharply focused picture. Such pictures or graphics can evoke a sense of nostalgia or loss. Rough background textures may denote something contentious, chaotic, or more significant. Conversely, smooth background textures may denote something calming, ordered, or less significant.

Direction

6-80. The direction of lines or graphics generally invokes certain ideas. Horizontal lines or layout of graphics along any left to right (or vice versa) axis are regarded by most cultures as calming and restful. Vertical lines or layout of graphics along any top to bottom (or vice versa) axis generally evokes thoughts of balance, formality, and alertness or loftiness in the spiritual, moral, or political sense. Oblique lines on any angular axis generally invoke ideas of movement and action.

Audio and Audiovisual Products

6-81. The basic rule of writing loudspeaker and radio scripts is brevity and conciseness. Input by PSYOP Soldiers on audiovisual products consists mainly of writing the script that marries up the video in the left-hand column and the audio in the right-hand column, as well as drawing or producing the storyboard for the product. (For a further discussion of audio and audiovisual product design, consult FM 3-05.301.)

6-82. A storyboard is a graphic, sequential presentation of the scenes of a film, television or theater product. A storyboard is necessary to conceptualize the before, during, and after events of a PSYACT. PSYACTs are carried out by agents other than PSYOP units and are supported by PSYOP product disseminations before, during, and after the PSYACT. The storyboard drawn for a PSYACT should include a brief scene-by-scene description of the product disseminations before and after the PSYACT and a detailed conceptualization of the flow of the PSYACT. This can be as simple as one or two frames for an event like an air strike, to many frames that "choreograph" the flow of a MEDCAP or police raid.

6-83. Storyboards are often hand drawn. They can be as simple as a rudimentary stick-figure drawing to one done with digital photos. Storyboards should include all necessary stage and camera directions. They may also include dialog cues. The view of each scene in the storyboard is drawn from the audience's viewpoint. If working with an outside agency or contractor, PSYOP units must obtain the agency or contractor's storyboard format or guidelines before beginning work. Unit SOP will dictate the format for all other storyboards.

6-84. Face-to-face communication products are designed using the FFEO to further articulate the concept that was written in Line 9 of the PAW. It should contain the arguments to be presented, any supporting information, and prepared responses to the predicted list of questions and objections from the TA. The FFEO contains the following four sections:

- Introduction and rapport building.
- Presentation of LOP.
- Answers to questions and discussion to overcome objections.
- Exit strategy or closing.

Seven-Phase PSYOP Process

6-85. The FFEO is intended to give the Soldier who is conducting the face-to-face encounter a "plan of attack" and the necessary "ammunition," so he can achieve his objective. Rehearsals are key, so he may quickly and smoothly react to all contingencies during the discussion. The format for an FFEO is provided in Figure 6-11; an actual example of an FFEO is provided in Figure 6-12, pages 6-28 and 6-29.

Tab AA (Product Prototype XX) to Enclosure XX (Product/Action Work Sheet XX) to Tab C (Product/Action Work Sheet Index) to Change 1 (Series XX) to Appendix 2 (Psychological Operations) to Annex P (Information Operations) to XX Operation Order Number X

FFEO Format

SPO – Specific behavior being sought.

LOP – Portion that will used in this encounter.

- A. Introduction and Rapport Building.
    1. Introduce self (and team if culture permits the introduction of subordinates).
    2. Discuss the reason for being there.
    3. Engage in culturally specific formalities, such as shaking hands, drinking tea, or conversing politely (about weather, health, sports, and so on).
- B. Presentation of LOP.
    1. Main Argument.
        a. Specific point or facts.
        b. Specific point or facts.
    2. Supporting Argument 1.
        a. Specific point or facts.
        b. Specific point or facts.
    3. Supporting Argument 2.
        a. Specific point or facts.
        b. Specific point or facts.
- C. Answers to Questions and Discussion to Overcome Objections.
    1. Predict possible question or objection.
        Answer with prepared response.
    2. Predict possible question or objection.
        Answer with prepared response.
    3. Predict possible question or objection.
        Answer with prepared response.
- D. Exit Strategy or Closing.
    1. Encounter has gone well.
        a. Leave a deliverable if appropriate.
        b. Extract a commitment to behave in desired manner.
    2. Encounter has gone poorly.
        a. Exit quickly without escalation.
        b. Determine if different approach would be successful. Document primary reason why encounter went poorly.

Figure 6-11. FFEO format

Tab AA (Product Prototype XXA02kaFF01) to Enclosure 12 (Product/Action Work Sheet XXA02kaFF01) to Tab C (Product/Action Work Sheet Index) to Change 1 (Series XXA02ka) to Appendix 2 (Psychological Operations) to Annex (Information Operations) to XX Operation Order Number X

FFEO

SPO: Increase insurgent activities reported.

LOP: XX Security Forces will arrest identified security forces.

A. Introduction and Rapport Building.
   1. TPT introduces itself.
   2. We are in the area disseminating handbills that address the need to report insurgent activity. Unobtrusively probe for relevant information—for example, do they have children?
   3. Engage in culturally specific formalities, such as shaking hands, drinking tea, or conversing politely (about weather, health, sports, and so on).

B. Presentation of LOP.
   1. Reporting insurgent activity will increase security.
      a. In XX city, reports from citizens have resulted in many arrests, resulting in a 20-percent drop in insurgent activities in the last month. Of those who reported the insurgent activities, only one faced repercussions.
      b. Insurgent bombings decreased 6 percent last month in XX, largely based on an increase in reports.
   2. XX Security Forces will arrest identified insurgents.
      a. XX Security Forces arrested four people in the raid in this city 2 days ago.
      b. XX Security Forces recently killed two XX militiamen.
      c. The XX *City Times* had four stories last week that emphasized the ability of the XX Security Forces to control crime.

C. Answers to Questions and Discussion to Overcome Objections.
   1. If I report insurgent activity, they will kill me.
      We are developing ways to report anonymously. There are several ways that this could be done. An anonymous phone line possibly or a drop box. Attempt to get the TA to offer ideas about what they would be most comfortable with. If you can engage them in the decision, they will be more committed.
   2. The XX Security Forces are corrupt.
      Understand that in the past this has been a problem. XX organization is committed to overcoming this problem, as all XX Security Force members are now required to attend 200 hours of training to international standards. This requirement was established by your new government last week and demonstrates everyone's commitment to solving this problem.
   3. The XX Security Forces are incompetent.
      Can use the same answer as the previous concern, plus several examples. They conducted a very successful raid 2 days ago where four insurgents were arrested.
   4. How do I report if I wanted to?
      We will be giving that information within the next week, as the details are still being worked out. You can always report to any coalition member or XX Security Force member, although I realize these are not anonymous procedures.

D. Exit Strategy or Closing.
   1. Encounter has gone well.
      a. Leave HB XXA02kaHB01 with TA.

Figure 6-12. Example FFEO

> b. Attempt to get commitment from TA to report and to be on the lookout for the anonymous method in the coming weeks.
> 2. Encounter has gone poorly.
>   a. Leave HB XXA02kaHB01 with TA.
>   b. Exit quickly without escalation. Determine if different approach would be successful. Document primary reason why encounter went poorly.

Figure 6-12. Example FFEO (continued)

6-86. Once the product prototype is completed and pretest and posttest guidance completed on the PAW, the pretest and posttest questionnaires can be developed. Pretest and posttest questionnaires are composed of two sections—the header data and the survey section.

6-87. The header data section of pretest and posttest questionnaires contains the following items:
- Product number.
- Interview date and location.
- Interviewer name.
- Interviewee name.
- Relation in TA.
- Applicable subgroup.
- Rapport building.
- Extraneous demographic questions.
- How viewed or received (posttest).
- Retained (yes or no) (posttest).
- Exposure to product (pretest).

6-88. Determining the relation of the test subject in the TA also serves to build rapport. This subsection is used administratively to determine relevant questions that identify which portion (if any) of the TA the subject is part of. Additional questions that otherwise have little or no PSYOP value may be included specifically to build rapport.

6-89. The header data should include the where, when, and how that the subject viewed, heard, or received the product. If the product was retainable, the subject should be asked if they did so. The last entry on the pretest questionnaire header data may include instructions on how to expose the product to the subject or simply a note to the tester to remind him to show the product to the test subject.

6-90. The survey section of the pretest and posttest questionnaire contains the following items:
- Warm-up questions (if applicable).
- Survey questions.
- Bottom line questions.
- General comprehension questions.
- Whether the SPO will be acted on (pretest).
- Whether interviewee be more likely to act (pretest).
- SPO accomplished (posttest).
- Future direction questions.

6-91. The survey section may or may not have "warm-up" questions at the start. Warm up questions are put in to reduce the impact of sensitive questions in the survey. The rapport building questions in the header section may serve this purpose. If a product will probably evoke an emotional response, it may be difficult and perhaps counterproductive to tone down that response. Several sensitive questions may need to be asked. When developing the questionnaire, "soft-ball" or even irrelevant questions may be placed between sensitive questions.

6-92. The survey section also includes a series of "bottom line" questions. This section should include one or more general comprehension questions to determine if the TA understood the product. For the pretest, the subject should be asked if they will act upon the SPO or if the product advances the argument for acting (in the desired manner) on the SPO. For posttesting the question of whether the SPO was acted upon must be asked. Both pretest and posttest questionnaires may include future direction questions. These can be specific to the type and content of the product—for example, "Do you like receiving information via the radio?" They can also be general questions that further refine the TAAW.

6-93. Questionnaires can use three types of questions—open-ended, closed-ended, and scaled response. When developing questions, avoid leading or weighted questions. A general rule of thumb is to use adjectives and adverbs sparingly and never use exaggerated expressions or derogatory terms; for example, best, worst, most, and least. Figure 6-13 provides an example pretest questionnaire, and Figure 6-14, page 6-31, is an example of a posttest questionnaire.

Tab AB (Pretest Questionnaire Stage 1 XXA02kaHB01) to Enclosure 1 (Product/Action Work Sheet XXA02kaHB01) to Tab C (Product/Action Work Sheet Index) to Change 1 (Series XXA02ka) to Appendix 2 (PSYOP) to Annex P (Information Operations) to XX Operation Order Number X

Pretest Questionnaire

Product/Action Number: XXA02kaHB01

Interview Date:

Interview Location:

Interviewer:

Subject:

Rapport Questions:

1. How many children do you have?

2. How old are the children?

3. What schools do they go to?

4. Has anyone you know, or even someone in your family, been harmed by the insurgents?

Give the subject a copy of Handbill 01. Allow sufficient time for the subject to read or view the handbill.

Survey Questions:

1. Do you remember the raid the XX Security Forces did on June 10th?

2. The insurgents are the chief threat to my children?
   Strongly Agree   Somewhat Agree   No Opinion   Somewhat Disagree   Strongly Disagree

3. The XX Security Forces can get rid of the insurgents?
   Strongly Agree   Somewhat Agree   No Opinion   Somewhat Disagree   Strongly Disagree

4. The XX Security Forces will act if I report a suspected insurgent?
   Strongly Agree   Somewhat Agree   No Opinion   Somewhat Disagree   Strongly Disagree

5. What does this handbill say to you?

6. Will you report insurgents?
   Definitely   Maybe   Unsure   Probably Not   Definitely Not

7. Will you be safer if the insurgents were gone?
   Definitely   Maybe   Unsure   Probably Not   Definitely Not

8. Do you like receiving information this way?
   Definitely   Maybe   Unsure   Probably Not   Definitely Not

Figure 6-13. Example pretest questionnaire

> Tab AC (Posttest Questionnaire Stage 1 XXA02kaHB01) to Enclosure 1 (Product/Action Work Sheet XXA02kaHB01) to Tab C (Product/Action Work Sheet Index) to Change 1 (Series XXA02ka) to Appendix 2 (PSYOP) to Annex P (Information Operations) to XX Operation Order Number X
>
> **Posttest Questionnaire**
>
> **Product/Action Number: Stage 1 XXA02kaHB01**
> **Interview Date:**
> **Interview Location:**
> **Interviewer:**
> **Subject:**
> **Rapport Questions:**
> 1. How many children do you have?
> 2. How old are the children?
> 3. What schools do they go to?
> 4. Has anyone you know, or even someone in your family, been harmed by the insurgents?
> 5. Did you hear about the XX Security Forces raid near the market on September 12th?
> 6. Have you heard of any other arrests of insurgents?
> 7. Have you seen this handbill before?
> 8. Did you save the handbill, give it away, or throw it away?
>
> **Survey Questions:**
> 1. Do you remember the raid the XX Security Forces did on September 12th?
> 2. The insurgents are the chief threat to my children?
>
>   Strongly Agree   Somewhat Agree   No Opinion   Somewhat Disagree   Strongly Disagree
> 3. The XX Security Forces can get rid of the insurgents?
>
>   Strongly Agree   Somewhat Agree   No Opinion   Somewhat Disagree   Strongly Disagree
> 4. The XX Security Forces will act if I report a suspected insurgent?
>
>   Strongly Agree   Somewhat Agree   No Opinion   Somewhat Disagree   Strongly Disagree
> 5. What does this handbill say to you?
> 6. Have you reported any suspicious characters?
> 7. Will you report insurgents?
>
>   Definitely   Maybe   Unsure   Probably Not   Definitely Not
> 8. Will you be safer if the insurgents were gone?
>
>   Definitely   Maybe   Unsure   Probably Not   Definitely Not
> 9. Do you like receiving information this way?
>
>   Definitely   Maybe   Unsure   Probably Not   Definitely Not

Figure 6-14. Example posttest questionnaire

ADDITIONAL TESTING CONSIDERATIONS

6-94. Producing an actual product prototype may not be practical due to cost and timeliness. In some cases, a substitute of the product may be used to submit for approval. With consumer goods, a large cost may be incurred to make initial molds, plates, or dyes, even if the unit cost is low. Few manufacturers or distributors will execute such work without an approved contract.

6-95. Manually producing a prototype or substitute of the product can be as simple as gluing paper graphics onto a soccer ball or school notebook. Frequently with audio products, the script for the product is pretested before production. Cost prohibits production of audiovisual prototypes before approval. This restriction can be overcome by submitting the storyboard and script for approval purposes.

6-96. Face-to-face communication and PSYACTs present pretest challenges as well. Face-to-face communication can be pretested by presenting the talking points to a focus group and getting their input. Pretesting face-to-face communication can also be accomplished by rehearsing the communication on a small group of the TA in an isolated area of the AO. PSYACTs may be pretested by presenting the storyboard of the PSYACT to a focus group and asking a series of hypothetical questions on the group's possible reaction to the actual PSYACT. Executing a small-scale version of the PSYACT in an isolated area of the AO may be possible as well. In this case, posttesting the exposed portion of the TA may or may not be possible. The observed behavior that happens after the execution of the PSYACT may be the only measure of success.

6-97. Product development is the process of conceptualizing the product on the PAW. It ends when Line 9 of the PAW is completed. Product design is the development of a prototype based on the PAW. Development is conducted by PSYOP Soldiers with occasional input from outside technical experts. While prototype design is done primarily by low-density military occupational specialties (MOSs) and outside technicians, the PSYOP Soldier is still responsible for supervision and creative input.

INTERNAL PRODUCT REVIEW BOARD

6-98. Once all product prototypes and substitutes within the series are complete, an internal product review board (Figure 6-15) is convened. The board is similar to the internal series review board where the initial series concept was approved. The board looks at all the prototypes and substitutes within the series and ensures that each accomplishes its intended goal. While reviewing each individual product or prototype, the board reviews the series documentation and the TAAW to ensure continuity. It also ensures that each product or prototype reinforces each other and that no contradictions exist. This review is the last review of the series before submitting it to the external approval authority, which is Phase V of the PSYOP process.

Figure 6-15. Conducting an internal product review board

6-99. The review board should be composed of the following representatives:
- Personnel from all sections of the TPDD.
- LNOs (dissemination battalion or contractors).
- Strategic studies detachment (SSD) personnel, if available.
- TPDD or TPC commander.

6-100. When all recommended changes to the prototypes are completed, pretest and posttest questionnaires can be finalized. Phase IV ends with the completion of all product prototypes and pretest and posttest questionnaires for the series. They are then submitted as a packet for approval.

APPROVAL (PHASE V)

6-101. The approval phase of the PSYOP process is where PSYOP receives approval to disseminate the products and conduct the actions necessary to change a single behavior of one TA. This is done as a series package. The central document of this package is the Change to the PSYOP appendix that, when issued as part of a supported unit's FRAGO, becomes an order for all elements of the supported unit to execute the series.

6-102. The Change to the PSYOP Appendix (Figure 6-16, pages 6-34 and 6-35) is issued in the standard five-paragraph format, with seven attachments (tabs):
- Paragraph 1 (Situation) of the Change contains any changes that have occurred in the PSYOP situation (friendly, enemy, neutral, or attachments or detachments) since the last change or the initial appendix was published. These variations in the situation may or may not be related to the execution of the series.
- Paragraph 2 (Mission) should not have any changes from the initial appendix unless the POs have changed.
- Paragraph 3 (Execution).
  - Paragraph 3a (Scheme of PSYOP) of the Change will identify the series to be executed, the stages and DPs of that series, the SPO, the TA, the start and end dates, the types of products to be used, and the area where the series will be executed.
  - Paragraph 3b (Tasks to Subordinate Units) of the Change will assign clear responsibility for all elements executing the series, including the element that is writing the Change.
  - Paragraph 3c (Coordinating Instructions) of the Change will discuss dissemination and usually references Tab B (SEM).
- Paragraph 4 (Service Support) of the Change will only contain changes if the series requires additional service and support requirements (for example, contracting and distribution) that were not covered in the initial appendix.
- Paragraph 5 (Command and Signal).
  - Paragraph 5a (Coommand) of the Change will detail any changes in reporting requirements or command relationships—for example, placing additional TPTs with a different TPD for a specific short-duration mission may not require attachment, but may require stating the support relationship in the division order for the execution of the series.
  - Paragraph 5b (Signal) of the Change typically references Tab G (PTM) for all PSYOP broadcasts occurring in the execution of the series. The initial appendix that this change is referencing is located in Appendix E of this manual.
- Tab A – Series Executive Summary (SES).
- Tab B – SEM.
- Tab C – PAW Index.
- Tab D – TAAW.
- Tab E – SCW.
- Tab F – Series Dissemination Work Sheet (SDW).
- Tab G – Psychological Operations Transmission Matrix (PTM).

XX PSYOP Company
XX, XX
DTG

Change 1 (Series XXA02ka) Appendix 2 (Psychological Operations) to Annex P (Information Operations) to XX Operation Order Number X

Time Zone used throughout the order: Local.

1. SITUATION.

    a. Hostile: Recent insurgent propaganda activity indicates that insurgents have acquired a limited, single color, mass print capability (30,000 per hour) employed in the XX area. Products produced by this capability and used with insurgent actions indicate the enemy propaganda objective is to reduce the effectiveness of the local XX government by exploiting the following arguments:

    (1) The XX Government is a puppet for the U.S. occupiers.

    (2) The XX Government cannot provide security for the citizens of XX.

    (3) The XX Government cannot provide basic services for the citizens of XX.

    b. Friendly. No change.

    c. Neutral. Because of the deteriorating security situation, the United Nation Humanitarian Relief Commission has suspended its information campaign in the XX ID AOR.

    d. Attachments and Detachments. No change.

2. MISSION. No change.

3. EXECUTION.

    a. Scheme of PSYOP (Add). Execute series XXA02ka to increase the number of insurgent activities reported by the parents of young XX children in XX. This series will be executed beginning NLT 1 September 2004 and ending no sooner than 01 October 2004. This series will be conducted in three stages with two DPs. The execution of Stage II will be dependent upon success in Stage I, and the execution of Stage III will be dependent upon success in Stage II. DP 1 is for the execution of Stage II and will be NLT 181200Z SEP 04. DP 2 is for the execution of stage III and will be NLT 251200Z SEP 04. This series will include the dissemination of handbills, radio broadcasts, loudspeaker broadcasts, newspaper inserts or editorials, and face-to-face communication. Individual product translation, pretesting, production, distribution, dissemination, and posttesting will be executed IAW the Series Execution Matrix (Tab B). Pretesting will be conducted using the panel of representatives method. Posttesting will be conducted IAW instructions contained in the Enclosures to Tab C of this change. Organic assets will produce audio and visual products. Distribution will be timely, and both the sender and the receiver will confirm receipt of electronic transmissions.

    b. Task to Subordinate Units.

    (1) TPC HQ: No change.

    (2) TPDD: Translate and produce audio and visual products in accordance with Tab B.

    (3) TPD XXX: Execute series XXA02ka in accordance with attachments.

    (4) PAO 2 Brigade: Will coordinate for the presence of XXXX imbedded reporter to be on location when XXA02kaAC01 is executed.

    c. Coordinating Instructions.

    (1) Presidential and SecDef themes. No change.

    (2) PTAs. No change.

    (3) Timelines for dissemination of PSYOP products will be IAW Tab B (SEM).

    (4) Requests for PSYOP support. No change.

Figure 6-16. Example of a change to the appendix

Seven-Phase PSYOP Process

> (5) Aerial delivery of PSYOP products. No change.
>
> (6) SITREP format. No change.
>
> 4. SERVICE SUPPORT. No Change.
>
> 5. COMMAND AND SIGNAL.
>
>   a. Command. TPT XXX (X Brigade) and XXX (X Brigade) will be OPCON to and receive CSS from X BDE from 110001Z SEP 04 thru 272359Z SEP 04.
>
>   b. Signal. Transmissions. See Tab G.
>
> Tab A – SES
> Tab B – SEM
> Tab C – PAW Index
> Tab D – TAAW
> Tab E – SCW
> Tab F – SDW
> Tab G – PTM

Figure 6-16. Example of a change to the appendix (continued)

TRANSMISSION MATRIX

6-103. The PTM is the document that lists all transmissions that will occur within a series. Examples of PSYOP transmission include radio, TV, Internet, telephone (fixed and cellular), and facsimile (FAX) machine. The PTM is the primary document to coordinate PSYOP transmissions with electronic warfare activity occurring in the supported unit's AO. Normally, this coordination is handled through the IO officer; however, at brigade level and below, the fire support element (FSE) may handle coordination. The technical information listed in the PTM originates from the TAAW. If the TAAW fails to identify this information, an RFI will be generated and that block on the PTM will be filled with a reference to the RFI. Figure 6-17 is an example PTM.

Tab G (Psychological Operations Transmission Matrix) to Change 1 (Series XXA02ka) Appendix 2 (PSYOP) to Annex (Information Operations) to XX Operation Order Number X							
Product Number	Transmission Times	Dates	Frequency	Transmitter Location	Power	Organization
XXA02ka RD01	0705-0706, 0805-0806, 0905-0906, 1905-1906, 2005-2006, 2105-2106	12-15 Sep 04	91.5 kHz	BD23679754	10KW	IKJF
	0715-0716, 0815-0816, 0915-0916, 1915-1916, 2015-2016, 2115-2116	12-15 Sep 04	880 kHz	BD23729688	5KW	IABC
	0725-0726, 0825-0826, 0925-0926, 1925-1926, 2025-2026, 2125-2126	12-15 Sep 04	98.5 MHz	RFI-PSY-041200ZAUG04	RFI-PSY-041200ZAUG04	ILVM

Figure 6-17. Example of a PSYOP transmission matrix

Chapter 6

SERIES EXECUTIVE SUMMARY

6-104. The next step in preparing the series for approval is to write the SES—a broad document laying out the concept of the series for the supported commander. The SES should, at a minimum, contain the PO, TA and behavior to be changed (SPO), media to be exploited, units to be involved, timeline (stages and DP) for the series in general terms, and the geographic locations where the series will be executed. Figure 6-18 presents a minimal example of a SES.

Tab A (Executive Summary) to Change 1 (Series XXA02ka) to Appendix 2 (Psychological Operations) to Annex P (Information Operations) to XX Operation Order Number X

Executive Summary for Series XXA02ka

Series XXA02ka will reduce the effectiveness of insurgent activity by increasing reporting of insurgent activity by the parents of young children in XX. Series XXA02ka will be executed from 12 September 2004 through 29 September 2004 in three stages with two DPs. The first DP (DP 1) is to execute Stage II and is NLT 181200Z SEP 04. DP 1 depends on the TA accepting that the XX Security Forces can and will arrest insurgents (Stage I) and will be determined by posttesting of Stage I. The second DP (DP 2) is to execute Stage III and is NLT 251200Z SEP 04. DP 2 depends on the TA accepting that they can anonymously report insurgent activity to XX Security Forces (Stage II) and will be determined by posttesting of Stage II. Stage III is getting the TA to accept that reporting insurgents is in the best interest and safety of their children and that they can increase their family's security in so doing. Series XXA02ka will include handbills, newspaper inserts, radio broadcasts (local radio stations), loudspeaker broadcasts, face-to-face communication, as well as one PSYACT by the XX Security Forces. The measure of effectiveness for Series XXA02ka is the number of calls to the telephone number provided exclusively for this series (Stage II) from 19 September 2004 through 16 October 2004, as measured weekly, as well as posttesting after the completion of each stage. To meet the planned timeline, as articulated in the SEM (Tab B), this series must receive approval NLT 010001Z SEP 04.

WILLIAM J. REASON
MAJ, PO
Commanding

Figure 6-18. Example of a series executive summary

TAB C (PRODUCT/ACTION WORK SHEET INDEX)

6-105. The PAW index tab will be Tab C (Figure 6-19) to the Change to the base PSYOP Appendix. This tab will list the product numbers for all products in the series. The PAW for each product number listed will be an enclosure to Tab C. The number of products and actions in the series determines the number of enclosures.

Tab C (Product/Action Work Sheet Index) to Change 1 to Appendix 2 (Psychological Operations) to Annex P (Information Operations) to XX Operation Order Number X

Product Numbers
Series XXA02ka
Enclosure 1 - XXA02kaHB01
Enclosure 2 - XXA02kaNP02
Enclosure 3 - XXA02kaCB01
Enclosure 4 - XXA02kaRD01
Enclosure 5 - XXA02kaRD02
Enclosure 6 - XXA02kaRD03

Figure 6-19. Tab C (PAW Index) to Change 1 to Appendix 2 (PSYOP)

6-106. Each enclosure to Tab C (PAW) will have three expanding tabs. These expanding tabs will be the product prototype or substitute, the pretesting questionnaire or survey, and the posttesting questionnaire or survey. Expanding tabs to an enclosure are written as double letter with the first and second letter being "A." For subsequent expanding tabs, the first letter remains constant, and the second letter follows in alphabetical order (AA, AB, AC, and so on). If the second letter reaches "Z," the first letter continues in alphabetical order (BA, BB, BC, and so on). The PSYOP planner should rarely have to expand beyond Tab AC.

6-107. The final step in preparing the series for approval is preparing the input to the FRAGO to the supported unit's base order. This input is normally in the form of identifying supported unit elements that are required to execute the series and referencing them to the change of the PSYOP appendix. This should include elements of the supported unit that are affected by changes in command relationship that are called for in executing the series. When this is complete, the series is prepared for approval.

6-108. Staffing of approval packets for series can become time consuming and cumbersome if staff bureaucracy is allowed to dictate the process. Parallel staffing, electronic staffing, and "silence implies consent" are all means to expedite the process. Ultimately, the commander or his designated representative is the only approval authority. Staff elements cannot veto individual products or the series itself. All staff comments and considerations of nonconcurrence by the senior PSYOP representative to the supported unit should be forwarded for consideration by the approving authority.

6-109. Once the approval authority has adjudicated the staff comments and any considerations of nonconcurrence and given his approval for the series, the supported unit's operations section issues the FRAGO. This FRAGO includes the Change to the PSYOP Appendix and order the execution of the series. This FRAGO is an order to all elements of the supported command to execute the series IAW the instructions contained in the Change to the PSYOP Appendix and all of its attachments.

PRODUCTION, DISTRIBUTION, AND DISSEMINATION (PHASE VI)

6-110. Once series and product approval are granted, Phase VI of the PSYOP process commences. This phase consists of translation, pretesting, production, distribution, dissemination, and posttesting. Pretesting and posttesting are conducted during this phase and evaluated during Phase VII. The SEM, SDW, and the change to the PSYOP appendix cover the timelines for Phase VI. Figure 6-20 diagrams the process of Phase VI.

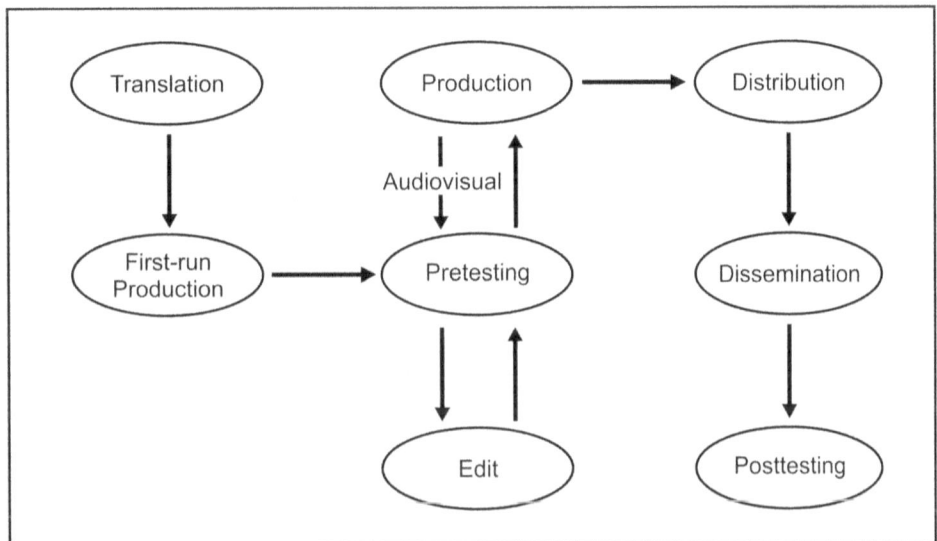

Figure 6-20. Phase VI of the PSYOP process

Chapter 6

TRANSLATION

6-111. Product prototypes are translated once they receive approval from the supported unit. Several factors must be taken into consideration prior to translation. Foremost among these factors is the availability of translators. Translators may come from various backgrounds and possess various types of experience. Ideally, the most qualified translator would be a U.S. citizen—highly educated, capable of translating from English to the target language and vice-versa without losing meaning, and possessing a security clearance. Unfortunately, not all of these characteristics can be found in every translator. Therefore, categories are assigned to translators to sort out various levels of reliability and experience. The following categories outline the types of translators; however, each translator as an individual may be better or worse than these generalizations:

- *Category I* – Have native proficiency in the target language (Levels 4 and 5) and an advanced working proficiency (Interagency Language Round Table [ILRT] Level 2+) in English. They may be locally hired or from a region outside the AO. They do not require a security clearance. Typically, they are the least reliable when translating complex English.
- *Category II* – Are U.S. citizens screened by Army personnel and are granted access to Secret-level material by the designated U.S. Government personnel security authority. They have native proficiency in the target language (Levels 4 and 5) and an advanced working proficiency (ILRT 2+) in English.
- *Category III* – Are U.S. citizens screened by Army personnel and are granted either Top Secret/sensitive compartmented information (TS/SCI) clearance or an interim TS/SCI clearance by the designated U.S. Government personnel security authority. They meet a minimum requirement of ILRT Level 3. They are capable of understanding the essentials of all speech in a standard dialect. They must be able to follow accurately the essentials of conversation, make and answer phone calls, understand radio broadcasts and news stories, and oral reports (both of a technical and nontechnical nature).

6-112. Completed product prototypes are translated into the language of the TA using PSYOP Soldiers, LN military members, or contracted linguists. The preferred method of translation is a "double-blind" process in which one translator or translation team translates from English to the target language, and another translator or team retranslates the translation back to English. Discrepancies between the two are then reconciled and a final version in the target language is approved.

6-113. Checking translations is an art that relies on the appropriate approach and questions. A reviewer should not be asked a broad question, such as "What do you think of this translation?" This question is not precise enough to pinpoint mistakes. It allows too much latitude for cultural reluctance to modify the reply. Politeness or cultural imperatives may lead the reviewer to spare PSYOP personnel embarrassment by not telling them the translation has serious mistakes. The significance of mistakes may be minimized for the same reasons. When a translation is checked, whether by the original linguist or by a second one, it should be checked in detail. PSYOP personnel should ask the linguist to compare the English and the translation word for word and determine if the translation is exact and complete. Is anything missing? Has anything been added? If liberties have been taken to make a translation idiomatic, as they often are and must be, the precise nature of the liberties should be reviewed to ensure that they truly convey the desired meaning.

6-114. The product should also be approached from a cultural perspective to ensure the product will be culturally appropriate for the TA. The translator may automatically make culturally dictated modifications; questions should be asked that reveal such changes and then determined whether they convey the intended meaning. The opposite may also occur—the first draft of a translation may be idiomatically and culturally swayed, perhaps making it difficult for a native speaker to understand or perhaps even making it laughable. The product might also be written in a vulgar idiom or grammatically incorrect style that might appeal to some TAs and offend others. The reviewer should be asked specific questions to determine if this is the case, and, wherever necessary, changes should be made to make the product appropriate to the intended TA.

6-115. All questions must be followed up in detail to make sure the reviewer is not simply being polite. All caveats and recommendations for change should be carefully noted. Additionally, after a product is produced, it should be carefully reviewed to ensure that no typographic errors or other changes have been

Seven-Phase PSYOP Process

inadvertently introduced during the production process. Minor font or accent mark changes can dramatically alter or even reverse the meaning of a word or phase in many languages.

PRETESTING

6-116. A product, once translated, is sent for pretesting (Figure 6-21, page 6-39) IAW pretest instructions on the PAW. The process for pretesting varies on the type of product. Visual products are fairly simple to pretest because the translated prototype or a limited production run can be used as the pretest sample, thereby reducing the amount of time and resources involved. Pretesting audiovisual and audio products, however, requires more resources. An initial storyboard should be pretested first. Then, if the results of that are positive, the product may be pretested again after production. After changes have been made based on pretest results, final production commences for the audiovisual or audio product. Pretesting questionnaires and guidance were discussed in Phase IV and the results of pretesting are addressed in Phase VII. During this phase, the pretest, as detailed on the PAW, is conducted and the results sent back to wherever it is stated in the pretest guidance.

Figure 6-21. Members of the Iraqi National Guard assisting in a pretest

PRODUCTION

6-117. After pretesting is completed and any changes incorporated, the series goes into production. During series development, the products that go to production first, IAW the SEM, are determined. The PAW also states the production means, which can be either organic or nonorganic assets. Detailed descriptions of organic PSYOP production assets are provided in Psychological Operations Handbook: Equipment Types, Specifications, and Capabilities. Nonorganic production assets include the following:

- Local and LN production facilities.
- Mobile public affairs detachments (MPADs).
- Other Services.
- OGAs.

6-118. Contracting with a local company during the initial stages of military operations is cost-effective and allows for timely, responsive production of PSYOP products. This coordination will be made through the contracting officer. An advantage to using LN assets is that they may have faster turnaround times for the finished product, which will free up PSYOP personnel to work on other series while approved products are being produced. When contracting with a nonorganic asset, however, PSYOP forces must be aware of operational security issues. PSYOP forces may want to produce any sensitive products with organic assets. LN assets can easily produce products that are ongoing and not sensitive. Some LN production facilities may not have the experience, knowledge, or resources to maintain their equipment. Print and audiovisual specialists may assist in training local personnel on the proper ways to repair and service their machines and equipment. This assistance may help establish rapport with the local facilities, thereby facilitating the production of PSYOP products.

6-119. PSYOP forces can also use the experience and expertise of other Services within the U.S. military. The Navy has the capability to produce audiovisual products from the Fleet Audiovisual Command, Pacific; Fleet Imagery Command, Atlantic; fleet combat camera groups; various film libraries; and Naval Imaging Command. Naval assets have the capability to broadcast amplitude modulation (AM)/frequency modulation (FM) radio and produce documents, posters, articles, and other materials for PSYOP. In addition, the Navy and Marine Corps EA-6B has the capability of broadcasting prerecorded .wav files from the USQ-113 against a wide variety of communication systems, including FM radio. Administrative capabilities ashore and afloat exist to produce various quantities of printed materials. Language capabilities exist in the naval intelligence community and among naval personnel for most Asian and European languages.

6-120. The United States Air Force (USAF) has a variety of aircraft with a vast range of capabilities that lend themselves to PSYOP across the range of military operations. Several types of military aircraft are specially modified and are thus PSYOP platforms. Air Force Special Operations Command (AFSOC) is equipped with a number of aircraft capable of accomplishing broadcast and leaflet operations. Six EC-130 (COMMANDO SOLO) aircraft, assigned to the Pennsylvania Air National Guard, broadcast PSYOP as their primary mission. These aircraft are equipped for airborne broadcasting of radio and TV signals. The Marine Corps also has Civil Affairs groups (CAGs) that are similar to Army CA units where some of their Marines are PSYOP-trained and may be working within the same AO as Army PSYOP personnel. These units may be able to provide some important information to assist PSYOP in the production or dissemination of PSYOP products.

6-121. Regardless of whether PSYOP forces use organic or nonorganic production assets, quality control must be conducted. Generally, a member of the TPDD and a translator will conduct a quality control check. The reason for the check is two-fold. For visual products, the TPDD must verify that the initial production run corresponds with the original approved prototype. The translator must also verify that none of the translated text has become obscured, distorted, or any of the words have run together. For audio products, the TPDD must ensure that the recording has no distortion and that it is in the correct format. The translator is responsible for verifying that the audio recording is understandable in the target language and the audio corresponds to the translated script. For audiovisual products, the TPDD verifies that the product corresponds with the approved storyboard, that the recording quality is good, and that it is produced in the correct format for broadcasting. The translator checks the product to verify that it is understandable in the target language, looks for cultural discrepancies, and ensures that the audio portion corresponds to the translated script. Once the quality control check is completed, full-scale production commences and the quantity is produced as stated on the SDW.

6-122. The last consideration for production is how the product will be packaged for distribution and dissemination. The following questions are considered:

- How many separate elements are going to disseminate the products and in what quantities?
- How will the products be disseminated?
- What will the products be exposed to during distribution?

6-123. Packaging of leaflets for distribution is determined by the dissemination means. For example, a static line box would be packed with about 25,000 leaflets. The standard static line box is 12 inches by 12 inches by 16 inches. Since the standard static line box is 12 inches by 12 inches by 16 inches, products by static-line leaflet dissemination will be packaged 25,000 per box. For leaflet bomb dissemination, the products will be packaged 30,000 per box. This arrangement saves significant man-hours in loading leaflet bombs, as each M129 holds about 60,000 leaflets and typically contains two or more products. The two types of leaflet bombs are the—

- M129 leaflet bomb, which holds about 60,000 leaflets and typically contains two or more products. The M129E1/E2 leaflet bomb is dropped from fixed-wing aircraft. It requires two to four 37F MOS Soldiers to assist in the loading of PSYOP leaflets. Leaflets may be machine-rolled or hand-rolled before placement inside the bomb. U.S. Air Force personnel are responsible for loading the bomb on aircraft and fusing it. The M129E1/E2 can be used only on aircraft requiring forced ejection for release from a bomb shackle. F-16, B-52, and FA-18 aircraft can carry the M129E1/E2.
- PDU-5/B, which is a modified MK-20 Rockeye II canister-type bomb that will replace the M129E1. It is used to drop leaflets from high-performance aircraft such as the F-16. Each PDU-5/B can deliver about 60,000 leaflets. It has been used in Operations ENDURING FREEDOM and IRAQI FREEDOM. In fact, in Operation IRAQI FREEDOM, PDU-5/Bs were dropped before artillery started hitting targets in Baghdad.

DISTRIBUTION

6-124. Distribution is the movement of approved products, either physically or electronically, from the production location to the point of dissemination. Distribution may also involve the temporary storage of products for later dissemination. PSYOP dissemination involves transmitting products directly to the TA via desired media. Timelines for distribution are determined during series development and incorporated into the SEM. Product distribution within the theater often consists of using surface or air assets for physical delivery of products to PSYOP units for dissemination, as directed by the SEM. The following are some of the various methods currently used for the distribution of PSYOP products:

- File transfer protocol (FTP).
- SIPRNET/NIPRNET.
- Electronic mail (E-mail).
- PDS.
- Psychological Operations automated system (POAS).
- Point-to-point file transfer.
- Air Mobility Command (AMC).

6-125. The aforementioned PSYOP-specific systems and their capabilities are explained in greater detail in the *Psychological Operations Handbook: Equipment Types, Specifications, and Capabilities*. PSYOP personnel can employ LN assets that may become available. PSYOP personnel should strive to build bonds with the LN by working together with their military, OGAs, or the NGOs. By working with the local military (if feasible) or NGOs, PSYOP forces will be able to coordinate combined distribution efforts to many of the areas that need to be reached. This coordination helps establish a greater working relationship between PSYOP forces and the LN and places PSYOP in a positive light with the local populace that sees these coordinated efforts as favorable.

6-126. PSYOP personnel may use local delivery companies to distribute products to various parts of an AO. This is an effective method where large quantities of magazines or posters must be delivered to different areas within the country. PSYOP personnel may contract out with a local company for distribution on a weekly, biweekly, or monthly basis. These contracts will ensure the distribution of the products and will not tie up military transportation assets. The contracting officer coordinates these actions and outside contracts. The contracting officer works out all the legal issues with payment and insurance with delivery companies. When using nonorganic assets for distribution, OPSEC must be maintained at all times. OPSEC is essential to ensure that products are not tampered with and prematurely disseminated, thereby jeopardizing series coordination.

6-127. Anytime supported unit assets are used for distribution, their use must be coordinated. Normally, coordination occurs between the PSYOP officer and the supported unit's S-4 or Deputy/Assistant Chief of

Staff for Logistics (G-4). Also, this relationship may be established during planning and articulated in the PSYOP appendix or a change to the appendix if it is for the execution of a specific series.

DISSEMINATION

6-128. Dissemination is the actual delivery of PSYOP products to the TA. Media analysis during the TAAP assists in determining the best method for reaching the TA. The means of dissemination is determined during series development and specified on the SDW. It is important to consider not only the factors that influence the dissemination method but also the activity of the TA. These considerations may cause a change in the execution timeline of a series and should be reported as soon as they are identified. Several factors which are discussed in the following paragraphs must be considered before the actual dissemination of products:

VISUAL DISSEMINATION CONSIDERATIONS

6-129. Weather can hamper efforts when disseminating visual products. Obtaining the most current weather data is essential to the accuracy of leaflet drops. Weather also factors into the dissemination of handbills and posters, especially if the plan called for handbills to be disseminated at a marketplace when a large amount of the TA is expected to be there.

6-130. Accessibility to the TA can change, based on fluid situations, especially in a combat environment or during an insurgency. For example, the TA normally frequents a marketplace in the town, but the day prior to a planned dissemination, a car bomb explodes at the marketplace. The TA may be reluctant to return to the marketplace for several days, which jeopardizes the dissemination plan.

6-131. Availability of airframes for leaflet drops may change due to changing priorities on the ATO. Quantity of products must also be taken into consideration. The quantity produced should be double-checked to ensure that there is neither too little nor too many. For example, handbill dissemination is planned at a local school. It is advisable to submit an RFI to the S-2 to ascertain whether the number of TA at the school has changed.

AUDIO DISSEMINATION CONSIDERATIONS

6-132. Environmental factors play an important role in the effective dissemination of audio products. When using tactical loudspeakers, wind, rain, and ambient noise can degrade the quality and reduce the effectiveness of the broadcast. Solar flares and radio interference can disrupt PSYOP radio broadcasts and cause the TA not to receive the broadcast.

6-133. Terrain must be considered prior to audio dissemination. Large terrain features may obscure loudspeaker and radio broadcasts, thus causing portions of the TA not to receive the broadcast. Electronic warfare or jamming of radio transmissions from opponent forces may affect the delivery of audio products to the TA.

6-134. Force protection is imperative when conducting audio dissemination with loudspeakers. Once the TPT initiates the loudspeaker broadcast, its position is immediately compromised. This factor is an extremely important consideration during combat operations, more so than in a permissive environment.

AUDIOVISUAL DISSEMINATION CONSIDERATIONS

6-135. Environmental factors also play an important role in the effective dissemination of audiovisual products, especially TV. Solar flares and radio interference can disrupt TV signals and cause the TA not to receive the broadcast. If the broadcast occurs via satellite, strong thunderstorms can impede the transmission of the PSYOP product to the TA.

6-136. Availability of broadcast assets is an important factor. Events may occur, which may cause an LN asset to change the time of a broadcast. Force protection is imperative when conducting face-to-face dissemination, even when the environment is permissive.

6-137. Although dissemination factors are considered during media analysis and series development, they must be double-checked before actual dissemination. The reason for double-checking is that many of the factors are fluid and may change at any time.

POSTTESTING

6-138. Conducting posttests and reporting the results are completed during Phase VI, IAW the posttest guidance on the PAW. Posttesting may or may not occur with dissemination. Observing the behavior of the TA during dissemination is always part of a disseminator's responsibility. These observations should be annotated, as they will be compiled with the results of questionnaires and surveys and be included in Phase VII, Evaluation.

EVALUATION (PHASE VII)

6-139. Evaluation consists of two interrelated activities. First, it encompasses testing (pretesting and posttesting), which typically deals with individual products. The goal of the testing (sampling and focus groups) is to ensure that LOPs, symbols, and design of the products of a series are achieving their intended goals. Testing is sometimes used to obtain information that can be used in TAA (Phase II). The second activity within evaluation focuses on determining the effectiveness of PSYOP over time. This is accomplished by analyzing impact indicators (answers to MOEs) and any spontaneous events related to the PSYOP effort and by determining to what extent the SPOs and ultimately the POs are being achieved. Because testing identifies deficiencies and suggests ways to improve a product, the products must be thoroughly pretested.

6-140. As each series of products is improved as a result of testing, the behavior of the TA is more successfully modified over time. Therefore, the relationship of the two activities within evaluation is interwoven. Important portions of evaluation occur during other phases of the PSYOP process. For example, writing questionnaires and testing guidance occur in Phase IV, with the conduct of that testing completed during Phase VI.

6-141. MOEs are written during Phase I and often refined during Phase II; however, the actual collation and analysis of data is completed during Phase VII (Evaluation). Evaluation is labor intensive and must be done throughout an operation to ensure that resources are correctly allocated and timely modifications are incorporated so that PSYOP are effective.

6-142. Evaluating impact indicators allows PSYOP to determine the success of PSYOP series. Supported commanders are interested in knowing if PSYOP are achieving the SPOs, and evaluation allows PSYOP to provide this assessment. Testing enables PSYOP forces to determine why they have been successful or unsuccessful.

TESTING

6-143. Testing was discussed in Phase IV and also in FM 3-05.301. The results of testing are reported to the TPDD or PSE where the data are analyzed and the appropriate action taken.

6-144. Pretest data may indicate that a product or series needs to be altered. Any changes to a product must be cross-referenced throughout the series to ensure cohesion. This is the most common danger to altering a product based on pretest data. If the change is something that impacts the whole series, that change must be made on all products within the series.

6-145. Posttesting also checks to see if the product or stage needs any adjustments to be more successful; however, that is not its primary function. A posttest is really trying to identify if the TA has accepted the portion of the LOP that was presented. Normally, this requirement is identified by the presence of a DP on the SEM. If the TA does not readily accept the first argument presented in the LOP, the PSYOP planner establishes a DP to determine if the series execution timeline needs to be adjusted. There is no need to begin disseminating the second argument if the first was rejected. Posttesting helps identify whether the TA is ready for the next stage of the series or perhaps that the TA needs further exposure to the first stage. Posttesting is therefore vitally important to gauging whether the TA is achieving the desired behavior. For example, it is often advantageous to expose the TA to all the products of one stage in a series and then conduct a thorough posttest to ensure that the TA has accepted the argument of one stage before beginning the dissemination of the next stage. This can be thought of as posttesting each stage of the series so that assets and resources are not wasted.

IMPACT INDICATORS

6-146. Impact indicators are simply the answers to MOEs. These answers are events or facts that aid in determining the effectiveness of a PSYOP series. An impact indicator represents a fact or an event that is known at a single moment in time and has relevance to the PSYOP series. For example, given the SPO "TA decreases support for insurgent activity" and the MOE "How many insurgent recruits have enlisted this month?" the impact indicator would be 12 on 01 February 2002 and a subsequent impact indicator would be 9 on 01 March 2002. The value of impact indicators is that they can be analyzed over time and therefore allow PSYOP forces to determine the effectiveness of a PSYOP series. If a baseline is not already known, the first impact indicator obtained will establish that baseline and then subsequent impact indicators are compared against the baseline. The combination of the MOEs (questions) and impact indicators (answers) establishes the scale that allows PSYOP forces to evaluate how well they are doing with respect to their objectives.

SPONTANEOUS EVENTS

6-147. Not all events that are important to PSYOP are anticipated. These spontaneous events must also be taken into consideration when evaluating the PSYOP effort. These can include unpredictable events (such as bombings or riots) that do not occur over time but may serve as a sign of the impact of a specific supporting PSYOP program. The spontaneous events must be considered with the impact indicators when determining to what degree an objective is being achieved. A direct correlation between a PSYOP series and a spontaneous event may be impossible to make.

ANALYSIS OF SERIES RESULTS

6-148. A series is disseminated to modify a TA's behavior. Various means are then employed (PSYOP units or ISR assets) to obtain impact indicators. All impact indicators are then analyzed in relation to the products disseminated and the PSYACTs conducted to see if there is a correlation between the PSYOP series and the behavior exhibited by the TA. This analysis will then give the PSYOP commander the ability to evaluate to what extent he has or has not achieved his objectives and thus allow him to determine whether an adjustment is necessary. Figure 6-22, page 6-45, is an example of a PSYOP plan that has used this system of MOEs, including impact indicators and spontaneous events.

6-149. The determination as to whether PSYOP forces are being effective or can only be assessed after an analysis of multiple impact indicators over a specified duration of time. This evaluation will indicate to the PSYOP commander or supported commander the degree to which the SPOs, and ultimately the POs, are being achieved.

6-150. Three TAs must be focused on to accomplish SPO 1, and two MOEs are determined for each TA. When answered, the MOEs give insight into whether behavior has changed. These MOEs (questions) were initially addressed on 1 February 2002. The impact indicators (answers to the MOEs) for 1 February 2002 are considered the baseline data and PSYOP forces will implement their plan in an attempt to decrease support from those levels. In the example, the MOEs are assessed again (some at weekly intervals and others monthly) so that PSYOP forces can monitor behavioral change over time.

6-151. For TA 1 the number of recruits declined the two months following 1 February 2002. The insurgent newspaper quit being circulated after 1 March 2002. This is explained by the spontaneous event of the facility being burned. Taking these impact indicators and the spontaneous event and assessing them against the PSYOP series disseminated may show the positive effect PSYOP are having in regards to this particular TA.

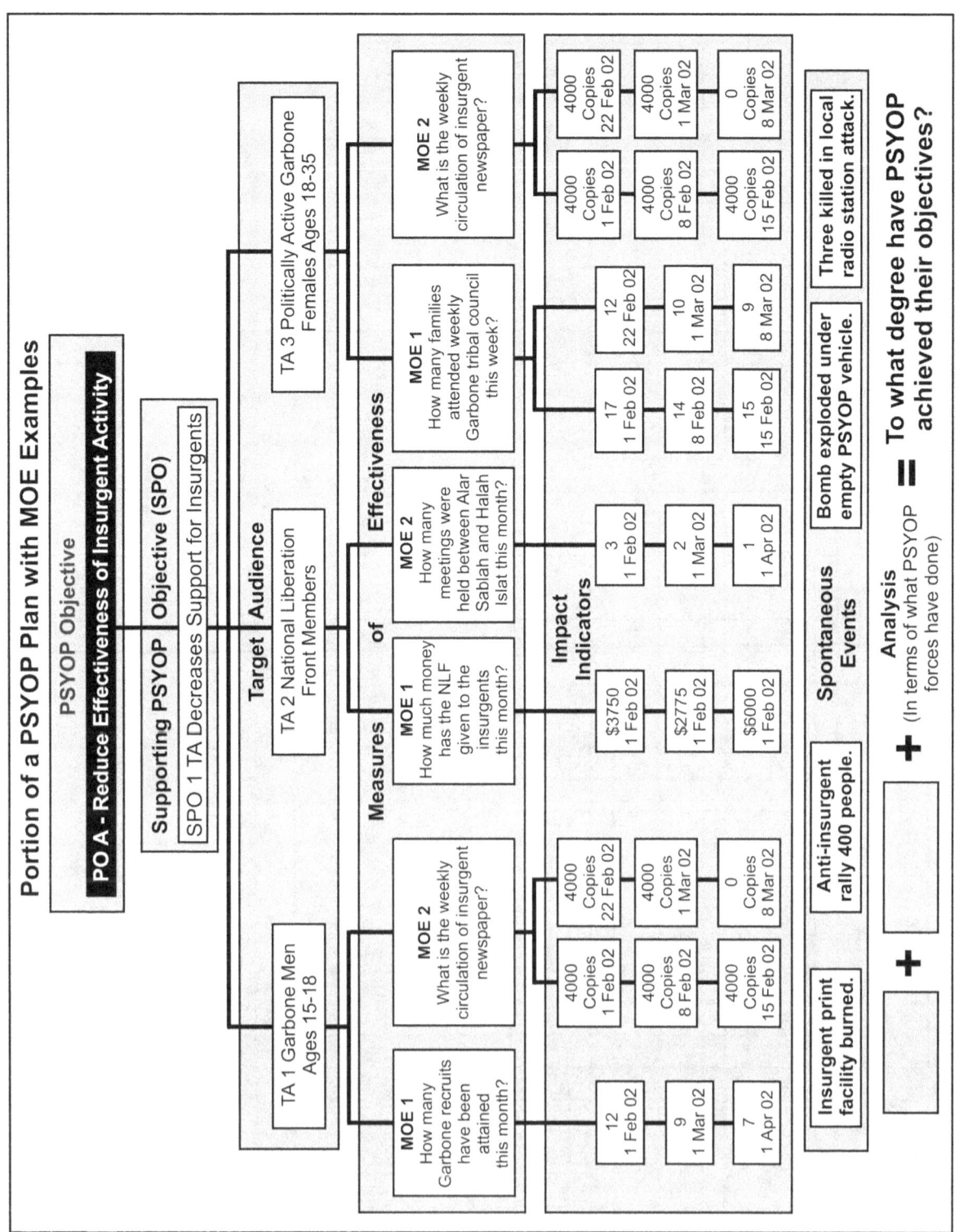

Figure 6-22. Example for evaluating PSYOP

Series 1ZA02ka	1	2	3	4	5	6	7	8	9	10	11	12	13	14	15	16	17	18	19	20	21	22	23	24	25	26	27	28	29	30	Dissemination
HB01												SA1																			
HB02																			SA2												
HB03																										SA3					
RD01												SA1	SA1	SA1	SA1	SA1	SA1	SA1													
RD02																			SA2	SA2	SA2	SA2	SA2	SA2	SA2						
RD03																										SA3	SA3	SA3	SA3	SA3	
LS01												SA1																			
LS02																			SA2												
LS03																										SA3					
NP01																			All							All					
NP02																						SA2							SA3		
FF01												SA1																			
FF02																			SA2												
FF03																										SA3					
AC01												SA1																			
MOE - How many insurgent activities reported each week?		Baseline 0						Week One - 0							Week Two - 1							Week Three - 4							Week Four - 7		
Posttest - 50 respondents (18 Sep) to supporting argument 1 question - The XX security forces will act if I report a suspected insurgent?		Strongly Agree 21	Somewhat Agree 16		No Opinion 7			Somewhat Disagree 2		Strongly Disagree 4		Posttest - 50 respondents (25 Sep) to supporting argument 2 question - Do you think anonymous phoning of insurgent activity is viable?			Definitely 39		Probably 7		Unsure 0		Probably Not 3	Definitely Not 1			Posttest - 50 respondents (30 Sep) to supporting argument 3 question - Does reporting insurgent activity help protect your family?		Definitely 34		Probably 12		Unsure 4; Probably Not 0; Definitely Not 0
Spontaneous Events	Task Force PAO received 2 calls on 22 Sep from people asking for the anonymous tip phone number																														
Posttest - 150 respondents (30 Sep) to bottom line question - Will you report insurgents?			Definitely - 39					Probably - 112			Unsure - 20					Probably Not - 7				Definitely Not - 6											
Posttest - 150 respondents (30 Sep) to bottom line question - Have you reported any suspicious characters?			Yes - 2				No - 148																								

Figure 6-23. Series evaluation grid example

6-152. The first MOE for TA 2 concerned National Liberation Front (NLF) financial support to the insurgents. The amount decreased as of 1 March 2002 but increased dramatically the following month. This may be to help finance the repair of the burned printing facility. Further measures may show this as a spike in support or perhaps a greater financial commitment. The impact indicators for the second MOE show that there has been diminished contact between the leader of the NLF and the leader of the insurgents. The PSYOP series aimed at dividing these two individuals may be working; however, in a real operation, further impact indicators would need to be analyzed to support this assessment. Perhaps an additional MOE about the number of phone conversations, letters, and E-mails is needed. For TA 2, PSYOP may want to concentrate on the financial support of the NLF and continue to monitor this area to see if the 1 April 2002 figures were indeed a spike or if the NLF is committing greater resources to the insurgent cause. If this is the case, PSYOP in future months may need to concentrate more heavily on this aspect.

6-153. Politically active females make up TA 3, and the impact indicators demonstrate a continuous decrease in meeting attendance by this group. MOE 2 for TA 1 and TA 3 shows that the fire in the print facility eliminated newspaper circulation. Although the correlation between the unanticipated elimination of the newspaper and meeting attendance by females is anecdotal, this provides evidence that the PSYOP series discouraging female participation in public meetings may be working.

6-154. When analyzing the six MOEs for the SPO "TA decreases support for insurgents," the impact indicators for five of the MOEs indicated that support is lessening. One area, financial support, was actually increasing, although that may be explained by an attempt to overcome the spontaneous event of the print facility burning. Also, the PSYOP analyst must factor in the anti-insurgent rally that supports the SPO. The bombing of the PSYOP vehicle must also be analyzed to see if it is connected with insurgents trying to decrease the PSYOP forces' ability to dwindle their support. The radio station was attacked after it agreed to increase the amount of PSYOP airtime. Considering all these impact indicators and spontaneous events and assessing them against the supporting PSYOP program of products and actions allow the PSYOP force to evaluate if they have succeeded over the 3 months in decreasing the support for insurgents. They also demonstrate that they may need to focus further effort to the financial support that the NLF is giving to the insurgents.

6-155. The example is hypothetical and does not include the complete breadth of factors normally taken into account in an actual operation. However, it gives an insight into what PSYOP forces must do to evaluate their efforts successfully.

MECHANICS OF EVALUATION

6-156. As demonstrated in the above example, the impact indicators and spontaneous events must be compared to the series conducted to determine the correlation between PSYOP and the TA's behavior. The SPO is the lowest level objective for PSYOP forces so the evaluation process is attempting to determine to what extent each SPO has been achieved. To accomplish this, each series, within a supporting PSYOP program, is evaluated separately and the results are combined to evaluate how successful PSYOP have been in relation to the given SPO. The evaluation is done at the lowest level to determine which series are being effective. To evaluate their SPOs, PSYOP forces must have the various series dissemination graphics, impact indicators, posttest results, and any spontaneous events that relate to the SPO being evaluated. Figure 6-23, page 6-46, is an example of a series evaluation grid that collates all this data, so that the relationship between the TA's behavior and PSYOP can easily be determined. Making a similar grid for each series within a SPO allows the PSYOP force to identify the series that are working and the ones that are not, as well as the reasons why.

6-157. To evaluate the SPO, PSYOP Soldiers must template each series. After each series is analyzed, the effectiveness of the PSYOP effort is evaluated and series that need to be allocated more time and resources are identified.

SUMMARY

6-158. The PSYOP process is a comprehensive, seven-phase process that, when followed, allows PSYOP forces to modify the behavior of foreign TAs successfully. This process is extremely involved, and success relies heavily upon comprehensive planning, detailed research, creative input, technical expertise, coordination, analysis, and a thorough evaluation.

This page intentionally left blank.

Chapter 7
Tactical Psychological Operations Team Operations

The TPT is a three-man team led by a staff sergeant. It normally provides tactical PSYOP support to battalion-sized units and below. Its primary purpose is to integrate and execute PSYOP series at the tactical level. The TPT also advises the supported unit commander and staff on the psychological effects of their operations on the TAs in their AO and answers all PSYOP-related questions.

INTRODUCTION

7-1. The TPT distributes and disseminates approved print, audio, and audiovisual products as part of a series. The TPT is instrumental in gathering PSYOP-relevant information, conducting town or area assessments, observing and reporting impact indicators, and obtaining pretesting and posttesting data. It also takes pictures and documents cultural behavior for later use in PSYOP products. The TPT often plays a major role in establishing rapport with foreign audiences and in identifying key communicators to achieve PSYOP objectives.

7-2. The TPT can be employed by the TPD in several ways. It is most often task-organized to a maneuver element in direct support for the duration of an operation. In HIC, the TPT is normally employed at the battalion level. In S&RO, the TPT is more effective at the company level.

7-3. This relationship allows the TPT the best opportunity to develop trust and familiarity with the supported unit (Figure 7-1, page 7-2). In peace operations, the TPT is often retained at the brigade and then given to a battalion in direct support for specific missions when required. This arrangement allows the PSYOP commander flexibility in making sure PSYOP series are thoroughly executed throughout the supported unit's sector.

INTEGRATION WITH SUPPORTED UNIT

7-4. The TPT leader's ability to integrate with a supported unit is key in the overall success of the TPT. As the supported commander's PSYOP staff planner, the TPT leader must have direct access to the S-3 and the commander. Without the trust and respect of a supported command, a TPT may be hindered in its ability to plan and conduct PSYOP effectively.

7-5. Upon linkup with a supported unit, the tactical PSYOP leader must integrate his team completely into the supported unit before he can effectively support any operations or become an integral part of the unit's battle rhythm. Coordination for logistical, communication, and intelligence support and establishing rapport with all staff elements must be done at the earliest opportunity. If the unit has an organic PSYOP planner, the coordination and integration process can be facilitated. The organic PSYOP planner may have already completed the majority of the coordination for the tactical PSYOP element before the linkup. The organic PSYOP staff planner, if present, should be the first point of contact for the tactical PSYOP element leader. Exchanging information is critical to successful integration. Before an effective capabilities brief can be constructed that is tailored to the supported unit and its mission, the TPT leader should know or provide the staff the following, as a minimum:
- Determine if the supported unit commander and staff have ever had tactical PSYOP support.
- Provide current PSYOP programs being executed in the supported unit's AI that can affect his current and future operations.

Chapter 7

- Provide additional PSYOP support that is available and the procedures for requesting the support.
- Determine reporting requirements and lines of communication for higher PSYOP elements.
- Provide production timeline and distribution plans and procedures.
- Provide approval chain and process.
- Determine past PSYOP programs executed in the supported unit's AOI and their effects.
- Provide prerecorded and approved loudspeaker messages.
- Provide organic PSYOP dissemination means, assets, and series available.
- Provide team equipment capabilities, limitations, and restrictions.
- Clarify the command relationship of the tactical PSYOP element.
- Determine the staff's battle rhythm and requirements for elements, such as fire and effects coordination cell (FECC).
- Determine MDMP steps and tasks currently being executed by supported unit staff.
- Determine targeting objectives for supported unit.
- Provide intelligence support requirements for PSYOP (for example, PSYOP PIR, MOE, TAA, propaganda).
- Determine unit's ROE and ROI.
- Obtain a copy of the unit tactical standing operating procedure (TACSOP), if possible.
- Determine unit's communication infrastructure and support for PSYOP reporting requirements and procedures.
- Determine or provide interpreter support requirements.
- Provide logistical support requirements (statement of requirement [SOR], maintenance, and PSYOP-specific equipment).
- Establish a thorough understanding of the commander's intent, as well as the role of subordinate and supporting forces.

Figure 7-1. TPT assisting supported unit during cordon and search in Iraq

Support Coordination

7-6. Upon linkup, the TPT leader must coordinate for necessary support, including logistical, communication, and intelligence support. For further guidance on conducting support coordination, see Appendix A.

Capabilities Brief

7-7. The team leader will attempt to solve all integration and coordination issues at the lowest level. Any critical unresolved issues must be presented to the supported unit commander during the capabilities brief. For guidance on constructing and delivering a capabilities brief, see Appendix F.

Tactical Operations Center Operations

7-8. The TOC is the center of activity for most deployed units. To integrate PSYOP properly with the supported unit, the TPT leader must be in the TOC whenever possible. Being in the TOC, the TPT leader can maintain awareness of the situation and of events in the supported unit's AO. This awareness ensures the integration of the TPT into the supported unit's missions when appropriate.

7-9. Missions can arise rapidly, and if the TPT leader is not in the TOC when an order is received, he will not be able to integrate PSYOP effectively into the plan. A supported commander or S-3 may not send a runner to find the TPT leader. Being in the TOC, the TPT leader is able to integrate PSYOP into the plan from inception through execution.

Advisory Role

7-10. One key role of the TPT leader is to advise the supported commander. The TPT leader should analyze proposed actions by the supported unit, as well as the effects of those actions on the TAs within the AO. For example, if the supported commander wants to destroy a bridge used by local civilians to transport goods to and from market, the TPT leader should advise the commander on the possible adverse effects of this action on the civilians. The TPT leader may also advise the commander on specific enemy forces to target with PSYOP to induce surrenders or to cause enemy forces to cease resistance.

Mission Planning

7-11. Detailed mission planning is critical to successful mission execution, and the standard for mission planning is the MDMP. Integrating PSYOP objectives early in the process is crucial to a successful coordinated effort; therefore, the TPT leader should understand the MDMP and be able to integrate the PSYOP process.

7-12. The MDMP is an in-depth process and is covered in detail in Chapter 4 of this publication and in FM 3-05.301. PSYOP planning must be integrated into the MDMP at all levels. It is covered in depth at the beginning of Chapter 6 of this publication. The TPT leader must be aware that at battalion level the MDMP is normally conducted in a time-constrained environment. As such, the TPT leader should remain in the TOC as much as possible. When the planning process is conducted, the TPT leader should be present throughout to ensure the integration and coordination of PSYOP objectives into the supported unit's plan.

7-13. The TPT leader should play an active role during the MDMP. He should analyze the roles of each BOS and identify where PSYOP objectives support the mission. He should brief the PSYOP support concept and how it supports the commander's intent and integrates PSYOP objectives into the overall plan.

7-14. The TPT leader should consider his role in supporting the TPD commander's mission and intent. When the TPD issues an appendix to the supported unit's OPORD or FRAGO, the TPT leader should identify the PSYOP requirements and integrate them into his supported commander's plan.

EMPLOYMENT

7-15. Tactical PSYOP should be employed throughout the range of operations across the full spectrum of conflict. There are multiple uses of tactical PSYOP, which are limited only by the experience and imagination of the TPT leader. The following paragraphs offer ideas and examples of methods of employment of tactical PSYOP. It is important to remember that the PSYOP process does not change between levels of employment; however, there are general considerations that tactical PSYOP Soldiers often encounter. (Appendix I describes TPT battlefield survival techniques.) None of the following examples are meant to exclude the TAA process or the series PSYOP execute to modify behavior based on TA-specific vulnerabilities. These are general guidelines on how tactical forces are often employed.

INTRODUCTION OF FORCES

7-16. During this phase, PSYOP prepare the local population for the arrival of U.S. and coalition forces. There are two distinct environments in which introduction of forces is executed—the permissive environment and the nonpermissive environment. The PSYOP approach is the same for each; however, the dissemination methods and how enemy or hostile forces are targeted differ, as follows:

- *Permissive environment.* In this situation, the TPT leader executes series that announce U.S. intentions in the AO and build civilian support. Civilian noninterference messages and safety instructions are series commonly used. The series typically require the TPT to conduct face-to-face communication and to gather information to support planning, TAA, and series development. This may include conducting area or town assessments, gathering information on the conditions affecting PTAs, and conducting media analysis.
- *Nonpermissive environment.* In this situation, civilians are targeted in the same manner as in a permissive environment. In addition, PSYOP series typically target enemy forces with the objectives—surrender, desert, or cease resistance. Typically, these series make extensive use of loudspeaker, radio, and leaflet products. Support to deception operations can also be conducted to deceive the enemy on entry points of U.S. forces. This can be done by coordinating leaflet drops advising civilians to stay out of the area or through loudspeaker operations broadcasting sounds in a false area.

PSYOP IN THE OFFENSE

7-17. TPTs often play a key role for a supported commander. By supporting deception operations, executing series that assist in the control of civilians on the battlefield (COBs), and causing enemy forces to cease resistance or surrender, TPTs help the supported commander gain the tactical advantage. In times of war, PSYOP objectives focus initially on reducing the enemy's effectiveness by undermining the enemy's will to fight. This is, in fact, the primary PSYOP objective during hostilities. PSYOP personnel use various media—such as loudspeakers, radio broadcasts, and leaflets—to exploit the enemy's vulnerabilities, identified through analysis of TA conditions; to instill fear of death, mutilation, or defeat in the enemy; and to undermine the enemy's confidence in its leadership, decreasing the enemy's morale and combat efficiency and encouraging surrender, defection, or desertion. The secondary PSYOP objective in warfare is to reduce interference with military operations. The modern battlefield is populated not only by enemy soldiers but also by civilians. PSYOP series set the conditions for the commander by causing civilians to avoid military operations and installations.

SUPPORT TO DECEPTION OPERATIONS

7-18. These types of missions can support a wide range of tactical operations. They can support the deception of avenues of approach and of breach sites and provide a force multiplier. The following are examples and are not all-inclusive:

- *Avenues of approach.* Tactical PSYOP can assist in deceiving the enemy about avenues of approach, routes of march, or direction of travel being used. PSYOP can target planned and unplanned avenues of approach. This may force the enemy to consider all avenues of approach, not just the most likely ones. The TPT leader can request or coordinate for series, which include

Tactical Psychological Operations Team Operations

radio or television broadcasts, aerial leaflet dissemination, and loudspeaker broadcasts to support the deception. Examples of the types of products that may be included in such a series are—
- Civilian noninterference.
- Cease resistance.
- Surrender appeals.
- Messages announcing the imminent arrival of U.S. forces and the reason for their arrival.

- *Breach sites.* TPTs can help deceive the enemy about the location and time of breaching operations. Multiple potential breach sites, planned and unplanned, should be targeted by PSYOP. This may force the enemy to consider all potential breach sites, not just the most likely ones. This can be achieved by executing one or more series that support the deception story. This can also be achieved by coordinating for aerial leaflet dissemination, radio or television broadcasts, and loudspeaker broadcasts. In addition, loudspeaker broadcasts can attempt to mimic sounds, such as troop movement, vehicles, and small arms.

- *Force multiplier.* As a force multiplier, TPTs may attempt to deceive the enemy into believing he is facing a larger force. Series may be developed to achieve this and typically include the following types of products:
  - Loudspeaker broadcasts to replicate the sounds of weapons systems (organic to the supported unit), vehicles, and aircraft. TPTs are very successful at masking movement when sonic deception is employed quickly.
  - Aerial leaflet dissemination and radio or television broadcasts that stress how the enemy is facing a larger, superior force.
  - Sonic deception to deceive the enemy into believing there are multiple pickup zones (PZs) or landing zones (LZs) in a certain area. Loudspeaker broadcasts off rotary-wing aircraft, conducted in appropriate terrain, can be very effective.

Civilians on the Battlefield

7-19. An effective method for controlling COBs is to conduct loudspeaker broadcasts. Series with civilian safety and noninterference objectives should be used.

Surrender Appeals

7-20. Surrender appeals are most effective against hostile forces that are degraded or surrounded or that have been exposed to other conditions that affect their will to fight. By inducing surrenders, the TPT can assist the supported commander by reducing the number of hostile forces he may have to face. Coordination must be conducted with the supported unit before executing a surrender appeal. The supported unit must be prepared to handle all hostile personnel who surrender. The members of the supported unit must also ensure that they adhere to any statements made to the TA.

Countermortar Sonic Deception Operations

A TPC supporting a division in a major city in Iraq used sonic deception to suppress Anti-Iraqi Forces' (AIF) use of mortars against MSC units. Two brigades in the division AOR used PSYOP loudspeakers to broadcast Apache helicopter noises at night to discourage AIF mortar teams from setting up. A pattern of aggressive patrolling by Apaches had conditioned AIF mortar crews to displace immediately when hearing helicopters in the area. Movement of the mounted loudspeakers gave the perception of helicopter movement. Loudspeaker broadcasts were only used at night to mirror night Apache patrols. Daytime Apache patrols were used to suppress daylight mortar attacks. The TTP was effective in reducing nighttime mortar attacks.

PSYOP in the Defense

7-21. As with PSYOP in the offense, TPTs are a valuable asset to the supported commander. Supporting deception operations, providing information, and controlling COBs are examples of TPT support.

Chapter 7

7-22. PSYOP support to deception operations during the defense is often through the use of loudspeakers to broadcast sounds that replicate engineer equipment and TOC operations and that create a double deception. Posters can be disseminated to help create a false minefield or to control COBs. TPTs can also augment a supported unit's quick-reaction force (QRF).

7-23. To support deception operations during the defense, loudspeakers can replicate the sounds of engineers digging in to deceive the enemy about where the actual defense is being prepared. They can also replicate the sounds common to TOC operations, such as vehicles and generators, to deceive the enemy on the actual TOC location.

7-24. The double deception technique can be used to support an ambush. In this technique, the TPT allows itself to be observed broadcasting armor sound effects, while the armored or mechanized forces are laagered elsewhere. During limited visibility, the loudspeaker and armor locations should be switched to allow for the element of surprise in an ambush.

7-25. Establishing a false minefield can potentially deceive the enemy into believing minefields are in the AO and thus possibly causing the enemy to advance slower, or not at all. Posters and warning signs must be emplaced where enemy reconnaissance units will find them. This tactic may also be used to funnel the enemy into a specific kill zone. The deception can be completed by also placing posters along likely avenues of approach warning civilians to use approved routes to enter the TOC area. The posters must also be placed along and up to a determined distance outside the perimeter of main supply routes (MSRs) to warn civilians to remain on known routes to avoid the dangers of mines.

7-26. Controlling COBs is critical to the defense of any supported unit. TPTs assist in this task by executing series that reduce civilian interference by supporting civil-military operations (CMO) and providing information about traffic control points (TCPs), dislocated civilian (DC) collection points, and location of other relief agencies. TPTs also disseminate information along MSRs via loudspeakers to assist in keeping the MSRs clear.

STABILITY AND RECONSTRUCTION OPERATIONS

7-27. TPTs are used to the greatest extent during support to S&RO. They routinely conduct face-to-face communication; disseminate handbills, newspapers, and other printed material; and conduct posttesting and area and media assessments. Seeking out and conversing with key communicators are essential during S&RO. The TPT leader should remain flexible and actively pursue missions that not only assist the supported commander, but also support the accomplishment of a SPO.

7-28. During S&RO, TPTs support CMO, such as civic-action programs (CAPs). With support from the TPDD, TPTs increase civilian participation in these programs—for example, through printed products and loudspeaker broadcasts. TPTs may also change the behavior of DCs as part of a humanitarian assistance package—for example, following natural disasters. TPTs may also assist in disseminating pertinent information to the civilian populace through printed products and face-to-face communication.

UNCONVENTIONAL WARFARE

7-29. UW often sets conditions for follow-on efforts or may achieve the goals without the introduction of additional forces. In either case, UW presents challenges to tactical PSYOP in direct support of the effort. It is often impractical for tactical PSYOP to provide active "on the ground" support to SOF units conducting entry operations in UW; however, it is possible. During entry into the AO, tactical PSYOP may accompany missions to establish link-up with potential guerrilla forces. Tactical PSYOP may use their face-to-face skills and cultural expertise to conduct link-up and to develop rapport with potential guerrilla leaders and recruits. When the security situation allows, tactical PSYOP may begin distributing products from PSYOP series to discredit the standing government; to encourage disaffection, desertion, and malingering; and to seek active support and recruitment for the guerrilla force. As the resistance movement progresses, tactical PSYOP can become more active in disseminating products in more areas. Tactical PSYOP advise the SOF commander and guerrilla leaders on potential PSYACTs, as well as the conduct of day-to-day military operations. Tactical PSYOP may support deception operations throughout the conduct of UW.

7-30. As population centers become accessible, tactical PSYOP support to SOF elements can continue to increase. Products such as "guerrilla theater," coupled with handbill or other product disseminations, may be executed as the security situation becomes more permissive. If possible, tactical PSYOP may disseminate badly needed consumer goods and PSYOP products in areas under resistance control. As guerrilla forces grow to sufficient numbers to begin diversifying unit types, including specialty units, tactical PSYOP may begin identifying individuals to train in the PSYOP process and, if authorized, train guerrillas to produce PSYOP series and disseminate products. Tactical PSYOP may act as an ADVON for a follow-on force for larger PSYOP elements if the resistance is successful. Tactical PSYOP units then begin to transition to S&RO.

FOREIGN INTERNAL DEFENSE

7-31. Initial restrictions in employing tactical PSYOP are generally far less a concern in FID than in UW; however, political restrictions on the use of PSYOP may effectively dampen the PSYOP effort more than security concerns. In all cases, tactical PSYOP must adapt to the restrictions of ROE and ROI. Thus, the chief role of tactical PSYOP is to assist their LN counterparts in conducting the PSYOP process. In FID, tactical PSYOP must be mindful of the necessity of legitimizing and bolstering LN forces and (typically) minimizing U.S. participation.

7-32. Typical PSYOP series executed in support of FID stress the illegitimacy of the insurgency and capitalize on any excesses or human rights violations committed by the insurgents. Stressing the legitimacy of the LN government and military is a typical FID line of persuasion. Tactical PSYOP may disseminate a wide range of media types in support of FID. Face-to-face communication may be very effective but should be conducted in conjunction with LN forces. Tactical PSYOP may conduct face-to-face communication along with cordon-and-search missions. Insurgents cannot operate without the support of the local populace; therefore, any PSYOP product (such as handbills or the guerrilla theater) that requires contact with the populace has the double effect of—

- Denying insurgents access to TAs that typically provide support and recruits.
- Reaching TAs with pro-LN products.

7-33. As insurgents typically attempt to produce propaganda as an asymmetrical response to superior LN or coalition firepower, tactical PSYOP conduct counterpropaganda operations against insurgent propaganda. Another asymmetrical advantage by insurgents is the use of mines and improvised explosive devices (IEDs). Countermine and counter-IED series are therefore often critical to mission success. Tactical PSYOP should advise the SOF unit commander and LN forces leadership on the use of PSYACTs and coordinate with any CA elements to conduct joint CMO-PSYOP missions or simply capitalize on CA projects.

LOUDSPEAKER OPERATIONS

7-34. Loudspeaker operations are an extension of face-to-face communication and can have an immediate impact on a TA. During combat operations, loudspeakers are the most effective PSYOP medium in high-intensity conflict or civil disorder environments. They can provide immediate and direct contact with a TA. As a result, tactical PSYOP rely heavily upon loudspeaker operations in high-intensity conflict or civil disorder environments.

7-35. Loudspeakers can move rapidly to wherever an exploitable PSYOP opportunity exists, and they can follow the TA when the TA moves. Loudspeakers achieve, in effect, face-to-face communication with the enemy. Loudspeakers transmit speeches, music, or sound effects to the audience. Tapes, minidisks, and CDs are preferred when conducting loudspeaker operations, because of their superior audio quality. Live performers are used whenever the situation necessitates a broadcast that has not been prerecorded (Figure 7-2, page 7-8). Loudspeaker broadcasts, even when live, should be rehearsed before being disseminated.

Chapter 7

Figure 7-2. TPTs conducting operations in Iraq

7-36. Loudspeakers are commonly mounted on a tactical high mobility multipurpose wheeled vehicle (HMMWV) or carried in a rucksack; however, they may also be placed on other vehicles such as armored personnel carriers (APCs), watercraft, or rotary-wing aircraft. Loudspeakers can broadcast to enemy forces that have been cut off, urging them to surrender or to cease resistance. Loudspeakers are often used to issue instructions to persons in fortified positions and locations. They are also used for deception operations to broadcast sounds of vehicles or other equipment. Loudspeakers are sometimes employed to control the flow of refugees and DCs and to reduce civilian interference on the battlefield.

> **Loudspeaker Operations During the Gulf War**
> An example of successful loudspeaker operations occurred during the Gulf War. Coalition forces effectively isolated a large element of the Iraqi forces on Faylaka Island. Rather than attack the island with a direct assault, a TPT from the 9th Battalion aboard a UH-1N helicopter flew aerial loudspeaker missions around the island, with Cobra gunships providing escort. The broadcast told the enemy below to surrender the next day in formation at the radio tower. The next day, 1,405 Iraqi soldiers, including a general officer, waited in formation at the radio tower to surrender to the Marine forces without a single shot being fired.

ADVANTAGES

7-37. The advantages of employing loudspeakers should be considered during mission planning, such as—
- *Flexibility.* Loudspeakers give a supported commander the ability to address several TAs with different messages in a short time. They also allow the supported commander the option of sending the TPT in dismounted or mounted or of using the ALS, based on METT-TC.
- *Mobility.* Through the use of vehicles or rotary-wing aircraft, the supported commander can quickly and effectively maneuver the TPT on the battlefield.
- *Exploitation of target.* Because of the mobility of loudspeakers, a supported commander can quickly exploit targets of opportunity, such as an enemy unit that has been defeated, isolated, or surrounded. Using their loudspeakers, TPTs can capitalize on the battlefield successes of friendly forces.

Tactical Psychological Operations Team Operations

- *Range of transmission.* Loudspeaker operations, when properly planned and employed, can cover a large area and reach a large part of the TA.
- *Effectiveness with illiterate audience.* Loudspeaker broadcasts, like radio broadcasts, do not require the TA to be literate. Any member of a TA should be able to hear and understand the message.
- *Ability to pinpoint targets.* Loudspeakers allow the TPT or supported commander to address pinpointed TAs or areas. An enemy element held up in a building is an example of a pinpointed target.
- *Immediate feedback.* Loudspeaker broadcasts allow for the gathering of immediate feedback or impact indicators. The TPT should determine the TA's reactions to the message, based upon the actions taken by the TA. If a crowd disperses upon or shortly after the dissemination of the message, then the TPT should be able to gauge the successfulness of the broadcast.

LIMITATIONS

7-38. Climatic conditions and enemy forces are the most common limiting factors to consider when planning loudspeaker operations. Other limitations include—

- *Vulnerability to hostile fire.* Because of the proximity of TPTs to the TA during loudspeaker broadcasts, hostile fire is a high threat. TPTs should make sure this threat is considered when planning all loudspeaker operations. TPTs often require security elements with them. Broadcast positions should also be locations that provide as much cover and concealment without compromising the quality or effectiveness of the broadcast.
- *Loss or distortion of messages over time.* Loudspeaker broadcasts are not permanent like visual products. Once the message is disseminated, the TA may forget the message or incorrectly communicate it to others. By the time a third or fourth party hears the relayed message, the message may no longer be what was originally disseminated.
- *Environmental conditions.* Loudspeakers are affected by weather and terrain. Wind can both adversely and positively affect loudspeaker broadcasts. Wind carries sound if it is blowing in the same direction as the broadcast. If it is blowing in the opposite direction, it will limit the range and effectiveness. Moisture—such as rain, fog, and high humidity—muffles sound and limits the effective range of a broadcast. The TPT leader should make sure nothing is between the speaker and the target area—such as trees, hills, or buildings. Sound cannot travel through these objects; therefore, the sound becomes distorted and unintelligible. On the other hand, open terrain and water allow sound to travel unimpeded. Low humidity also helps amplify sound, allowing sound to travel further. Figure 7-3 shows the adverse and positive environmental conditions.

Adverse Conditions	Positive Conditions
Wind	Wind
Hills	Open Terrain
High Humidity and Moisture	Water
Vegetation	Low Humidity
Structures	

Figure 7-3. Environmental conditions

PLANNING AND COORDINATION

7-39. Loudspeaker operations require detailed planning and coordination. TPT leaders must make sure all environmental conditions are considered. Proper selection of a broadcast position is critical to the success of any loudspeaker operation. Routes and rallying points should also be considered, along with expected impact indicators. TPT leaders should also plan for follow-on dissemination, based upon the TA's reaction.

Chapter 7

7-40. Close coordination by the loudspeaker team with personnel of the supported unit and other supporting elements is essential. Commanders within audible range of the broadcasts must be informed about loudspeaker operations being conducted in their AO. Commanders must make sure troops are briefed on the opponent's possible reaction to the broadcast, which may include enemy soldiers attempting to surrender. The supported unit must be aware of the procedures for accepting enemy soldiers who surrender. If this is not done, potential enemy prisoners of war (EPWs) may lose their lives while attempting to surrender. There should be a coordinated plan should hostile fire be directed at the loudspeakers. Troops must also be briefed on what procedures to follow in the event of possible TA reactions. If the loudspeaker message is an ultimatum, threatening artillery fire or air attacks, arrangements must be made so the threatened action can be executed. Lack of follow-through contributes to decreased credibility.

7-41. Without thorough and continuing coordination of activity, PSYOP series cannot achieve maximum effectiveness. Coordination is required in several directions. Command and staffs at higher, lower, and adjacent echelons must be aware of the PSYOP series and its results. If artillery and air support are required for loudspeaker operations, the PSYOP planner must coordinate precisely and thoroughly with the supported unit's staff. Coordination may involve the fire support coordinator (FSCOORD), theater airlift liaison officer (TALO), tactical air control party (TACP), and the maneuver element commander. PSYOP personnel must make sure requirements are clearly spelled out in the unit's CONOPS and execution portion of the OPORD so that all involved elements understand the mission. Without coordination, the many hours of planning and preparation that precede a loudspeaker operation are wasted or are counterproductive.

7-42. TPT leaders, using the PSYOP process, ensure that loudspeaker scripts are carefully worded, are short, and, if possible, have shock effect. Loudspeaker scripts must be well planned, must be coordinated, and must comply with the objectives and policies of all higher HQ.

7-43. Because of the TPT's limited firepower, coupled with its proximity to the enemy, loudspeaker operations necessitate a clear security and extraction plan. Examples of areas of consideration when planning a loudspeaker mission are—
- Environmental conditions.
- Message.
- Location and mission of friendly units.
- Security element.
- Insertion and extraction plan.
- Signal or method to initiate broadcast.
- Method of broadcast (mounted, dismounted, ALS).

7-44. In an urban setting, loudspeakers are used to communicate with assembled groups. Loudspeakers effectively extend the range of face-to-face communication and are the most responsive medium that can be used to support combat operations. When necessary, unsophisticated loudspeaker messages can be developed on the spot and delivered live in very fluid situations; however, loudspeaker broadcasts are best when prerecorded to ensure accuracy, clarity, and quality. TPTs normally deploy with a variety of general prepackaged loudspeaker scripts in the TA language that support approved PSYOP objectives.

BROADCAST POSITION

7-45. To occupy a broadcast position successfully, a TPT must be aware of several considerations. The TPT leader should obtain a map of the potential broadcast area (1:50,000 scale) and the location of the TA to be affected. He should select the potential broadcast position—based upon terrain, distance to the target, and environmental conditions. He should also select a location in which to conduct a temporary halt before the broadcast position. The TPT leader must also assess potential security threats, based on a map reconnaissance and intelligence updates. Once the broadcast position is selected, the TPT leader should coordinate with the supported unit for security. Because a TPT has only a limited amount of organic weapons systems to defend itself against a hostile force, it should always go on combat operations with a security element provided by the supported unit. The TPT leader should then determine the best route to the broadcast area and check the engineer map and mine overlay of known routes in the AO. To prevent fratricide, the TPT leader should inform the unit commander of the broadcast position and the selected

Tactical Psychological Operations Team Operations

route. Once the supported unit has granted permission to initiate movement, the TPT begins movement to the broadcast position.

7-46. The TPT conducts a temporary halt before reaching the broadcast position. During the temporary halt, the TPT establishes security, and the TPT leader gets out of the vehicle (if mounted) while the assistant TPT leader mans the M249. The driver (if mounted, or PSYOP specialist if dismounted) observes terrain and maintains security, always considering the best evacuation route if the team is engaged. The TPT leader then reconfirms the suitability of the planned broadcast position and calls in new coordinates if he changes location from the original determination. (*Note*. The TPT leader asks himself if it is better to broadcast from a remote position.) Once the position is confirmed, the TPT leader gives the order to prepare for broadcast.

7-47. The assistant TPT leader then powers up the system and notifies the TPT leader that he is ready to broadcast. Using the route that gives the most cover and concealment possible, the TPT then moves forward and occupies its broadcast position. The driver (PSYOP specialist when dismounted) scans the sector, maintaining situational awareness at all times. Once the TPT occupies the broadcast position, the TPT leader reports to higher HQ. The TPT leader must verify the target area, assess wind and other environmental factors, and then direct the assistant TPT leader to sight the loudspeaker cones in the proper direction for the target area to receive the message. Once the assistant TPT leader sights the cones, the TPT leader reports to higher HQ that the team is in position and requests permission to broadcast. The TPT maintains 360-degree security throughout the entire process. The TPT should also maintain communications with higher HQ throughout the entire broadcast.

BROADCAST DELIVERY

7-48. To achieve maximum effect in the loudspeaker broadcast, PSYOP personnel should observe certain rules governing speech delivery. They should make sure they or their translators—

- Speak loudly, but do not shout.
- Speak deliberately and take time for message delivery.
- Maintain a constant voice volume, with an even rate of delivery.
- Never slur or drop words.
- Avoid a singsong delivery.
- Sound out every syllable of each word.
- Sound the final consonant of each word.
- Think of each word as it is spoken.
- Speak into the microphone.

PRINTED PRODUCT DISSEMINATION

7-49. In a permissive or semipermissive environment, dissemination of printed products by TPTs is a highly effective way of disseminating the PSYOP message to TAs. TPTs usually disseminate printed products by hand, in a face-to-face manner, which lends credibility to the product (Figure 7-4, page 7-12).

PRODUCT TYPES

7-50. There are various types of printed products. The following paragraphs discuss some of the types of printed products a TPT might disseminate.

Posters

7-51. TPTs place posters up within their specific AO, using tape, staples, or poster paste. Poster paste is the preferred method, as paste makes tearing the product down more difficult. PSYOP personnel should consult with local leaders before disseminating posters, as these leaders can provide PSYOP personnel information about the best locations that guarantee maximum visibility. Care should also be taken when placing posters at sensitive locations, such as religious facilities. PSYOP personnel should check with the facility manager, as there may be specific guidelines for where, how, and when a poster is put up because of fears of retribution or other perceived threats. A technique that has proved effective in disseminating posters is to place the posters at night. Operations in Bosnia and Kosovo have shown that when the populace is not present when the poster is placed, the poster often remains for a much longer time.

Figure 7-4. TPT member disseminating handbills in Iraq

Novelty Items

7-52. Handing out novelty items with a PSYOP message printed on them—for example, notebooks, soccer balls, pens and pencils, and T-shirts—are an extremely effective means to reach a TA, especially children. Another example of novelty items is illustrated in Figure 7-5, "Rewards for Justice" matchbooks. The front and back covers of the matchbooks show Saddam Hussein and Abu Musab al-Zarqawi; the inside covers provide a phone number and E-mail address for tips. The matchbooks were distributed throughout Iraq by tactical PSYOP teams.

Figure 7-5. Rewards for justice matchbooks

7-53. An effective dissemination technique, when the force protection and OPSEC allow, is to hand out products at the same time and place on a regular schedule. When TPTs disseminate these products, they should, if the security situation permits, inform the local populace that they will return on a certain date and time. This practice sets up a specific dissemination location where the TA knows they will receive new products and information on a regular basis. The TPT leader should make sure his team observes all local cultural nuisances. For example, some cultures frown on adults, other than parents, having direct contact with or talking to children. Cultural awareness is key to gaining the trust and respect of the TA.

Leaflets and Handbills

7-54. TPTs can effectively disseminate leaflets and handbills in a face-to-face environment. Several methods may be used to disseminate these products. For example, the TPT leader can distribute the products to a key communicator, who then disseminates them to the TA. This method adds credibility to the products; however, the key communicator must be trusted to disseminate the products. Another method for disseminating leaflets and handbills is to leave the products at a key location for the TA to pick up. This method is most often used in disseminating newspapers, but it is also effective in disseminating leaflets and handbills. Locations that provide excellent opportunities for disseminating leaflets and handbills are community centers, religious centers, market centers, and places where rallies or demonstrations are held. When disseminating leaflets or handbills, TPTs should apply the same cultural awareness rules they use when disseminating novelty items.

Newspapers

7-55. Newspapers should be disseminated in the same manner as other printed products. They should also be disseminated on a regular schedule at the same time and place. TAs may become reliant upon information within the product; therefore, not having the newspapers available regularly lessens their effectiveness.

DISSEMINATION METHOD

7-56. Several factors influence the dissemination method. The type of product, the message, and its sensitivity all play a part in choosing the best method for dissemination. The TPT can hand out the products, post or leave the products at a designated location, or use a key communicator to disseminate the products. Careful consideration should be made as to which of the following methods should be employed:

- *Handing out products.* The TPT can hand out the products themselves. This method works best with novelties, leaflets, handbills, and newspapers. It allows the TPT to ensure that the products get into the hands of the TA. This method is the most time consuming; however, it allows the team to get some feedback and can also be used as a springboard to face-to-face communication, which is often the most effective type of PSYOP dissemination.
- *Posting or leaving products.* Products can be posted or left at designated locations for the TA to read or take. This method is the least time-consuming method, allowing the TPT to conduct other missions once the products are dropped off. This method works best with posters, newspapers, leaflets, and handbills. This method does not ensure that the TA reads or takes the products, or that opposition elements do not confiscate them.

DISSEMINATION LOCATION

7-57. The location for disseminating printed products is determined by the amount, the TA, the message, and the risk that the product will be censored. Religious centers, markets, community centers, and street corners are some of the optional locations. The TPT leader should consider any cultural nuances before deciding on a location. A religious center may be a good place; however, it may not be well received or may be viewed as an intrusion by the Americans. Markets are good locations when there is a large quantity of the product, but community centers are better locations when there is a smaller quantity.

FACE-TO-FACE COMMUNICATION

7-58. Face-to-face communication is the most common and potentially effective mission conducted by TPTs. Increasing rapport, trust, and credibility with the TA is accomplished through effective face-to-face communication. This method also allows PSYOP Soldiers the best way of engaging with a TA about complex issues (Figure 7-6). The give-and-take of personal communication is best suited for discussing such issues as politics and economics. The importance of this TPT mission necessitates a detailed discussion.

Figure 7-6. TPT conducting face-to-face communication with Iraqi locals

7-59. TPTs conduct face-to-face communication whenever they are handing out products and talking with local leaders or the general population. Face-to-face communication is the conveyance of a message by the sender in the sight or presence of the receiver. This communication may be by one individual to another or by one speaker addressing a large group of people. Face-to-face communication ranges from two or more individuals in informal conversation to planned persuasion among groups. The credibility of PSYOP products delivered by face-to-face communication is increased when the communicator is known and respected. Disseminating the product through face-to-face communication gives the PSYOP forces the opportunity to interact with the local populace and to get direct, immediate feedback and reactions from the TA that would normally not be available as quickly.

CULTURAL AWARENESS

7-60. A keen awareness of the TA's culture, coupled with skillful face-to-face communication, can lead to successful PSYOP. PSYOP personnel can use face-to-face communication to present persuasive appeals and complex material in detail. They can repeat portions of the communication as required and use slight variations to influence a specific TA. The importance of appropriate gestures and physical posture in the communication process must not be overlooked. What may be an appropriate gesture in one culture may be viewed quite differently in another. The most important part of face-to-face communication is the immediate feedback that can be obtained from the TA.

7-61. PSYOP personnel can obtain valuable information from this feedback and may immediately identify product content that is culturally or politically insensitive to the TA. This information may change the message intent or the message itself. PSYOP personnel should take every opportunity to hone and enhance their ability to conduct effective face-to-face communication. PSYOP personnel need to rehearse face-to-face communication to practice favorable body language while eliminating unfavorable gestures and

Tactical Psychological Operations Team Operations

posture. Body language is as important as the verbal message and should appear natural, not labored or uncomfortable.

7-62. To learn more about gestures, posture, and other mannerisms used when communicating face-to-face, PSYOP personnel should consult individuals who have lived in the LN and are aware of these customs (Figure 7-7). A good source of this information is to talk with and ask questions of the interpreters assigned in the AO. Another excellent source of information is the Culturgram series published by Brigham Young University. Each Culturgram lists the latest information about greetings, eating, gestures, and travel under the "Customs and Courtesies" heading and also includes the headings "The People," "Lifestyle," "The Nation," and "Health." *The Do's and Taboos Around the World* book contains chapters on hand gestures and body language, giving and receiving gifts, a quick guide to the ways of the world, and information about the importance of colors, jargon, slang, and humor. The ethnic composition of a working PSYOP team should be as diverse as possible. This practice will prevent hostile propaganda about the use of a specific ethnic group to achieve certain goals. A diverse ethnic composition within the TPT demonstrates a willingness to work with all races.

Figure 7-7. PSYOP Soldier interfacing with members of a target audience

ADVANTAGES

7-63. There are many advantages of face-to-face communication. Some examples include—
- *Relationship.* Face-to-face communication employs an interpersonal relationship.
- *Audience selection.* The audience can be deliberately selected and the appeal directed and tailored for the audience.
- *Assessment of impact.* Feedback is immediate. The communicator can immediately assess the impact of his message and adjust his approach to obtain the desired response.
- *Requirement for limited support.* Limited technical and logistical support is required.
- *Credibility.* Face-to-face communication can be more credible than other methods because the TA can evaluate the source.

Chapter 7

- *Presentation.* Complex material can be presented in detail. Frequent repetition and slight variations can be readily used to influence the audience.
- *Efficiency.* In some instances, particularly in primitive areas, face-to-face communication may be the most efficient and expedient means to disseminate.

DISADVANTAGES

7-64. There are also disadvantages of face-to-face communication. Some examples include—

- *Limited use in tactical situations.* Face-to-face communication is limited in war, with the exception of loudspeaker operations, because of the inaccessibility of the target individual or group. Likewise, in combat, face-to-face communication is limited, because the PSYOP Soldier has little face-to-face communication with the enemy until the enemy is captured or is defected.
- *Close control necessary.* Face-to-face dissemination must be controlled, especially at the lowest levels where each communicator has the responsibility to interpret policy and objectives. The control factor is best illustrated by trying to pass an oral message, one person at a time, throughout a group. By the time the message reaches the end of the group, it does not resemble the original message. Reinforcement by other media is necessary to mitigate this problem.
- *Limited use in secure areas.* Security considerations limit the conduct of face-to-face communication. As the security situation improves and more areas are secure, area coverage can be extended.
- *Able communicators required.* Effective communication requires knowledgeable, orally persuasive individuals who can convince the TA to change a specific behavior.
- *Indigenous personnel required.* For effective communications, indigenous personnel are normally required.
- *Limited range of voice.* The range of the human voice and the need for visual contact limit this method to relatively small audiences.

PLANNING

7-65. Before conducting a face-to-face mission, the TPT leader must confirm the local threat and the impact of prior operations or dissemination by coordinating with the battalion S-2 or company commander of the supported unit. The TPT leader should know the name of the village or town leader, if possible. The TPT leader and the security element should communicate face to face with the leader, to ease dissemination within the area. The TPT leader should also coordinate with any friendly or adjacent units within the AO to ensure that ongoing operations will not adversely affect the mission. The TPT leader should determine the disseminator (usually himself), security (usually the assistant TPT leader), recorder (usually the PSYOP specialist), and translator (usually a native speaker) for the mission. The TPT verifies security posture, informs the supported unit of the operating location, and performs communications checks before the mission to minimize any possibility of fratricide. The disseminator and translator should discuss potential topics, articulate clear meaning of certain key words or phrases, establish certain parameters before the mission, and review the FFEO contained in the PAW for the face-to-face product.

7-66. The interviewer should be aware of any restrictions on the local populace, such as curfews and restricted movement. He should also be knowledgeable of any rewards programs, such as cash rewards for weapons and how they work.

7-67. The interviewer should try to find out if there has been any exposure to PSYOP or propaganda. This is a great opportunity to conduct a posttest or to collect propaganda. Before going into the area, the TPT leader should find out what PSYOP products have been previously disseminated in the area. Identifying previous PSYOP products will be helpful in assessing the effectiveness of the dissemination plan.

7-68. If the purpose of the face-to-face mission is to persuade a key communicator to disseminate products, then the interviewer should ensure he has at least a prototype with him. Giving the prototype to the key communicator provides an excellent opportunity to pretest the products.

Tactical Psychological Operations Team Operations

SECURITY POSTURE

7-69. As a tactical element, security should always be in the minds of the TPT members. Security can be a challenging requirement when conducting face-to-face communication. TPT members should keep the individual they are talking to at ease, without compromising the safety of the TPT. The TPT leader should make sure he has a security plan. If TPT members are separated—for example, when two team members go inside a building and one stays outside—there should be a plan in place that ensures communication within the team. The tactical situation and command guidance dictate the security posture.

INDIVIDUAL RESPONSIBILITIES

7-70. As with other operations, the TPT has individuals with specific responsibilities when conducting face-to-face communication. The TPT generally consists of the following individuals:

- *Interviewer.* The interviewer is usually the TPT leader. He should present himself in a nonthreatening manner and try to make his subject feel at ease. If an interpreter is used, a rehearsal should be conducted before executing the mission. The interviewer should always talk to his audience, not the interpreter. The interviewer should make sure he is aware of all cultural nuances. The TPT leader must continually assess the security posture throughout the engagement.
- *Recorder.* The recorder is usually the PSYOP specialist. He is responsible for taking notes during the mission. He should take note of any references to propaganda, effects of previous friendly PSYOP, grievances or conditions that affect the TA, and actions of those in the area. The recorder documents information and takes photos or videos for future products. He must also maintain situational awareness and security responsibilities. When propaganda is encountered, the PSYOP specialist must prepare an initial SCAME and forward it to the TPD as soon as possible.
- *Interpreter.* The interpreter is usually a native speaker who may be a civilian from the LN, a U.S. military member, or a member of a friendly military force. Interpreters are discussed further in Appendix J.
- *Security personnel.* The security person is usually the assistant TPT leader. He is responsible for maintaining security for the TPT. He should coordinate with any security element provided by the supported unit that may be present. He observes the situation and advises the TPT leader if the threat level increases. He should remain back from the TPT leader and the PSYOP specialist, but not so far away that he cannot control the situation.

PRESENTATION

7-71. Face-to-face communication is an important facet of TPT operations. Effective face-to-face communication can help build the rapport and trust of a local population. Ineffective face-to-face communication can have the opposite effect, destroying any faith in U.S. or coalition forces.

7-72. Face-to-face communication is one of the most difficult tasks to master. Preparation is of utmost importance to ensure a successful meeting. Many considerations should be made about the presentation, including the following:

- The interviewer should not use colloquialisms during the conversation, as the use of American slang may confuse the interpreter and thus potentially cause the loss of the meaning through translation. The interviewer should also speak clearly in a deliberate manner. He and other TPT members should present themselves in a nonthreatening or nonconfrontational manner.
- Cultural nuances should be observed. Offending the individual being spoken to can quickly cause a loss of trust or respect on the part of the interviewee. Such practices as removing shoes when entering a building, crossing one's legs when seated, and accepting a glass of tea may be very important to the culture.
- The interviewer should also be aware of the types of words and or phrases he uses. The use of authoritative phrases such as "we need or want you…" and "you need to…" may be extremely offensive to the interviewee. The interviewer should make sure he does not sound like he is begging. Phrases such as "we really need you…" may display a position of weakness that the

interviewee may attempt to exploit. The interviewee should know that his help helps his people, not the United States or the coalition.

PRETESTING AND POSTTESTING

7-73. PSYOP personnel pretest and posttest products or series to predict and assess the effectiveness on the TA. Testing criteria are developed during Phase IV of the PSYOP process. Testing is executed during Phase VI and the results are evaluated during Phase VII (Chapter 6 covers the PSYOP process). An important function of the TPT is to test products or series. A higher PSYOP HQ, through command or PSYOP channels, may direct the TPT to conduct a pretest or posttest of PSYOP products or series. For example, after the development and design of a potential symbol or a series of PSYOP products, PSYOP personnel may conduct testing to answer important questions about PSYOP materials, such as—

- Should this LOP be used?
- Are the symbols meaningful to the TA?
- Are the colors used offensive in any way?
- Does the material address the correct TA?
- Is the medium used the most effective way to present the material?
- Does each product in the series complement the others?

7-74. PSYOP personnel use pretesting to assess the potential effectiveness of a series of PSYOP products on the TA. The information derived from testing is also used to refine and improve PSYOP products. Posttesting is a process that evaluates products after they have been disseminated. PSYOP personnel use the same methods in posttesting as used in pretesting.

PLANNING AND COORDINATION

7-75. The TPT leader should receive testing guidance and a pretest or posttest questionnaire from the TPD, along with the product being tested, its English translation, and a copy of the PAW. Upon receipt of these materials, the TPT leader should begin planning how he will obtain information. With guidance from the TPD, the TPT leader should decide the type of interview he will conduct. For detailed information on interviews, see FM 3-05.301.

7-76. The TPT leader begins by selecting the best location for an interview. Depending on the method selected, the location may be outdoors, in a room within an I/R camp, in a building coordinated for in a town or village, or in any other place that lends itself to an effective setting. An effective setting is one that is free of distractions, is safe, and is accessible to the TA.

7-77. The TPT leader should coordinate with the supported unit for any support he may need, such as—

- Security.
- Access to EPWs.
- Transportation.

7-78. In addition to evaluating answers to the actual questions, TPT members must also be aware of cues not reflected in the answers given by a TA member. Evaluating verbal and nonverbal cues, as well as emotion, is as important as the questions themselves.

VERBAL COMMUNICATION

7-79. Verbal communication includes words and the way they are spoken. The interviewer must remember that every word has a denotation (its literal, dictionary meaning) and a connotation (its suggested meaning). The way in which people say a word has a distinct influence on its meaning. The interviewer (PSYOP team leader) needs to look for vocal cues—for example, emphasis, volume, tempo, pitch, enunciation, and breaks in speech.

NONVERBAL COMMUNICATION

7-80. Nonverbal communication, or body language, is the second part of communication. The interviewer must properly interpret the body language—facial expressions, territory, body position, gestures, visual behavior, and appearance—of the person being interviewed to understand fully what is being said. During an interview, the interviewer should look for body language that indicates negative emotions. Examples include—

- Facial expressions, which include lowered brows, narrowed eyes, and a tightened mouth or frown.
- Territory, which involves violating space relationships by standing too close.
- Body position, which includes "closing-up" positions, such as clenched fists, tightly crossed arms or legs, or shifting of body weight from one foot to the other.
- Gestures, which include shaking the head, covering the mouth with the hand, or rubbing the ear.
- Visual behavior, which includes staring or not maintaining eye contact.
- Appearance, which includes dress and behavior inappropriate for the situation.

INTERPRETING EMOTIONS

7-81. Adding both verbal and nonverbal communication, the interviewer should follow these general guidelines when interpreting emotions during an interview:

- Look for cooperation, respect, and courtesy. This behavior may indicate trust.
- Look for embarrassment, crying, or a withdrawn attitude. This behavior may indicate hurt.
- Look for aggression; hostile, sarcastic, loud, or abusive language; lack of cooperation; or a stiff, strong face. This behavior may indicate anger.
- Look for sweating, sickness, running away, freezing in place, nervousness, physical or mental inability to cooperate, excessive cooperation, or submission. This behavior may indicate fear.
- Look for the offering of aid and comfort through word or deed, by listening, or by nodding agreement. This behavior may indicate concern.

TEST RESULTS

7-82. Testing is usually a short-suspense mission for the TPT; therefore, test results must be forwarded to higher HQ as soon as possible. Incorporating the TPT's assessment of verbal and nonverbal cues and the emotions of those interviewed is critical to acquiring accurate results. Forwarding the assessment and the actual survey or answered questions helps higher PSYOP echelons make accurate assessments of PSYOP series effectiveness. Chapter 8 of this publication discusses reporting procedures.

CIVIL DISTURBANCE

7-83. The U.S. Army can provide military assistance to civil authorities in civil disturbances when it is requested or directed IAW prevailing laws. When such assistance is requested, the military forces assist local authorities in the restoration and maintenance of law and order. Additionally, in S&RO, the U.S. military may be the only recognized authority and may also have to respond unilaterally to civil disturbances in the areas under their authority and control.

7-84. Crowd behavior during a civil disturbance is essentially emotional and without reason. The feelings and the momentum generated typically make the whole group act like its worst members. Skillful agitators or subversive elements can exploit these psychological factors during these disturbances. Regardless of the reason for violence, the results may consist of indiscriminate looting and burning or open and violent attacks on officials, buildings, and innocent passersby. Rioters may set fire to buildings and vehicles to—

- Block the advance of troops.
- Create confusion and diversion.
- Achieve goals of property destruction, looting, and sniping.

7-85. In addition, organized rioters or agitators may use sniper fire to cause security forces to overreact. In these situations, TPTs may assist in controlling crowds and defusing a potentially hostile situation. Proper planning and situational awareness are essential in these situations.

7-86. The TPT leader should attempt to gather as much information about the situation as possible. The clearer the operational picture, the better the plan can be conceived and executed. The intelligence assets and the supported unit should be used to identify friendly units in the area and to gather more information. These assets may be operational detachments A (ODAs), Civil Affairs teams (CATs), or military police (MP). Examples of the type of information that should be gathered during planning include—

- Location.
- Size of crowd.
- Apparent grievance.
- Goals of the crowd.
- Known potential key communicators.
- Agitators.

7-87. When planning is completed, the TPT is ready to execute its mission. If the TPT is surrounded, the TPT leader attempts to discuss the situation or grievance with the key communicator or agitator. Effective use of the interpreter is essential during this attempt at defusing the situation. If unsuccessful, the TPT leader then attempts to reason with known sympathetic individuals. If the TA poses a threat to personnel or to U.S. Government property, the TPT leader can implement graduated-response techniques IAW ROE and ROI (Appendix K). The TPT maintains security and communication throughout. Upon mission completion, the TPT leader forwards a SITREP that summarizes his actions in response to the civil disturbance and makes notes of any impact indicators.

7-88. If the face-to-face communication is not well received by the TA, the TPT leader determines whether to continue and if any additional security measures need to be taken. If the TA grows hostile and no local maneuver elements are present, the TPT should attempt to leave the area.

7-89. The TPT leader makes sure all doors, windows, and hatches on the vehicle are secured. A security person should remain with the vehicle at all times in the objective area. If an interpreter is present, the TPT leader should use him to issue commands to the TA. Noninterference messages should be used. The TPT should attempt to maneuver out of the area by way of the quickest route available. FOL (vehicle-mounted loudspeaker system) may be used to facilitate retrograde movement. The siren, trill, or other loud, irritating noises may be used to assist in clearing a path in a nonlethal manner. The supported unit and higher HQ must be notified of the situation and the route being used.

7-90. If dismounted, the TPT must retrograde out of the area as quickly as possible. The supported unit and higher HQ must be contacted immediately so that assistance can be provided. Security is paramount and must be maintained at all times. The supported unit and higher HQ must be kept informed of the route being used.

7-91. When being deployed to a situation that is deteriorating into a disturbance, the TPT leader should quickly reiterate the ROE to his team and conduct linkup with the supported commander, as necessary. He should then receive an update on the current situation from the supported unit and establish liaison with other QRF or graduated-response-measure (GRM) components, as required. The team should assess the situation on the ground, maintain communications with higher HQ, and submit SITREPs, as required. The TPT should maintain security at all times, regardless of whether another element is present. During the initial stages of the disturbance, the team monitors and attempts to identify facts and assumptions about the TA (crowd). The TPT uses the following questions as a guide to get a complete picture of the disturbance:

- What is the lead agitator's message?
- What is the general attitude or behavior of the group?
- How many people are present in the group?
- What are the demographics (age and gender)?
- What is the cultural composition of the group?
- What language are they speaking?
- How are they moving (mounted or dismounted)?
- Are signs or banners present, and, if so, what is the message?
- Are any media on site? If so, what people do they represent?
- Are any weapons present among the demonstrators?
- Who else is present at the location (police, elected public officials, NGOs, CA, other forces)?

Tactical Psychological Operations Team Operations

- Is the group from that location or from another location? If from another location, where and why?
- How did the people know or hear about the gathering, rally, or demonstration?
- What are their underlying grievances or stated objectives for the event?

Note. Once these questions are answered, the team should have a well-documented picture of the situation.

7-92. The team should then consult the specified and implied tasks of the supported unit (commander's intent, scheme of maneuver, and coordinating instructions) to see how the disturbance fits into the command guidance. The TPT must know the series available to address the needs and grievances of the crowd, and the ROE. The TPT leader should consider conducting face-to-face communication with the key communicator in an isolated area, as this, many times, is the most successful approach to diffusing a crowd situation. The TPT should be prepared to create a message for broadcast, if needed.

7-93. When the commander directs the TPT to broadcast in this environment, the team should—

- Give simple directions that are clear and concise.
- Maintain composure.
- Avoid using the word "please" when constructing messages, so the team does not display a passive appearance.
- Do not issue ultimatums not approved by the commander.
- Make sure the crowd has time to conform to the conditions of any ultimatum approved by the commander.
- Make sure the supported commander is prepared to act upon his ultimatum if the crowd fails to respond favorably.
- Use approved LOPs when possible and conduct impromptu broadcasting only as a last resort.
- Conduct rehearsals with the translator before going "live," unless the situation makes rehearsing absolutely impossible.
- Make sure the gender and other social aspects of the translator are credible in the eyes of the TA.
- Pick a broadcast position that communicates effectively with the crowd and does not compromise the security of the team.
- Direct the broadcast toward the primary agitators.
- Limit the volume of the broadcast so it is not overbearing; do not harass the crowd—such action only exacerbates the situation.

7-94. The team must maintain communication with the supported commander or his representative on the ground throughout the situation. Also, the TPT leader must make sure PSYOP-relevant information, human intelligence (HUMINT), and PIR are forwarded through appropriate channels.

SUMMARY

7-95. Tactical PSYOP forces are responsive to the ground commander's needs. Their ability to execute PSYOP series provides a means to address changing and unusual tactical situations rapidly and effectively. Tactical PSYOP forces also provide the commander the ability to communicate directly and indirectly with combatants and hostile or potentially hostile noncombatants, ensuring they take actions that support the maneuver commander's intent.

This page intentionally left blank.

Chapter 8
Intelligence Support

For PSYOP, intelligence support implies a mutual exchange of information between PSYOP units and traditional intelligence elements and systems. This reciprocal relationship is critical not only to the success of the PSYOP effort but also to the overall accomplishment of the supported commander's mission. This chapter explains the integration of PSYOP into the Army's IPB structure, the Army's information categories, and the procedures for reporting valuable information through the chain of command.

INTELLIGENCE PREPARATION OF THE BATTLEFIELD

8-1. The IPB process supports commanders and their staffs in the decision-making process. The IPB is a continuous process that combines all available information and determines the common operational picture (COP) that commanders use in conducting their missions. The IPB process is conducted at all echelons and follows a standard four-step procedure; however, each type of Army unit must make special considerations to ensure the information needed to conduct its mission successfully is included. The four steps of the IPB are—

- Define the battlefield environment.
- Describe the battlefield effects.
- Evaluate the threat.
- Determine threat courses of action.

STEP 1: DEFINE THE BATTLEFIELD ENVIRONMENT

8-2. In Step 1 of the IPB process, the Deputy/Assistant Chief of Staff for Intelligence (G-2) or the S-2—
- Identifies characteristics of the battlefield that will influence friendly and threat operations.
- Establishes the limits of the AOI.
- Identifies gaps in current intelligence holdings.

8-3. The G-2 or S-2 identifies characteristics of the battlefield that require in-depth evaluation of their effects on friendly and threat operations, such as terrain, weather, logistical infrastructure, and demographics. Defining the significant characteristics of the battlefield environment also aids in identifying gaps in current intelligence holdings and the specific intelligence required to fill them. Similarly, the G-2 or S-2 identifies gaps in the command's knowledge of the threat and the current threat situation. Once approved by the commander, the specific intelligence required to fill gaps in the command's knowledge of the battlefield environment and threat situation becomes the command's initial intelligence requirements.

8-4. For PSYOP, the emphasis during this first step of IPB is to identify weather, terrain, infrastructure, area and media assessments, and PTAs within the AOR. The G-2 or S-2 completes most of these functions along with the PSYOP planner or the TPDD. Identification of these essential elements is normally completed during initial IPB, which is Task 2 of Step 2 of the MDMP.

STEP 2: DESCRIBE THE BATTLEFIELD EFFECTS

8-5. Step 2 evaluates the effects of the environment with which both sides must contend. The G-2 or S-2 identifies the limitations and opportunities the environment offers on the potential operations of friendly and threat forces. This evaluation focuses on the general capabilities of each force until COAs are developed in later steps of the IPB process. This assessment of the environment always includes an examination of terrain and weather but may also include discussions of the characteristics of geography and infrastructure and their effects on friendly and threat operations.

8-6. Characteristics of geography include general characteristics of the terrain and weather, as well as such factors as politics, civilian press, local population, and demographics. An area's infrastructure consists of the facilities, equipment, and framework needed for the functioning of systems, cities, or regions.

8-7. For PSYOP, Step 2 of IPB is critical and expansive. In Step 2, the PPD determines the MOEs for each PTA under each SPO. Once determined, the MOEs—which are in the form of questions—are submitted to the supported unit's G-2 or S-2 for inclusion in the collection plan. The answers to the MOEs (impact indicators) establish a baseline and measure PSYOP effectiveness. They are the key component of assessment for targeting and for judging PSYOP impact on the battlefield. As such, they are always an IR. Without the answers to the MOEs, PSYOP will be unable to gauge the effectiveness of the series conducted and there can be no assessment of the PSYOP effort.

8-8. The G-2 or S-2 must analyze the weather and terrain and determine how these will affect the dissemination of PSYOP products by both friendly and hostile forces. Infrastructure analysis for PSYOP considers the information environment and the media outlets that disseminate information. This analysis must determine which outlets are available for use by friendly PSYOP forces and those that are being used or could be used by opponent forces. The POTF or PSE G-2 or S-2, in conjunction with the supported unit's intelligence section, is primarily responsible for this portion of Step 2. The TAAT takes the PTAL from Step 1 of IPB, and the SPO written during planning, and begins to analyze each target set and SPO combination to determine the effectiveness of each PTA. This process determines each PTA's ability to affect the battlefield. The TAAT determines the ability of each PTA to influence the PSYOP and supported commander's stated objectives.

STEP 3: EVALUATE THE THREAT

8-9. In Step 3 of Army IPB, the G-2 or S-2 and his staff analyze the command's intelligence holdings to determine how the threat normally organizes for combat and conducts operations under similar circumstances. During this stage of IPB, PSYOP specialists focus on propaganda analysis and counterpropaganda. They monitor the competing agencies within the AOR that disseminate information and determine the effects of the information on the conduct of the operation. This analysis is done by the TAAD but with significant assistance from the G-2 or S-2 who interfaces with the various intelligence agencies to obtain PSYOP-relevant information. One technique that facilitates propaganda analysis is to have TAAD and G-2 or S-2 personnel located in proximity to one another. This function of propaganda analysis is unique to PSYOP IPB and when done effectively can be of great interest and assistance to a supported commander.

STEP 4: DETERMINE THREAT COURSES OF ACTION

8-10. Step 4 integrates the results of the previous steps into a meaningful conclusion. Likely objectives and COAs available to the threat are determined, based on what the threat normally prefers to do and the effects of the specific environment in which he is operating. After the first three steps, PSYOP specialists have defined the operational environment, conducted TAA, and analyzed competing information. This information taken together allows the PSYOP force to modify behavior and counter other information to achieve PSYOP and, ultimately, the supported commander's objectives. In short, the IPB process allows commanders to make informed decisions that ensure mission success.

INFORMATION MANAGEMENT CATEGORIES

8-11. During the conduct of military operations, staffs routinely obtain large amounts of information. Processing and categorizing that information ensure that the appropriate recipient receives the information in a timely manner. The Army uses several categories and procedures to prioritize information.

RELEVANT INFORMATION

8-12. Relevant information includes all information that may impact on a commander's ability to accomplish his mission. The immense amount of information in today's world necessitates that only information relevant to the mission is considered. PSYOP are information-intensive, and understanding the Army's categories facilitates one's ability to ensure that the commander obtains the answers he needs to make important decisions.

INFORMATION REQUIREMENTS

8-13. IRs are all information elements the commander and staff require to conduct operations successfully—that is, all elements necessary to address the factors of METT-TC. A HQ must focus IRs on relevant information. From all data that are available, the staff retains only that which is relevant. Once the staff has analyzed all relevant information, it develops questions that need to be answered to exercise C2. These questions become IRs, which are the basis for beginning the process of allocating assets to collect mission-essential information. However, Army units have successfully generated far too many IRs to allocate resources to each one; therefore, IRs must be further refined.

PRIORITY INTELLIGENCE REQUIREMENTS

8-14. Once a staff receives IRs, it must designate PIR and friendly forces information requirements (FFIRs). PIR are the intelligence requirements for which a commander has an anticipated and stated priority in his task of planning and decision making. PIR involve both the enemy and the environment. PIR focus on how the commander sees the enemy.

FRIENDLY FORCES INFORMATION REQUIREMENTS

8-15. FFIRs are information the commander and staff need about the forces available for the operation. FFIRs consist of information on the mission and troops, time, and support available for friendly forces. FFIRs focus on how the commander sees his forces. Common PSYOP-specific FFIRs may include the availability of COMMANDO SOLO, organic linguistic support, and dissemination battalion production assets, such as SOMS-B.

COMMANDER'S CRITICAL INFORMATION REQUIREMENTS

8-16. CCIR are elements of information required by commanders that directly affect decision making and dictate the successful execution of military operations. CCIR belong to the commander alone and can be derived from his own cognitive abilities or chosen from the list of PIR and FFIRs the commander receives from his staff. The designation of CCIR clearly sets the priorities for allocating resources to answer IRs. Resources are allocated first to answer CCIR, then to PIR, next to FFIRs, and only then to remaining assets tasked to collect all other IRs. CCIR and PIR normally involve tasking intelligence, surveillance, and reconnaissance assets. PSYOP-specific issues the commander may deem to be CCIR include—

- Enemy radio and TV jamming capability or use.
- New enemy propaganda production capacity or use of specific types of media.
- Reprisals against possession of U.S. or coalition PSYOP products.
- Presence of trained propaganda-producing enemy units or individuals within the AO.

ESSENTIAL ELEMENTS OF FRIENDLY INFORMATION

8-17. Essential elements of friendly information (EEFI) are the critical aspects of a friendly operation that, if known by the enemy, would subsequently compromise, lead to failure, or limit success of the operation and, therefore, must be protected from enemy detection. When established, EEFI have a priority on the level with CCIR. EEFI are neither IRs nor part of the CCIR. EEFI establish information to protect, not information to obtain. EEFI answer the question, "How can I (the commander) prevent the enemy force from seeing me?"

8-18. PSYOP-specific EEFI always include any release of information on products awaiting dissemination. Other EEFI may be the release of information on PSYOP-specific support requests—for example, if the enemy learns that PSYOP planners are inquiring about airtime costs on radio but not TV, they can infer the media mix that PSYOP are planning to use.

INTEGRATING INTO SUPPORTED UNIT'S INTELLIGENCE PROCESS

8-19. To be involved with the intelligence process, the PSYOP element must integrate itself into the supported unit's intelligence process. Often, the battalion S-2 that a TPT supports is very helpful in terrain and weather analysis, enemy strength and dispositions, and the position of displaced civilians. The TPT, as a passive collector, often shares with the supported battalion S-2 information gathered from higher PSYOP elements or from conducting missions. For example, the TPT may share with the supported unit the knowledge of a culturally specific activity a certain TA does every Monday night within a certain town. This sharing of information can establish a very productive working relationship between the PSYOP unit and the supported unit. Such relationship is crucial and facilitates integration into the supported unit's MDMP.

DETERMINING WHERE TO SEND REQUESTS FOR INFORMATION

8-20. Within the Army's information categories, RFIs are the least important. A critical piece of required information is categorized as an IR at the lower levels. A staff may then integrate that IR into its PIR. If the information is important enough, it is then further reclassified as a CCIR. Therefore, RFIs, which are outside the information requirement realm, are pieces of information that are good to know but are not important enough to be classified as an IR. When a higher echelon receives an RFI, it responds with the answer if known; however, it most likely cannot allocate resources to collect the information. For PSYOP-specific information, it is more likely to receive attention if requested through POTF channels. For traditional IPB types of information, RFIs should be sent through the supported S-2. More attention is always given to IRs than to RFIs.

TACTICAL PSYOP CONSIDERATIONS DURING IPB METT–TC

8-21. In the context of information management, the six factors of METT-TC (mission, enemy, terrain and weather, troops and support available, time available, civil considerations) make up the major subject categories into which relevant information is grouped for military operations. The commander and staff consider relevant information for each category in all military operations. The relative impact of each category may vary, but the commander and C2 system consider all of them. The following paragraphs consider each category and give a quick example of what tactical PSYOP Soldiers may look for in each category.

MISSION

8-22. The mission is the task, together with the purpose, that clearly indicates the action to be taken and the reason therefore. It is always the first factor commanders consider during decision making. A thorough understanding of the mission focuses decision making throughout the operations process.

8-23. Commanders analyze their missions and decisions in terms of the higher commander's intent, mission, and CONOPS. As commanders allocate tasks and resources to subordinates, they make sure their decisions support the decisive operation and the higher commander's intent. Commanders and staffs view all the other factors of METT-TC in terms of their impact on mission accomplishment.

8-24. At the tactical level, PSYOP leaders must determine if and how they can assist the supported unit in the accomplishment of its stated mission. They must ensure the employment of the best-suited system and avoid using a system that will not be beneficial in accomplishing the stated mission.

ENEMY

8-25. The second factor to consider is the enemy—disposition (including organization, strength, location, and tactical mobility), doctrine, equipment, capabilities, vulnerabilities, and probable COAs. FM 34-130, *Intelligence Preparation of the Battlefield*, provides further information.

8-26. The enemy factor is larger for PSYOP Soldiers than it is perhaps for other units. The enemy for PSYOP is any foreign entity that may impede mission accomplishment through attempts to change behavior. ROE often do not allow for many units to attack a noncombatant hindering a military mission; however, this restriction is not the case for PSYOP Soldiers. One of the main functions of tactical PSYOP Soldiers is to minimize civilian interference in military operations.

TERRAIN AND WEATHER

8-27. Terrain and weather are natural conditions. Commanders have only a limited ability to influence them, although terrain includes manmade structures, such as roads and cities. Human modification of terrain can change the shape of the land or its trafficability. It can also change local weather effects by modifying local wind or water pathways. Commanders consider manmade features and their effects on natural terrain features and climate when they analyze terrain. Commanders also consider the effects of manmade and natural terrain and the weather on friendly and enemy operations. The second step of IPB helps commanders with this complex task. Terrain and weather are relatively neutral—they favor neither side unless one is better prepared to operate in the environment or is more familiar with it (for example, fighting on friendly territory). Commanders analyze terrain and weather for favorable and unfavorable conditions. Enemy commanders do the same.

8-28. Weather and climatic conditions play an important role in planning PSYOP missions. Loudspeaker ranges differ under certain climatic conditions. For example, a loudspeaker has much greater range on a cool, clear night across water, than it does on a hot, rainy night in the jungle. Wind can also play an important role in loudspeaker operations, as well as in leaflet dissemination.

TROOPS AND SUPPORT AVAILABLE

8-29. The fourth factor of METT-TC is the number, type, capabilities, and condition of available friendly troops and support. These include supplies and support available from joint, multinational, and interagency forces. They also include support from Department of Defense and Department of the Army civilians and from contractors employed by military organizations, such as, the Defense Logistics Agency and the Army Materiel Command.

8-30. Commanders consider available troops and support when analyzing whether they have enough resources to accomplish a mission. If commanders determine that they do not, they request more from the higher commander. Increasing assets in one area may compensate for a shortage of assets in another. Under mission command, commanders make sure their subordinates have the right mix of troops and support to accomplish the assigned missions.

8-31. Commanders consider tangible and intangible factors when assigning missions. Differences in mobility, protection, firepower, equipment, morale, experience, leadership, and training make some units more suitable for certain missions than others. The personalities of subordinate commanders are also important. For example, a bold commander may be a good choice for a pursuit mission, but a methodical commander may be a better choice for a deliberate breaching operation.

8-32. PSYOP leaders must make sure they are completely integrated with the supported unit to receive the maintenance and Army-common supplies necessary to conduct their mission. For example, a tactical team should always deploy with its vehicle Unit-Level Logistics System (ULLS) data to ensure that the supported unit can order all necessary supply parts. When considering friendly troops and support available, TPTs determine which element within the supported unit will allow them to support the commander's intent best and to accomplish their mission.

TIME AVAILABLE

8-33. Commanders assess the time available for planning, preparing, and executing the mission. They consider how friendly and enemy adversary forces will use the time and the possible results. Proper use of the time available can fundamentally alter the situation. Time available is normally explicitly defined in terms of the tasks assigned to the unit and implicitly bounded by enemy or adversary capabilities.

CIVIL CONSIDERATIONS

8-34. Civil considerations comprise the influence of manmade infrastructure, civilian institutions, and attitudes and activities of the civilian leaders, populations, and organizations within an AO on the conduct of military operations. They are a factor in all types of military operations—offense, defense, stability and reconstruction, and civil support. If the military's mission is to support civil authorities, civil considerations define the mission.

8-35. Civil considerations generally focus on the immediate impact of civilians on operations in progress; however, they also include larger, long-term diplomatic, informational, and economic issues at higher levels. At the tactical level, they directly relate to key civilian areas, structures, capabilities, organizations, people, and events within the AO. Discounting these can tax the resources of follow-on elements. The world's increasing urbanization means that the attitudes and activities of the civilian population in the AO often influence the outcome of military operations. Civil considerations of the environment can either help or hinder friendly or enemy forces—the difference lies in which commander has taken time to learn the situation and its possible effects on the operation. These considerations can influence the choice of a COA and the execution of operations.

8-36. This category of information is where PSYOP and CA personnel can be of tremendous value-added to a supported commander. PSYOP personnel spend proportionately more time studying these issues than any supported unit G-2 or S-2. PSYOP Soldiers can pass certain TAA data that may be beneficial to the supported staff.

GATHERING PSYOP-RELEVANT INFORMATION

8-37. Perhaps the most important mission for tactical PSYOP Soldiers is to gather PSYOP-relevant information. Tactical PSYOP Soldiers are often in direct contact with the TA, giving the PSYOP Soldier the opportunity to obtain specific and accurate information. This contact is a critical link to the PSYOP development process, and when done correctly helps to ensure the success of many PSYOP programs. Tactical PSYOP elements continuously assess the PSYOP situation in the AO to determine the effects of the programs on friendly, enemy, and neutral TAs. Gathering PSYOP-relevant information includes, but is not limited to—

- Pretesting and posttesting PSYOP products, LOPs, and symbols.
- Conducting PSYOP area assessments.
- Making casual contact and conversation with local populations.
- Observing the conditions of local populations, focusing the approved SPOs, and identifying PTAs, particularly secondary groups within a local area.
- Gathering information about and from local TV, newspapers, radio, and other media.
- Identifying and communicating with key communicators.
- Conducting interviews with EPWs, civilian internees (CIs), and DCs.

8-38. PSYOP Soldiers must always be aware of the CCIR and PSYOP PIR so they can pass this information on when observed. PSYOP-relevant information must be passed from TPTs to higher echelons as quickly as possible for adjustments to be made to the appropriate series or supporting program. Conditions affecting a TA can change, which makes gathering PSYOP-relevant information highly time sensitive.

EVALUATION METHODS

8-39. Three types of evaluation data are used to determine the effectiveness of the PSYOP effort—impact indicators, spontaneous events, and testing results. The following paragraphs explain these three types.

IMPACT INDICATORS

8-40. Impact indicators are answers to MOEs, which are fundamental to evaluating the success of the PSYOP effort. They are used to determine the degree to which the TA has been influenced by the PSYOP series. Since tactical PSYOP Soldiers are most often in direct contact with the TA, they must completely understand impact indicators.

8-41. Impact indicators are a scale for evaluating PSYOP. They are the most reliable determinants for assessing achievement of the SPO. To determine behavior change, a baseline or starting point must be established. For example, if the SPO is "TA increases insurgent activities reported" and the MOE is "How many insurgent activities were reported over the week?" the initial impact indicators will establish a baseline for subsequent impact indicators to be measured against. This baseline is established by answering the MOEs, which are created for each SPO-TA pair during planning.

SPONTANEOUS EVENTS

8-42. Spontaneous events involve the assessment of events in the target area that can be related to the PSYOP effort. Any independent external factors that may have influenced events in the target area must be identified and evaluated before any firm conclusions can be drawn. Spontaneous events may be identified by the following types of evidence:

- Physical actions barring reception of the PSYOP product by the TA.
- Psychological conditioning of the TA.
- Events occurring in the target area that can be related to the PSYOP effort.

8-43. Hostile forces may also precipitate spontaneous events. Such events can assist in evaluating PSYOP objectives. These events may expose a vulnerability to dissemination that can later be exploited. Once dissemination has begun, hostile forces may try to prevent PSYOP material from reaching the TA. Some typical techniques used to stop reception include—

- Barring entry of printed material.
- Organizing takeovers or attacks on TV and radio stations.
- Forbidding newspapers to be printed.
- Banning social gatherings.
- Jamming radio broadcasts.

8-44. A hostile government or other power group can initiate actions that cause the TA to avoid PSYOP products. These actions are carried out after the initial messages are transmitted. They include attempts to convince the TA that the source of the material cannot be believed or that the message is untrue. The hostile government may penalize TA personnel who possess PSYOP materials, listen to PSYOP radio transmissions, or watch PSYOP TV broadcasts. Sources of indirect indicators showing governmental or power group attempts to limit access or showing influence of PSYOP may include—

- Radio communications.
- Newspapers and other publications.
- Captured documents.
- Opponent propaganda.

- In-depth interviews.
- Other intelligence reports.

TESTING RESULTS

8-45. After a TPT conducts testing, the results must be sent up the chain of command immediately. Testing is often a very time-sensitive mission for TPTs. Pretest results that are negative are used to change products or symbols, so that ineffective products are not disseminated. Posttest results are used to assess a series' effectiveness. When TPTs are asked to conduct surveys that are not product-specific, the results are often used to support TAA.

8-46. Test results must be sent through the same channels that they were received through. The test results may also help the supported unit's staff answer an IR from some other element and therefore should be made available to the supported unit's S-2. Test results can then be incorporated into the intelligence process and shared with other capabilities.

PSYOP SITUATION REPORTS

8-47. SITREPs are submitted from lower PSYOP units to higher HQ. Often, a TPT must also submit a SITREP to the supported unit in a different format (Appendix G), based upon that unit's SOP. The two SITREPs can differ widely, but they are essential to their respective recipients.

SUMMARY

8-48. The intelligence process is critical to conducting an effective PSYOP effort. Important pieces of information can be garnered from the Army's intelligence systems, especially once the different categories of information are understood. PSYOP elements also have valuable information that when shared with supported units enhance the ability of those units to conduct effective operations. The interdependence of intelligence to both PSYOP and supported units cannot be overstated.

Chapter 9
Support and Sustainment

The supply and maintenance requirements of PSYOP units differ from those of most other units because of the mission and configuration of PSYOP units. Frequently, a tactical PSYOP unit is organized into small detachments or teams. These detachments or teams are often dependent upon the units they are attached to for maintenance and supply support; however, they may also be self-supporting.

MAINTENANCE CATEGORIES AND RESPONSIBILITIES

9-1. Maintenance categories and responsibilities are—
- *Organizational maintenance.* Units perform scheduled and unscheduled preventive maintenance tasks, including tightening, adjusting, cleaning, lubricating, and testing. Units replace minor items—such as knobs, lamps, fuses, and interconnecting cables—and make operational checks to verify equipment readiness.
- *Direct support maintenance.* Designated maintenance activities perform maintenance in DS of using organizations. DS maintenance is limited to the repair of end items, components, and assemblies on a return-to-user basis and is performed at corps level. Broad-level controlled substitution is authorized at the DS level.
- *General support maintenance.* Designated activities perform GS maintenance in support of Army area supply requirements. Personnel perform repairs or overhauls to restore materiel to a ready-for-issue condition, based upon published Army maintenance standards for the particular item of equipment. Theater Support Command (TSC) units perform GS maintenance at theater level. The Television Audio Support Activity (T-ASA) provides disposition instructions for warranty items. Component and part-controlled substitution is authorized at the GS level.
- *Depot maintenance.* An industrial-type facility performs depot maintenance, the highest category of materiel maintenance. Depot maintenance includes necessary disassembling, overhauling, rebuilding, testing, and inspecting of operating components; servicing of items for desired performance; and returning items to the Army supply system when they meet maintenance standards established for the equipment.

Note. Because of anticipated supply and maintenance problems caused by low-density and nonstandard equipment, commanders must keep their supported unit constantly aware of the status of their equipment. Immediate action must be taken to train and cross-train personnel to operate and maintain the equipment.

GARRISON MAINTENANCE REQUIREMENTS

9-2. The units conduct weekly preventive maintenance checks and services (PMCS) on all vehicles, including trailers, unless precluded by events outside their control. PMCS includes driving the vehicles around the motor pool and then checking them for proper operation. If the units cannot perform proper weekly maintenance, they must make sure someone else—such as the battalion maintenance section or the company—checks the equipment. This action is critical for vehicles left sitting for longer than 30 days. Units conduct PMCS IAW appropriate technical manuals and higher HQ maintenance SOPs.

9-3. Major maintenance events—such as semiannual services, lubrication orders, and major repairs—must be planned IAW operational and training requirements. The unit members conduct all services and repairs themselves, with minimal assistance from the battalion maintenance section. Such actions provide unit members experience that may be necessary when operating without mechanic support.

DEPLOYMENT MAINTENANCE REQUIREMENTS

9-4. When a tactical battalion deploys, the S-4, the HSC commander, and the first sergeant, in coordination with the battalion XO, are responsible for forecasting, planning, and executing logistical support. When a company deploys as a whole unit, the supply sergeant acts as the company logistician. He coordinates with the supported unit's G-4 or the S-4 for company supplies and services and serves as the distribution point for supplies. TPD NCOICs submit requests for supply items (Table 9-1) through the company supply sergeant.

Table 9-1. Classes of supply

Class	Supplies
I	Subsistence, gratuitous health and comfort items (includes rations and water).
II	Clothing, individual equipment, tentage, organizational tool sets and kits, hand tools, unclassified maps, administrative and housekeeping supplies and equipment.
III	Petroleum, fuels, lubricants, hydraulic and insulating oils, preservatives, liquids and gases, bulk chemical products, coolants, deicer and antifreeze compounds, components, and additives of petroleum and chemical products, and coal.
IV	Construction materials, including installed equipment, and all fortification and barrier materials.
V	Ammunition of all types, bombs, explosives, mines, fuzes, detonators, pyrotechnics, missiles, rockets, propellants, and associated items.
VI	Personal demand items—such as health and hygiene products, soaps and toothpaste, writing material, snack food, beverages, cigarettes, batteries, and cameras (nonmilitary sales items).
VII	Major end items—such as launchers, tanks, mobile machine shops, and vehicles.
VIII	Medical materiel, including repair parts peculiar to medical equipment.
IX	Repair parts and components, including kits, assemblies, and subassemblies (repairable or nonrepairable) required for maintenance support of all equipment.
X	Material to support nonmilitary programs—such as agriculture and economic development (not included in Classes I through IX).

9-5. When TPDs or TPTs deploy separately or are detached from the company main body to support another unit, the TPD NCOIC or TPT leader coordinates with the supported unit's S-4 for logistics support. PSYOP-specific items, including supplies for attached dissemination POB elements, must be requested through PSYOP coordination or communication channels from the deployed PSYOP element to the next-higher PSYOP element.

9-6. When the company is deployed as a whole, the supply sergeant submits requests to or through the next-higher PSYOP element. When TPDs and TPTs are deployed without the company HQ, they must submit requests directly to the next-higher PSYOP element. In addition to submitting requests through logistics channels, requests for PSYOP-specific items must be submitted as part of the daily SITREP to higher PSYOP HQ. Submitting requests as part of the daily SITREP ensures that the commander of the next-higher PSYOP unit is aware of the shortages and the possible impact on mission readiness.

LOGISTICS PREPARATION

9-7. Resupplying, maintaining, and issuing special supplies or equipment and repositioning logistic assets occur during preparation. Other activities occur during preparation—such as identifying and preparing forward bases, selecting and improving lines of communication, and identifying resources available in the area and making arrangements to acquire them. Commanders direct OPSEC measures to conceal preparations and friendly intentions.

Support and Sustainment

COORDINATION WITH SUPPORTED UNIT'S LOGISTICIANS

9-8. The S-4 at the battalion level and the senior leader at the company level making initial linkup with the supported unit should provide the following information, as a minimum, to the supported unit's logistician:

- Number of POB personnel attached.
- Number and types of vehicles and generators.
- Estimated daily fuel consumption for vehicles and generators.
- Number and types of weapons systems.
- Battery requirements.
- Special logistical requirements.

9-9. During initial linkup, the S-4 or the senior leader should obtain the following information from the supported unit's logistician:

- Unit SOP for requesting supplies.
- Availability of PSYOP-specific supplies in the supported unit's supply chain.
- Unit SOP and requirements for logistics reporting (daily logistics status [LOGSTAT] report).
- Location of fuel point.
- Location of water point.
- Availability of sundry and comfort packages.
- Location of supported unit's aid station.
- Location of ammunition supply points (ASPs) and ammunition basic load or force-protection basic load per weapon system.

MAINTENANCE SUPPORT

9-10. United States Army Special Operations Command (USASOC) and United States Army Civil Affairs and Psychological Operations Command (USACAPOC) monitor ongoing logistics support to PSYOP forces and provide the initial support that may not be available from the ASCC. The following organizations perform maintenance support functions:

- *Special operations support command (SOSCOM).* The SOSCOM plans, coordinates, and, when required, executes CSS for PSYOP forces through its forward-deployed SOTSE and organic special operations support battalion (SOSB). The SOSCOM may also attach logistics LNOs to the POTF when its sustainment operations are expected to require complex multi-Service, interagency, and contractual support. The SOTSE and the SOSB may provide the following support:
    - *SOTSE.* The SOTSE has a coordination cell with the ASCC staff. It provides SO staff expertise and coordinates access to the support infrastructure. The SOTSE ensures PSYOP requirements are included in the support plan. It also provides the capability for deploying PSYOP to gain access to the theater Army support structures upon arrival in-theater.
    - *SOSB.* The SOSB, when required, provides limited DS to PSYOP. It provides support from the early arrival and employment of PSYOP forces until the theater support structure capability can take over. The SOSB provides supply and maintenance support similar to that provided to conventional units. It also provides low-density and PSYOP-peculiar item support. The SOSB is capable of deploying anywhere in the world to provide early support. It provides support only until the theater support structure is established and capable of meeting PSYOP requirements. Once the theater support structure is in place, the SOSB elements prepare to redeploy in preparation for other contingencies.
- *Theater special operations command (SOC).* The theater SOC supports PSYOP forces for any PSYOP-peculiar requirements the ASCC identifies as a shortfall. It validates the SOR of PSYOP forces. It also works closely with the unified command staff, the theater ASCC, and PSYOP logisticians to convey the PSYOP requirements, depending upon the theater's organizational structure. SOC and PSYOP logisticians coordinate with the ASCC to develop plans and subsequent orders to implement directives the ASCC issues to support the PSYOP forces

assigned to the unified command. The SOC, in conjunction with the POTF S-4, advises the ASCC commander on the appropriate logistics command and support relationships for each PSYOP mission. The SOTSE keeps SOSCOM and USASOC informed of the status of ASCC supporting plans.

- *Tactical Psychological Operations battalion.* Tactical POB elements draw support for all standard Army equipment through the supported unit's maintenance channels. Maintenance support for PSYOP-specific equipment is through the supported unit or next-higher PSYOP element. Whenever possible, companies deploy with necessary technicians attached.
- *PSYOP commander or leader.* The commander or leader of the PSYOP element is responsible for evacuating PSYOP equipment to higher-level maintenance, monitoring repairs, and returning repaired equipment to the user. He is also responsible for making initial contact with the supported unit's maintenance officer to coordinate for support.

PREVENTIVE MAINTENANCE CHECKS AND SERVICES

9-11. The commander or leader of the PSYOP element establishes a maintenance schedule for his unit. The schedule should include, at a minimum, daily PMCS of vehicles and radio and weapons systems; every-other-day PMCS for loudspeakers; and weekly maintenance day for PMCS on other equipment, as specified by the commander or leader.

9-12. Soldiers deploy with a complete 10-level technical manual (TM)—or the civilian-produced equivalent—for vehicles, radio systems, loudspeakers, computers, and camera equipment. Following PMCS, the commander or leader completes DA Form 2404 (Equipment Inspection and Maintenance Worksheet) or the automated ULLS version of the form—DA Form 5988-E (Equipment Inspection Maintenance Worksheet [EGA])—and coordinates with the supported unit's maintenance section for parts and repairs.

SPECIAL MAINTENANCE CONSIDERATIONS

9-13. METT-TC determines the nature and extent of external logistics support. Local procurement support depends on the resources in the area. The support provided should be continuous, and plans to provide that support must be kept flexible to meet changing conditions. To achieve flexibility, the tactical PSYOP unit should—

- Have primary, alternate, and contingency plans.
- Identify the location of all possible support installations throughout the AO.
- Find adequate reserves of supplies and of personnel, equipment, communication, and transportation assets from which prompt deliveries can be made.
- Have several principal and alternate points and routes for pickup and delivery of equipment and supplies.

9-14. When contracting logistics support, the PSYOP unit should consider the following questions:

- What funding is required to support initial contracting and other local procurement efforts other than International Merchant Purchase Authorization Card (IMPAC) purchases?
- Has the commander identified a Class "A" agent and a contracting or ordering officer?
- Has the commander named and appointed a field ordering officer?
- Is the support of linguists required? If so, is an SOR approved?

RECOVERY

9-15. Postoperations are the actions taken to restore units to a combat-effective level. PSYOP units in garrison and the field use postoperations maintenance and recovery (POMR) procedures. These procedures consist of actions and deadlines to return the unit to a state of mission readiness by accomplishing tasks in order of priority.

Support and Sustainment

9-16. POMR should be performed upon completion of all missions, including field-training exercises, emergency deployment readiness exercises, Army training and evaluation programs, or other operational missions. Adherence to POMR procedures ensures equipment reliability and readiness.

EXECUTION OF POSTOPERATIONS MAINTENANCE AND RECOVERY

9-17. PSYOP units follow a 5-day recovery plan (Figure 9-1, page 9-6) when executing POMR. Before the PSYOP unit departs from the field or deployment site, the TPT leader must—

- Account for all Soldiers.
- Account for all equipment and supplies, including—
    - Component items.
    - Sensitive items (by serial number).
- Account for all classified material.
- Turn in all Class V, brass, and residue.

9-18. When returning from the field or the deployment site, the PSYOP unit must—

- Clean all weapons and night vision goggles (NVGs). Wipe down and secure M240 and M249 bipods and tripods and M240 and M249 mounts. Turn in all weapons and night-vision equipment to the arms room. Identify inoperative weapons to the company supply sergeant. Conduct a 100-percent inventory of the arms room.
- Conduct postoperation PMCS of all vehicles, trailers, and generators. Remove all equipment and trash from vehicles and trailers. Refuel vehicles to three-quarters of a tank.
- Zero all communications security (COMSEC) fills in tactical radios and ANCYZ-10s. Make sure all radios and components are locked down in vehicles or secured in containers express (CONEXs) or cages. Turn in and properly secure ANCYZ-10s.
- Account for and turn in or secure all sensitive items (computers, cameras).
- Account for and secure in a General Services Administration (GSA)-approved safe all classified material.
- Turn in closing report to the company commander of all above tasks completed.
- Turn in closure report to the battalion S-3.

PERSONNEL RECOVERY TASKS

9-19. The commander, first sergeant, and detachment NCOICs must make sure postdeployment administrative tasks for personnel recovery are completed, or are scheduled for completion, within the required working days of return to home station. These tasks include—

- Submitting an after-action report/review (AAR), a trip report, and travel vouchers.
- Updating immunizations and shot records.
- Scheduling dental appointments.
- Undergoing basic airborne refresher training, if required.
- Conducting urinalysis.
- Conducting weapons qualification.
- Conducting the Army Physical Fitness Test (APFT).
- Making sure special entitlement payments are stopped.
- Taking Defense Language Proficiency Test (DLPT).
- Updating family care plan.
- Turning in field meal cards.
- Writing and submitting award recommendations.
- Turning in and updating passports.
- Family reintegration training.

Chapter 9

FIVE-DAY RECOVERY PLAN
Day 1
• *Wheeled vehicles.* Wash, conduct full PMCS of, and lubricate all vehicles and trailers. Check company parts bin in the POB maintenance office and install any parts on hand (TM-10 maintenance only). Inventory, clean, and service vehicle basic issue items (BIIs). Turn in DA Form 2404/5988-E. Turn in shortage annexes for BIIs to the detachment NCOIC.
• *Communications equipment.* Clean, PMCS, and inventory communication equipment (tactical radios, OE254 antennas, field telephones, communication wire). Turn in damaged or inoperative communication equipment to electronic maintenance shop (EMS). Turn in shortage annexes for component parts to the detachment NCOIC.
• *Weapons.* Clean and PMCS all individual and crew-served weapons, vehicle mounts, and tripods.
• *NVGs.* Clean, PMCS, and inventory PVS-7s and PVS-4s. Identify inoperative weapons to company supply sergeant.
• *Protective masks.* Clean, PMCS, and inventory component items of protective masks. Prepare DA Form 2404s on and identify inoperative promasks to company NBC NCO.
• *Closing report.* Turn in closing report (tasks completed) to the company commander and battalion S-3.
Day 2
• *Loudspeakers.* Clean, PMCS, and inventory loudspeakers. Turn in inoperative communication equipment to EMS. Turn in shortage annexes for component parts to detachment NCOIC.
• *Audiovisual and computer equipment.* Clean, PMCS, and inventory cameras, computers, minidisk players. Turn in inoperative equipment to EMS. Turn in shortage annexes for component parts to detachment NCOIC.
• *Closing report.* Turn in closing report (tasks completed) to the company commander and S-3.
Day 3
• *NBC equipment.* Clean, PMCS, and inventory all NBC equipment (M22 chemical alarms, chemical agent monitors [CAMs], AN/VDR-2s). Prepare DA Form 2404s on and identify inoperative NBC equipment to company NBC NCO.
• *Camouflage nets.* Set up, clean, dry, and inventory camouflage net systems. Submit shortage annex to detachment NCOIC.
• *Tents.* Set up, clean, dry, and inventory tents. Submit shortage annex to detachment NCOIC.
• *Closing report.* Turn in closing report (tasks completed) to commander and S-3.
Day 4
• *TA-50.* Clean and inventory individual TA-50. Return to company supply, as necessary, damaged company-issued items.
• *Hand receipts and shortage annexes.* Update detachment hand receipts and shortage annexes. Detachment commander or NCOIC reports all shortages and field losses to supply sergeant. Supply sergeant prepares statements of charges or cash collection vouchers as necessary.
• *Additional duty areas.* Review additional duty areas. Update books and logs. Identify to the company commander any required training not accomplished during deployment or due during the next 3 months.
• *Closing report.* Turn in closing report (tasks completed) to commander and S-3.
Day 5
• *Items inspection.* Company commander or detachment commanders conduct inspection of selected items.
• *TA-50 inspection.* The first sergeant conducts layout and inspection of individual TA-50.

Figure 9-1. POMR plan

SUMMARY

9-20. All units require services to sustain equipment and personnel needs. As with other Army supplies, exact determinations of requirements for supplies and equipment and careful requisitioning are essential. This chapter discussed equipment and systems, equipment planning, supplies and repair parts, and maintenance.

Appendix A
Coordination and Liaison

This appendix discusses how PSYOP units conduct coordination. Coordination must occur between units to achieve synchronization. One of the most effective means of achieving coordination is liaison. This appendix also describes the types of coordination and the importance of coordination in the conduct of PSYOP. The appendix ends with a description of liaison—or the "how" of conducting coordination.

COORDINATION

A-1. Coordination is the action necessary to ensure adequately integrated relationships between separate organizations located in the same area. It may include such matters as fire support, emergency defense measures, area intelligence, and other situations in which coordination is considered necessary (Army-Marine Corps). Coordination takes place continuously throughout operations. Commands do not operate in isolation—they synchronize their actions with those of others. Coordination is essential to this synchronization. Coordination has four objectives:

- Ensure a thorough understanding of the commander's intent, as well as subordinates' and supporting forces' roles.
- Ensure all affected and interested personnel have been consulted or informed as time permits, so they may respond as desired or adjust their plans and actions.
- Avoid conflict and duplication of effort among units, reducing fratricide and expending resources.
- Ensure commanders and staffs consider as many relevant factors as time permits and effectively employ all available assets.

A-2. Locations, times, and functions may all require coordination. Coordinating begins during planning; however, a plan alone does not guarantee coordination. Exchanging information is critical to successful coordination.

A-3. During preparation, commands coordinate with higher, lower, adjacent, supporting, and supported units. Coordination includes—

- Sending and receiving liaison teams as necessary.
- Establishing communications links that assure continuous contact during execution.
- Exchanging SOPs as needed.
- Synchronizing security and reconnaissance plans to prevent breaks in coverage.

A-4. Coordination requirements fall into two categories:

- *Internal.* Internal coordination occurs within HQ. It starts activities within and among staff sections that the plan requires to succeed. It ensures staff members remain fully informed of relevant information affecting their functional responsibilities. During preparation, internal coordination ensures that staffs refine plans based on updated relevant information. It helps resolve problems of external coordination. Internal coordination also supports subordinate units' preparations by resolving problems, conflicts, and resource allocations.
- *External.* External coordination includes coordinating with subordinate units, adjacent units, higher HQ, and supported and supporting units for resources or forces that may not be immediately under the command's control during planning. Places where two HQ must

Appendix A

coordinate their actions are potential weak points. Enemies may exploit them, or commanders may commit too many or too few resources there. These points include unit boundaries, where unit interdependence may delay execution.

PSYOP Coordination

A-5. The POTF normally has coordinating authority over tactical PSYOP units operating in its AOR. This authority allows the POTF to establish PSYOP policy at the combatant commander or JFC level. The POTF communicates that policy to lower level PSYOP units, directs and coordinates theater-level PSYOP programs, and delineates approval authority for disseminating PSYOP products.

A-6. PSYOP must be coordinated and deconflicted at all levels. Regardless of the relationship between the tactical PSYOP element and the supported unit, a PSYOP communications and coordination chain exists from the POTF down to the smallest tactical PSYOP element operating in the AO (normally a TPT). This arrangement is not a chain of command—it is a channel through which PSYOP-relevant information and plans are passed from upper echelons to lower echelons to ensure coordination of all PSYOP actions (unity of effort) in the AO.

A-7. The JPOTF develops the PSYOP support plan to the GCC's or JFC's campaign plan. The PSYOP support plan includes PSYOP objectives, supporting PSYOP objectives, MOE, PTAs, and themes to stress and to avoid. The PSYOP support plan provides tactical POB elements with the guidance needed to conduct tactical PSYOP. It also provides limitations on what the element can do for the supported unit.

Coordination With a Supported Unit

A-8. When a tactical PSYOP unit is notified it will be supporting a maneuver commander, one of the first steps in its deployment is the initiation of contact with the supported unit. The following are some necessary steps in establishing initial coordination:

- *Step 1.* The battalion S-3 or his representative or the leader of the PSYOP element (company or detachment commander, team leader) must initiate coordination with the supported unit as soon as possible.
- *Step 2.* Before deployment, initial contact can be made in person, by telephone or over the Internet. If contact with the supported unit is not possible before deployment, face-to-face linkup must occur as soon as possible at the deployed location.
- *Step 3.* Postdeployment coordination with the supported unit before actual attachment requires authorization (direct liaison authorized [DIRLAUTH]) from the higher PSYOP element.

A-9. Staff officer, company or detachment commander, or TPT leader tasks are as follows:

- Contact the supported commander or designated representative (chief of staff or XO and the J-3/G-3/S-3) and—
  - Brief the supported commander on PSYOP capabilities (capabilities brief, Appendix F), including the battalion, company, TPD, or TPT organization, equipment, personnel, and employment options; available dissemination means, assets, or products; constraints and restrictions (approval process or themes and audiences to be used and avoided); and PSYOP assets on hand or available through coordination with higher PSYOP units.
  - Stress that attached PSYOP forces are a form of nonlethal fire support working through the J-3/G-3/S-3. Attached tactical PSYOP forces work with the organic PSYOP staff planner(s) in the G-7/S-7 at corps/unit of employment (corps) (UEy), division/unit of engagement (division) (UEx), and brigade combat team (BCT) to coordinate and synchronize PSYOP.
  - Ensure PSYOP are included in the mission planning.
  - Ensure PSYOP are included in the air-targeting meeting.
  - Ask for a briefing on the staff's battle rhythm. Coordinate for PSYOP to take part in the decision-making process, staff planning for missions, and daily briefings or meetings.
  - Ask for a copy of the supported unit's ROE or ROI.
  - Determine unit SOP or requirement for daily SITREPs.

Coordination and Liaison

- Contact the supported unit J-2/G-2/S-2 and—
  - Provide a memorandum from the Psychological Operations Group (POG) or POB S-2 confirming the security clearances of all PSYOP Soldiers involved in the mission.
  - Provide a copy of current PSYOP PIR.
  - Request access to maneuver unit SITREPS and spot reports (SPOTREPs), EPW interrogations, and interrogation reports.
- Contact the supported unit IO officer and—
  - Ensure PSYOP are coordinated in mission planning with other nonlethal fires.
  - Provide an LNO to the IO section.
- Contact the supported unit Deputy/Assistant Chief of Staff for Civil-Military Operations (G-9) or battalion or brigade civil-military operations staff officer (S-9) and—
  - Ascertain if LN assets are available for product production and dissemination.
  - Identify civilian issues or problems in the AOR that were not identified during TAA or initial assessments.
- Contact the supported unit J-6 or Deputy/Assistant Chief of Staff, Command, Control, Communications, and Computer Operations (C4 Ops) (G-6) or signal officer and—
  - Determine the communications systems the supported unit has available, especially Internet, SIPRNET, and NIPRNET connectivity.
  - Determine the radio frequencies the supported unit operates on and coordinate on or for a PSYOP internal radio frequency.
  - Coordinate for AN/CYZ-10 secure fills.

A-10. S-1, first sergeant, detachment NCOIC, or TPT assistant team leader tasks are as follows:
- Contact the J-1, Deputy/Assistant Chief of Staff for Personnel (G-1), or S-1 and—
  - Provide a copy of attachment orders and information on the Soldiers to be attached to the supported unit; provide two copies (one paper and one electronic); include (for each attached Soldier) the Soldier's full name, rank, duty position, social security number, battle roster number, security clearance, blood type, next of kin and next of kin contact information; determine (from the J-1/G-1/S-1) which of the supported unit's subordinate units the company element will be attached to for administrative and logistics support (normally the supported unit's HQ company); provide unit SOP for personnel reporting (for example, daily personnel status [PERSTAT] report).
  - Confirm with the J-1/G-1/S-1 or HSC executive officer the supported unit's plan for or availability of mail services and Internet accesses, chaplain or religious services, finance services, and personnel or administrative services.
- Contact the J-4/G-4/S-4 and—
  - Provide information on the number of battalion, POTF, or company personnel being attached; the number and types of vehicles and generators; the estimated daily fuel consumption for vehicles and generators; the number and types of weapons systems; and the battery requirements. Submit an SOR, as necessary.
  - During initial linkup, learn from the J-4/G-4/S-4 or HSC executive officer the unit SOP for requesting supplies; the availability, if any, of PSYOP-specific supplies in the supported unit's supply chain; the unit SOP for logistics reporting (for example, daily LOGSTAT reports); the location of fuel points; the location of water points and bath and laundry facilities; the availability of sundry and comfort packages; the location of supported unit's aid station; and the location of ASP and ammunition basic load or force protection basic load per weapon.

A-11. Establishing and maintaining liaison are vital to external coordination. Liaison provides a means of direct communications between the sending and receiving HQ. It may begin with planning and continue through preparing and executing, or it may start as late as execution. Available resources and the need for

Appendix A

direct contact between sending and receiving HQ determine when to establish liaison. The earlier liaison is established, the more effective the coordination.

LIAISON OFFICER

A-12. The LNO plays a key role in conducting PSYOP. An LNO facilitates understanding and synchronization between different levels of command and, specifically for PSYOP, between the POTF, other functional components, and any deployed tactical PSYOP elements. When using LNOs or teams, commanders must use organic, uncommitted personnel. The senior PSYOP commander in the AO exchanges PSYOP liaison personnel with the supported units, U.S. nonmilitary agencies (as appropriate), and allied military organizations. The exchange of liaison personnel provides a network of proper mutual support and synchronization. PSYOP personnel at all levels must be ready to assume liaison duties. The following paragraphs address liaison principles and the responsibilities of liaison officers and parties. Liaison checklists and a sample outline for a liaison officer handbook are included.

A-13. Liaison is the contact or intercommunication maintained between elements of military forces or other agencies to ensure mutual understanding and unity of purpose and action (JP 3-08, Interagency Coordination During Joint Operations). It is the most commonly employed technique for establishing and maintaining close, continuous physical communication between commands. Commanders use liaison during operations and normal daily activities to help facilitate communication between organizations, to preserve freedom of action, and to maintain flexibility. Liaison provides senior commanders with relevant information and answers to operational questions. It ensures they remain aware of the tactical situation. They include establishing and maintaining physical contact and communication between elements of military forces and, as directed, nonmilitary agencies. Liaison activities ensure—

- Cooperation and understanding between commanders and staffs of different HQ.
- Coordination on tactical matters to achieve unity of effort.
- Understanding of implied or inferred coordination measures to achieve synchronized results.

A-14. Liaison is a tool that enhances the commander's confidence. It helps commanders overcome friction and synchronize operations. Effective liaison assures commanders that subordinates understand implicit coordination.

LIAISON RESPONSIBILITIES

A-15. Both the sending and receiving units have liaison responsibilities before, during, and after operations. The sending unit's most important tasks include selecting and training the Soldiers best qualified for liaison duties. Liaison personnel should have the characteristics and qualifications discussed in the following paragraphs. Figure A-1, pages A-4 through A-6, shows a sample outline for an LNO handbook that addresses knowledge and skills LNOs require.

- Table of contents, with the sending unit's proponency statement.
- Purpose statement.
- Introduction statement.
- Definitions.
- Scope statement.
- Responsibilities and guidelines for conduct.
- Actions to take before departing from the sending unit.
- Actions to take upon arriving at the receiving unit.
- Actions to take during liaison operations at the receiving unit.
- Actions to take before departing from the receiving unit.
- Actions to take upon return to the sending unit.

Figure A-1. Sample outline of a liaison officer handbook

Coordination and Liaison

- LNOs should be able to answer the following types of questions:
  - Does the sending unit have a copy of the receiving unit's latest OPLAN, OPORD, and FRAGO?
  - Does the receiving unit's plan support the plan of the higher HQ, including logistics and the tactical concept? Are MSRs known?
  - What are the receiving unit's CCIR? At what time, phase, or event are they expected to change? Are there any items the CCIR do not contain that the sending unit can help with?
  - Which sending commander's decisions are critical to executing the receiving unit operation?
  - What are the "no-later-than" times for those decisions?
  - What assets does the unit need to acquire to accomplish its mission? How would they be used? How do they support attaining the more senior commander's intent? Where can the unit obtain them—from higher HQ? other Services? multinational or coalition partners?
  - How are aviation assets (rotary- and fixed-wing) being used?
  - How can the LNO communicate with the sending unit? Are telephones, radios, facsimile machines, computers, and other information systems (INFOSYS) available? Where are they located? Which ones are secure?
  - What terrain has been designated as key? Decisive?
  - What weather conditions would have a major impact on the operation?
  - What effect would a chemical environment have on the operation?
  - What effect would large numbers of refugees or EPWs have on the receiving unit's operations?
  - What is the worst thing that could happen during execution of the current operation?
  - How would the LNO handle a passage of lines by other units through the LNO's own force?
  - What conditions would cause the LNO's unit to request OPCON of a multinational force?
  - If the LNO's unit is placed under OPCON of a larger multinational force, or given OPCON of a smaller such force, what special problems would it present?
  - If going to a multinational force HQ, how do the tactical principles and command concepts of that force differ from those of U.S. forces?
  - What LN support is available to the sending unit? IRs?
- Required reports (from higher and sending units' SOPs).
- Packing list:
  - Credentials (including permissive jump orders, if qualified).
  - Forms: DA Form 1594 (Daily Staff Journal or Duty Officer's Log) and other blank forms as required.
  - References.
  - Excerpts of higher and sending HQs' orders and plans.
  - Sending unit SOP.
  - Sending unit's command diagrams and recapitulation of major systems. The unit MTOE, unit status report (if its classification allows), and mission briefings can be used. The G-3 (S-3) or the force modernization officer is an excellent source of these.
  - Computers and other INFOSYS required for information and data exchange.
  - Signal operating instructions extract.
  - Security code encryption device.
  - Communications equipment, including remote frequency modulation radio equipment.
  - Sending unit telephone book.
  - List of commanders and staff officers.

Figure A-1. Sample outline of a liaison officer handbook (continued)

Appendix A

- Telephone calling (credit) card.
- Movement table.
- Administrative equipment—for example, pens, paper, scissors, tape, and hole punch.
- Map and chart equipment—for example, pens, pins, protractor, straight edge, scale, distance counter, acetate, and unit markers.
- Tent (camouflaged net, cots, stove, and other CTA-50 equipment as appropriate).
- Foreign phrase book and dictionary.
- Local currency as required.

Figure A-1. Sample outline of a liaison officer handbook (continued)

A-16. The sending unit provides a description of the liaison party (number and type of vehicles and personnel, call signs, and radio frequencies) to the receiving unit. The LNO or team must also have—
- Identification and appropriate credentials for the receiving unit.
- Appropriate security clearance, courier orders, transportation, and communications equipment.
- The SOP outlining the missions, functions, procedures, and duties of the sending unit's liaison section.
- Individual weapons and ammunition.
- Rations for the movement to the receiving unit.

A-17. Figure A-2 lists tasks for liaison personnel to accomplish before departing the sending unit.

- Understand what the sending commander wants the receiving commander to know.
- Receive a briefing from operations, intelligence, and other staff elements on current and future operations.
- Receive and understand the tasks from the sending unit staff.
- Obtain the correct maps, traces, and overlays.
- Arrange for transport, communications and cryptographic equipment, codes, signal instructions, and the challenge and password—including their protection and security. Arrange for replacement of these items, as necessary.
- Complete route-reconnaissance and time-management plans so the LNO party arrives at the designated location on time.
- Make sure liaison personnel and interpreters have security clearances and access appropriate for the mission.
- Verify that the receiving unit received the liaison team's security clearances and will grant access to the level of information the mission requires. Verify courier orders.
- Know how to destroy classified information in case of an emergency during transit or at the receiving unit.
- Inform the sending unit of the LNO's departure time, route, arrival time, and, when known, the estimated time and route of return.
- Pick up all correspondence designated for the receiving unit.
- Conduct a radio check.
- Know the impending moves of the sending unit and the receiving unit.
- Bring INFOSYS needed to support LNO operations.
- Pack adequate supplies of Classes I and III for use in transit.
- Arrange for the liaison party's departure.

Figure A-2. Liaison checklist, before departing the sending unit

Coordination and Liaison

RECEIVING UNIT

A-18. The receiving unit—
- Provides the sending unit with the LNO's reporting time and place, point of contact (POC), recognition signal, and password.
- Provides details of any tactical movement and logistics information relevant to the LNO's mission, especially while the LNO is in transit.
- Makes sure the LNO has access to the commander, chief of staff (XO), and other officers for important matters.
- Gives the LNO an initial briefing and allows the LNO access necessary to remain informed of current operations.
- Protects the LNO while at the receiving unit.
- Publishes an SOP outlining the missions, functions, procedures, and duties of the LNO or team at the receiving unit.
- Provides access to communications equipment (and operating instructions, as needed) when the LNO needs to communicate with the receiving unit's equipment.
- Provides administrative and logistics support.

DURING THE TOUR

A-19. Figure A-3, pages A-7 and A-8, summarizes liaison duties during the tour. LNOs also inform the receiving unit's commander or staff of the sending unit's needs or requirements. The LNO's ability to clarify questions about the sending unit rapidly can keep the receiving unit from wasting planning time.

DURING THE LIAISON TOUR, LNOS—

- Arrive at the designated location on time.
- Promote cooperation between the sending and receiving unit.
- Accomplish their mission without becoming actively involved in the receiving unit's staff procedures or actions; however, they may assist higher staffs in war gaming.
- Follow the receiving unit's communication procedures.
- Actively obtain information without interfering with the receiving unit's operations.
- Facilitate understanding of the sending unit's commander's intent.
- Help the sending unit's commander assess current and future operations.
- Remain informed of the sending unit's current situation and provide that information to the receiving unit's commander and staff.
- Expeditiously inform the sending unit of the receiving unit's upcoming missions, tasks, and orders.
- Make sure the sending unit has a copy of the receiving unit's SOP.
- Inform the receiving unit's commander or chief of staff (XO) of the content of reports transmitted to the sending unit.
- Keep a record of their reports, listing everyone met (including each person's name, rank, duty position, and telephone number), as well as primary operators and their telephone numbers.
- Attempt to resolve issues within the receiving unit before involving the sending unit.
- Notify the sending unit promptly if unable to accomplish the liaison mission.
- Report their departure to the receiving unit's commander at the end of their mission.
- Arrive at least 2 hours before any scheduled briefings.
- Check in with security and complete any required documentation.

Figure A-3. Liaison duties during the liaison tour

Appendix A

- Present their credentials to the chief of staff (XO).
- Arrange for an "office call" with the commander.
- Meet the coordinating and special staff officers.
- Notify the sending unit of arrival.
- Visit staff elements, brief them on the sending unit's situation, and collect information from them.
- Deliver all correspondence designated for the receiving unit.
- Annotate on all overlays the security classification, title, map scale, grid intersection points, effective date-time group (DTG), DTG received, and from whom received.
- Pick up all correspondence for the sending unit when departing the receiving unit.
- Inform receiving unit of the LNOs' departure time, return route, and expected arrival time at the sending unit.

Figure A-3. Liaison duties during the liaison tour (continued)

AFTER THE TOUR

A-20. After returning to the sending unit, LNOs promptly transmit the receiving unit's requests to the sending unit's commander or staff, as appropriate. They also brief the chief of staff (XO) on mission-related liaison activities and prepare written reports, as appropriate.

A-21. Accuracy is paramount. Effective LNOs provide clear, concise, complete information. If the accuracy of information is not certain, LNOs quote the source and include the source in the report. LNOs limit their remarks to mission-related observations. They—

- Deliver all correspondence.
- Brief the chief of staff (XO) and the appropriate staff elements.
- Prepare the necessary reports.
- Clearly state what they learned from the mission.

Appendix B
Assessments

PSYOP Soldiers conduct assessments to gather and organize PSYOP-relevant information. Assessments provide detailed information that is critical to conducting the PSYOP process. There are two primary types of assessments conducted by tactical PSYOP—local and media.

LOCAL ASSESSMENTS

B-1. Conducting local assessments can provide detailed information that is critical in the execution of the PSYOP process. Depending on time and security constraints, local assessments can be either deliberate or rapid. Deliberate assessments (Figure B-1, pages B-1 through B-7) are, by nature, in-depth and provide the maximum amount of information. When a deliberate assessment cannot be conducted, an abbreviated or rapid assessment (Figure B-2, pages B-8 and B-9) is conducted to provide the priority information critical to the PSYOP process.

B-2. A TPT assigned the task of conducting a local assessment, whether deliberate or rapid, must ensure it is as complete as possible. As these assessments are submitted to the next-higher level of command, the information they provide can be incorporated into the PSYOP process and shared with other staff sections, as well as the intelligence community. The deliberate local assessment format and the rapid local assessment format can be used for either an area or a town.

B-3. When conducting a local assessment, the TPT should adhere to security and interview techniques. The TPT leader should attempt to coordinate with a key communicator or a senior or prominent member of the area or town to assist in gathering his information. Additionally, the assessment should include the responses from several individuals to achieve a broader understanding of the overall environment.

PSYOP GEOGRAPHIC ASSESSMENT (DELIBERATE)

Location:
Province:_____
District:_____
Alternate district:_____
Settlement name (English):_____
Settlement name (LN language):_____
AIMS geocode:_____
Alternate name 1:_____
Alternate name 2:_____
Alternate name 3:_____
Latitude:_____
Longitude:_____
DATUM/coordinate system (for example, WGS84/decimal degrees)_____
(Or MGRS with grid zone designator)_____
Coordinate location (where was the GPS waypoint taken; for example, from the center of the settlement)_____
Physical size (approximate radius in meters from town center)_____
Settlement is province center: Y   N
Settlement is district center: Y   N

Figure B-1. PSYOP geographic assessment (deliberate)

Appendix B

Type of settlement (circle all that apply):
 Urban Suburban Rural Compact Dispersed Seasonal Nomadic Unknown
 Other:_____
Subdivided settlement: Y   N
Sub-settlement(s):
Name 1:_____
Name 2:_____
Name 3:_____
Name 4:_____

Population:
Total population:_____
% pro-U.S._____% neutral_____% pro-enemy_____
Total number of families: _____ Average family size:_____ % male:_____ % female:_____
% children:_____
Number of female-headed households:_____
Ethnicity by %:_____
Religious makeup by %:_____
Literacy %:_____
Number by ethnicity of permanent resident families:_____
Number by ethnicity of refugee returnee families:_____
Number by ethnicity of internally displaced person families:_____
From where are they displaced (approximate proportion by location)?_____
Reasons for displacement (approximate proportion by reason):_____
Conditions for resettlement (approximate proportion by condition): _____
Population structure:

AGE	MALE	FEMALE
0-4		
5-9		
10-14		
15-19		
20-24		
25-29		
30-34		
35-39		
40-44		
45-49		
50-54		
55-59		
>59		

Local government and institutions:
Type of government (tribal, elected, or so on):_____
How chosen?_____
Key leaders (names and titles):_____

Police or security force?   Y   N
Key leaders:_____
Number of police:_____ Armed? Y N   Reliable? Y N
If no police, how is security and order kept?_____
Legal system:_____
Reliable? Y   N

Figure B-1. PSYOP geographic assessment (deliberate) (continued)

Security:
Settlement access restricted because of—

Landmines?	Y	N
Roadblocks?	Y	N
Other:_____		
I) Weapons in evidence?	Y	N
II) Evidence of recent fighting?	Y	N
III) Evidence of criminal activity?	Y	N
IV) Local rivalry leading to hostility?	Y	N
V) Was the team made to feel welcome?	Y	N
VI) Any open hostility?	Y	N
VII) Pro- or anti-central government?	Y	N

Explanation or remarks reference I-VII above:
_____
_____
_____
_____

Media services:
Radio station(s)?　Y　N　　Orientation:　Pro-U.S.　Anti-U.S.　Neutral
Location(s):_____
Owner(s):_____
Frequency(ies):_____
Type of programs:_____
Times of programs:_____
Newspapers(s)?　Y　N　　Orientation:　Pro-U.S.　Anti-U.S.　Neutral
Location:_____
Owner:_____
Frequency of editions:_____
Television?　　Y　N　　Orientation:　Pro-U.S.　Anti-U.S.　Neutral
% of populace with access to television?_____ % of household:_____
Channel(s):_____
Program(s):_____
Language(s):_____

Information environment:
Propaganda encountered?_____
What influence does the settlement have upon or from other settlements? (Include names.)
_____
Means of communication (internal and external):_____
_____
How is information posted or exchanged?_____
Who are the key communicators?_____
_____
What are the most prestigious symbols of wealth?_____
What PSYOP products has the populace encountered? Any impact indicators?_____
_____
_____
What effect have these had? (Observable behavior, statements made, and so on.):_____
_____
_____
Unique conditions affecting the populace?_____
_____

Figure B-1. PSYOP geographic assessment (deliberate) (continued)

Appendix B

Vulnerabilities per these conditions?_____
_____
Appeals to avoid or stress:_____
Symbols to avoid or stress:_____
Accessibility to the populace:_____
Prior contact with U.S. Soldiers?   Y   N
General audience summary:_____
_____
_____

Economy:
LN currency:_____
Attitude toward LN currency: Positive   Negative   Indifferent
Preferred currency or alternate currencies:_____

Primary economic base: Food crops   Commercial crops   Livestock   Industry
Services   Government   Other (describe):_____
Markets and shops:
Available?   Y   N
Type: Permanent   Weekly   Other
Number of stalls and shops:_____
What other communities use this market?_____
If no market, where do they go for market access?_____
For specific goods?_____
Distributions:
What goods and supplies?_____

Local warehouse or storage facilities available?   Y   N
Agriculture:
Livestock: Number of households having livestock_____
Total number of sheep in the settlement:_____
Total number of goats in the settlement:_____
Total number of cattle in the settlement:_____
Total number of poultry in the settlement:_____
Principal crop:_____
Secondary crop:_____
Self-sufficient in food?   Y   N
Mechanization used in farming? Y   N
Customers and markets (location name) _____

Evidence of illegal crop cultivation? Y   N
Attitude toward illegal crop cultivation:_____
Natural resources:
Mineral deposits: Y   N
Describe:_____
Oil and gas?   Y   N
Describe:_____
Gem stones?   Y   N
Describe:_____
Local industry?   Y   N
Describe:_____
Major employer:_____

Figure B-1. PSYOP geographic assessment (deliberate) (continued)

Infrastructure:
Housing (for description of Categories 1-4, see below):
Total number of houses:
Category 1:_____Category 2:_____
Category 3:_____Category 4:_____
Electricity available?   Y   N
Number of hours per day:_____
Source of supply:_____
Sewage disposal system:_____
Trash removal system:_____
Safe water sources (for example, closed well with hand pump, piped system from protected source with standposts, protected spring, and so on):_____
Reliable?   Y   N
Number of wells:_____
Number of standposts:_____
Perceived water quality: Good   Bad
Actual water quality: Adequate   Inadequate
Grid locations of operational wells:
a._____
b._____
c._____
Petroleum, oil, lubricants available?   Y   N
Reliable?   Y   N

Category 1
- Broken windows, door locks and hinges, and roof tiles.
- Cut-off from electricity, water.
- *Can be repaired.*

Category 2
- Up to 30 percent roof damage.
- Light shelling or bullet impact on walls.
- Partial fire damage.
- *Can be repaired.*

Category 3
- Over 30 percent roof damage.
- Severe fire damage.
- Need for replacement of floors.
- Doors and windows destroyed.
- All piping, wiring destroyed.
- *Can be repaired.*

Category 4
- Destroyed.
- Needs reconstruction.
- *Cannot be repaired.*

Figure B-1. PSYOP geographic assessment (deliberate) (continued)

Appendix B

Schools:
Number of primary schools for boys:_____ Category: 1 2 3 4
Number of primary schools for girls:_____ Category: 1 2 3 4
Number of primary coeducational schools:_____ Category: 1 2 3 4
Number of secondary schools for boys:_____ Category: 1 2 3 4
Number of secondary schools for girls:_____ Category: 1 2 3 4
Number of secondary coeducational schools:_____ Category: 1 2 3 4
Name(s) and grid location(s) of schools:_____
_____

Roads:
Route to district center:
Name:_____From:_____To:_____
Distance from district center (kilometers):_____
Time from district center (four-wheel drive [4WD]):_____
Distance from province center:_____
Time from province center (4WD):_____
Road condition (summer):
 Usable by: Donkey Motorcycle Car 4WD 6 x 6 truck
Road condition (winter):
 Usable by: Donkey Motorcycle Car 4WD 6 x 6 truck
Road type: Track Paved

Bridges:
Location(s):_____
Latitude:_____
Longitude:_____
 Or grid reference:_____
 Between Settlement 1 (name):_____
 And Settlement 2 (name):_____
 Distance from Settlement 1:_____
 Distance from Settlement 2:_____
Type(s) of bridge: (Circle all that apply.) Road Emergency Floating Auxiliary
    Foot Ford
Condition:
 Summer usable by: Donkey Motorcycle Car 4WD 6 x 6 truck
 Winter usable by: Donkey Motorcycle Car 4WD 6 x 6 truck
Capacity (maximum weight and dimensions):_____

Medical services:
Hospital(s):
Name(s):_____
Ownership:_____Population size served_____
Coordinates: Latitude:_____Longitude:_____
Grid location:_____
Population size served:_____
Capability:
 Inpatient beds: _____Male:_____ Female: _____
Operating rooms:
Type surgeries performed:
 Gynecology? Y N General? Y N Orthopedic? Y N
Diagnostic capability:
 X ray? Y N Laboratory? Y N Blood bank? Y N

Figure B-1. PSYOP geographic assessment (deliberate) (continued)

Outpatient clinic:
    Primary care?   Y   N
    Dental?   Y   N
    Obstetrics?   Y   N
    Pediatrics?   Y   N
Doctors:
    Male:_____
    Female:_____
    Surgeons:_____
    Obstetrics:_____
    Midwives:_____
    Nurses:_____
    Other:_____
Ambulance services?   Y   N
    Number of vehicles:_____
    Dispatch method:_____
General comments on condition of facility and shortfalls in equipment and supplies:_____
_____
_____

Organizations working in the settlement:
NONE
Name 1:_____
Projects: Health   Education   Water and sanitation   Agriculture   Shelter
Orientation: Pro-U.S.   Anti-U.S.   Neutral
Name 2:_____
Projects: Health   Education   Water and sanitation   Agriculture   Shelter
Orientation: Pro-U.S.   Anti-U.S.   Neutral
Name 3:_____
Projects: Health   Education   Water and sanitation   Agriculture   Shelter
Orientation: Pro-U.S.   Anti-U.S.   Neutral
Name 4:_____
Projects: Health   Education   Water and sanitation   Agriculture   Shelter
Orientation: Pro-U.S.   Anti-U.S.   Neutral

Description and grids of other religious, cultural, and historical sites:
    1._____
    2._____
    3._____
    4._____
    5._____
    6._____
    7._____
    8._____
    9._____
    10._____

Summary and additional remarks:
_____
_____
_____
_____
_____

Figure B-1. PSYOP geographic assessment (deliberate) (continued)

Appendix B

RAPID LOCAL ASSESSMENT

POINT OF CONTACT:_____
RANK/NAME:_____
UNIT:_____
DTG COMPLETED:_____

General Information.

   a. Village name: _____
   b. Location: _____
   c. Population total: _____ Male: _____ Female: _____
   d. Pro-U.S., neutral, pro-enemy: _____
   Comments:_____
   _____
   e. Languages: _____
   f. Currency: _____
   g. Refugees: Yes/No   Total: _____ From: _____
   h. Ethnic makeup: _____
   i. Religious makeup: _____
   j. Tribe: _____
   k. Key communicators:(1)_____Title:_____
      (2)_____Title:_____
      (3)_____Title:_____
   l. Mayor or leader: _____
   m. Police chief: _____
   n. Local military leaders:_____
   o. School leaders: _____
   p. Types of dwellings: _____Overall category: _____

Category 1
- Broken windows, door locks and hinges, and roof tiles.
- Cut-off from electricity, water.
- *Can be repaired.*

Category 2
- Up to 30 percent roof damage.
- Light shelling or bullet impact on walls.
- Partial fire damage.
- *Can be repaired.*

Category 3
- Over 30 percent roof damage.
- Severe fire damage.
- Need for replacement of floors.
- Doors and windows destroyed.
- All piping, wiring destroyed.
- *Can be repaired.*

Category 4
- Destroyed.
- Needs reconstruction.
- *Cannot be repaired.*

Figure B-2. Rapid local assessment format sample

Assessments

q. Number of dwellings: _____
r. Average number in dwellings: _____
s. Power: _____ Reliability: _____ Percent dwellings with power: _____
t. Water supply type: _____ Reliability: _____ Percent dwellings with power: _____
u. Sewage: _____ Reliability: _____ Percent dwellings with sewage: _____
v. Transportation between villages: _____
w. Contact with other villages: Yes/No   Reason: _____
x. Medical facilities: Yes/No   Description: _____
   Limitations: _____
   Doctors: (1)_____(2)_____

Economic Characteristics.
   a. Natural resource types: (1) _____ (2) _____ (3) _____
   b. Monetary system used: _____
   c. Black market activities: Yes/No   Type: _____
   d. Agriculture and domestic food supply main crop: _____
   e. Industry type:_____
   f. Unemployment rate: _____ Percent: _____
   g. Fuel supply: Type: _____ Availability: _____
   h. NGO activity: Type: _____ Name: _____
      POC: _____ Traditions, customs, and taboos:_____

   Comments:_____
   _____
   _____
   _____

Media:
   a. Television: Number per household or village:_____Channel: _____
      Location: _____
   b. Radio: Number per household or village: _____ Frequency: _____-
      Location: _____
   c. Newspaper: Yes/No   Name: _____ Owner: _____-
      Frequency: _____

Contact With Forces:
   a. U.S.: DTG: _____ Who: _____ Why: _____
   Positive/NegativeComments:_____
   _____
   _____

   b. Coalition: DTG: _____ Who: _____ Why: _____
   Positive/Negative Comments:_____
   _____
   _____

   c. Enemy: DTG: _____ Who: _____ Why: _____
   Positive/Negative Comments: _____
   _____
   _____

   d. PSYOP: DTG: _____ Product type: _____
   Positive/Negative Comments: _____
   _____
   _____

Figure B-2. Rapid local assessment format sample (continued)

MEDIA ASSESSMENTS

B-4. Tactical forces also conduct an in-depth assessment of media assets operating in their AO whenever possible. Figure B-3, pages B-10 through B-12, provides a sample media assessment format. The information from this assessment is crucial in supporting the interaction of tactical PSYOP Soldiers with local media assets, such as newspapers, radio and TV stations. This list of questions is not all-inclusive—additional questions may be necessary in some situations. Some of these questions may not be relevant to all media assets or cannot be initially answered, especially those pertaining to information about employees and business relationships of the media asset. These questions may be too sensitive to inquire about directly, especially on initial visits to the facility.

B-5. Once tactical forces make contact with a station manager or an editor-in-chief, the relationship must be developed and carefully maintained. Establishing a good, habitual working relationship is an effective way to ensure continued use of that media asset.

B-6. When visiting a newspaper office or a TV or radio station, tactical forces must not make promises that cannot be supported. Unfulfilled promises can quickly destroy any relationship with the facility and its manager.

Media Assessment

Radio/Television Stations

What is the location of the radio station?
- Town name:_____ Street name:_____
- Neighborhood:_____
- Universal transverse mercator [UTM] coordinates:_____
- Geographic coordinates:_____
- Proximity to landmarks:_____

Who is the manager?
- Owner, or POC: _____
- Professional background: _____
- Languages spoken: _____
- Ethnic group: _____
- Tribal affiliations: _____
- Family background: _____
- Religion: _____
- Political agenda: _____

How can we contact the station manager or POC?
- Telephone number: _____
- E-mail: _____
- Residence: _____

Who else can act as a facilitator in doing business with this radio station?
- Village headman, political party official, and so on: _____

What other media facilities are collocated with this radio station?
(For example, a TV station or audio recording studio in the same or adjacent building.)
_____

What are program times and formats?
(For example, music, 0600-1000; news, 1000-1200; music, 1200-1600; talk radio, 1600-2200.)
_____

What are the demographics for the station's audience? (Ethnicity, ages, socioeconomic standing, and so on.)
_____

Figure B-3. Sample media assessment format

Assessments

What are the station's sources of broadcast material?
(Internet downloads, satellite network rebroadcasts, commercially purchased programs or CDs, black market materials, recordings of local artists, live performers, gifts from NGOs, and so on.)
_____
_____
_____

What are the station's sources of news broadcast material?
   Commercial news services:_____
   Local newspapers:_____
   Reporters:_____
   Internet:_____
   Local journalists:_____

What advertisers are currently doing business with the station?
   Political parties:_____
   Local businesses:_____
   NGOs and so on:_____

How does the station charge advertisers? (Barter for free airtime? Price per minute? What national currencies does the radio station accept? What form of payments does the station accept?)
_____
_____

What broadcast equipment does the station use? Format? (CD, DVD, MP3, Betamax, PAL, or NTSC? Manufacturer and model number? Recommend taking a digital photograph of the radio station's broadcast equipment. We want to provide compatible media for broadcast and maybe replacement parts or upgrades; a photograph will facilitate this.)
_____
_____

What electrical power source does the station use? (Commercial power or generator. What type of electrical outlets is used in the radio station—American or European, 110V or 220V?)
_____
_____

What are the parameters of the station's electrical power supply?
   Voltage:_____Hertz [Hz]:_____

What is the reliability of the station's electrical power supply? (How often do blackouts, brownouts, and surges occur?)_____

Where is the station's antenna located? (Is the antenna collocated with the broadcast studio or is it in a remote location?) UTM:_____ Geographic coordinates:_____

What type of antenna does the station use? (Dipole, single pole, and so on.)_____

What type of soil is prevalent at the antenna site? (Sand, loam, clay, and gravel.)_____

What is the station's broadcast output? (In watts)_____

What is the radio station manager's estimate of the broadcast footprint? _____

What is the total estimated audience size, and what are the peak audience hours and days?
_____

What nearby terrain features affect the station's broadcast footprint? (Mountains, steep valleys, large buildings.) _____
_____

What is the operating frequency or channel designation for the station? _____

Newspaper/Print
   What is the location of the newspaper/print office?
   Town name:_____ Street name:_____
   Neighborhood:_____
   Universal Transverse Mercator (UTM) coordinates: _____Geographic coordinates:_____
   Proximity to landmarks:_____

Figure B-3. Sample media assessment format (continued)

Appendix B

>   Who is the manager? _____
>   Owner or POC: _____
>   Professional background:_____
>   Languages spoken: _____
>   Ethnic group:_____
>   Tribal affiliations:_____
>   Family background:_____
>   Religion:_____
>   Political agenda:_____
> How can we contact the editor/manager or POC?
>
>   Telephone number:_____E-mail:_____
>   Residence:_____
>
> Who else can act as a facilitator in doing business with this organization? (Village headman, political party official, and so on.)_____
>
> What is the overall format and tone of the print source? (Local/town newspaper, national, international, entertainment, general interest, black and white, full color, and so on.)
> _____
> _____
> _____
>
> What is the orientation of the newspaper/print source? (Pro-U.S., anti-, or central government and so on.)
> _____
> _____
> _____
>
> What are the station's sources of news material?
>   Commercial news services:_____
>   Staff Reporters:_____
>   Internet:_____
>   Local journalists:_____
> What advertisers are currently doing business with the newspaper/print source?
>   Political parties:_____
>   Local businesses:_____
>   NGOs:_____
>   Others:_____
> How does the newspaper/print source charge advertisers? (Barter for free ad space? Price per cm2? What national currencies do they accept? What form of payment do they accept?)
> _____
> _____
>
> What editing equipment does the newspaper/print source use? (PC or Macintosh, hardcopy typesetting, and so on. We want to provide compatible media, so ensure we find out what format is needed.)
> _____
> _____
>
> What is the publishing frequency? (Daily, 5 days/week, weekly, monthly, and so on.) _____
>
> What is the approximate readership? (Readers per issue or per week.) _____
>
> What are the demographics of their readership? (Ethnicity, socioeconomic standing, and so on.)
> _____
> _____
>
> What are the most heavily read publishing days (if applicable)? _____

Figure B-3. Sample media assessment format (continued)

Appendix C
Support to Internment/Resettlement Operations

Unlike enemy prisoner of war/civilian internee (EPW/CI) operations in the past, I/R operations include additional detained persons. They include handling, protecting, and accounting for the classifications of detained persons—EPWs, CIs, retained persons (RPs), other detainees (ODs), DCs, and U.S. military prisoners. Tactical PSYOP forces are trained and equipped to support all I/R, except the handling of U.S. military prisoners. This appendix provides techniques, procedures, and considerations for employment of tactical PSYOP forces and other PSYOP units task-organized to support I/R operations.

INTERNMENT/RESETTLEMENT DETACHMENT

C-1. The tactical PSYOP unit assigned to support the I/R mission first plans and conducts PSYOP in support of theater, JTF, or corps-level I/R operations in any mission environment. The purpose of the mission is to assist MP or other units assigned an I/R mission to maintain order and to provide the POTF with information relevant to the ongoing PSYOP programs.

MISSION-ESSENTIAL TASKS

C-2. Tactical PSYOP units provide the POTF with a unique and useful capability by collecting timely PSYOP-relevant information from representatives of actual TAs within an I/R facility. In addition, tactical PSYOP units provide the GCC or JTF commander with a valuable asset by executing SPPs that pacify I/R camp populations. These programs reduce MP guard requirements, freeing scarce MP resources to conduct other missions. To support I/R effectively, tactical PSYOP units must perform the following essential tasks:

- Pretest and posttest PSYOP products and series as directed by the POTF.
- Assist the guard force I/R holding facility in controlling the facility population during emergencies.
- Collect, analyze, and report PSYOP-relevant information.
- Assist in the production of products in support of POTF operations, such as EPW-recorded surrender appeals.
- Collect and refine TAA data through the use of questionnaires.
- Determine the effectiveness of the opponent's internal propaganda, such as propaganda directed by the opponent at his own forces.
- Ascertain targets and objectives of hostile propaganda.
- Execute series to pacify, obtain cooperation of, and condition the population of the I/R holding facility to accept U.S. authority.
- Conduct PSYOP, when directed, to achieve other POTF objectives, such as reorientation of the population of the I/R holding facility.
- Assist in improving relations with the local populace to minimize interference with camp operations.

OPERATIONAL CONCEPTS AND PROCEDURES

C-3. Because I/R operations can vary greatly in many aspects, including PSYOP support requirements, each mission must be planned and tailored to meet unique mission requirements. The basis for planning

Appendix C

support to I/R operations is the TPD. One TPD can support an I/R facility operated by a battalion with a maximum capacity of 8,000 detainees. An element from the TPDD may be required to provide series development, design, and production support based on the mission. Ideally, the span of control for the TPC supporting I/R should not exceed three TPDs. Each TPD requires audiovisual augmentation from the TPDD. Audiovisual teams need to be attached to TPDs, or retained under TPDD control, to support specialized dissemination requirements.

C-4. If mission requirements exceed the ability of the TPC to provide C2 and administrative support, an element from the tactical POB HQ supporting the I/R operation can be organized with the minimum necessary personnel to meet mission requirements (Figure C-1). Any additional support teams required for the mission are attached directly to the company or battalion HQ.

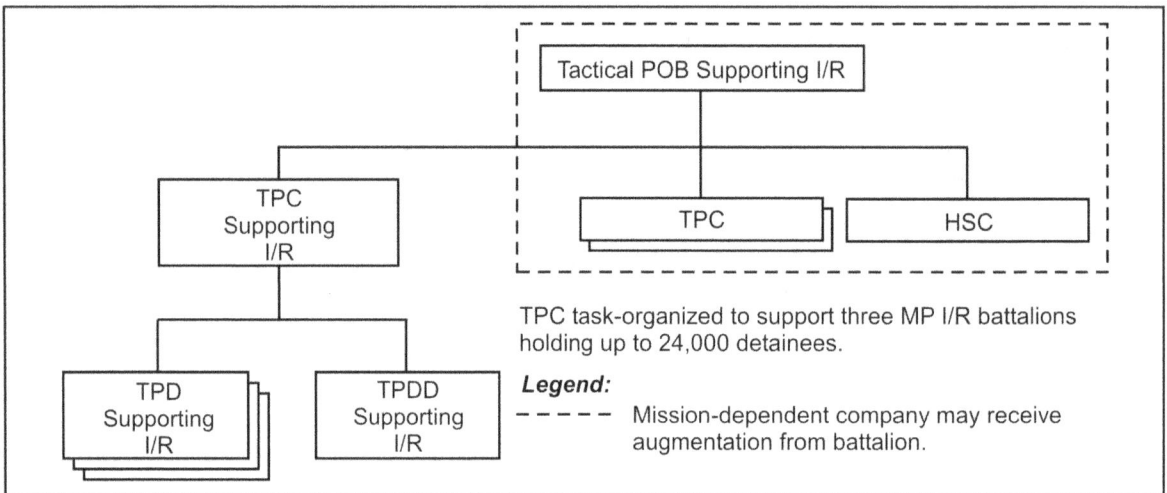

Figure C-1. Example of task organization to meet mission requirements

TACTICAL PSYOP DETACHMENT TASK ORGANIZATION

C-5. The TPD (Figure C-2) deploys to I/R facilities during the construction phase. Figure C-3, page C-3 and FM 3-19.40, *Military Police Internment/Resettlement Operations*, include examples of typical I/R facility layouts. The TPD is attached to the I/R MP battalion (or other unit) responsible for the camp. Arrival at the camp during the construction phase ensures adequate time for the TPD to coordinate operating procedures, communications, and logistical support with the supported battalion. Early arrival also allows time to develop and produce the products necessary to support camp operations, such as printed and recorded camp rules in the language of the facility population.

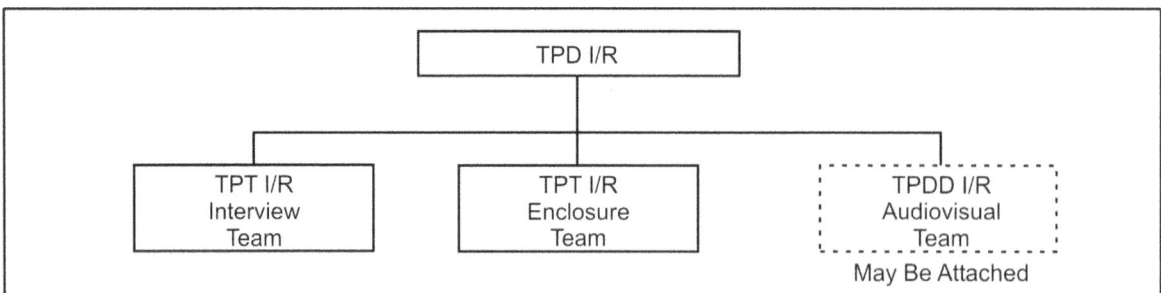

Figure C-2. TPD organization supporting internment/resettlement

C-6. The TPD commander functions as the PSYOP staff officer for the camp commander. The detachment commander advises the camp commander on the psychological impact of all actions within the camp and all actions external to the camp that affect the camp population. This support is critical to prevent

Support to Internment/Resettlement Operations

misunderstandings that may lead to subsequent disturbances by the facility population. Differences in culture, customs, language, religious practices, and dietary habits can be of such magnitude that misunderstandings are not always completely avoidable. However, investigation, information briefings, and proper handling can minimize misunderstandings.

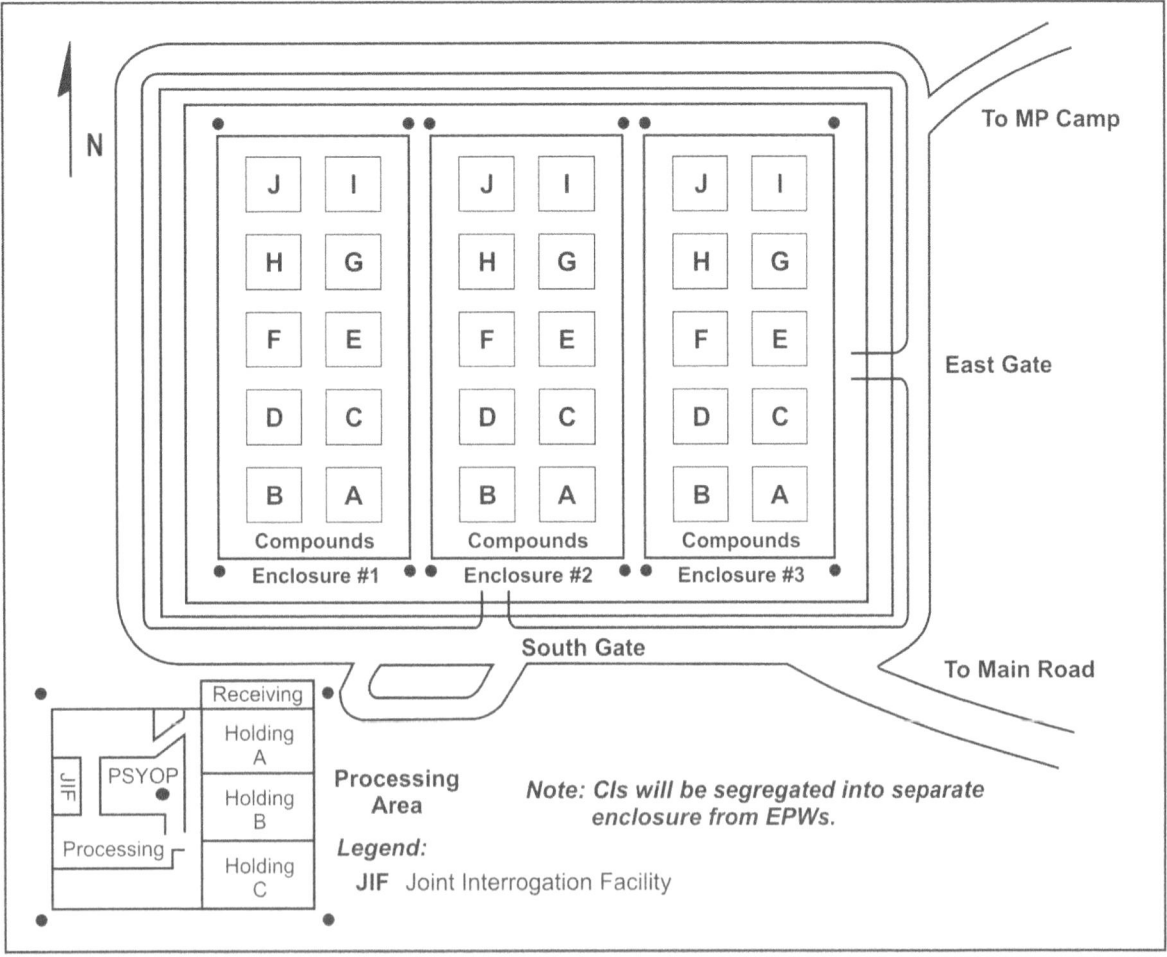

Figure C-3. Typical I/R facility layout

C-7. Upon arrival at the camp, the TPD commander briefs the camp commander and subordinate enclosure commanders on the detachment's mission and capabilities. He, or his designated representative, attends all camp command and staff meetings. These meetings provide the most effective means to communicate on a daily basis with the various facility commanders, their staffs, and other supporting units. Before the arrival of detainees at the camp, the detachment commander and enclosure team leader brief the MP guards (who will work directly with the facility population) on the mission and capabilities of the teams.

C-8. All PSYOP personnel must be thoroughly familiar with the laws, regulations, and current policies governing the treatment of detainees. Chief among these are the following:
- Geneva Convention of 12 August 1949, Paragraph 1, Article 3: The Hague Conventions.
- Army Regulation (AR) 190-8, *Enemy Prisoners of War, Retained Personnel, Civilian Internees, and Other Detainees*.
- FM 3-19.40.
- FM 27-10, *The Law of Land Warfare*.

Appendix C

C-9. Making sure all facility personnel observe these rules validates the team's credibility with the facility population, as well as with facility guards. In addition, following these rules prevents embarrassing incidents that can be exploited by hostile actors or that can discredit the United States. These rules apply even when hostilities are not declared.

C-10. During S&RO, special rules for handling civilians apply. Procedures for treatment of CIs and DCs should be coordinated with the camp commander and the Judge Advocate General or competent legal authority.

C-11. The TPD executes supporting PSYOP programs using a variety of media. Music and news (from approved sources), camp rules, and in-processing instructions are broadcast using semipermanent camp loudspeaker systems. Supporting audiovisual teams produce and disseminate audio, video, and audiovisual products. Print products are produced by supporting light print teams or through reachback capability. All products not directly related to camp command information are subject to the established approval process.

C-12. By international convention and Army regulation, all information presented to the facility population must be in the population's language. Translators must be fully integrated into TPD operations. These personnel provide the capability to address the facility population in their native language and to screen products for language accuracy and content. U.S. or allied military personnel, contracted civilians, or cooperative detainees may provide translator support. Detachment members must exercise caution to safeguard classified material and sensitive POTF operations.

C-13. Limitations on resources available for camp construction, combined with large surges of detainees arriving at the camp, may result in temporary overcrowding. Potential for disturbances increases dramatically when I/R facilities experience overcrowded conditions. The TPD commander should make sure enclosure commanders include PSYOP loudspeaker support in all activities involving mass transfers between compounds—for example, health and welfare inspections. PSYOP personnel provide an MP force-multiplier in these I/R situations.

INTERVIEW TEAM

C-14. The interview team consists of TPT personnel trained to conduct interviews. If available, the team should be augmented with qualified 97E interrogators to increase team effectiveness. The interview team normally operates in the facility processing area screening all, or a representative sample, of the incoming detainees. Although military intelligence (MI) units are most likely present in the facility, the interview team must maintain a separate operation. Nevertheless, the team must coordinate closely with MI and other assets to obtain any PSYOP-relevant information those assets may gather.

C-15. The team uses interview notes and database software to collect information about each detainee and provides the data to the TPD. The data is compiled and forwarded to the company or directly to the POTF for TAA. Information collected includes—

- Race or ethnicity.
- Sex.
- Age.
- Political affiliation.
- Religious affiliation.
- Geographic origin.
- Education levels.
- Length, depth, and type of involvement.
- Previous or current occupation.
- Standard of living and personal finances.
- Previous military training.
- Political and military indoctrination.
- PSYOP vulnerabilities and susceptibilities.

C-16. Detainees who are cooperative or who possess information, skills, or characteristics of interest to the TPT are interviewed in depth, as time permits. Interview team personnel look specifically for—

- Malcontents, rabble-rousers, trained agitators, and political officers who may attempt to organize resistance or create disturbances within the camp. Once these individuals are identified, the guards normally confine them in isolated enclosures to deny them access to the general population.
- Detainees willing to cooperate with setting up informant networks. These detainees should be referred to counterintelligence personnel, as they are responsible for running informant networks within the facility.
- Detainees with special skills who can assist with camp operations. Such skills include language, construction, engineering, medical, education, entertainment, and so on.
- Detainees willing to assist with product development, such as taping audio surrender appeals.
- Detainees willing to participate in pretesting or posttesting.

C-17. Ready access to members and former members of the TA allows the interview team to conduct pretesting and posttesting that provides accurate, meaningful feedback to the POTF. Data collected during these surveys are passed to the POTF through the TPC and battalion. The interview team must maintain secure, reliable communications with higher HQ and ensure the timely, secure transport of the product prototype and testing results.

C-18. The interview team, along with other camp personnel, must take precautions to safeguard the identities of cooperative detainees to protect them from reprisal. PSYOP personnel must always exercise discretion when dealing with cooperative detainees. Guards must be thoroughly briefed on proper handling procedures.

C-19. Discovering detainees with false identities is an important security measure that can reduce potential problems and ensure smooth camp operations. Interview team personnel can discover false identities during initial processing or subsequent interviews. They look for—

- Documents that do not match or agree.
- An interview response that does not match the response given during an earlier interview.
- Identification that does not agree with another document or information from another source, such as the International Committee of the Red Cross (ICRC).
- Slow verbal response to simple questions, such as date of birth. The detainee may be making up responses or trying to remember false information.
- A detainee without documentation. This situation requires careful investigation. Did detainee throw away identification card?
- A detainee who suddenly refuses to cooperate at any point during processing.
- Detainee names that appear in the "black book," or on list of sought-after persons.

ENCLOSURE TEAM

C-20. The enclosure TPT conducts face-to-face PSYOP and collects vital information within the facility. To perform their mission, enclosure team personnel must have unrestricted access to the camp population. Close coordination with MP guards is necessary to ensure the safety of PSYOP personnel when operating inside the camp. Enclosure team personnel and MP guards develop a system of signals before conducting operations.

C-21. Enclosure team personnel build rapport with detainees by distributing recreational equipment, conducting morale support activities, informing detainees of the rights provided them under the Geneva Convention, and performing other actions designed to gain the trust of detainees. Although the enclosure team must maintain close communication with other PSYOP team elements, such communication should be discreet and conducted away from the view of the camp population. If enclosure team personnel are not identified with the authoritarian elements of camp administration, they usually enjoy greater rapport with the camp population.

Appendix C

C-22. Information is critical to the effective management of an I/R PSYOP program. Enclosure team personnel capitalize on their access to the camp population to collect information about the population and to watch for any potential problems. Enclosure team personnel look for—
- Leaders, not necessarily those wearing higher rank.
- Low-ranking individuals, such as privates, being paid high respect. They may be high-ranking people who are hiding their identity.
- Detainees who are the center of attention in a group.
- Loners who shun others. They may be mentally ill or may be hiding their true identity. They may also be intelligence operatives or members of an SO unit.
- Unusual groups. The presence of unusual groups may indicate someone is organizing.
- Items passed from one person to another.
- New soil in the compound. Someone may be tunneling.
- Lookouts. Does this person warn others? Does a group scatter at the approach of a guard?
- Signals and codes. Are detainees tapping out messages, waving rags, or using hand signals? The use of codes is common in I/R facilities and usually indicates something is going on that requires secrecy.
- Individuals who move from one group to another and whose presence forces the topic of conversation to change. They may be political officers or intelligence officers.
- Individuals who speak for a group but maintain eye contact with another person in that group. The speaker may be a front man for the real leader.
- Individuals who immediately make friends with MP guards and are readily accepted back into the camp population. They may be key communicators.
- Detainees who express interest in camp construction or materials and equipment used in camp construction. These detainees could be planning escape or weapons manufacture.

C-23. Enclosure team personnel must be alert for detainees who attempt to contact them discreetly. Contact attempts may be manifested in the following manner:
- Detainee hails the guard and asks for asylum.
- Detainee is unusually friendly or cooperative.
- Detainee feigns illness.

C-24. Guard and PSYOP enclosure TPT personnel must watch for missing items. Dining facility items—such as knives, forks, spoons, and most other common kitchen items—can be used as weapons or digging tools. I/R facilities usually have construction of some sort underway. All construction materials and tools must be accounted for daily. Any other items that detainees can use for escape—such as ropes, ladders, uniform items, documents, and cameras—must also be accounted for daily.

AUDIOVISUAL TEAM

C-25. The TPDD audiovisual team normally supports three TPD supporting I/R operations. The audiovisual team uses the Product Development Workstation–Light (PDW-L) to produce and disseminate products to the facility population. The team supports the facility PSYOP program by disseminating entertainment products, such as videos and music. This asset gives the TPD the ability to influence detainee behavior by providing or withholding something of value to the facility population. When directed, the audiovisual team disseminates products that support other POTF programs, such as reorientation and posthostility themes.

QUICK-REACTION FORCE

C-26. The TPD commander coordinates with enclosure commanders to include PSYOP loudspeaker support as part of the facility's QRF. The QRF is a predesignated element that serves as an emergency tactical response force for the compounds or other locations determined by higher command. This force is ready 24 hours a day, every day.

C-27. The TPD commander maintains contact with the QRF element through the supported unit's radio net or by other means. Soldiers designated to support the QRF must be prepared to execute the QRF mission rapidly. The TPD commander or his designated representative must accomplish these premission tasks:

- Brief the QRF leader on PSYOP capabilities and employment.
- Coordinate linkup plan with the QRF.
- Rehearse linkup procedures with each new QRF element.
- Rehearse likely emergency scenarios and perform reconnaissance of the sites.
- Prepare audio products and scripts for likely scenarios.
- Make sure translators are briefed and are available.

IMPACT OF TACTICAL PSYOP FORCES

C-28. Tactical PSYOP forces not only provide a force multiplier to the forces tasked to support I/R missions, but also are critical in collecting PSYOP-related information and in assisting the product development process through pretesting and posttesting. Careful adherence to all provisions of the Geneva Conventions and relevant laws and regulations must be maintained. Legal consultation may prevent incidents that could be used against the United States in opponent propaganda. In addition, the attitudes and opinions of former detainees toward the United States can have a long-term impact on relations with their nation in the future. A positive attitude may lessen the chance of future-armed conflict.

This page intentionally left blank.

Appendix D
Propaganda Assessment

Propaganda is any form of communication in support of national objectives designed to influence the opinions, emotions, attitudes, or behavior of any group in order to benefit the sponsor, either directly or indirectly. By policy and practice, PSYOP forces use the term to indicate PSYOP, or information activities, conducted by enemy or hostile forces, elements, or groups against U.S. or coalition forces.

> **Propaganda Examples**
> The broadcasts of Lord Haw Haw (William Joyce) to the British Isles during the Battle of Britain and of Tokyo Rose in the Pacific theater during World War II are excellent examples of skewed information. The programs were deliberately designed to attack the will of nations to resist and the will of Soldiers to fight. These propagandists attempted to mix truth and lies in a way that was imperceptible to the listener.

COUNTERPROPAGANDA EFFORT

D-1. Support to the counterpropaganda effort is usually a responsibility of PSYOP units within an AOR and a joint operations area (JOA). Other government agencies counter propaganda on an international scale and within the United States. Often, PSYOP forces must depend upon the information networks of U.S. allies to counter propaganda within their own borders. However, PSYOP forces may provide assistance when requested. The ideal counterpropaganda plan incorporates a loose network of organizations with common objectives. Many elements of IO can play a role in supporting the counterpropaganda plan; however, PSYOP and public affairs normally play the most active roles in countering propaganda.

D-2. The Internet has presented PSYOP units with a new medium for exploitation by both friendly and opposing forces. Figure D-1 shows an example of electronic media propaganda.

Figure D-1. Example of electronic media propaganda

OPPOSING INFORMATION

D-3. Opposing information is intentional or unintentional truth based on information coming from anyone who represents an opposing view based upon factual evidence. This counterinformation may also be directed against the U.S. military, U.S. allies, key audiences within the JOA or AOR, or even U.S. adversaries and potential adversaries or nonaligned parties.

D-4. Key U.S. decision makers must understand the impact of U.S. forces in a JOA or an AOR and must react in a way that minimizes negative images and amplifies positive images of U.S. policy and operations.

Appendix D

All good policies and actions taken by a military, the government, and coalitions will have equal and opposite adverse impacts and reactions within a JOA or an AOR. When American troops are deployed OCONUS, they can create problems by their presence. For example, during humanitarian operations to build schools and hospitals in Central America, indigenous populations demonstrated against the U.S. forces because the construction did not facilitate their needs. Local populations complained that the Americans bought all the construction materials in the area and escalated prices. Local businessmen complained that Americans were signing contracts and working with minority and small businesses while not attempting to work with them, although they offered lower prices in many instances. These opposing attitudes and beliefs, if not monitored and addressed quickly, can create an image of the force that nullifies the success of an operation. Normally, the PSYOP unit crafts the image of the force in a JOA or an AOR with support from the assigned public affairs and CA staff.

SCAME TECHNIQUE OF ANALYSIS

D-5. PSYOP personnel often use the SCAME technique of analyzing opponent propaganda. PSYOP personnel should avoid "forcing" information into this format if they do not know the actual information. Often, the true information appears after the propaganda has been analyzed or after other forms of intelligence data have been revealed.

SOURCE

D-6. A source is the individual, organization, or government that sponsors and disseminates the propaganda. Source analysis should consider all of the various players involved in the design, development, and dissemination of the propaganda or information. Correct identification of the various sources behind a particular item of propaganda can assist in providing a clearer picture of the opponent's capabilities and intent. The source may also be classified as white, gray, or black, if known. The following are types of sources:

- *Actor.* An actor may be a true "actor" in the film or stage sense, or an actor may be the individual, animal, or representative the opponent has selected to use to convey the propaganda message.
- *Author.* The author is the individual who created or wrote the message or propaganda. The author is readily identifiable in many media forums. In addition to the individual authors, PSYOP personnel should attempt to identify the production location where the propaganda was created or developed—for example, a TV studio or print plant.
- *Authority.* Authority is the propaganda source's means to establish credibility in the eyes of the intended TA. Authority can be manifested by means of individuals, symbols, slogans, or representations of items that resonate with the TA. An example is the use of the presidential seal on written documents produced in the U.S. Government. Another example is the Iraqi Minister of Information during Operation IRAQI FREEDOM. While the Iraqi Minister of Information's inaccurate statements minimized impact on any Western audiences, his position as a member of the government did establish his authority to the Iraqi people initially. As it became obvious that Iraq was losing the conflict, his stubborn defiance (and continued misrepresentation of the situation) became a source of pride to some in the Arab world.

D-7. PSYOP personnel should try to identify who disseminated the propaganda. Sometimes, the dissemination means is obvious, as in the retransmission of a TV product via terrestrial retransmission sites. In many cases, PSYOP personnel can identify the dissemination source by applying other known facts about events in the AO to the situation. Potential dissemination sources include—

- Government agencies.
- Police.
- Political parties.
- Mass media.
- Military organizations.
- Hired personnel.
- Volunteers.

Propaganda Assessment

- International media.
- Underground networks.

CONTENT

D-8. Analysis reveals what the propaganda message says and what is trying to be achieved regarding the TA. This analysis can also reveal the source's intent, motives, and goals. Content analysis reveals the meaning of the message, the reason the message was disseminated, the intended purpose or objective, and the manner in which the message was presented to the TA. PSYOP personnel analyze the content of propaganda by evaluating—

- Objectives.
- Lines of persuasion used.
- Morale.
- Involuntary information.
- Biographic information.
- Economic data.
- Propaganda inconsistencies (Figure D-2).
- Geographic information.
- Intentions.

This anti-NATO propaganda contains inconsistencies. If the intended target audience is Americans, then the message of global domination by the United States via NATO does not resonate. If the target audience is other than Americans, the symbol of the pyramid and eye from a U.S. one dollar bill is unknown to most non-Americans and means nothing. Although the product is graphically of high quality, the execution is flawed. Proper planning by PSYOP personnel prevents obvious errors of this sort.

Figure D-2. Example of propaganda inconsistencies

AUDIENCE

D-9. In this aspect of propaganda analysis, PSYOP personnel attempt to determine which TAs are being reached by the propaganda and which TAs were specifically selected by the opponent. By viewing the TA via propaganda, PSYOP personnel may become more aware of lines of persuasion and symbols that are more effective. Those lines of persuasion and symbols can later be used in the development of PSYOP products. This aspect of propaganda is critical, as it will, to a large part, determine which TA that PSYOP forces will target in their counterpropaganda campaign. Audience analysis must be conducted in concert with content analysis, as content analysis will discover what behavior or attitude the opponent seeks in the TA.

D-10. The establishment of a Taliban web site in English represents a viable attempt to harness a worldwide dissemination tool. Further examination of the web site reveals themes targeting the Muslim community as the ultimate TA. The use of English as a language could be an attempt to use a common, worldwide language to reach Muslims around the world who may not speak Afghan or Arabic. Western (sympathetic)

Appendix D

Muslims are an additional potential TA. Another TA may be the English-speaking Afghan diaspora, though such a small TA seems hardly worth the effort. Propaganda analysis involves the exploration of all possible TAs targeted by the opponent. Audience analysis identifies four major classifications of TAs:

- *Apparent.* Upon first observation, the propaganda appears to be intended for the apparent TA. The audience may or may not be the real intended or final targets of the propaganda. The opponent may have selected the apparent TA deliberately or may be trying to deceive PSYOP forces. Closer examination and analysis may reveal a true TA beneath the obvious one (Figure D-3).
- *Intermediate.* The opponent uses the intermediate TA to assist in getting the message across to the ultimate TA. The intermediate audience may or may not be part of the ultimate TA.
- *Unintended.* The unintended TAs are those audiences for whom the propaganda was not intended, but nonetheless received it.
- *Ultimate.* The ultimate TAs are those audiences for whom the opponent intended the message to get to, or those targets in which the opponent desires a change of behavior or attitude.

Upon initial observation, the apparent target audience of this propaganda is the French population; however, after some initial analysis, the impact of a famous monument in flames in the heart of a major European capital possibly strikes a chord in the minds of all Europeans. Europeans well remember the bombings of capital cities during WW II; this appears to be the theme sought by the creators of this product. The ultimate target audience may potentially then be the European population. This product was also used as a backdrop behind a location from which international reporters were forced to report.

Figure D-3. Example of questionable propaganda audience

MEDIA

D-11. This aspect of propaganda analysis determines why a particular medium was selected, what media capabilities the opponent has, and how consistent the message was across a variety of media. Propaganda can be disseminated via visual, audio, and audiovisual means. Propaganda transmission modes may also be overt or covert.

D-12. Disseminated propaganda can show opponent weaknesses. Propaganda printed on inferior grades of paper may indicate supply shortages. Weak broadcast signals, interrupted programs, poor production techniques, and a shortage of broadcast platforms may also indicate a lack of support, both logistically and from the opponent's HQ. PSYOP personnel should not evaluate the effectiveness of the propaganda based only on production quality. The opponent may have deliberately lowered the quality of the propaganda to make it more acceptable to the TA. The following common terminology is used when analyzing media selection:

- *Frequency.* Frequency refers to how often a medium is disseminated. Newspapers or magazines may be daily, weekly, or monthly. Radio and TV may be daily, hourly, or weekly broadcasts. Propaganda may appear multiple times across different mediums.
- *Placement.* Placement is the physical location of opponent propaganda in a medium. In printed media, propaganda may be located in various parts of the paper. In audio and audiovisual mediums, propaganda can be located in a wide variety of places. PSYOP personnel are able to evaluate the legitimacy of the propaganda by its placement in media.

Propaganda Assessment

- *Place of origin.* The place of origin is the production source of the propaganda. Examples are print plants, TV production studios and broadcast stations, radio production studios and broadcast stations, advertising agencies, marketing firms, and print media firms.
- *Technical characteristics.* Technical characteristics include such information as frequency, channel, modulation, signal strength, bandwidth, and other electronic signature means. TV propaganda characteristics include picture quality, sound quality, and color (Figure D-4). Printed media may be classified by size and quality of paper, print colors, and print quality.
- *Method of dissemination.* Method of dissemination is similar to dissemination source, as stated earlier in the source analysis.

Belgrade television developed several television spots like this one in English and broadcast them on their TV stations daily. International media, such as CNN and British Broadcasting Corporation (BBC), then rebroadcast the spots onto Western stations, assisting the Serbs in disseminating their messages. The spots were of very high quality and were produced by a Serbian marketing firm in Belgrade using state-of-the-art digital technology.

Figure D-4. Example of television propaganda

EFFECTS

D-13. The most important, and often the most difficult, aspect of propaganda analysis to determine is its effectiveness on the ultimate TA. The ultimate measure of opponent propaganda effectiveness is the change in behavior or attitude of the TAs involved. Effects analysis is similar to determining the impact of friendly PSYOP on its intended TAs; direct and indirect impact indicators are significant indicators of effectiveness.

D-14. PSYOP planners may not always be able to gather actual impact indicators to evaluate the effects of an opponent's propaganda and may have to evaluate its impact analytically. Below is a portion of an analysis by Richard Williams Bulliet of Columbia University of Osama bin Laden's recruitment video. The evaluation goes beyond effects and evaluates many other aspects of the video. Such input can be very helpful to PSYOP personnel in propaganda analysis.

There is no way to calculate the effectiveness of this videotape. Some young Arab men who watch it find it gripping; some feel it contains nothing new. Effective propaganda often contains nothing new, however. It works by triggering latent feelings, by manipulating familiar words and images. Looked at strictly from a structural standpoint, the bin Laden videotape shows a highly professional mind at work. The psychological understanding of how propaganda can move people to action is of a very high order, as are the technical skills deployed in the video and sound editing. Though some propagandists for the American side in the current conflict portray Osama bin Laden as the enemy of America's modern technological civilization, this tape proves that he is capable of using both the techniques and the professional production skills of the modern television industry to convey his message. Though never named in the tape or accorded a rank or title confirming his implicit leadership, Osama bin Laden's face, voice, and thinking dominate it throughout. Whoever the actual producer, the animating intelligence is that of bin Laden, a man who shows himself here as a master of propaganda and an intelligent, ruthless, and, yes, modern adversary.

Richard Williams Bulliet, Columbia University

Appendix D

D-15. If necessary, PSYOP units may decide to test the propaganda on the TAs by survey sampling, focus groups, or any of the other means of product pretesting and posttesting. A drawback of this action is that PSYOP personnel actually are further disseminating the propaganda. Another means of determining the effect of opponent propaganda is to execute surveys of the TAs involved.

D-16. PSYOP personnel may often find that the behavior or attitudes of the TAs are impacted by a variety of sources, one of which is opponent propaganda. PSYOP personnel should evaluate the impact of opponent propaganda on all applicable TAs—apparent, intermediate, unintended, and ultimate. This analysis may reveal errors or vulnerabilities for future exploitation.

D-17. While conducting effects analysis, PSYOP personnel also identify any linkages between the propaganda being analyzed and other known items of similar design. This step marks the beginning of a transition from individual propaganda analysis to analysis of a potential propaganda program.

D-18. PSYOP personnel advise the supported commander and coordinating staff of the current situation regarding the use or anticipated use of adversary propaganda in the AO. PSYOP personnel advise commanders on the recommended defense against adversary propaganda and recommend the appropriate material to be included in command information programs. This task also includes advice on available options for use of counterpropaganda.

D-19. PSYOP personnel analyze propaganda and conduct a comprehensive analysis of SCAME reports. Figure D-5, pages D-6 and D-7, provides a sample SCAME format.

Source Analysis: What is the real source?   **DTG:** When last updated?

1. Elements of the source.
    a. Actor.
    b. Authority.
    c. Author.
2. Type. White _____ Gray _____ Black _____
3. Credibility of each source element.
    a. Actor.
    b. Authority.
    c. Author.

Content Analysis: What does the propaganda say? What is it trying to get the TA to do?

4. Objective of the message.
5. Line of persuasion used.
6. Morale of the source.
7. Involuntary information in the message (news, opinions, and entertainment).
8. Biographical information (new leader, and so on).
9. Economic information.
10. Propaganda inconsistencies.
11. Intentions or agenda of the source.
12. Geographic information.

Audience Analysis: Who are the audiences?

1. Apparent audience.
    a. Perception of the message.
    b. Reason selected.
2. Ultimate audience.
    a. Perception of the message.
    b. Reason selected.
3. Intermediate audience.
    a. Perception of the message.
    b. Reason selected.

Figure D-5. Sample SCAME format

4. Unintended audience.
    a. Perception of the message.
    b. Reason selected.

Media Analysis: What media are used and why?

1. Type. Radio _____ Television _____ Print (specific type) _____
   Newspaper/Magazine _____ Internet _____ Other _____
2. Frequency.
3. Placement.
4. Place of origin.
5. Technical characteristics.
6. Method of dissemination.
7. Transmission mode.

Effects Analysis: What impact is this propaganda having?

1. Methods used in analysis.
2. Impact indicators (direct and indirect).
3. Conclusions.

Figure D-5. Sample SCAME format

This page intentionally left blank.

Appendix E
Sample PSYOP Appendix

At the tactical level, the PSYOP planner writes the PSYOP appendix to the supported unit's plan. Figure E-1, pages E-1 through E-5, provides a sample PSYOP appendix.

CLASSIFICATION

APPENDIX 2 (PSYCHOLOGICAL OPERATIONS) TO ANNEX P (INFORMATION OPERATIONS) OPERATIONS ORDER NUMBER:

1. SITUATION:
   a. Hostile: Insurgent forces in the metropolitan areas around XXX, XXX, and XXX have propaganda capability. Primary capability is rudimentary visual production. Recent propaganda found in XXX has had the primary objective of trying to convince the populace that local and national governments are unable to protect the citizens.
   b. Friendly: X TPC supporting X Division/UEx. XX POB supporting XX. POTF supporting JTF XXX. No PSYOP programs are being conducted in the AOI at this time. COMMANDO SOLO and print facilities aboard naval vessels are available to support the production and dissemination of PSYOP products. These capabilities are coordinated for through the POTF (see paragraph 3c[4]).
   c. Neutral: XXXX TV network. Has ability to be either pro- or anti-U.S. policy. Tends to broadcast material detrimental to U.S. objectives.
   d. Attachments and Detachments:
      (1) One DAPS team attached.
      (2) TPD XXX is detached from X TPC effective DTG and attached to the JSOTF effective DTG.
      (3) TPD XXX is detached from X POB effective DTG, and further attached to 3d Brigade XX effective DTG. Responsible for the distribution and dissemination of audio, visual, and audiovisual products within their AO. Responsible for series testing within their AO.
      (4) TPD XXX attached to 2d Brigade XX effective DTG. Responsible for the distribution and dissemination of audio, visual, and audiovisual products within their AO. Responsible for series testing within their AO.
      (5) TPD XXX attached to 1st Brigade XX effective DTG. Responsible for the distribution and dissemination of audio, visual, and audiovisual products within their AO. Responsible for series testing within their AO.
2. MISSION: X TPC conducts PSYOP in support of XX Division/UEx within AO XXXX by increasing participation in democratic institutions, reducing effectiveness of insurgent activity, and decreasing casualties due to mines and unexploded explosive ordnance (UXO) no earlier than DTG.
3. EXECUTION:
   a. Scheme of PSYOP: X TPC will conduct PSYOP by executing series that support each supporting PSYOP objective (see Tab A).
   b. Tasks to Subordinate Units:
      (1) TPC HQ: Responsible for the distribution of the series to the TPDs.
      (2) TPDD: Responsible for all contracts for airtime of audio and audiovisual products. Responsible for the development of PSYOP series.
      (3) DAPS team: Reports to the TPDD OIC.
   c. Coordinating Instructions:
      (1) Presidential and SecDef themes to stress or avoid:

CLASSIFICATION

Figure E-1. Sample PSYOP appendix

CLASSIFICATION

    (a) Themes to stress:

- Coalition forces will act decisively in response to attacks upon its forces, installations, or civilian agencies operating under International sanction.
- Coalition forces are operating under robust ROE and have the authorization and capability to respond rapidly and proportionately in response to any acts of violence.
- Coalition forces will take every precaution to minimize collateral damage and will act only as a last resort to prevent violence or loss of life.
- Continued violence will not accomplish the objective of any organization or group.
- Coalition forces are professional, subordinate to internationally recognized codes of conduct.
- Commitment to peace is in the best long-term interests of the region.
- Those who advocate continued violence are acting against the interest of the citizens of XXXXX.

    (b) Themes to avoid:

- Any theme that implies support for or legitimizes the XXX Regime.
- References to coalition forces as an occupying Army.
- Minority group independence.
- Portrayal of all religious leaders as terrorist supporters.
- Any reference to religious affiliations.
- Any ultimatum that cannot be immediately carried out.
- Portrayal of favoritism or special treatment for a particular group.

  (2) SEM will be published once a series is approved. The SEM will be placed on the division's/UEx's shared drive and updated daily.

  (3) Reachback will be used for the distribution of products not produced in theater. The TPDD may coordinate directly with the CPSE for reachback support.

  (4) TPDD will coordinate for support from assets referenced in paragraph 1b through the POTF S-3.

  (5) All propaganda will be reported to the TPDD for immediate analysis. This will be accomplished through the unit's supporting PSYOP forces and S-2 channels. If a supporting PSYOP force is not available, propaganda will be reported to the division/UEx through S-2 and G-2 channels.

  (6) Additional POs, SPOs, PTAs, TAs, and MOEs can be added through a change to this appendix as necessary.

  (7) Any targets nominated by subordinate commands for engagement by a PSYOP capability must be vetted through the TPC no later than 96 hours before engagement. This lead time will allow for development of supporting PSYOP programs to support these target nominations.

4. SERVICE SUPPORT:

  a. Command-Regulated Classes of Supply: Additional printing and audio materials will be requested through the G-4 and purchased through contracts.

  b. Supply Distribution Plan: XX supply channels will provide all Army common items. PSYOP-peculiar equipment will be requested through PSYOP channels to the SOTSE. Division/UEx logistical network will be used to distribute PSYOP series whenever possible.

5. COMMAND AND SIGNAL:

  a. Command:

    (1) Succession of command is X TPC commander, TPDD commander, TPD XXX commander, TPD XXX commander, and TPD XXX commander. TPC HQ and TPDD are collocated with XX.

    (2) PSYOP approval process is outlined in Tab B. Tactical PSYOP elements, when necessary, can create impromptu provisional loudspeaker and face-to-face products concerning only deception, force protection, or civilian noninterference.

  b. Signal: Division/UEx communication support will be provided for all subordinate PSEs. Daily SITREPs will be digitally sent through S-3 channels and to the TPDD by 1900 Zulu each day.

Tab A – PSYOP Objectives, Supporting PSYOP Objectives, Potential Target Audiences, and Measures of Effectiveness
Tab B – PSYOP Approval Process
Tab C – PSYOP SITREP

CLASSIFICATION

Figure E-1. Sample PSYOP appendix (continued)

CLASSIFICATION

TAB A

DTG

PO A – Reduce effectiveness of insurgency.

SPOs:

1. TA ceases insurgent activity.
    a. PTA: Hussein United National Tribe (HUNT). MOE: How many HUNT members arrested for insurgent activity each week?
    b. PTA: Fedayeen Insurgent Support Horde (FISH). MOE: How many FISH members arrested for insurgent activity each week?
    c. PTA: Baathist Association for the Advancement of Saddam (BASS). MOE: How many BASS members arrested for insurgent activity each week?
2. TA increases insurgent activities reported.
    a. PTA: Iraqi parents. MOE: How many insurgent activities reported each week?
    b. PTA: Utility workers. MOE: How many insurgent activities reported each week?
    c. PTA: Schoolteachers. MOE: How many insurgent activities reported each week?
    d. PTA: Sunni sheikhs. MOE: How many insurgent activities reported each week?
    e. PTA: Sunni Imams. MOE: How many insurgent activities reported each week?

PO B – Decrease casualties due to mines and UXO.

SPOs:

1. TA increases reporting of the location of mines and UXO.
    a. PTA: Iraqi school-age children. MOE: How many mines or UXO reported each week?
    b. PTA: Postal workers. MOE: How many mines or UXO reported each week?
    c. PTA: School teachers. MOE: How many mines or UXO reported each week?
    d. PTA: Farmers. MOE: How many mines or UXO reported each week?
2. TA decreases handling of mines and UXO.
    a. PTA: Iraqi school-age children. MOE: How many injuries due to handling reported each week?
    b. PTA: Farmers. MOE: How many injuries due to handling reported each week?
    c. PTA: School teachers. MOE: How many injuries due to handling reported each week?

PO C – Increase participation in democratic institutions.

SPOs:

1. TA uses national democratic institutions.
    a. PTA: Kurd males. MOE: On a daily basis, how many registered to vote?
    b. PTA: Kurd females. MOE: On a daily basis, how many registered to vote?
    c. PTA: Sunni males. MOE: On a daily basis, how many registered to vote?
    d. PTA: Sunni females. MOE: On a daily basis, how many registered to vote?
2. TA participates in the electoral process.
    a. PTA: Kurd females (18+). MOE: How many voted in the most recent elections?
    b. PTA: Sunni males (18+). MOE: How many voted in the most recent elections?
    c. PTA: Sunni females (18+). MOE: How many voted in the most recent elections?
    d. PTA: Shia males (18+). MOE: How many voted in the most recent elections?
    e. PTA: Shia females (18+). MOE: How many voted in the most recent elections?

CLASSIFICATION

Figure E-1. Sample PSYOP appendix (continued)

Appendix E

CLASSIFICATION

TAB B
DTG

PSYOP APPROVAL PROCESS

1. SITUATION: This appendix outlines the internal approval process within XX HQ for the staffing and approval of PSYOP series.
2. MISSION: See base appendix.
3. EXECUTION:
    a. Concept of the Operation: To make PSYOP timely and responsive in XX operations, the internal staffing and approval process must be as quick and simple as possible. Commander XX, or his designated approval authority, is the sole decision maker on the approval or disapproval of PSYOP series
    b. Where Approval Maintained at the XX Level:
    c. Staffing and Approval Process:
        (1) Staffing: The A/9POB TPDD Commander is responsible for the packaging, staffing, and final disposition of all staffed PSYOP series. The A/9POB TPDD commander will conduct internal staffing per SOP and then staff all series approval requests, simultaneously, with the Information Operations Coordinator (IOCOORD), Staff Judge Advocate (SJA), and public affairs officer. These staffing agencies will not have approval or disapproval authority over any PSYOP series. For planned operations, the A/9POB TPDD commander will submit PSYOP series staffing requests at 0800. **IF NO RESPONSE IS RECEIVED BY CLOSE OF BUSINESS ON THE DAY OF SUBMISSION, CONCURRENCE IS ASSUMED AND THE SERIES APPROVAL REQUEST WILL ENTER THE APPROVAL CHAIN.** After completion of the staffing process, the A/9POB TPDD commander will consolidate comments and prepare the request for entry into the approval process. Staffing sections will make comments on the form provided or will attach a point paper with their comments about the series. **SERIES STAFFING REQUESTS WILL NOT RETURN TO THE TPDD FOR CHANGES AT ANY POINT IN THIS PROCESS UNTIL FINAL APPROVAL OR DISAPPROVAL.** After completion of the staffing process, the A/9POB TPDD Commander will consolidate comments and prepare the request for entry into the approval process, including any Considerations of Nonconcurrence as a result of staffing.
        (2) Approval: After all staffing actions are completed, PSYOP series approval requests are submitted to the G-3 for review and comment. All staffing sections' comments will be available for review with explanations or comments from the A/9POB TPDD commander. The G-3 recommends approval or disapproval and forwards the request through the chief of staff to the XX commander or his designated approval authority for final approval.
        (3) Postapproval or disapproval actions: Following the XX commander 's final decision, the A/9POB TPDD commander will incorporate any changes directed by the approval chain and will prepare the series for execution. If the series is disapproved, the A/9POB TPDD commander will file the request and determine if an alternate means to achieve the same desired effect can be developed. All staffing and approval sheets will be maintained on file with the A/9POB TPDD commander for the duration of the operation.
        (4) SERVICE SUPPORT: See base appendix.
        (5) COMMAND AND SIGNAL: See base appendix.

CLASSIFICATION

Figure E-1. Sample PSYOP appendix (continued)

CLASSIFICATION

TAB C
DTG

PSYOP SITREP

MISSION: Operation Raging Eagle

SUBJECT: TPD SITREP Number

PERIOD COVERED:

1. PSYOP FORCES: Include status of personnel here; ensure that total numbers are included. Include PSYOP support systems and sensitive items—such as weapons, NVGs, pro-masks, loudspeakers, risographs, print presses, or radio stations, by element.

    a. Deployed.
    b. Attached.
    c. Detached.
    d. Principal Duty.

2. PAST OPERATIONS: Summarize the key activities of the last 24 hours in which PSYOP forces participated. Do not provide details here, as they will be covered elsewhere.

3. CURRENT OPERATIONS: List the major focus of ongoing and planned PSYOP the next 24 hours.

4. FUTURE OPERATIONS: List any missions that are upcoming in the next 48 hours that PSYOP will be supporting. Inform higher HQ if there will be any problems with executing PSYOP series as directed.

5. IMPACT INDICATORS AND SUMMARY: Detail the results of any patrols, dissemination missions, surveys, media meetings, and any impact indicators (answers to MOEs). Also attach any requested pretest and posttest results in tabular data here. This paragraph is the location to detail any PSYOP-relevant information for future use. List all products disseminated, locations of dissemination, and quantities of products disseminated per location.

6. LOGISTICS:

    a. Maintenance Status: Identify any deadline equipment here. If needing help with maintenance, request that here.
    b. Supply Status: List any supplies needed here, by quantity and priority.
    c. Available Assets: All available PSYOP assets—such as loudspeakers, radio equipment, and vehicles.
    d. Sensitive Items Report: Initial report: Entire inventory, by serial number. Subsequent reports: Status only.

7. PRODUCT REQUEST: Identify any products needed from the existing inventory in this location. Request products by product number and quantity.

8. COMMANDER'S COMMENTS: The senior PSYOP representative makes any necessary comments here.

CLASSIFICATION

Figure E-1. Sample PSYOP appendix (continued)

This page intentionally left blank.

Appendix F
Capabilities Brief

The first capabilities brief presented to a supported unit commander can set the tone for the future relationship of a tactical PSYOP force with the supported unit. First impressions are often lasting impressions, and the capabilities brief is key to establishing credibility and trust initially with the supported unit. It complements, if not completes, the integration process. The briefing must be planned, rehearsed, and tailored to the supported commander. Time available, type of unit, mission, and the commander's experience with PSYOP are the four main factors that influence the structure of the briefing. By tailoring the brief to the individual commander, the tactical PSYOP leader ensures that PSYOP have a role in the supported unit's concept of operations. The way the briefer presents himself and the briefing itself plays a critical role in the success or completion of his integration with the supported unit.

TECHNIQUES

F-1. Depending on the time available, the briefing can range from a full slide presentation or desk-side briefing to an oral presentation. Regardless of the briefing type or location, the briefing must be planned, rehearsed, and tailored to the individual supported commander.

PRESENTATION

F-2. The most important aspect of the capabilities brief is the presentation of the appropriate information. The briefer must prepare and deliver a professional brief (content, appearance, delivery). A professional brief will ensure that PSYOP capabilities will be fully nested in the supported unit's concept of operations.

F-3. Before presenting the briefing, the briefer should take time to observe other personnel in the area, specifically in the operations center. He should make sure he is in the same uniform as the uniform of supported unit personnel.

F-4. During his presentation, the briefer should speak clearly and confidently. He should be well rehearsed and have a complete understanding of the material in the briefing. Rehearsal increases the confidence level of the briefer and results in a more relaxed presentation. Prior preparation is critical to leaving an impression of professionalism and competency with the supported commander.

TAILORING THE CAPABILITIES BRIEF

F-5. The capabilities brief should be tailored for the individual commander. During integration, the briefer should inquire about the commander's exposure to PSYOP. If the briefer cannot find out this information ahead of time, he should address this subject at the beginning of his briefing.

F-6. The capabilities brief should be tailored for the type of unit and its mission. For example, if the tactical PSYOP element is supporting an MP unit with a mission to conduct I/R, then the briefer should specifically address how he can support that mission.

F-7. The briefer should limit his briefing to 3 to 5 minutes, if possible. He need not give a complete lesson on PSYOP—he should present only the essential information. For example, if the tactical PSYOP leader is conducting a battle handover or transfer of authority with another tactical PSYOP element, the brief may be focused on any changes in capabilities.

F-8. The briefer must be prepared to present his briefing to other members of the staff and subordinate commanders. In most cases, briefing the S-3 first will result in a brief that focuses on the information critical to the commander.

Appendix F

KEY INFORMATION

F-9. Several key pieces of information should be presented in the briefing. The briefer should advise the commander that he is the commander's subject-matter expert on PSYOP. The briefer must identify the command and support relationships, including where in the staff the briefer falls—for example, S-3 or FECC. The supported unit's SOP may dictate these relationships.

F-10. The briefing should start with the PSYOP mission statement. The statement should contain the supported unit's mission (based on the OPORD) and the SPOs that support mission accomplishment. The PSYOP mission statement for the briefing is similar to the mission statement in the PSYOP appendix.

F-11. The PSYOP element will provide the supported unit commander an operational picture from the PSYOP perspective. The operational picture should include—
- Propaganda and the ability of hostile elements to conduct propaganda within the supported unit commander's AI.
- Ongoing PSYOP programs within the supported unit commander's AI.
- Additional PSYOP support available, including support capabilities and limitations.

F-12. The briefer should explain his dual reporting chain—he has a coordinating chain for PSYOP-specific support, yet falls under the supported commander's chain of command. PSYOP approval will vary by echelon, so approval authorities at each level must be clarified if the supported unit has not had previous experience with the approval process in theater.

F-13. When presenting the capabilities brief, the briefer should advise the commander on the types of series he is currently resourced to execute, the series that are available, and the process and timeline for resourcing new series. The briefer should not go into great detail—he need not present a product book at this time. Upon request, the briefer should coordinate a time to present the series to the commander, staff, or subordinate commanders. The goal of the briefer is to ensure the command group understands the PSYOP capabilities that are currently available to the supported unit and the way additional PSYOP capabilities can be resourced.

CAPABILITIES BRIEF CONTENT

F-14. PSYOP capabilities and the supported unit's mission will determine the format and content of the capabilities brief. However, the PSYOP mission statement is critical because it links the SPOs with the supported unit's objectives. The brief may contain the following information; however, the actual content of the brief will be tailored to the specific supported commander:
- PSYOP mission statement (for example: On order TPT/TPD/TPC XXX will support the unit's mission by providing tactical PSYOP support to SPO A and SPO B).
- Command relationships.
- Person PSYOP are working for in the supported unit.
- PSYOP coordination chain.
- Propaganda assessment.
- Ongoing PSYOP programs and their effects in the supported unit's AOI.
- Additional organic capabilities.
- Higher PSYOP capabilities.
- Limitations on PSYOP and higher capabilities.
- Approval process and authority.
- Preapproved series that PSYOP are resourced to execute.
- Preapproved series that PSYOP are not resourced to execute.
- PSYOP MOEs.
- Series development timeline.
- Unresolved issues that require the supported commander's attention.

Appendix G
Tactical PSYOP Report and Request Formats

This appendix describes standardized formats for reporting information from TPT to TPD; TPD to company HQ; company to supported unit, PSE, or battalion HQ; and battalion to group or higher element. Various reports and their formats are discussed.

PSYOP SITUATION REPORT

G-1. PSYOP elements submit SITREPs to their higher HQ on a regular basis (daily or weekly, depending on the unit SOP). During battalion operations—where the companies and TPDs are not collocated with the battalion HQ, the company HQ, or the PDD—TPD commanders submit the SITREP to the company commander and he submits the report to the battalion or the POTF. When a TPD or TPT is deployed, it submits a SITREP (Figure G-1) daily or weekly (METT-TC) to its company HQ and S-3.

DTG
MISSION: Operation IRAQI FREEDOM
SUBJECT: TPT SITREP Number _____
PERIOD COVERED: _____

1. PSYOP FORCES. Include status of personnel (make sure total numbers are included). Include PSYOP support systems and sensitive items (such as weapons, NVGs, pro-masks, FOL, risographs, print presses, and radio stations) by element.
    a. Deployed.
    b. Attached.
    c. Detached.
    d. Principal Duty.

2. PAST OPERATIONS. Summarize the key activities of the last 24 hours in which PSYOP forces participated. Do not provide details here, as they will be covered elsewhere.

3. CURRENT OPERATIONS. List the major focus of ongoing and planned PSYOP the next 24 hours.

4. FUTURE OPERATIONS. List any missions upcoming in the next 48 hours that PSYOP will be supporting. Inform higher HQ if there will be any problems with executing PSYOP series as directed.

5. IMPACT INDICATORS AND SUMMARY. Detail the results of any patrols, dissemination missions, surveys, and media meetings, and any impact indicators (answers to MOE). Also attach, in tabular data, any requested pretest and posttest results. Also detail any PSYOP-relevant information for future use. List all products disseminated, locations of dissemination, and quantities of products disseminated per location.

6. LOGISTICS.
    a. Maintenance status. Identify any deadline equipment. Request any help needed with maintenance.
    b. Supply Status. List any supplies needed, by quantity and priority.
    c. Available Assets. Identify all available PSYOP assets (FOL, radio equipment, vehicles).
    d. Sensitive Items Report. In initial report, list entire inventory, by serial number. In subsequent reports, identify status only.

7. PRODUCT REQUEST. Identify any products needed from the existing inventory. Request products by product number and quantity.

8. COMMANDER'S COMMENTS. The senior PSYOP representative makes any necessary comments here.

Figure G-1. Sample SITREP format

Appendix G

MINE AND UNEXPLODED EXPLOSIVE ORDNANCE REPORT

G-2. The report format used to identify the location and type of mine or unexploded explosive ordnance (UXO) to units or HQ tasked to remove mines and UXO is as follows:

- Line 1. Date-Time Group: DTG item was discovered.
- Line 2. Reporting Activity: Unit identification code (UIC) and location (grid of UXO).
- Line 3. Contact Method: Radio frequency, call sign, POC, and telephone number.
- Line 4. Type of Ordnance: Dropped, projected, placed, or thrown. If available, supply the subgroup. Give the number of items, if more than one.
- Line 5. NBC Contamination: Be as specific as possible.
- Line 6. Resources Threatened: Report any equipment, facilities, or other assets that are threatened.
- Line 7. Impact on Mission: Provide a short description of current tactical situation and how the presence of the UXO affects status.
- Line 8. Protective Measures: Describe any measures taken to protect personnel and equipment.
- Line 9. Recommended Priority: Recommend a priority for response by explosive ordnance disposal technicians or engineers.
- Priority Basis:
  - *Immediate:* Stops the unit's maneuver and mission capability or threatens critical assets vital to the mission.
  - *Indirect:* Slows the unit's maneuver and mission capability or threatens critical assets important to the mission.
  - *Minor:* Reduces the unit's maneuver and mission capability or threatens noncritical assets of value.
  - *No Threat:* Has little or no effect on the unit's capabilities or assets.

Note. The priority requested must correspond with the tactical situation described on Line 7 of the report (Impact on Mission).

MEDICAL EVACUATION REQUEST

G-3. The medical evacuation (MEDEVAC) request includes the information shown in Figure G-2, pages G-2 and G-3.

---

1. LOCATION OF PICKUP.
2. RADIO FREQUENCY, CALL SIGN, AND SUFFIX.
3. NUMBER OF PATIENTS BY PRECEDENCE.
   - URGENT – Must be evacuated immediately and, in no case, more than 2 hours to save life, limb, and eyesight.
   - PRIORITY – Patient must be evacuated within 4 hours, or medical condition will deteriorate to urgent.
   - ROUTINE – Requires evacuation, but condition not expected to deteriorate within next 24 hours.
   - TACTICAL IMMEDIATE – Medical condition is not urgent or priority, but evacuation is needed as soon as possible (ASAP) to not endanger unit's tactical mission.
4. SPECIAL EQUIPMENT NEEDED. For example, hoist, ventilator, or jungle penetrator.
5. NUMBER OF PATIENTS BY LITTER AND AMBULATORY.

Figure G-2. MEDEVAC request

6. SECURITY TO PICKUP SITE (In peacetime, becomes TYPE OF INJURY, WOUND, OR ILLNESS).
   - No enemy troops in the area.
   - Possible enemy troops in the area.
   - Enemy troops in the area (approach with caution).
   - Enemy troops in the area (armed escort required).
7. METHOD OF MARKING PICKUP SITE.
8. PATIENT NATIONALITY AND STATUS.
   - U.S. Military.
   - U.S. Civilian.
   - Non-U.S. Military.
   - Non-U.S. Civilian.
   - EPW.
9. NBC CONTAMINATION (In peacetime, becomes TERRAIN DESCRIPTION).

Figure G-2. MEDEVAC request (continued)

This page intentionally left blank.

Appendix H
Leaflet Operations

This appendix describes leaflet dissemination operations and calculations from air platforms. Included are techniques for leaflet packing, calculations, plotting, and mission planning requirements for actual and training missions with dissemination aircraft.

GENERAL

H-1. Leaflet dissemination planning must be done after target analysis. The target analysis will determine the suitability of leaflet drops, the appropriate density on the ground, and the frequency of delivery. For example, a TAA determined that there are few literate people in a town being targeted. The social structure is such that there are fewer than 10 key communicators who make up the leadership. In this situation, only a few leaflets would be necessary. Leaflet density per 100 square meters would be appropriate at the minimum of 10 because the inhabitants of the village would take them to the leadership or to the few members who could read.

H-2. In preparation, the best size and weight for the leaflets should be determined. The content has no effect on the dissemination, but the size and weight are critical elements in determining the leaflets' ballistic data. If the mission dictates a leaflet characteristic that is not listed, personnel should choose the closest size and weight.

H-3. Successful leaflet-drop missions depend on an understanding of the behavior of leaflets falling through the air. Once released, leaflets are subject to drift and diffusion. Drift is the movement of the center of the leaflet cloud. Diffusion is the spread of the leaflets caused by wind turbulence and the ballistic characteristic of the leaflet. Identical leaflets do not fall at an identical rate. Individual differences between the leaflets and variations in the air cause identical leaflets to fall at slightly different rates. This creates a cloud that is taller than it is wide, making an oblong pattern on the ground (Figure H-1, page H-2). Plotting the ground pattern is essential to ensure that the target area is completely covered. Multiple release points may be required.

MISSION-PLANNING FACTORS

H-4. The following information must be known before any of the calculations are done, to aid the planner in determining the release point, proper dissemination pattern, and leaflet density:

- Density desired (10 to 30 leaflets per 100 square meters, depending on terrain and population of target area).
- Size and weight of the leaflet being used (needed for the appropriate descent and spread factors).
- Type of platform.
- Location of the target.
- Size of the target.
- Wind speed and azimuth around the target area in 1,000-foot increments below 10,000 feet and 2,000-foot increments above 10,000 feet.

H-5. At least 48 hours prior to dissemination, coordination must be effected through a mission-planning meeting with the aircrews flying the mission. On the day of the mission, the mission planner from the PSE must meet with the aircrews to go over last-minute data.

Appendix H

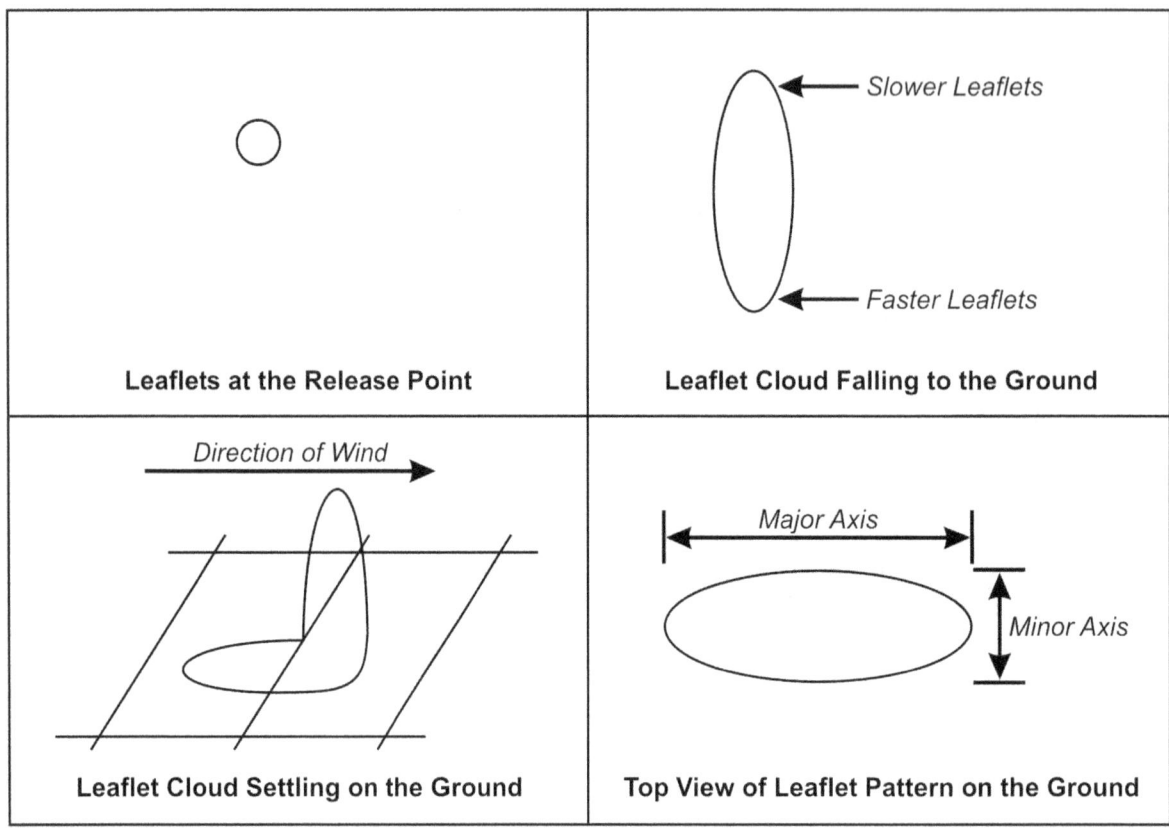

Figure H-1. Oblong pattern of leaflets on the ground

PLOTTING

H-6. The following items are needed:
- Pencil.
- Protractor (a navigation plotter works well for this and as a scale ruler).
- Map (preferably 1/100,000).
- Leaflet calculation worksheet.
- Tables with rates of descent, leaflet spread factors, and descent time factors.
- Calculator.
- Scale ruler.
- Overlay paper or acetate.
- Current weather data from the staff weather officer (SWO).

STEP 1

H-7. The first step in the leaflet drop calculation is to determine the size of the leaflet and the weight of the paper being used, which have a direct influence on how the leaflets will fly. Personnel fill in the information on the top of the leaflet work sheet (Figure H-2, page H-3). The work sheet and tables detailed on pages H-3 through H-9 show all the required information and the manual calculation process. Several automated spreadsheet programs are in use in the field to simplify leaflet calculations. Regardless, those responsible for leaflet calculations need to be familiar with and prepared to calculate leaflet data manually, if necessary.

Leaflet Operations

1. Mission Data:
   a. Mission number _____
   b. Product number _____
   c. Release altitude _____
   d. Release coordinates _____
   e. Target altitude _____
   f. Target coordinates _____

2. Leaflet Data:
   a. Size _____
   b. Paper weight _____
   c. Autorotator? Yes   No
   d. Rate of descent _____
   e. Spread factor _____
   f. Leaflets per pound _____
   g. Number of pounds _____
   h. Number in mission _____
   (Multiply item 2f by item 2g)

3. Descent Data:

Altitude (k = 1,000)	Descent Time Factor	x	Wind Speed (in Knots [kt])	=	Drift Distance (in Nautical Miles [NM])	@	Wind Azimuth (in Grid)
25k		x		=		@	
23k		x		=		@	
20k		x		=		@	
18k		x		=		@	
16k		x		=		@	
14k		x		=		@	
12k		x		=		@	
10k		x		=		@	
9k		x		=		@	
8k		x		=		@	
7k		x		=		@	
6k		x		=		@	
5k		x		=		@	
4k		x		=		@	
3k		x		=		@	
2k		x		=		@	
1k		x		=		@	
Surface		x		=		@	

4. Total Drift Distance _____ NM
   Sum of Drift Distance column

5. Maximum Deviation _____ NM
   Farthest distance from the net drift azimuth

6. Major Axis _____ NM
   .5 x release altitude / 6,076.115 + total drift x spread factor = NM

7. Minor Axis _____ NM
   .5 x release altitude / 6,076.115 + maximum deviation x spread factor = NM

8. Area in Square (sq) NM _____ sq NM
   .785 x minor axis x major axis = sq NM

9. Mean Density per Square NM _____
   Number of leaflets (item 2h) / sq NM (item 8) = mean density

10. Density per 100 Meters Square _____
    Mean density per sq NM (item 9) / 343

Figure H-2. Example of leaflet calculation work sheet

Appendix H

STEP 2

H-8. Personnel determine the rate of descent and spread factor from Table H-1, based on the size and weight of the leaflet. They fill in the information at the top of the work sheet.

Example: Using a 6- x 3-inch leaflet of 20-pound paper, the rate of descent is 2.5, the spread factor is 1.11, and the leaflet autorotates.

STEP 3

H-9. Using the leaflet descent time factor tables (Tables H-1 through H-4, pages H-4 through H-6), personnel write the time factors for each altitude from the surface to the projected release point, making sure to use the autorotating or non-autorotating table as appropriate. Using the wind data that the SWO provided, personnel write the wind speeds (in knots) in the wind speed column of the work sheet so they coincide with the altitudes that are in the first column. Personnel must change the wind directions provided by the SWO from magnetic to grid azimuths and place them in the azimuth (AZ) column of the work sheet.

Table H-1. Standard leaflet rates of descent and spread factor

Paper Size (in Inches)	Paper Weight (in Pounds)				
	9	13	16	20	60
8.5 x 8.5	2.9 / 0.24	2.5 / 0.31	2.7 / 0.26	2.8 / 0.35	
8.5 x 4.25	2.7 / 0.20	3.4 / 0.25	3.8 / 0.68	5.2 / 0.71	
8.5 x 3.09	3.0 / 0.15	3.2 / 0.15	3.6 / 0.65	_1.9_ / 0.42	
7.5 x 3				_1.8_ / 0.51	
6 x 4	2.3 / 0.26	2.7 / 0.37	3.3 / 0.63	4.0 / 0.46	
6 x 3	3.1 / 0.48	3.6 / 0.89	4.7 / 1.04	_2.5_ / 1.11	_1.8_ / 0.54
6 x 2	_2.3_ / 0.67	_1.3_ / 0.59	_1.6_ / 0.36	_1.7_ / 0.22	
6 x 1.5	_1.8_ / 0.30	_1.5_ / 0.09	_2.1_ / 0.17	_2.1_ / 0.22	
4 x 4	2.0 / 0.31	2.2 / 0.12	2.4 / 0.20	2.6 / 0.19	
4 x 3.2	2.2 / 0.18	2.4 / 0.12	2.6 / 0.11	3.0 / 0.16	
4 x 2.67	2.2 / 0.30	2.6 / 0.13	2.8 / 0.20	3.1 / 0.16	
4 x 2	2.1 / 0.13	_1.8_ / 0.27	_1.5_ / 0.05	_1.7_ / 0.05	
4 x 1.6	_1.3_ / 0.56	_1.3_ / 0.16	_1.4_ / 0.23	_1.7_ / 0.05	
4 x 1.23	_1.3_ / 0.24	_1.5_ / 0.34	_1.6_ / 0.28	_1.6_ / 0.65	
4 x 1	_1.3_ / 0.18	_1.6_ / 0.50	_1.9_ / 0.63	_2.1_ / 0.54	
NOTES: 1. The first number is the rate of descent; the second number is the spread factor. 2. Underlined numbers are leaflets that autorotate.					

Table H-2. Standard leaflets per pound

Paper Size (in inches)	Paper Weight (in Pounds)				
	9	13	16	20	60
8.5 x 8.5	288	199	162	129	
8.5 x 4.25	575	398	324	259	
8.5 x 3.09	791	548	445	<u>356</u>	
7.5 x 3				<u>416</u>	
6 x 4	866	599	487	390	
6 x 3	1,154	799	649	<u>519</u>	<u>440</u>
6 x 2	<u>1,731</u>	<u>1,199</u>	<u>974</u>	<u>779</u>	
6 x 1.5	<u>2,309</u>	<u>1,598</u>	<u>1,299</u>	1,039	
4 x 4	1,299	899	730	584	
4 x 3.2	1,623	1,124	913	730	
4 x 2.67	1,948	1,349	1,096	877	
4 x 2	2,597	<u>1,798</u>	<u>1,461</u>	1,169	
4 x 1.6	<u>3,247</u>	<u>2,248</u>	<u>1,826</u>	<u>1,461</u>	
4 x 1.23	<u>4,220</u>	<u>2,922</u>	<u>2,374</u>	<u>1,899</u>	
4 x 1	<u>5,194</u>	<u>3,596</u>	<u>2,922</u>	<u>2,338</u>	

NOTE: Underlined numbers are leaflets that autorotate.

Table H-3. Autorotating leaflet descent time factors

Autorotating Descent Rate	Surface	Thousands of Feet															
		1	2	3	4	5	6	7	8	9	10	12	14	16	18	20	23	25
1.3	.11	.21	.21	.21	.21	.20	.20	.20	.20	.19	.28	.37	.35	.34	.33	.39	.37	.48
1.4	.10	.20	.20	.19	.19	.19	.19	.18	.18	.18	.26	.34	.33	.32	.30	.36	.34	
1.5	.09	.18	.18	.18	.18	.18	.17	.17	.17	.17	.24	.32	.31	.29	.28	.34	.32	.42
1.6	.09	.17	.17	.17	.17	.17	.16	.16	.16	.16	.23	.30	.29	.28	.27	.32	.30	.40
1.7	.08	.16	.16	.16	.16	.16	.15	.15	.15	.15	.21	.28	.27	.26	.25	.30	.28	.37
1.8	.08	.15	.15	.15	.15	.15	.14	.14	.14	.14	.20	.26	.25	.25	.24	.28	.27	.35
1.9	.07	.15	.14	.14	.14	.14	.14	.14	.13	.13	.19	.25	.24	.23	.22	.27	.25	.33
2.1	.07	.13	.13	.13	.13	.12	.12	.12	.12	.12	.17	.23	.22	.21	.20	.24	.23	.30
2.3	.06	.12	.12	.12	.12	.12	.11	.11	.11	.11	.16	.21	.20	.19	.18	.22	.21	.27
2.5	.06	.11	.11	.11	.11	.11	.10	.10	.10	.10	.10	.15	.19	.18	.18	.17	.20	.19
2.0	.05	.14	.14	.14	.14	.13	.13	.13	.13	.13	.19	.25	.24	.23	.22	.26	.24	.31
2.1	.05	.13	.13	.13	.13	.13	.13	.13	.12	.12	.18	.24	.23	.22	.21	.25	.23	.30
2.2	.04	.13	.12	.12	.12	.12	.12	.12	.12	.12	.10	.22	.22	.21	.20	.24	.22	.28
2.3	.04	.12	.12	.12	.12	.12	.12	.11	.11	.11	.17	.21	.21	.20	.19	.23	.21	.27
2.4	.04	.12	.11	.11	.11	.11	.11	.11	.11	.11	.16	.21	.20	.19	.18	.22	.20	.26
2.5	.04	.11	.11	.11	.11	.11	.11	.11	.10	.10	.15	.20	.19	.18	.18	.21	.19	.25
2.6	.04	.11	.11	.11	.10	.10	.10	.10	.10	.10	.15	.19	.18	.18	.17	.20	.19	.24
2.7	.04	.10	.10	.10	.10	.10	.10	.10	.10	.10	.14	.18	.18	.17	.16	.19	.18	.23
2.8	.03	.10	.10	.10	.10	.10	.10	.09	.09	.09	.14	.18	.17	.16	.16	.19	.17	.22
2.9	.03	.10	.09	.09	.09	.09	.09	.09	.09	.09	.13	.17	.16	.16	.15	.18	.17	.22

Appendix H

Table H-4. Non-autorotating leaflet descent time factors

Non-Autorotating Descent Rate	Surface	Thousands of Feet																
		1	2	3	4	5	6	7	8	9	10	12	14	16	18	20	23	25
3.0	.03	.09	.09	.09	.09	.09	.09	.09	.09	.09	.13	.16	.16	.15	.15	.17	.16	.21
3.1	.03	.09	.09	.09	.09	.09	.09	.09	.08	.08	.12	.16	.15	.15	.14	.17	.16	.20
3.2	.03	.09	.09	.09	.09	.08	.08	.08	.08	.08	.12	.15	.15	.14	.14	.16	.15	.20
3.3	.03	.08	.08	.08	.08	.08	.08	.08	.08	.08	.12	.15	.14	.14	.13	.16	.15	.19
3.4	.03	.08	.08	.08	.08	.08	.08	.08	.08	.08	.11	.15	.14	.13	.13	.15	.14	.18
3.6	.03	.08	.08	.08	.08	.07	.07	.07	.07	.07	.11	.14	.13	.13	.12	.14	.14	.17
3.8	.03	.07	.07	.07	.07	.07	.07	.07	.07	.07	.10	.13	.13	.12	.12	.14	.13	.16
4.0	.02	.07	.07	.07	.07	.07	.07	.07	.07	.06	.10	.12	.12	.11	.11	.13	.12	.16
4.7	.02	.06	.06	.06	.06	.06	.06	.06	.05	.08	.11	.10	.10	.09	.11	.10	.13	.17
5.2	Data not available																	

STEP 4

H-10. To determine the drift in nautical miles, personnel should multiply the descent time factor by the wind speed at each altitude, as shown in the example in Table H-5. The drift identifies how far the leaflets will move laterally through that altitude.

Table H-5. Example of leaflet drifts

Altitude	Descent Time Factor	Wind Speed	Drift (NM)	at	AZ (Degrees)
Surface	.06	5 kt	.30	at	180
1,000 feet	.11	7 kt	.77	at	196
2,000 feet	.11	10 kt	1.1	at	210
Total Drift = 2.17					

STEP 5

H-11. Personnel start at the center of the target on a map. The USAF provides wind azimuths for the direction the wind is coming from, so when plotting from the surface up, it is not necessary to calculate back azimuths. Using the example, personnel start with the surface drift distance (.30) and azimuth (180). Using the protractor or plotter, personnel mark a 180° line from their starting point. They use the scale ruler or plotter and mark a point .30 nautical miles away from the center point along the 180° azimuth. Next, they mark a 196° line from the last point they marked. Personnel measure .77 nautical miles along this azimuth and plot the 2,000-foot drift distance. The example in Figure H-3, page H-7, shows the path of the leaflet cloud.

STEP 6

H-12. The maximum deviation is the greatest distance between the net drift line and the actual flight pattern of the leaflets. The maximum deviation line shows how far the leaflets will stray from the net drift line and is used to determine the minor axis of the ground pattern. In the example (Figure H-3, page H-7), the maximum deviation is 1.02 nautical miles.

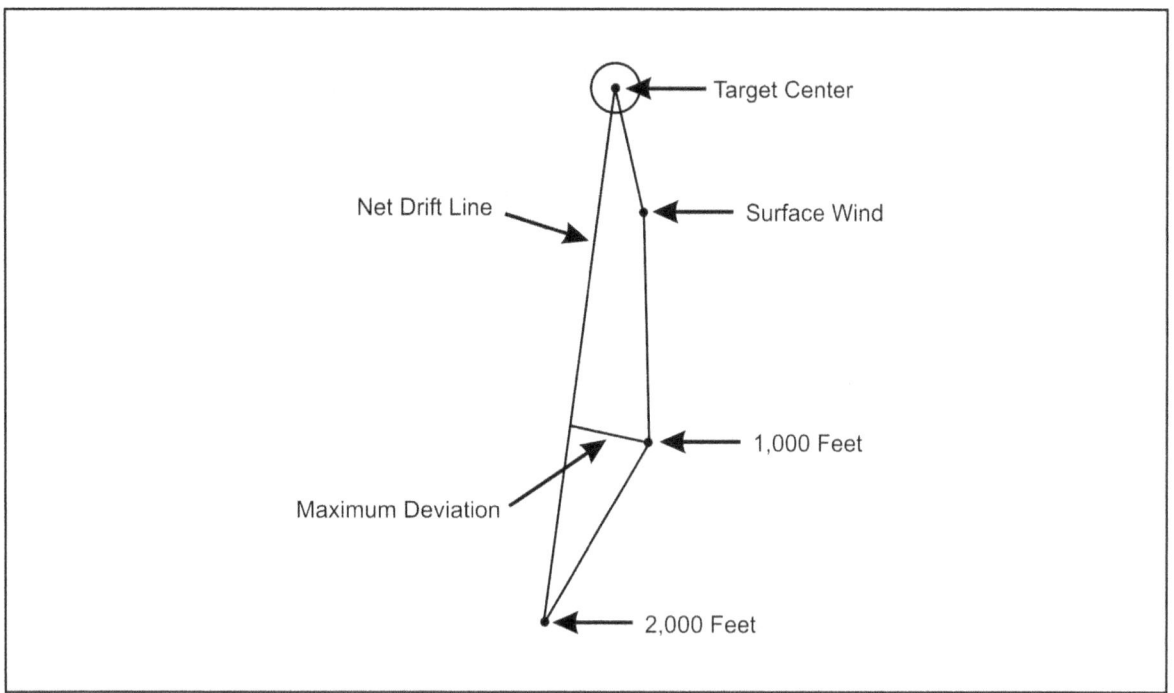

Figure H-3. Path of the leaflet cloud

STEP 7

H-13. Personnel determine the major axis. The major axis is the long axis that follows the leaflet path. As shown in Table H-6, the major axis is calculated using this formula: .5 (release altitude) / 6,076.115 + (total drift) spread factor = NM. The total drift distance for this example is 2.17 NM; 6,076.115 is used to convert feet to nautical miles.

Table H-6. Example of major axis determination

Release Altitude	+	(Total Drift) Spread Factor	=	NM
.5 (2,000) / 6,076.115	+	(.3 + .77 + 1.1) 1.11	=	2.565
1,000 / 6,076.115	+	(.3 + .77 + 1.1) 1.11	=	2.565
0.165	+	(.3 + .77 + 1.1) 1.11	=	2.565
0.165	+	(2.17) 1.11	=	2.565
0.165	+	2.4	=	2.565 NM

STEP 8

H-14. Personnel determine the minor axis. The minor axis is the greatest width of the short axis of the leaflet pattern. As shown in Table H-7, page H-8, the minor axis is calculated similarly to the major axis. The only difference is that the maximum deviation distance is substituted for the total drift distance. The minor axis is calculated by using this formula: .5 (release altitude) / 6,076.115 + (maximum deviation) spread factor = NM. It is plotted by taking the total from the formula and plotting it perpendicular to the major axis and over the target area. The maximum deviation for this example is 1.02 NM. Figure H-4, page H-8, shows the final pattern in which 90 percent of the leaflets will land.

Appendix H

Table H-7. Example of minor axis determination

Release Altitude	+	(Maximum Deviation) Spread Factor	=	NM
.5 (2000) / 6076.115	+	(1.02) 1.11	=	1.297
1000 / 6076.115	+	(1.02) 1.11	=	1.297
0.165	+	(1.02) 1.11	=	1.297
0.165	+	1.132	=	1.297

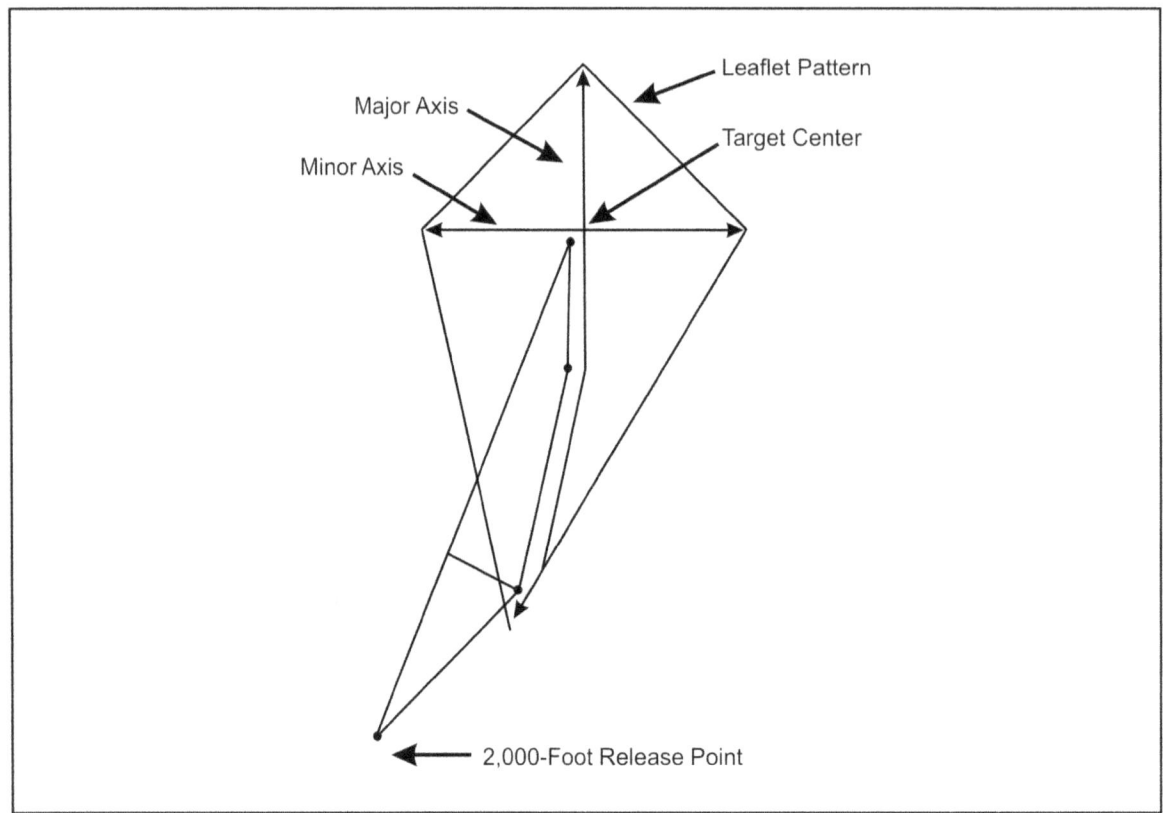

Figure H-4. Pattern in which 90 percent of the leaflets will land

STEP 9

H-15. The final steps show if the leaflet density coincides with the commander's intent of 10 to 30 leaflets per 100 square meters. First, personnel determine the area of the leaflet pattern on the ground. The formula to determine the area is .785 (major axis) minor axis = NM; .785 is used to calculate an ellipse and is p (pi, or 3.14) divided by 4.

Example: .785 (2.565) 1.297 = 2.612 NM

STEP 10

H-16. Personnel determine the mean density per square nautical mile. For this formula, the area of the pattern (2.612) must be used. The formula is number of leaflets / area = leaflets per nautical mile.

Example: 20,000 / 2.612 = 7656.968 leaflets per NM

STEP 11

H-17. Personnel determine the density per 100 square meters. This portion tells the commander if the 10 to 30 leaflet requirements are met. Using the mean density (7,656.968), the formula is mean density / 343 = leaflets per 100 square meters. Personnel should note that there are 343 units of 100 square meters in 1 square nautical mile.

Example: 7,656.968 / 343 = 22.324 rounded off to 22 leaflets per 100 square meters

STEP 12

H-18. All the calculations and map plotting are now completed. The key point in the calculation process is the release altitude. The plotter should ask himself the following questions:

- Does the release altitude fit in with the flight requirements of the air platform being used?
- Does the ground pattern cover the desired target area, and does the number of leaflets per 100 square meters meet the commander's requirements?

H-19. If these questions are answered with a "yes," the mission should be successful. If not, there are some ways to meet the mission requirements. If the ground pattern does not cover the target, personnel should go up in altitude. The higher the altitude, the larger the area covered. If the number of leaflets per 100 square meters is not enough, two things can be considered—increase the number of leaflets being dropped or lower the altitude of the drop. If the leaflets per 100 square meters are over the limit, personnel should stay with the original release point using fewer leaflets or go up in altitude and make the ground pattern larger. Before the altitude is changed, personnel must ensure that the air planners and pilots are informed and that they agree to the change in altitude. Figure H-2, page H-3, provides an example of a leaflet calculation work sheet used for leaflet dissemination planning.

H-20. Attention must be paid to the possibility of violating sovereign international boundaries during leaflet operations. Notification and coordination must be made whenever there is potential that either aircraft or leaflets may cross into or land in a third country.

AIRCRAFT

H-21. Most Department of Defense fixed- and rotary-wing platforms can be used to disseminate leaflets. Tactical PSYOP forces normally disseminate leaflets by hand, by trash bag, or by leaflet box, depending on the aircraft type and tactical situation.

H-22. The C-130 is used when there is minimal threat in the area and the airplane can fly at low altitudes. This is beneficial because the lower the drop, the less effect wind gusts will have on the flight of the leaflet. The C-130 has the ability to carry more than 1 million leaflets in 20 boxes. When dropping leaflets out of a C-130, a PSYOP NCO or officer should be on board in case the winds shift in flight and last-minute calculations are needed to determine a new release point. Also, 81Ls may be required to help the loadmaster in hooking and kicking the boxes out of the airplane. The airplane should fly at about 190 knots when the leaflets are kicked out. Anything faster causes the leaflets to get sucked back into the airplane. The aircraft commander determines the speed, so he should be made aware of speed requirements. The release altitude on a C-130 drop is always left up to the pilots flying the mission. They know the safety issues of the aircraft and the current intelligence and air threat from the target area. In the meeting 48 hours out, the OIC or NCOIC of the leaflet mission should discuss what the optimum altitude should be with the navigator. They should determine a "no higher than" and a "no lower than" limit. Once these altitudes are determined, they can be used for planning purposes. The actual altitude will not be known until the winds are determined for the actual day of the drop. On the mission day, the altitude that suits the required leaflet coverage is used.

H-23. Rotary-wing aircraft—such as the CH-47, UH-60, and others—can be used to disseminate leaflets. Leaflet boxes, trash bags, and simply tossing leaflets out by hand are some common dissemination methods used. In some cases, the aircrew will not allow static-line leaflet boxes to be used because of the risk of the boxes (after deployment) being sucked up into the rotors due to the rotor wash. Personnel should check with the aircrew or liaison prior to mission execution. Trash bags are a very effective means of dissemination.

Appendix H

This method alleviates the risk of anything attached to the aircraft coming into contact with the rotors. To use this method, personnel should—

- Untie the opening of the trash bag.
- With one hand on the opening, push forward with the other hand from the bottom toward the opening, turning the trash bag inside out.
- Once emptied, secure the trash bag out of the way and continue.

H-24. Improvised leaflet boxes are another effective method of disseminating leaflets from rotary wing aircraft. As with the trash bags, this method alleviates the risk of anything attached to the aircraft encountering the rotors. In addition, the boxes add a measure of protection for the leaflets and prevent leaflets from coming loose inside the aircraft. To use this method, personnel should—

- Hold the box by the handle at the edge of the door.
- On command, execute a quick jerking motion, causing the bottom of the box to open and the leaflets to disseminate.
- Once emptied, secure the box out of the way and continue.

STATIC-LINE BOX

H-25. At high altitudes, the use of leaflet bundles or boxes opened by a static line has proved effective. Through use of rollers on the deck of the aircraft, boxes weighing up to 49.90 kilograms can be ejected with minimum exertion. The box is rolled out of the aircraft, and as the container comes to the end of the static line, the sides of the box split (Figure H-5). In effect, the box is turned inside out, and the leaflets fall away from the empty box. Figure H-6, page H-11, shows the steps required in preparing boxes for high-altitude, static-line dissemination.

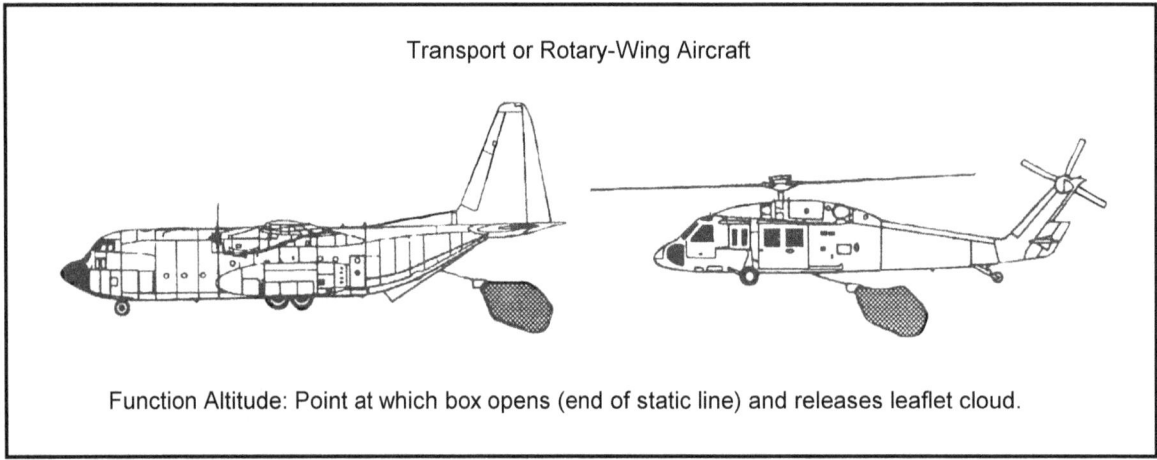

Figure H-5. Static-line box employment

Leaflet Operations

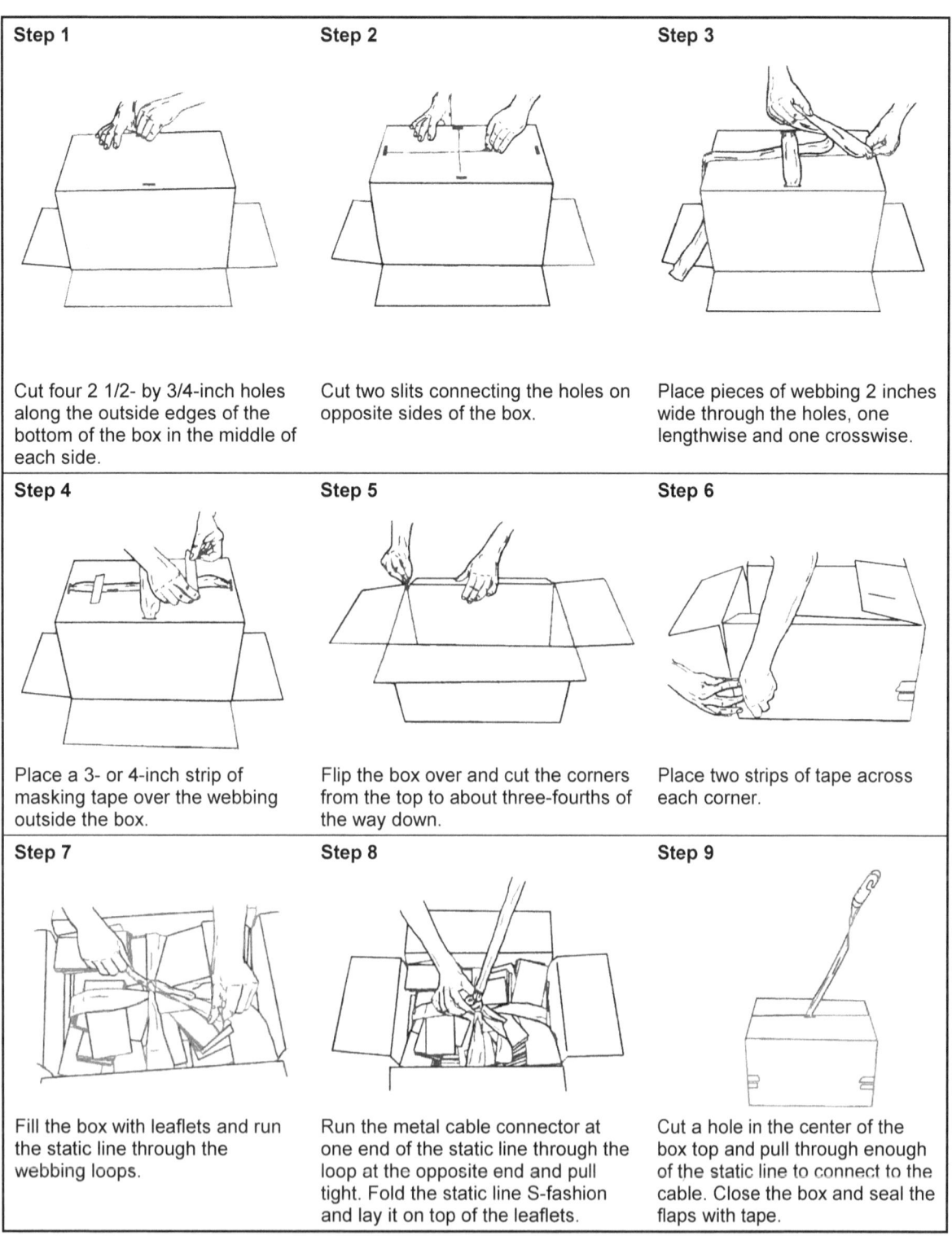

Figure H-6. Steps in the assembly of the static-line box

This page intentionally left blank.

Appendix I
Tactical Psychological Operations Team Battlefield Survival Techniques

TPTs must be adept at moving as an element of a mounted or dismounted tactical formation. TPTs must also be prepared to move and operate autonomously when required. Movement formations, techniques, and battle drills may vary, depending on the type of unit and an individual unit's SOP. To function effectively in a tactical environment, PSYOP leaders and Soldiers must have a basic knowledge of the tactical doctrine of the unit they are supporting. This appendix provides a basic overview of movement and land navigation techniques in current Army doctrine. These techniques and battle drills focus on squad and platoon elements based on the concept of making contact with the smallest element possible and subsequently developing the situation.

TACTICAL PSYCHOLOGICAL OPERATIONS TEAM PREPARATIONS

I-1. When conducting premission planning, TPTs consider the—
- *Mission.* The mission determines the required PSYOP-specific equipment, ammunition, and classes of supply.
- *Enemy and friendly situation.* Routes of marches, obstacles (friendly and enemy), danger areas, and possible ambush sites and kill zones should all be considered when planning a movement.
- *Troops available.* TPTs must be proficient in mounted and dismounted tactical operations. Tactical PSYOP personnel require repetitive training in dismounted and mounted navigation during day and night movement, cross-country and night driving with and without night vision devices, mounted navigation, vehicle maintenance, assisted and self-recovery operations, and crew-served weapons usage.
- *Terrain and weather.* Terrain and weather affect route planning, required personal equipment, and special equipment needs. Light conditions determine the time available for movement with regard to the enemy situation.
- *Time and distance.* Time and distance affect the amount of fuel, packaged POL, repair parts, food, and water required for the mission.
- *Civilian populace.* Mission planning must consider the local civilians in the AO, their effect on mission success, and the psychological impact of friendly operations on local civilians.
- *Equipment and supplies.* METT-TC considerations determine the TPT's equipment and logistical requirements. Identifying and projecting resupply requirements are critical for continuous operations. PSYOP-specific equipment must be cross-leveled among the TPT for dismounted operations. For mounted operations, a functional load plan for the vehicle should be in place.

EQUIPMENT AND PERSONNEL PREPARATION

I-2. All TPT equipment must be inspected and tested to ensure it is functional before mission execution. TPT leaders ensure the completion of all premission requirements.

Appendix I

VEHICLE PREPARATION

I-3. TPT personnel make all preparations necessary for airland, airdrop, amphibious, and cross-country movement. They must plan for and spend sufficient time to prepare their vehicles for mounted operations.

I-4. TPTs prepare their vehicles using a standard load plan from the unit SOP and tailored from mission requirements. The load plan standardizes the location of equipment on vehicles, thus ensuring that any personnel can locate or pack equipment on any unit vehicle.

I-5. TPTs plan for sufficient fuel supplies as well (Figure I-1). If a TPT is operating independently, fuel trucks or fuel points may not be available. A standard amount is 9 miles per gallon (mpg) for estimating fuel requirements.

```
                _____ Total miles of mission (mission distance)
Divide by       _____ Vehicle mpg average
                            Light load highway       = 12 mpg
                            Heavy load highway       = 10 mpg
                            Light load cross-country = 10 mpg
                            Heavy load cross-country =  7 mpg
                            Fully loaded trailer     = subtract 5 mpg
Equals          _____ Gallons necessary per vehicle
Plus            _____ Percent of gallons necessary
                            1:250,000 = 15 percent
                Added for map error 1:100,000 = 10 percent
                            1:50,000  =  5 percent
Equals          _____ Adjusted gallons necessary per vehicle
Multiply by     _____ Number of vehicles on mission
Equals          _____ Gallons necessary for detachment
Plus            _____ 15 percent safety factor
Equals          _____ Total detachment fuel requirements
Minus           _____ Gallons carried in vehicle fuel tanks
                      (25 gallons per vehicle tank)
Equals          _____ Gallons of fuel to be carried in 5-gallon fuel cans
Divide by       _____ Gallons per can (U.S. fuel can = 5 gallons)
Equals          _____ 5-gallon cans necessary for remaining fuel requirements
```

Figure I-1. Fuel estimation formula

ADEQUATE WATER, FOOD, AND AMMUNITION

I-6. A standard quantity for planning water supply is 4 to 6 quarts of water per Soldier per day for mounted operations. Additional water may be required for dismounted operations. Water carried on individual load-bearing equipment is not included in this estimate. Water from vehicle stores should be consumed before using personal stores. The formula in Figure I-2 may be used for planning the needed water supply. TPTs plan for adequate food supplies. A general rule of thumb is to have a 3-day ration for each man on the vehicle.

```
                _____ Number of personnel
Multiply by     _____ Number of quarts per day (minimum 4 to 6 quarts)
Multiply by     _____ Number of days of mission duration
Equals          _____ Mission water requirements
Plus            _____ 15 percent safety factor
Equals          _____ Total water requirement
Divide by       _____ Gallons per can (U.S. water can = 5 gallons)
```

Figure I-2. Water estimation formula

Tactical Psychological Operations Team Battlefield Survival Techniques

I-7. TPTs should make sure ammunition is placed where it can be accessed quickly. Personnel should secure large ammunition cans to prevent injury from shifting loads due to accidents or rough terrain. Signal munitions should be positioned near the TPT leader's position.

FUNDAMENTALS OF MOVEMENT

I-8. A commander's estimate of the situation helps him decide how to move his unit most effectively. However, no set method exists for making this determination. The fundamentals in the following paragraphs provide guidance for planning effective tactical movements.

MOVEMENT VERSUS MANEUVER

I-9. Maneuver is movement supported by fire to gain a position of advantage over the enemy. At company and battalion level, the two overlap considerably. When planning company movements, the commander ensures the unit is moving in a way that supports a rapid transition to maneuver. Once contact with the enemy is made, squads and platoons execute the appropriate battle drill leaders design to maneuver their units.

TERRAIN AND WEATHER

I-10. Maneuver elements should move on covered and concealed routes. Moving during periods of reduced visibility provides more concealment, and the enemy may be less alert during these periods. TPTs should avoid known danger areas.

CAMOUFLAGE

I-11. For the TPT, camouflage can mean the difference between life and death. Camouflage measures are important because the team must not be detected at any time when moving alone, operating as part of another element, or operating from a loudspeaker position. Knowing how and when to camouflage can enable the TPT to escape becoming a target. The team must be camouflage-conscious from the time it departs on a mission until returning. Paying attention to camouflage fundamentals is a mark of a well-trained TPT. FM 20-3, Camouflage, Concealment, and Decoys, provides detailed information on camouflage.

I-12. TPTs must pay careful attention when using camouflage clothing and equipment (natural and artificial). They should apply the following fundamental rules when determining their camouflage needs:
- Take advantage of all available natural concealment, such as trees, bushes, grass, earth, man-made structures, and shadows.
- Alter the form, shadow, texture, and color of objects.
- Camouflage against ground and air observation.
- Camouflage a loudspeaker position, as it is prepared:
    - Study the terrain and vegetation in the area. Arrange grass, leaves, brush, and other natural camouflage to conform to the area.
    - Use only as much material as is needed. Excessive use of material (natural or artificial) can reveal a TPT's position.
    - Obtain natural material over a wide area. Do not strip an area, as this may attract the enemy's attention.

SECURITY

I-13. A primary responsibility of the TPT leader is to protect his TPT at all times. Protection is especially critical during movement because the TPT is extremely vulnerable to enemy fires. In addition to the fundamentals listed earlier, the TPT leader provides security for the TPT by—
- Using the proper movement formation and technique.
- Moving as fast as the situation will allow. (This tactic may degrade the enemy's ability to detect the TPT and the effectiveness of his fires once detected.)

Appendix I

- Ensuring that security elements are positioned to the flanks, front, and rear at a distance that prevents enemy direct fire on the main body. (Normally, the company formation and movement technique provide greater security to the front. The flanks and rear that must be secured by these security elements. The company SOP should state who is responsible for providing the security elements.)
- Enforcing noise and light discipline.
- Ensuring all personnel camouflage themselves and their equipment.

MOVEMENT FORMATIONS

I-14. Mounted and dismounted formations are similar and often differ only in the rate of travel and distance between elements in the formation. Supported unit SOPs, force protection postures, unit battle drills, and other factors will determine placement and movement techniques of the TPT. Regardless of the size of the element, the TPT is generally placed in proximity to the element leader, similar to the positioning of the radio/telephone operator (RTO). However, it is up to the TPT leader to ensure he is placed where he can best support the commander, as determined by the supported commander.

TACTICAL PSYCHOLOGICAL OPERATIONS TEAM EMPLOYMENT

I-15. When traveling with a larger unit (mounted or dismounted), the TPT is positioned in a movement formation where it can best accomplish its mission. The TPT travels near the supported unit's command group when not engaged in a mission. The supported unit should provide security; however, the TPT should be prepared to react to contact if required. The movement commander dictates the specific location of the TPT within a formation, as advised by the TPT leader.

I-16. TPTs may move with a small security element separate from a larger formation in order to execute a PSYOP mission. In this instance, the TPT leader and the senior member of the security element need to coordinate how the movement will be executed and who will be the movement commander. The TPT leader must inform the senior member of the security element of his requirements in order to support the execution of the PSYOP mission.

MOVEMENT TECHNIQUES

I-17. Movement techniques (Table I-1) are the manner in which a unit traverses terrain. The three types of movement techniques are traveling, traveling overwatch, and bounding overwatch. The selection of a movement technique is based on the likelihood of enemy contact and the need for speed. Factors to consider for each technique are control, dispersion, speed, and security. Movement techniques are not fixed formations. They refer to the distances between Soldiers, teams, squads, platoons, and companies that vary based on mission, enemy, terrain, visibility, and any other factor that affects control. Soldiers must be able to see their immediate leader. A squad leader must be able to see his fire team leaders. A platoon leader should be able to see his lead squad leader. A TPT chief should be able to see all members of the TPT and the leader of the element with which he is moving. Company and battalion commanders position themselves where they can best see and control their units. Leaders control movement with arm-and-hand signals. They use radios only when needed. Any of the three movement techniques can be used with any formation.

Table I-1. Movement techniques and characteristics

Movement Techniques	When Normally Used	Characteristics			
		Control	Dispersion	Speed	Security
Traveling	Contact not likely	More	Less	Fastest	Least
Traveling Overwatch	Contact possible	Less	More	Slower	More
Bounding Overwatch	Contact expected	Most	Most	Slowest	Most

Tactical Psychological Operations Team Battlefield Survival Techniques

NAVIGATION TECHNIQUES

I-18. There are many different methods for moving from one location to another, just as there are many environments in which the TPT may move. Mounted navigation and nighttime movements are common operational environments. The use of navigational aids is also changing. GPSs are quickly becoming more common; however, they do not replace a map and a compass.

GLOBAL POSITIONING SYSTEM

I-19. The global positioning system (GPS) is a satellite-based, radio navigational system. It consists of a constellation with 24 active satellites that interface with a ground-, air-, or sea-based receiver. Each satellite transmits data that enable the GPS receiver to provide the user the precise position and time. GPS receivers come in several configurations—handheld, vehicle-mounted, aircraft-mounted, and watercraft-mounted. FM 3-25.26, *Map Reading and Land Navigation*, provides detailed information on the GPS. The following paragraphs discuss some of the basic information on GPS capabilities, limitations, and employment.

I-20. The GPS is based on satellite ranging. It figures the user's position on earth by measuring the distance from a group of satellites in space to the user's location. For accurate three-dimensional data, the receiver must track four or more satellites. Most GPS receivers provide the user with the number of satellites it is tracking and whether the signals are good. Some receivers can be manually switched to track only three satellites if the user knows his altitude. This method provides the user with accurate data much faster than that provided by tracking four or more satellites. Each type of receiver has mode keys with a variety of functions. (*Note.* The GPS operator's manual provides detailed information on how the GPS receiver operates.)

I-21. The GPS provides worldwide, 24-hour, all-weather, day-or-night coverage when the satellite constellation is complete. The GPS can locate the position of the user accurately to within 21 meters—95 percent of the time. In some cases, the GPS has accurately located the position of the user within 8 to 10 meters. It can determine the distance and direction from the user to a programmed location or the distance between two programmed locations called way points. The GPS provides exact date and time for the time zone in which the user is located.

I-22. Unlike the compass, the GPS receiver set on navigation mode guides the user to a selected way point by actually telling the user how far left or right the user has drifted from the desired azimuth. With this option, the user can take the most expeditious route possible, moving around an obstacle or area without replotting and reorienting. While in the navigation mode, the user can navigate to a way point using steering and distance, and the receiver can tell him how far he has left to travel and for how long, at the current speed.

I-23. A constellation of 24 satellites broadcasts precise signals for use by navigational sets. The satellites are arranged in six rings that orbit the earth twice each day. The GPS navigational signals are similar to light rays, so anything that blocks the light reduces or blocks the effectiveness of the signals. The more unobstructed the view of the sky, the better the system performs.

LAND NAVIGATION TECHNIQUES

I-24. Land navigation techniques can greatly enhance a tactical PSYOP element's effectiveness in the field. Using the techniques can ensure that TPTs successfully plan and conduct movement during dismounted and mounted operations. A TPT should be able to navigate from one point on the ground to another, with or without a compass, to arrive at the correct location at the right time. Staying on the route is accomplished through the use of one navigation technique or a combination of two—dead reckoning and terrain association. These techniques, along with other proven land navigation techniques, are discussed in the following paragraphs.

Appendix I

Deliberate Offset

I-25. Deliberate offset is a planned magnetic deviation to the left or right of an azimuth. It is used when approaching a linear object from an oblique angle. A drift of 18 meters exists for every degree at 1,000 meters.

Steering Marks

I-26. Steering marks should not be determined from a map study. They are selected as movement progresses and are commonly on or near the highest points seen along the azimuth line followed when they are selected. They may be uniquely shaped trees, rocks, hilltops, posts, towers, and buildings—any object that can be easily identified. If a good steering mark to the front is not seen, a back azimuth to some feature behind should be used until a good steering mark appears in front. Characteristics of a good steering mark include the following:

- A good steering mark must have some characteristics about it—such as color, shade of color, size, or shape (preferably all four)—that will assure the navigator that the mark will continue to be recognized as he approaches it.
- If several easily distinguished objects appear along the line of march, the navigator should select the most distant object as the steering mark. This procedure enables the navigator to travel farther with fewer references to the compass. If the navigator has many options, he should select the highest object. A higher mark is not as easily lost to sight as is a lower mark that blends into the background as it is approached. A steering mark should be continuously visible as the navigator moves toward it.
- Steering marks selected at night must have unique shapes more distinguishable than those selected during daylight. As darkness approaches, colors disappear and objects appear as black or gray silhouettes. Instead of seeing shapes, the navigator sees only the general outlines that may appear to change as he moves and sees the objects from slightly different angles.

Handrails

I-27. Handrails are linear features—such as roads or highways, railroads, power transmission lines, ridgelines, or streams—that run roughly parallel to the direction of travel. Instead of a precision compass, a rough compass without steering marks may be used if the feature travels to the right or left. It acts as a handrail to guide the way.

Backstops

I-28. A backstop is a linear terrain feature—such as a river or a road—used to prevent overshooting the target. It should be no more than 100 meters beyond the destination.

Catching Feature

I-29. A catching feature is a prominent, preselected feature that warns the navigator he has gone too far. When reaching this point, the navigator must change direction.

Attack Point

I-30. The catching feature may also be a navigational attack point—the place where area navigation ends and point navigation begins. From this last easily identified checkpoint, the navigator moves cautiously and precisely along a given azimuth for a specified distance to locate the final objective. The selection of this navigational attack point is important. A distance of 500 meters or less is most desirable.

Dead Reckoning

I-31. Dead reckoning consists of two fundamental steps. The first step is to use a protractor and graphic scales to determine the direction and distance from one point to another on a map. The second step is to use a compass and some means of measuring distance to apply this information on the ground. In other words, the step begins with determining a polar coordinate on a map and ends with finding the location on the ground.

I-32. Dead reckoning along a given route is the application of the same process used by a mapmaker as he establishes a measured line of reference upon which to construct the framework of his map. Therefore, triangulation exercises (either resection or intersection) can be easily undertaken by the navigator at any time to determine or confirm precise locations along or near his route. Between these position-fixes, the navigator establishes his location by measuring or estimating the distance traveled along the azimuth being followed from the previous known point. The navigator may use pacing, a vehicle odometer, or the application of elapsed time for this purpose, depending upon the situation.

I-33. Most dead-reckoning movements do not consist of single straight-line distances because the tactical and navigational aspects of the terrain, enemy situation, natural and man-made obstacles, time, and safety factors cannot be ignored. Another reason most dead-reckoning movements are not single straight-line distances is that pace counts and compasses are imprecise measures. Error from these measurements compounds over distance and, therefore, takes someone far from his intended route, even if the procedures are performed correctly. The only way to counteract this occurrence is to reconfirm the location by terrain association or resection. Routes planned for dead reckoning generally consist of a series of straight-line distances between several checkpoints with perhaps some travel running on or parallel to roads or trails.

Advantages

I-34. There are two advantages to dead reckoning. First, dead reckoning is easy to teach and to learn. Second, dead reckoning can be a highly accurate way of moving from one point to another if done carefully over short distances, even when few external cues are present to guide the movements.

I-35. During daylight, across open country, and along a specified magnetic azimuth, the navigator should not walk with the compass in the open position and in front of him. Because the compass does not stay steady or level, it does not give an accurate reading when held or used this way. The navigator should begin at the start point and face with the compass in the proper direction, then sight in on a landmark located on the correct azimuth to be followed. He should then close the compass and proceed to the landmark. The process should be repeated as many times as necessary to complete the straight-line segment of the route.

I-36. The landmarks selected for these purposes are steering marks and are crucial to success in dead reckoning. Dead reckoning without natural steering marks is used when the area through which the navigator is traveling is devoid of features or when visibility is poor. This procedure can be performed mounted or dismounted. Mounted movements are discussed later in this appendix. For dismounted movements, the navigator—

- Moves forward of the rest of the team in the direction of a back azimuth, and adjusts himself until he is on the desired azimuth.
- Gives the signal (hand-arm, radio, or other predetermined travel).
- Faces the team, computes an azimuth, converts the azimuth (signal), and the rest of the team moves forward.
- Repeats the process until the objective is reached or identifiable steering marks can be used.

I-37. When encountering obstacles or detours on the route, the navigator should follow these guidelines:

- When an obstacle forces the navigator to leave his original line of march and take a parallel one, he must return to the original line as soon as the terrain or situation permits.
- When turning clockwise (right) 90°, the navigator must add 90° to his original azimuth. When turning counterclockwise (left) 90° from his current direction, the navigator must subtract 90° from his present azimuth.
- When making a detour, the navigator must be sure only paces taken toward the final destination are counted as part of his forward progress. These paces should not be confused with the local pacing that takes place when traveling perpendicular to the route to avoid the problem area or when returning to the original line of march after the obstacle is passed.

Appendix I

I-38. Sometimes, a steering mark on the azimuth of travel can be seen across a swamp or some other obstacle to which the navigator can simply walk around. Dead reckoning then begins at that point. If no obvious steering mark can be seen across the obstacle, a steering mark might be located to the rear. A back azimuth should then be computed to this point and later sighted back to it when the obstacle is passed.

I-39. The deliberate offset technique may be used. Highly accurate distance estimates and precision compass work may not be required if the destination or an intermediate checkpoint is located on or near a large linear feature that runs nearly perpendicular to the navigator's direction of travel. Examples include roads or highways, railroads, power transmission lines, ridges, or streams. In these cases, the navigator should apply a deliberate error (offset) of about 10° to the azimuth he planned to follow. He should then move, using the lensatic compass as a guide, in that direction until he encounters the linear feature. The navigator then knows exactly which way to turn (left or right) to find his destination or checkpoint, depending upon which way he planned his deliberate offset.

I-40. Because no one can move along a given azimuth with absolute precision, the navigator should plan a few extra steps and not just begin an aimless search for the objective once he reaches the linear feature. Planning should also cope with minor compass errors and the slight variations that occur in the earth's magnetic field.

Disadvantages

I-41. There are disadvantages to dead reckoning. For instance, the farther the navigator travels by dead reckoning without confirming his position in relation to the terrain and other features, the more errors he will have in his movements. The navigator should therefore confirm and correct his estimated position whenever he encounters a known feature on the ground that is also on the map. He should periodically accomplish a resection triangulation using two or more known points to pinpoint and correct his position on the map. He should redo pace counts or any type of distance measurement each time he confirms his position on the map.

I-42. Also, selecting a single steering mark, such as a distant mountaintop, and then moving blindly toward it can be dangerous. For example, the navigator may have problems if he suddenly must call for fire support or a medical evacuation. Therefore, the navigator must periodically use resection and terrain association techniques to pinpoint his location along the way.

I-43. Another disadvantage is that during darkness, in fog, or in areas of dense vegetation, steering marks must be close together. This necessity to calculate numerous measurements increases the chance for error.

I-44. Finally, dead reckoning is time-consuming and demands constant attention to the compass. Errors accumulate easily and quickly. Every fold in the ground and a detour as small as a single tree or a boulder also complicate the measurement of distance.

Terrain Association

I-45. The technique of moving by terrain association is more forgiving of mistakes and far less time-consuming than dead reckoning. It best suits situations that call for movement from one area to another. Once an error is made in dead reckoning, the navigator is off track. However, errors made using terrain association are easily corrected, because what is seen on the map can be compared to what is actually seen on the ground. Errors are anticipated and do not go unchecked. The navigator can easily make adjustments based upon what he encounters. Periodic position-fixing through plotted or estimated resection also allows the navigator to correct his movements, to call for fire, or to call in the locations of enemy targets or any other information of tactical or logistical importance.

Identifying and Locating Selected Features

I-46. Identifying and locating the selected features on the map and on the ground are essential to success in moving by terrain association. The navigator should—

- Be sure that the map is properly oriented as he moves along the route and that the terrain and other features are used as guides. To prevent confusion, the orientation of the map must match the terrain.
- Look for the steepness and shape of the slopes, the relative elevations of the various features, and the directional orientations in relation to his position and the position of the other features he sees.
- Use the additional cues provided by hydrographic features, culture, and vegetation.

Interpreting and Analyzing Features

I-47. The major disadvantage to navigation by terrain association is that the navigator must be able to interpret the map and to analyze his surroundings. He must be skilled in recognizing terrain and other features, determining and estimating direction and distance, and quickly computing a fixed position.

Combining Techniques

I-48. The most successful navigation is obtained by combining the techniques described above. The navigator should not depend entirely upon compass navigation or map navigation—either or both may be lost or destroyed.

NIGHT NAVIGATION

I-49. Darkness presents its own requirements in land navigation because of limited or no visibility. However, the techniques and principles for night navigation are the same as those for day navigation. The success in nighttime land navigation depends on rehearsals during the planning phase before the movement—for example, thoroughly analyzing the appropriate map to determine the type of terrain where navigation will occur and predetermining azimuths and distances. Night vision devices can greatly enhance night navigation.

I-50. The basic technique in nighttime land navigation is dead reckoning, with the use of several compasses recommended as well. The point man should be in front of the navigator, but just a few steps away, for easy control of the azimuth. Smaller steps should be taken during night navigation, thus causing the pace count to be different. Preferably, a pace count should be obtained using a predetermined 100-meter pace course during both day and night. Navigation using the stars is recommended in some areas; however, a thorough knowledge of constellations and location of stars is needed.

MOUNTED LAND NAVIGATION

I-51. When preparing to move, the navigator must determine the effects of terrain on navigating mounted vehicles. Because great distances will be covered quickly, the navigator must be able to estimate distances traveled. (A distance of 0.1 mile is about 160 meters, and 1 mile is about 1,600 meters or 1.6 kilometers. In converting kilometers per hour to miles per hour, the number of kilometers [kmph] is multiplied by .62—for example, 9 kmph is multiplied by 0.62 = 5.58 mph. In converting miles per hour to kilometers per hour, the number of miles per hour [mph] is divided by .62—for example, 10 mph is divided by 0.62 = 16.12 kmph). When determining terrain effects, the navigator—

- *Considers vehicle capabilities.* When determining a route for mounted land navigation, the capabilities of the vehicles should be considered. Most military vehicles are limited in the degree of slope they can climb and the type of terrain they can negotiate. Swamps, thickly wooded areas, or deep streams may present no problems to dismounted Soldiers; however, the same terrain may completely stop mounted Soldiers. The navigator should consider the following factors when selecting a route:

- Most vehicles can knock down a tree. The bigger the vehicle, the bigger the tree it can knock down. Vehicles cannot knock down several trees at once. Paths between trees that are wide enough for the vehicles to maneuver should be located. Military vehicles are designed to climb 60 percent slopes on a dry, firm surface.
- Approximate slope can easily be determined, just by looking at the selected route. If there is a contour line in any 100 meters of map distance on the route, it is a 10 percent slope. If there are two contour lines, it is 20 percent, and so forth. If there are four contour lines in any 100 meters, the navigator should look for another route.
- Side slopes are more important than slopes that can be climbed. Normally, a 30 percent slope is the maximum in good weather. A side slope should be traversed slowly and without turns. For tactical reasons, movement should be in draws or valleys because they provide cover.

Note. The above figures are correct for a 10-meter or a 20-foot contour interval. If the map has a different contour interval, the arithmetic should be adjusted—for example, with one contour line in 100 meters, a 20-meter interval gives a 20-percent slope.

- *Knows the effects of weather on vehicle movement.* Weather can halt mounted movement. Snow and ice are obvious dangers, but more significant is the effect of rain and snow on the load-bearing ability of soil. Cross-country vehicles may be restricted to road movement in heavy rain. In areas where rain has recently occurred, the route should be adjusted to avoid flooded or muddy areas.
- *Prepares map before movement.* The start point and the finish point should be located on the map. The grid azimuth from the start point to the finish point on the map should be determined and converted to a magnetic azimuth. The distance between the start point and the finish point or any intermediate points on the map should be determined and a thorough map reconnaissance of that area made.

TERRAIN ASSOCIATION MOUNTED NAVIGATION

I-52. Terrain association is the most widely used method in mounted navigation. The navigator should plan his route for movement from terrain feature to terrain feature. The selected route must be capable of sustaining the travel of the vehicles. It should be relatively direct and easy to follow. In a typical move, the navigator determines his location, computes the location of his objective, notes the position of both locations on his map, and then selects a route between the two locations. After examining the terrain, the navigator adjusts the route by—

- *Considering tactical aspects.* Skyline objects should be avoided, key terrain selected for overwatch positions, and concealed routes identified.
- *Considering ease of movement.* The easiest possible route should be used and difficult terrain bypassed. A difficult route is harder to follow, is noisier, is physically demanding, and requires increased movement time. Tactical surprise is achieved by doing the unexpected—for example, selecting an axis or a corridor, instead of a specific route. The selected area should provide maneuver room for the vehicles.
- *Using terrain features as checkpoints.* Terrain features selected for checkpoints must be easy to recognize in light, under weather conditions, and from almost any location. The best checkpoints are linear features that cross the selected route—for example, streams, rivers, hardtop roads, ridges, valleys, and railroads. The next best checkpoints are elevation changes, such as hills, depressions, spurs, and draws. Less than two contour lines of change cannot be spotted. In wooded terrain, checkpoints should be at no more than 1,000-meter intervals. In open terrain, checkpoints may be at 5,000-meter intervals.
- *Following terrain features.* Movement and navigation are easiest along a valley floor or near the crest of a ridgeline.

- *Determining directions.* The route should be broken down into smaller segments, and the rough directions to be followed should be determined. The main points of direction (north, northeast, east, and so forth) may be used to determine direction. The location of the sun should be noted. Changes of direction at the selected checkpoints should also be noted.
- *Determining distance.* The total distance to be traveled and the approximate distance between checkpoints should be determined. The vehicle odometer should be used to keep track of distance traveled. The pace-count method should be used, and a record of the distance traveled should be kept. When the pace-count method is used, the map distance should be converted to ground distance by adding the conversion factors of 20 percent for cross-country movement.
- *Making notes.* Making mental notes is usually adequate. The navigator should imagine the route and try to remember its features.
- *Planning to avoid errors.* The route selected should be restudied. The navigator should determine where errors are most likely to occur and how to avoid any trouble.
- *Using a logbook.* When the routes have been selected and the distance to be traveled divided into legs, the navigator should prepare a logbook. The logbook is an informal record of the distance and azimuth of each leg, with notes to aid the navigator in following the correct route. The notes identify easily recognizable terrain features at or near the point where the direction of movement changes.

DEAD RECKONING MOUNTED NAVIGATION

I-53. Dead reckoning involves moving a set distance along a setline. Generally, dead reckoning is movement in specified meters along the setline, usually an azimuth in degrees. Movement may be with or without steering marks:

- *With steering marks.* The procedure for movement with steering marks is the same for travel by vehicle as it is for travel by foot. Specifically, the navigator dismounts from the vehicle and moves away from the vehicle (at least 18 meters). He sets the azimuth on the compass and selects a steering mark (rock, tree, hilltop) in the direction on the azimuth. He remounts, has the driver identify the steering mark, and then proceeds in a straight line to the steering mark. Upon arrival at the steering mark or upon any changes in direction, he repeats the procedure for the next leg of travel.
- *Without steering marks.* The procedure for movement without steering marks is used on flat, featureless terrain only. The navigator dismounts from the vehicle, which is oriented in the direction of travel, and moves at least 18 meters to the front of the vehicle. He faces the vehicle and reads the azimuth to the vehicle. By adding or subtracting 180°, he determines the forward azimuth (direction of travel). Upon order from the navigator, the driver drives in a straight line to the navigator. The navigator remounts the vehicle, holds the compass as it will be held while the vehicle is moving, and reads the azimuth in the direction of travel.

Note. The compass swings off the determined azimuth and picks up a constant deviation. For example, the azimuth might be 75° while the navigator is away from the vehicle, but when he remounts and his driver drives straight forward, the navigator's compass would show 67°—a deviation of -8°. In that situation, the navigator would simply maintain the 67° compass heading and travel on a 75° magnetic heading.

I-54. At night, the navigator should—
- Determine, from the map, the azimuth to be traveled.
- Convert the grid azimuth to a magnetic azimuth.
- Line up the vehicle on the magnetic azimuth.
- Move well in front of it.
- Be sure it is aligned correctly.
- Mount the vehicle, have the driver move slowly forward, and note the deviation.

Appendix I

> *Note.* The above procedure works if the vehicle has a turret, unless the turret is traversed, which changes the deviation.

I-55. To determine the distance factor in dead reckoning, the navigator simply computes the map distance to be traveled and adds 20 percent to convert to ground distance. The navigator should use the vehicle odometer to be sure he has traveled the proper distance.

NAVIGATION IN URBAN AREAS

I-56. Major urban areas represent the power and wealth of a particular country in the form of industrial bases, transportation complexes, economic institutions, and political and cultural centers—all of which may need to be secured and neutralized. In navigation of urban areas, man-made features—such as roads, railroads, bridges, and buildings—become important, while terrain and vegetation become less useful.

Interpretation and Analysis

I-57. Military operations on urbanized terrain require detailed planning that provides for decentralized execution. As a result of the rapid growth and changes occurring in many urban areas, the military topographic map is likely to be outdated. Supplemental use of commercially produced city maps may be helpful, or an up-to-date sketch may be made.

I-58. Urbanized terrain normally offers many approach areas for mounted maneuver well forward of and leading to urban centers. In the proximity of these built-up areas, however, such approach routes generally become choked by urban sprawl and perhaps by the nature of adjacent natural terrain. Dismounted forces then make the most of available cover by moving through buildings and underground systems, along edges of streets, and over rooftops. Urban areas typically separate and isolate units, requiring the small-unit leader to take the initiative and demonstrate his skill to prevail.

I-59. The urban condition of an area creates many obstacles, and the destruction of many buildings and bridges as combat power is applied during a battle further limits freedom of movement. Cover and concealment are plentiful, but observation and fields of fire are greatly restricted.

Navigation Cues

I-60. Navigation in urban areas can be confusing; however, many cues can be useful in navigating the area—for example, streets and street signs; building styles and sizes; urban geography of industrial, warehousing, residential housing, and market districts; man-made transportation features other than streets and roads (rail and trolley lines); and the terrain features and hydrographic features located within the built-up area. Strategies for staying on the route in an urban area include—

- *Processing route descriptions.* Write down or memorize the route through an urban area as a step-by-step process—for example, "Go three blocks north, turn left (west) on a wide divided boulevard until going over a river bridge . . . ."
- *Understanding conceptually the urban area.* Study the map and develop an understanding (mental map) of the entire area when operating in a built-up area. This practice allows navigation over multiple routes to any location. It also precludes getting lost when a turn is missed or when obstacles or the tactical situation alter the planned route.
- *Using resection.* Use estimated or plotted resection to pinpoint one's position whenever a vantage point to two or more known features portrayed on the map is present. These opportunities are often plentiful in an urban setting.

I-61. Using the following techniques, TPTs can be successful in the urban environment. TPTs generally operate in overwatch positions to support maneuver elements. TPTs conduct broadcasts to assist in building clearing, to degrade enemy morale, to induce surrender, and to harass enemy troops. TPTs also assist in controlling and providing information to local civilians.

URBAN TERRAIN MOVEMENT

I-62. When moving in an urban area, squads and platoons may use variations of traveling, traveling overwatch, and bounding overwatch movement techniques. Often, squads and fire teams use the modified wedge (file or column) to move. Leaders must be aware of the three-dimensional aspect of urban terrain and anticipate enemy contact from all directions. Squads and platoons are extremely vulnerable to sniper fire; therefore, countersniper TTP must be well-rehearsed and implemented to prevent excess casualties.

I-63. The assault force (squad or platoon) can minimize the effects of the enemy's defensive fires during movement by—
- Using covered and concealed routes.
- Moving only after enemy fires have been suppressed or enemy observation obscured.
- Moving at night or during other periods of reduced visibility.
- Selecting routes that will not mask friendly suppressive fires.
- Crossing open areas quickly under concealment of smoke and suppressive fires.
- Moving on rooftops not covered by enemy fires.

I-64. In lightly defended areas, the type of operation may dictate moving along streets and alleys without clearing all the buildings. The squads move along streets and alleys on one side of the street supported by an overwatch element. Each man is assigned a specific sector to observe and cover. To avoid exposure on the street or to provide mutual support, the squads should move through the buildings if possible.

I-65. When armored vehicles are attached, the platoon moves on foot with two squads leading, one on each side of the street, using bounding overwatch movement techniques. This technique is used to locate, identify, engage, and eliminate any antiarmor threat quickly.

Note. When armored vehicles are employed with the infantry, the platoon leader must brief his personnel to the dangers associated with vehicles engaging targets close to them (explosive effects, fragmentation fallout, and blast over-pressure).

Crossing a Wall

I-66. Each Soldier must learn the correct method of crossing a wall. After he has reconnoitered the other side, he quickly rolls over the wall, keeping a low silhouette. The speed of his move and a low silhouette deny the enemy a good target.

Moving Around Corners

I-67. The area around a corner must be observed before the Soldier moves beyond it. The most common mistake a Soldier makes at a corner is allowing his weapon to extend beyond the corner, exposing his position. He should show his head below the height where an enemy Soldier would expect to see it. When looking around a corner, the Soldier should lie flat on the ground and be sure he does not extend his weapon beyond the corner of the building. He should wear his Kevlar helmet and expose his head (at ground level) only enough to permit him to observe his surroundings.

Moving Past Windows

I-68. Windows present a hazard to the Soldier and small-unit leader. The most common mistake in passing a window is to expose the head. If the Soldier shows his head, an enemy shooter inside the building could engage the Soldier through the window without exposing himself to friendly covering fires.

I-69. When passing a window, the Soldier should stay below the window level. He should make sure he does not silhouette himself in the window—he should "hug" the side of the building. An enemy shooter inside the building would then be exposed to covering fires if he tried to engage the Soldier.

I-70. The techniques in passing first-floor windows are also used in passing basement windows; however, the most common mistake in passing a basement window is not being aware of the window. A Soldier should not walk or run past a basement window, because he becomes a target to an enemy shooter inside the building. When negotiating a basement window, the Soldier should stay close to the wall of the building and step or jump past the window without exposing his legs.

Using Doorways

I-71. Doorways should not be used as entrances or exits, because they are normally covered by enemy fire. If a Soldier must use a doorway as an exit, he should move quickly through it to his next position, staying as low as possible to avoid silhouetting himself. Preelection of positions, speed, a low silhouette, and the use of covering fires must be emphasized in exiting doorways.

Moving Parallel to Buildings

I-72. Soldiers and small units may not be able to use the inside of buildings as a route of advance. Therefore, they must move on the outside of the buildings. Smoke, covering fires, cover, and concealment should be used to hide movement. When moving on the outside of a building, the Soldier should "hug" the side of the building, stay in the shadow, present a low silhouette, and move rapidly to his next position. If an enemy shooter inside the building fires on a Soldier, he exposes himself to fire from other squad members. An enemy shooter farther down the street, as well, would have difficulty detecting and engaging the Soldier.

Crossing Open Areas

I-73. Open areas, such as streets, alleys, and parks, should be avoided. They are natural kill zones for enemy crew-served weapons. They can be crossed safely if the individual or small-unit leader applies certain fundamentals.

I-74. When crossing an open area, the Soldier should develop a plan for his own movement—for example, smoke from hand grenades or smoke pots should be used to conceal the movement of all Soldiers. He should run the shortest distance between the buildings and move along the building to the next position. By doing so, he reduces the time he is exposed to enemy fire.

I-75. Before moving to another position, the Soldier should make a visual reconnaissance and select the position for the best cover and concealment. At the same time, he should select the route that he will take to get to that position.

BATTLE DRILLS

I-76. In a worst-case scenario, the TPT will find the enemy at a time and place most advantageous to the enemy. To counter this threat, the TPT employs methods to avoid detection. The TPT may move at night using routes that allow the best chance to remain undetected. Despite these precautions, the TPT must be prepared should it make contact with the enemy. It prepares itself for contact by keeping the weapons systems manned, keeping vehicle interval, and maintaining movement discipline.

I-77. The TPT can increase its ability to avoid compromise by using NVGs during halts and movement. Infrared lights should be used only when necessary, as many countries have this capability as well. Making contact at night, even under the best of illumination, involves some difficulty in determining the number of enemy involved in the contact. During unexpected enemy contact, the TPT should try to break contact and place as much distance between itself and the enemy as the terrain and light conditions allow. TPT and supported unit SOPs, along with experience, establish immediate action drills (IADs). Generally, the most effective way to break contact is to bound away from the enemy. The following paragraphs explain some additional methods TPTs may use to avoid detection.

Visual Contact

I-78. If the TPT sees the enemy and the enemy does not see the team, the team freezes. If the team has time, it—
- Assumes the best covered and concealed position.
- Remains in position until the enemy has passed.

Contact From the Front or Rear

I-79. The lead or trail element normally makes contact with the enemy first. This element immediately engages the enemy, while the other elements in the movement move to each side of the direction of movement to provide covering fire. The first element in contact then maneuvers away from the enemy by passing through or past the other elements. As the lead element moves past, the other elements, in turn, engage the enemy and then maneuver and follow. This maneuver is simply a reverse direction of bounding overwatch.

Contact From the Flank, Near or Far

I-80. The TPT is not designed to engage in decisive firefights with the enemy, so again breaking contact is desirable. The TPT must use the mobility and speed of the vehicle in moving to avoid observation and therefore enemy fire. The action taken upon contact from the flank (far contact) is to break contact. The same basic techniques apply as in making contact from the front or rear. Upon contact from the flank when the enemy is too close (near contact) to break contact, the engaged unit turns into the enemy and attempts to fight its way through with all weapons available. The elements move by team and link up at the last en route rally point.

Ambush-Dismounted Contact

I-81. If the unit enters a kill zone and the enemy initiates an ambush with a casualty-producing device and a high volume of fire, the unit takes the following actions:
- In a near ambush (within hand grenade range), Soldiers receiving fire immediately return fire, take covered positions, and throw fragmentation concussion and smoke grenades.
- Immediately after the grenades detonate, Soldiers in the kill zone assault through the ambush, using fire and movement.
- Soldiers not in the kill zone immediately—
    - Identify enemy positions.
    - Initiate immediate suppressive fires against the enemy.
    - Take covered positions.
    - Shift fires as Soldiers in the kill zone assault through the ambush.
- In a far ambush (beyond hand grenade range), Soldiers receiving fire immediately return fire, take covered positions, and suppress the enemy by—
    - Destroying or suppressing enemy crew-served weapons first.
    - Obscuring the enemy position with smoke.
    - Sustaining suppressive fires.
- Soldiers not receiving fires move by a covered and concealed route to a vulnerable flank of the enemy position and assault using fire and movement techniques.
- Soldiers in the kill zone continue suppressive fires and shift fires as the assaulting team fights through the enemy position.
- The forward observer calls for and adjusts indirect fires as directed. On order, he lifts or shifts fires to isolate the enemy position or attacks the enemy with indirect fires as the enemy retreats.
- The team leader reports, reorganizes as necessary, and continues the mission.

Appendix I

AMBUSH-MOUNTED CONTACT

I-82. If the unit is mounted and enters a kill zone and the enemy initiates an ambush with a light antiarmor weapon and a high volume of fire, the unit should take the following actions:
- Soldiers in vehicles in the kill zone immediately return fire, while moving out of the kill zone or moving to covered positions within the kill zone and continue to fire on the ambush position with the highest possible volume of fire.
- Soldiers in disabled vehicles in the kill zone dismount immediately, assume covered and concealed positions, and add their suppressive fires against the enemy.
- The unit in the kill zone—
  - Gains suppressive fire.
  - Destroys or suppresses enemy weapons firing most effectively against the section.
  - Obscures the enemy position with smoke.
  - Sustains suppressive fires.
- The unit not in the kill zone—
  - Moves by a covered and concealed route to a vulnerable flank of the enemy position.
  - Assaults mounted across the enemy position.
- Infantry fighting vehicles (IFVs) and Soldiers in the kill zone continue suppressive fires and shift fires as the assaulting unit fights through the enemy position.
- The platoon leader—
  - Calls for and adjusts indirect fires.
  - Lifts or shifts fires to isolate the enemy position or attacks the enemy with indirect fires as the enemy retreats.
  - Reports, reorganizes as necessary, and continues the mission. If the platoon cannot continue the assault, it breaks contact.

INDIRECT FIRE

I-83. If a TPT comes under indirect fire, the leader immediately moves the unit out of the impact area by designating a direction and distance move. Indirect fire can cause the team to move out of the area as quickly as possible and may result in its exact location and the pinpointed direction. Therefore, the team must not only react to indirect fire but also take the following actions to conceal its movement once it is out of the impact area:
- The team leader moves the team out of the impact area, using the quickest route by giving the direction and distance.
- All members move out of the impact area to the designated distance and direction.
- The team leader then moves the team farther away from the impact area by using the most direct concealed route. The team continues the mission using an alternate route.
- If team members become separated, they should link up at the objective rallying point (ORP) or move to the next designated rallying point.

AIR ATTACK

I-84. If the TPT is caught in an air attack or its position is about to be destroyed, it should—
- Assume the best available covered and concealed positions.
- Move between passes of aircraft to a position that offers better cover and concealment.
- Not engage the aircraft (leader's decision).
- Remain in position until the attacking aircraft departs.
- Link up at the ORP or move to the next designated rallying point if the members become separated.

Tactical Psychological Operations Team Battlefield Survival Techniques

BREAKING CONTACT

I-85. If a unit is under enemy fire and must break contact—
- The platoon leader—
  - Gives the order to break contact.
  - Directs TPTs to support the disengagement of the dismounted element. If TPTs cannot support the disengagement of the dismounted element, the platoon leader directs one squad or fire team to suppress by fire to support the disengagement of the remainder of the element.
  - Orders a distance and direction, a terrain feature, or the last ORP for the movement of the first squad or fire team.
- The TPT squad or fire team increases the rate of fire to suppress the enemy.
- The maneuver element—
  - Moves to assume the overwatch position.
  - Uses fragmentation, concussion, and smoke grenades to mask its movement.
  - Takes up the designated position and engages the enemy position.
- The platoon leader directs the TPT squad or fire team to move to its next location. Based on the terrain and the volume and accuracy of the enemy's fire, the maneuver squad or fire team may need to use fire and movement techniques.
- The platoon or squad continues to bound away from and suppress the enemy until it—
  - Breaks all contact.
  - Passes through a higher-level base-of-fire position.
  - Is in the assigned position to conduct the next mission.

Note. In the absence of a leader's instructions, the platoon or squad moves to the last designated rallying point.

FORCE PROTECTION

I-86. During movement, each element is responsible for a sector, depending on its position in a formation. Fire teams are assigned sectors of fire to give companies and battalions full security.

I-87. During short halts, Soldiers spread out and assume prone positions behind cover. They watch the same sectors that were assigned while moving. Leaders set up observation posts, machine guns, and antiarmor weapons on likely enemy approaches into the position. Soldiers remain alert and speak (quietly) only when necessary. They keep movement to a minimum. Soldiers with night vision devices scan areas where the enemy may be concealed during limited visibility.

I-88. During long halts, the company sets up a perimeter defense. The commander chooses the most defensible terrain (with good cover and concealment). The company SOP should address the actions required during long halts.

I-89. For additional security, small ambush teams may be concealed and remain in position after short halts. Ideally, these teams should be provided by the platoon in the center of the company formation. These teams should remain in position to ambush any enemy following the company. The linkup of these teams must be coordinated and understood by all.

I-90. Before the team occupies a static position (ORP, patrol base, or assembly areas), the commanding officer should make sure the enemy is unaware of the location of the team. In addition to using the ambush teams, the commanding officer may also conceal security teams in or near the tentative static position as the unit passes. The company continues movement, preferably until darkness, and then circles back to link up with and guide the security teams, which have reconnoitered the position.

I-91. TPTs operating independently from a main body generally require security augmentation during mission execution. Most TPT missions require the team to be focused on the TA. Two or more TPTs operating together can provide their own local security, depending upon the threat. TPTs moving with a larger element do not require a specific or dedicated security element. For example, a TPT moving with a platoon does not need a separate security element—its security comes from its proximity to the platoon.

IMPROVISED EXPLOSIVE DEVICES

I-92. Most of the casualties suffered by tactical PSYOP forces during Operations ENDURING FREEDOM and IRAQI FREEDOM were a result of IED detonations. The nature of tactical PSYOP puts TPTs among the populace, often with minimal security. This exposure increases the risk of exposure to IEDs. Tactical PSYOP forces, especially TPTs, need to know the IED risks, the ways to identify potential IEDs, and what to do if one is detonated.

I-93. IEDs are nonstandard and usually fabricated from common materials. They may be constructed out of any available material and contain various fillers, including explosive, chemical, biological, or hazardous materials. IEDs may range in size from a cigarette pack or carton to the size of a large vehicle. The only limitations an enemy bomber faces are availability of resources, personal ingenuity, and the degree or extent of know-how required to facilitate construction and, in some cases, application of an IED. TC 9-21-01, *Soldiers Improvised Explosive Device (IED) Awareness Guide: Iraq and Afghanistan Theaters of Operation*, contains examples of IED employment.

GENERAL MITIGATION MEASURES

I-94. There are 10 general mitigation measures in relation to the IED threat:
- Trust one's instincts. If something does not seem right, it probably is not. Be aware of the surroundings (situational awareness).
- Watch the locals in the AO. Are familiar locals in the area? Are people who are moving away from the PSYOP element acting or appearing nervous? Most bombers do not blow up their own neighborhoods.
- Be aware of news crews in the area for no apparent reason. Most bombers like their work filmed, but they do not like pictures of themselves.
- Before every convoy or patrol, brief PSYOP personnel on the latest IED threat intelligence, including—
    - Types of items currently in use.
    - Known techniques, patterns, and likely locations of emplacement.
    - Areas where items have previously been placed.
    - Intelligence on current PSYOP route of march (primary and alternates).
- Rehearse actions (battle drill) for reacting to a possible IED.
- Wear personal protective equipment (vests, helmets and eye protection).
- Maintain speed and movement whenever possible.
- Maintain dispersion while conducting either mounted or dismounted operations.
- Be cautious of choke points, vehicle breakdowns, bridges, one-way roads, traffic jams, and sharp turns.
- If something stops movement, either mounted or dismounted, survey immediate area for possible IEDs.

REACTION TO POSSIBLE IMPROVISED EXPLOSIVE DEVICES

I-95. Several steps should be taken when a possible IED is identified:

Note. These steps do NOT supersede any SOPs, orders, or military directives. Tactical PSYOP forces should adhere to their supported unit's SOPs or directives.

- STOP all movement toward the possible IED and immediately evaluate the surrounding area for possible secondary IEDs:
    - Do not approach the possible IED.
    - Do not attempt to move the possible IED.
    - If possible, avoid using any communication or electronic equipment within the previously established and secure exclusion area.
- Establish security:
    - Establish an area around the possible IED. Adjust the exclusion area, based on METT-TC, local command policy and guidance, TTP, and SOPs.
    - Search initial secure area for possible secondary explosive devices and hazards, while maintaining security.
    - Identify potential enemy force observation or vantage points.
    - Seek all available man-made or natural frontal and overhead cover.
    - Avoid establishing a "reaction" pattern.
    - Forward information to higher HQ using the standard 9-line UXO Report.
    - Continue the mission IAW guidance from higher HQ.

This page intentionally left blank.

Appendix J
Use of Interpreters

During PSYOP, PSYOP Soldiers sometimes lack the linguistic ability to communicate personally and effectively with the local populace in the AO. The use of interpreters is often the best or only option. The proper use and supervision of interpreters can play a decisive role in the mission.

INTERPRETER SELECTION

J-1. Whenever possible, the interpreters used should be U.S. military personnel or at least U.S. citizens. In some operational or training settings abroad, PSYOP Soldiers are not faced with the problem of selecting an interpreter—they simply are assigned one by the chain of command or the host government. In other cases, interpreters are chosen from a pool provided by the host government. Finally, in many operational situations, interpreters are hired from the general LN population. Whatever the case, the following guidelines are critical to the success of mission accomplishment. The PSYOP Soldier can use this opportunity to influence the outcome of the mission effectively. Interpreters should be selected based on the following criteria:

NATIVE SPEAKER

J-2. The interpreters should be native speakers of the socially or geographically determined dialect. Their speech, background, and mannerisms should be completely acceptable to the TA so that no attention is given to the way they talk, only to what they say.

SOCIAL STATUS

J-3. In some situations and cultures, interpreters may be limited in their effectiveness with a TA if their social standing is considerably lower than that of the audience. Examples include significant differences in military rank or membership in an ethnic or religious group. Regardless of the PSYOP Soldier's personal feelings on social status, he should remember the job is to accomplish the mission, not to act as an agent for social reform in a faraway land. The PSYOP Soldier must accept local prejudices as a fact of life.

ENGLISH FLUENCY

J-4. An often-overlooked consideration is how well the interpreter speaks English. As a rule, if the interpreter understands the PSYOP Soldier and the PSYOP Soldier understands the interpreter, then the interpreter's command of English should be satisfactory. The PSYOP Soldier can check that "understanding" by asking the interpreter to paraphrase, in English, something the PSYOP Soldier said. The PSYOP Soldier then restates the interpreter's comments to ensure that both persons are in synchronization. In addition, interpreting goes both ways. The interpreter must be able to convey the information expressed by the interviewee or TA.

INTELLECT

J-5. The interpreter should be quick, alert, and responsive to changing conditions and situations. He must be able to grasp complex concepts and discuss them without confusion in a reasonably logical sequence. Although education does not equate to intelligence, generally speaking, the better educated the interpreter, the better he will perform due to increased exposure to diverse concepts.

Appendix J

TECHNICAL ABILITY

J-6. In certain situations, the PSYOP Soldier may need an interpreter with technical training or experience in special subject areas. This type of interpreter will be able to translate the "meaning" as well as the "words." For instance, if the subject is very technical or specialized (with terms such as nuclear physics) background knowledge is useful.

RELIABILITY

J-7. The PSYOP Soldier should beware of the potential interpreter who arrives late for the interview. Throughout the world, the concept of time varies widely. In many less-developed countries, time is relatively unimportant. The PSYOP Soldier should make sure the interpreter understands the military's preoccupation with punctuality.

LOYALTY

J-8. If the interpreter is a local national, his first loyalty is most likely to the LN or subgroup, not to the U.S. military. The security implications are clear. The PSYOP Soldier must be very cautious in how he explains concepts to give interpreters a greater depth of understanding. Additionally, some interpreters, for political or personal reasons, may have ulterior motives or a hidden agenda when they apply for the interpreting job. If the PSYOP Soldier detects or suspects such motives, he should tell his commander or security manager.

GENDER, AGE, RACE, CULTURE, ETHNICITY, AND NATIONALITY

J-9. Gender, age, race, culture, ethnicity, and nationality have the potential to seriously impact the interpreter's effectiveness. One example is the status of females in Muslim society. In predominantly Muslim countries, cultural prohibitions may render a female interpreter ineffective in certain circumstances. Another example is the Balkans, where the ethnic divisions may limit the effectiveness of an interpreter from outside the TA's group. Since traditions, values, and biases vary from country to country, the in-country assets or area studies should be checked for specific taboos or favorable characteristics.

COMPATIBILITY

J-10. The PSYOP Soldier and the interpreter must work as a team. For the interpreter to be most effective, he should become a psychic extension of the PSYOP Soldier. The TA is quick to recognize personality conflicts between the PSYOP Soldier and the interpreter, which can undermine the effectiveness of the communication effort. If possible, when selecting an interpreter, the PSYOP Soldier should look for compatible traits and strive for a harmonious working relationship.

J-11. If several qualified interpreters are available, the PSYOP Soldier should select at least two. This practice is of particular importance if the interpreter will be used during long conferences or courses of instruction. The exhausting nature of these types of jobs makes approximately 4 hours of active interpreting about the maximum for peak efficiency. Whatever the mission, with two or more interpreters, one can provide quality control and assistance to the active interpreter. Additionally, this technique is useful when conducting coordination or negotiation meetings, as one interpreter is used in an active role and the other pays attention to the body language and side conversations of the others present. Many times, the PSYOP Soldier gains important side information that assists in negotiations from listening to what others are saying among themselves outside the main discussion.

EVALUATION CRITERIA

J-12. Interpreters must be honest and free from unfavorable notoriety among the local inhabitants. Their reputation or standing in the community should be such that persons of higher rank and standing do not intimidate them.

J-13. If the interpreter is not U.S. military or at least a U.S. citizen, his first loyalty is presumably to his country or subgroup and not to the United States. The security implications of using local nationals are clear. The PSYOP Soldier must be cautious about what information he gives his interpreter. The PSYOP Soldier must always keep possible security issues in mind. Certain tactical situations may require the use of uncleared indigenous personnel as "field expedient" interpreters. Commanders should be aware of the increased security risk involved in using such personnel and carefully weigh the risk versus the potential gain. If uncleared interpreters are used, any sensitive information should be kept to a minimum.

RAPPORT ESTABLISHMENT

J-14. The interpreter is a vital link to the TA. Without a supportive interpreter, the mission could be in serious jeopardy. Mutual respect and understanding are essential to effective teamwork. The PSYOP Soldier must establish rapport early in the relationship and maintain rapport throughout the joint effort. Personal contact is key to establishing rapport.

J-15. The PSYOP Soldier begins the process of establishing rapport before he meets the interpreter for the first time. The Soldier should do his homework. Most foreigners are reasonably knowledgeable about the United States. The PSYOP Soldier should obtain some basic facts about the AO. Useful information may include population, geography, ethnic groups, political system, prominent political figures, monetary system, business, agriculture, and exports. A good general outline can be obtained from a recent almanac or encyclopedia. More detailed information is available in the area handbook for the country and in current newspapers and magazines.

J-16. The PSYOP Soldier should understand the interpreter's background. He should show a genuine concern for the interpreter's family, aspirations, career, education, and so on. Many cultures place great emphasis on family over career, so the PSYOP Soldier should start with understanding the interpreter's home life. He should also research cultural traditions to understand the interpreter and the AO better. Although the PSYOP Soldier should gain as much information on culture as possible before entering an AO, his interpreter can be a valuable source to fill gaps.

J-17. The PSYOP Soldier should gain the interpreter's trust and confidence before addressing sensitive issues, such as religion, likes, dislikes, and prejudices. The PSYOP Soldier should approach these areas carefully and tactfully. Although deeply personal beliefs may be very revealing and useful in the professional relationship, the PSYOP Soldier must gently and tactfully gather that information from his interpreter.

ORIENTATION

J-18. Early in the relationship with interpreters, the PSYOP Soldiers should make sure interpreters are briefed on their duties and responsibilities. The PSYOP Soldier should orient the interpreters as to the nature of their duties, standards of conduct expected, techniques of interview to be used, and any other requirements necessary. The orientation may include the following:

- Current tactical situation.
- Background information obtained on the source, interviewee, or TA.
- Specific objectives for the interview, meeting, or interrogation.
- Method of interpretation to be used:
  - Simultaneous. Interpreter listens and translates at the same time.
  - Alternate. Interpreter listens to an entire phrase, sentence, or paragraph, and then translates during natural pauses.
- Conduct of the interview, lesson, or interrogation.
- Need for interpreters to avoid injecting their own personality, ideas, or questions into the interview.
- Need for interpreter to inform interviewer (PSYOP Soldier) of inconsistencies in language used by interviewee. During interrogations or interviews, this information is used as part of the

Appendix J

assessment of the information obtained from the individual. For example, someone claims to be a college professor, yet speaks like an uneducated person.
- Physical arrangements of site, if applicable.
- Possible need for interpreter to assist in AARs or assessments.

INTERPRETER TRAINING

J-19. As part of the initial training with the interpreter, the PSYOP Soldier should tactfully convey that the instructor, interviewer, or interrogator (PSYOP Soldier) must always direct the interview or lesson. The PSYOP Soldier should put the interpreter's role in proper perspective and stress the interpreter's importance as a vital communication link between the PSYOP Soldier and the TA. The PSYOP Soldier should appeal to the interpreter's professional pride by clearly describing how the quality and quantity of the information sent and received are directly dependent upon the interpreter's skills. Also, the PSYOP Soldier should mention how the interpreter functions solely as a conduit between the PSYOP Soldier and the subject.

J-20. The PSYOP Soldier must be aware that some interpreters, because of cultural differences, may attempt to "save face" by purposely concealing their lack of understanding. They may attempt to translate what they think the PSYOP Soldier said or meant without asking for a clarification or vice versa.

J-21. Because this situation can result in misinformation and confusion and can impact on credibility, the PSYOP Soldier should let the interpreter know that when in doubt he should always ask for clarification. The PSYOP Soldier should create a safe environment for this situation as early in the relationship as possible.

J-22. Other points for the PSYOP Soldier to cover while orienting and training the interpreter are—
- Importance of the training, interview, or interrogation.
- Specific objectives of the training, interview, or interrogation, if any.
- Outline of lesson or interview questions, if applicable.
- Background information on the interviewee or TA.
- Briefing, training, or interview schedules. Double or triple time may be needed when using an interpreter to convey the same information. For that reason, the interpreter may be helpful in scheduling enough time.
- Copy of the briefing, questions, or lesson plan, if applicable. Special attention should be given to develop language proficiency in the technical fields in which the interpreters will be employed. In general, a copy of the material gives the interpreter time to look up unfamiliar words or ask questions to clarify anything confusing.
- Copies of handout material, if applicable.
- General background information on subject.
- Glossary of terms, if applicable.

FORCE PROTECTION

J-23. The interpreter must be thought of and treated as a member of the team. Just as force protection is considered for team members, so should it be for interpreters. Alternating work schedules and varying routes when going to and from work will help increase their safety. Interpreters should receive instruction on antiterrorism and force protection. Interpreters should also receive individual equipment like that of the other team members. When possible, interpreters should receive body armor, uniforms, helmet, and weapon. They should also be taught how to use communication systems, in the event it is necessary.

INTERVIEW PREPARATION

J-24. The PSYOP Soldier selects an appropriate site for the interview. He positions and arranges physical setup of the area. When conducting interviews with very important persons (VIPs) or individuals from different cultures, this arrangement can be significant.

J-25. The PSYOP Soldier instructs the interpreters to mirror the PSYOP Soldier's tone and personality of speech. He instructs the interpreters not to interject their own questions or personality. He also instructs the interpreters to inform him if they notice any inconsistencies or peculiarities from sources.

INTERVIEW CONDUCT

J-26. Whether conducting an interview or presenting a lesson, the PSYOP Soldier should avoid simultaneous translations; that is, both the Soldier and the interpreter talking at the same time. The PSYOP Soldier should speak for a minute or less in a neutral, relaxed manner, directly to the individual or audience. The interpreter should watch the PSYOP Soldier carefully and, during the translation, mimic the PSYOP Soldier's body language and interpret the verbal meaning. The PSYOP Soldier should observe the interpreter closely to detect any inconsistencies between the interpreter's and PSYOP Soldier's manners. The PSYOP Soldier must be aware not to force the interpreter into literal translation by being too brief. The PSYOP Soldier should present one major thought in its entirety and allow the interpreter to reconstruct it in his language and culture.

J-27. Although the interpreter does some editing as a function of the interpreting process, he must transmit the exact meaning without additions or deletions. As previously mentioned, the PSYOP Soldier should insist that the interpreter always ask for clarification, before interpreting, whenever not absolutely certain of the PSYOP Soldier's meaning. However, the PSYOP Soldier should be aware that a good interpreter, especially if he is local, can be invaluable in translating subtleties and hidden meanings.

J-28. During an interview or lesson, if questions are asked, the interpreter should immediately relay them to the PSYOP Soldier for an answer. The interpreter should never attempt to answer a question, even though he may know the correct answer. Additionally, neither the PSYOP Soldier nor interpreter should correct the other in front of an interviewee or class—all differences should be settled away from the subject or audience.

J-29. Just as establishing rapport with the interpreter is vitally important, establishing rapport with interview subjects or the TA is equally important. The PSYOP Soldier and the interpreter should concentrate on rapport. To establish critical rapport, the subjects or audiences should be treated as mature, important human beings who are capable and worthy.

COMMUNICATION TECHNIQUES

J-30. An important first step for the PSYOP Soldier in communicating in a foreign language is to polish his English language skills. These skills are important even if no attempt is made to learn the indigenous language. The clearer the Soldier speaks in English, including diction, the easier it is for the interpreter to translate. Other factors to consider include use of profanity, slang, and colloquialisms. In many cases, such expressions cannot be translated. Even those that can be translated do not always retain the desired meaning. Military jargon and terms such as "gee whiz" or "golly" are hard to translate. In addition, if a technical term or expression must be used, the PSYOP Soldier must be sure the interpreter conveys the proper meaning in the target language. The PSYOP Soldier should speak in low context, simple sentences. For instance, he may want to add words usually left off, such as "air" plane, to ensure the meaning is obvious and he is not talking about the Great Plains or a wood plane.

J-31. When the PSYOP Soldier is speaking extemporaneously, he must think about what he wants to say. He should break his thoughts down into logical bits and say them a small piece at a time, using short, simple words and sentences and low context, which can be translated quickly and easily. As a rule, the PSYOP Soldier should never say more in one sentence than he can easily repeat word for word immediately after saying it. Each sentence should contain a complete thought without being verbose.

TRANSITIONAL PHRASES AND QUALIFIERS

J-32. Transitional phrases and qualifiers often confuse and waste valuable time. Examples are "for example," "in most cases," "maybe," and "perhaps." The PSYOP Soldier should be cautious about using American humor. Cultural and language differences can lead to misinterpretations by foreigners. The

PSYOP Soldier should determine early on what the interpreter finds easiest to understand and then translate meaningfully. In summary, the PSYOP Soldier should—
- Keep the entire presentation as simple as possible.
- Use short sentences and simple words (low context).
- Avoid idiomatic English.
- Avoid tendency toward flowery language.
- Avoid slang and colloquial expressions.

J-33. Whenever possible, the PSYOP Soldier should identify any cultural restrictions before interviewing, instructing, or conferring with particular foreign nationals. For instance, he should know when it is proper to stand, sit, or cross one's legs. Because gestures are learned behavior, they vary from culture to culture. The interpreter should be able to relate a number of these cultural restrictions, which, whenever possible, should be observed in working with the particular group or individual.

DOS AND DON'TS

J-34. The following are some dos and don'ts for the PSYOP Soldier to consider while working with an interpreter. The PSYOP Soldier should—
- Position the interpreter by his side (or even a step back). This method keeps the subject or audience from shifting its attention or from fixating on the interpreter and not on the PSYOP Soldier.
- Always look at and talk directly to the subject or audience. Guard against the tendency to talk to the interpreter.
- Speak slowly and clearly. Repeat as often as necessary.
- Speak to the individual or group with culturally appropriate tone, gestures, and body language. Considerable nonverbal meaning can be conveyed through voice and body movements. Encourage the interpreter to reflect the PSYOP Soldier's tone and body language.
- Periodically check the interpreter's accuracy, consistency, and clarity. Have another American, fluent enough in the language, sit in on a lesson or interview to make sure the translation is not distorted, intentionally or unintentionally. Another way to be sure is to learn the target language so that the interpreter's loyalty and honesty can be personally checked.
- Check with the audience whenever misunderstandings are suspected and clarify immediately. Using the interpreter, ask questions to elicit answers that will tell whether the point is clear. If not clear, rephrase the instruction differently and illustrate the point again. Use repetition and examples whenever necessary to facilitate learning. If the class asks few questions, it may mean the instruction is "over the heads" of the audience or the message is not clear to the audience.
- Make the interpreter feel like a valuable member of the team. Give the interpreter recognition commensurate with the importance of his contribution.

J-35. The PSYOP Soldier should—
- **Not** address the subject or audience in the third person through the interpreter. Avoid saying, "Tell them I'm glad to be their instructor." Instead say, "I'm glad to be your instructor." Address the subject or audience directly.
- **Not** make side comments to the interpreter that he should not translate. This action usually creates the wrong atmosphere for communication.
- **Not** be a distraction while the interpreter is translating and the subject or audience is listening. The PSYOP Soldier should not pace the floor, write on the blackboard, teeter on the lectern, drink beverages, or carry on any other distracting activity while the interpreter is actually translating.

Appendix K
Rules of Engagement

The ROE reflect the requirements placed on the military by the law of war, operational concerns, and political considerations when the situation shifts throughout the full spectrum of conflict. ROE are the primary means by which the commander conveys legal, political, diplomatic, and military guidelines to his forces.

Operational requirements, policy, and law define ROE. ROE always recognize the right of self-defense, the commander's right and obligation to protect assigned personnel, and the national right to defend U.S. forces, allies, and coalition participants against armed attack. Well-defined ROE are enforceable, understandable, tactically sound, and legally sufficient. Furthermore, explicit ROE are responsive to the mission and permit subordinate commanders to exercise initiative when confronted by an opportunity or by unforeseen circumstances.

PSYOP SUPPORT TO ROE

K-1. PSYOP often help minimize ROE violations by ensuring that HN civilians are aware of what behaviors are or are not acceptable to U.S./coalition forces. Violations of the ROE can cause the TA to develop animosity and negativity toward U.S. forces. TAs hostile to U.S. forces may attempt to use ROE violations to further their cause. PSYOP Soldiers should be prepared to minimize repercussions through carefully coordinated supporting PSYOP programs. Reinforcing previous accomplishments and assistance provided by U.S. forces are examples of the types of supporting programs that can help sustain a positive attitude of the TAs.

K-2. The type of ROE will depend on the type of mission. During wartime, the ROE are usually lethal in nature. In MOOTW, the ROE are usually nonlethal in nature and should closely resemble the standing rules of engagement (SROE).

LETHAL VERSUS NONLETHAL RULES OF ENGAGEMENT

K-3. The type of ROE depends on the type of mission. During wartime, the ROE are usually lethal in nature. In MOOTW, the ROE are usually nonlethal in nature and should closely resemble the standing rules of engagement (SROE).

WARTIME RULES OF ENGAGEMENT

K-4. In general, ROE during wartime permit U.S. forces to engage all identified enemy targets, regardless of whether those targets represent an actual or immediate threat. Wartime ROE are familiar to units and Soldiers because battle-focused training concentrates on combat tasks.

MOOTW RULES OF ENGAGEMENT

K-5. During MOOTW, the SROE merely permit engagement in individual, unit, or national self-defense. The ROE in MOOTW are generally more restrictive, detailed, and sensitive to political concerns than they are in wartime. Restrained, judicious use of force is necessary; excessive force undermines the legitimacy of the operation and jeopardizes political objectives. MOOTW ROE considerations may include—
- Balancing force protection with potential harm to innocent civilians or nonmilitary areas.

Appendix K

- Balancing mission accomplishment with political considerations.
- Protecting evacuees while not having the authority to preempt hostile actions by proactive military measures.
- Enabling Soldiers to balance initiative and restraint properly.
- Determining the extent to which Soldiers may protect LN or third nation civilians.
- Using riot-control agents.
- Using PSYOP.

K-6. In multinational operations, developing ROE acceptable to all troop-contributing nations is important. Responsiveness to changing ROE requirements is also important.

K-7. The principles of necessity and proportionality help define the peacetime justification to use force in self-defense and are thus fundamental to understanding ROE for MOOTW. The principle of necessity permits friendly forces to engage only those forces committing hostile acts or clearly demonstrating hostile intent. This formulation—a restrictive rule for the use of force—captures the essence of peacetime necessity under international law. The rule of necessity applies to individuals, as well as to military units or sovereign states.

> In 1840, Secretary of State Daniel Webster described the essence of the necessity rule as the use of force in self-defense justified only in cases in which "the necessity of that self-defense is instant, overwhelming and leaving no choice of means and no moment for deliberation."

K-8. A hostile act is an attack or other use of force. Hostile intent "is the threat of imminent use of force." ROE take into consideration the important distinction between "hostile act" and "hostile intent." ROE describe specific behaviors as hostile acts or equate particular objective characteristics with hostile intent. For instance, the ROE might define a foreign uniformed soldier aiming a machine-gun from behind a prepared firing position as a clear demonstration of hostile intent, regardless of whether that soldier truly intends to harm U.S. forces.

K-9. The principle of proportionality requires that the force is reasonable in intensity, duration, and magnitude. The type of force should be based on all available facts known to the commander at the time to counter the hostile act or hostile intent decisively and to ensure the continued safety of U.S. forces. As with necessity, the proportionality principle reflects an ancient international legal norm.

PSYCHOLOGICAL IMPACT

K-10. ROE are legal, political, and diplomatic in nature. These fundamental ideas can have a psychological effect when ROE are observed and when they are not. The PSYOP Soldier needs to understand ROE fully and the effects the execution of ROE has on the various TAs within the operational area. The PSYOP Soldier should assist the SJA and the commander to develop the ROE by advising them on the psychological impact of certain actions based on culture and traditions.

K-11. Violations of the ROE can cause animosity and negativity on the part of the TAs toward U.S. forces. TAs hostile to U.S. forces may attempt to use ROE violations to further their cause. PSYOP Soldiers should be prepared to minimize repercussions through carefully coordinated messages. Reinforcing previous accomplishments and assistance provided by U.S. forces is an example of the type of message that can help sustain a positive attitude of the TAs.

K-12. The U.S. forces' successful compliance with the ROE can be a basis for furthering acceptance and trust by the TAs. PSYOP Soldiers can emphasize the respect for protected sites, such as religious shrines, hospitals, and schools. They can also emphasize the respect for the TA, its culture, its history, and its future.

RULES OF INTERACTION

K-13. ROI apply to the human dimension of S&RO. They spell out with whom, under what circumstances, and to what extent Soldiers may interact with other forces and the civilian populace. ROI, when applied with good interpersonal communication (IPC) skills, improve the Soldier's ability to accomplish the mission while reducing possible hostile confrontations. ROI founded on firm ROE provide the Soldier with the tools to address unconventional threats, such as political friction, ideologies, cultural idiosyncrasies, and religious beliefs and rituals. ROI must be regionally and culturally specific. They lay the foundation for successful relationships with the myriad of factions and individuals who play critical roles in operations. ROI encompass an array of interpersonal communication skills, such as persuasion and negotiation.

K-14. ROI enhance the Soldier's survivability; therefore, their reinforcement is critical. PSYOP planners contribute to the development of ROI by providing culture- and TA-specific expertise. Participation in the ROI development process can mitigate the potential negative impact of Soldiers violating the accepted standards of behavior, dress, or speech in the given AO.

K-15. Restrictions imposed by ROI may have significant impact on PSYOP. ROI may dictate TA or media selection, as well as time and manner of dissemination. Input in planning proposed ROI will help minimize restrictions on PSYOP's ability to access TAs.

This page intentionally left blank.

Glossary

SECTION I – ACRONYMS AND ABBREVIATIONS

4WD	four-wheel drive
AAR	after-action report/review
ADA	air defense artillery
ADP	automated data processing
ADVON	advanced echelon
AFSOC	Air Force Special Operations Command
AI	area of interest
AIF	Anti-Iraqi Forces
ALS	aerial loudspeaker system
AM	amplitude modulation
AMC	Air Mobility Command
AO	area of operations
AOR	area of responsibility
APFT	Army Physical Fitness Test
AR	Army regulation
ARSOF	Army special operations forces
ASAP	as soon as possible
ASCC	Army Service component command
ASP	ammunition supply point
ATO	air tasking order
AZ	azimuth
BBC	British Broadcasting Corporation
BCT	brigade combat team
BFV	Bradley Fighting Vehicle
BII	basic issue item
BMNT	begin morning nautical twilight
BOS	battlefield operating system
C2	command and control
C4I	command, control, communications, computers, and intelligence
CA	Civil Affairs
CAG	Civil Affairs group
CAM	chemical agent monitor
CAP	Civic Action Program
CAT	Civil Affairs team
CCIR	commander's critical information requirements
CD	compact disc

Glossary

CDR	commander
CI	civilian internee
CJCS	Chairman of the Joint Chiefs of Staff
CJCSI	Chairman of the Joint Chiefs of Staff Instruction
CJPOTF	combined joint Psychological Operations task force
CJTF	combined joint task force/commander, joint task force
CLS	combat lifesaver
cm2	square centimeter
CMO	civil-military operations
COA	course of action
COB	civilian on the battlefield
COCOM	combatant command
COMSEC	communications security
CONEX	container express
CONOPS	concept of operations
CONUS	continental United States
COP	common operational picture
CPOTF	combined Psychological Operations task force
CPT	captain
CS	combat support
CSM	command sergeant major
CSS	combat service support
DA	direct action
DAPS	Deployable Audio Production System
DC	dislocated civilian
DENTCAP	Dental Civic Action Project
DEPORD	deployment order
DET	detachment
DIRLAUTH	direct liaison authorized
DLPT	Defense Language Proficiency Test
DMS	demobilization station
DP	decision point
DPPC	Deployable Print Production Center
DS	direct support
DTG	date-time group
DVDS	Digital Video Distribution System
DZ	drop zone
EEFI	essential elements of friendly information
EENT	end evening nautical twilight
E-mail	electronic mail

EMS	electronic maintenance shop
EPW	enemy prisoner of war
EPW/CI	enemy prisoner of war/civilian internee
FABS	Flyaway Broadcast System
FAX	facsimile
FDC	fire direction center
FECC	fire and effects coordination cell
FFEO	face-to-face encounter outline
FFIR	friendly forces information requirement
FHA	foreign humanitarian assistance
FID	foreign internal defense
FM	field manual; frequency modulation
FO	forward observer
FOL	family of loudspeakers
FRAGO	fragmentary order
FSCOORD	fire support coordinator
FSE	fire support element
FTP	file transfer protocol
G-1	Deputy/Assistant Chief of Staff for Personnel
G-2	Deputy/Assistant Chief of Staff for Intelligence
G-3	Deputy/Assistant Chief of Staff for Operations and Plans
G-4	Deputy/Assistant Chief of Staff for Logistics
G-6	Deputy/Assistant Chief of Staff, Command, Control, Communications, and Computer Operations (C4 Ops)
G-7	Deputy/Assistant Chief of Staff for Information Operations
G-9	Deputy/Assistant Chief of Staff for Civil-Military Operations
GCC	geographic combatant commander
GPS	global positioning system
GRM	graduated-response measure
GS	general support
GSA	General Services Administration
GSR	general support-reinforcing
HF	high frequency
HFM	high-frequency module
HHC	headquarters and headquarters company
HIC	high intensity conflict
HMMWV	high mobility multipurpose wheeled vehicle
HQ	headquarters
HSC	headquarters and support company
HUMINT	human intelligence
Hz	hertz

IAD	immediate action drill
IAW	in accordance with
ICRC	International Committee of the Red Cross
IED	improvised explosive device
IFV	infantry fighting vehicle
ILRT	Interagency Language Round Table
IMPAC	International Merchant Purchase Authorization Card
INFOSYS	information systems
IO	information operations
IOCOORD	Information Operations Coordinator
IPB	intelligence preparation of the battlefield
IPC	interpersonal communication
IR	information requirement
I/R	internment/resettlement
ISR	intelligence, surveillance, and reconnaissance
J-1	Manpower and Personnel Directorate
J-2	Intelligence Directorate
J-3	Operations Directorate
J-4	Logistics Directorate
J-5	Civil Affairs Directorate
J-6	Command, Control, Communications, and Computer Systems Directorate
JCET	joint combined exercise for training
JCMOTF	joint civil-military operations task force
JCS	Joint Chiefs of Staff
JFACC	joint force air component commander
JFC	joint force commander
JFLCC	joint force land component commander
JFMCC	joint force maritime component commander
JFSOCC	joint force special operations component commander
JIF	joint interrogation facility
JOA	joint operations area
JP	joint publication
JPOTF	joint Psychological Operations task force
JSCP	Joint Strategic Capabilities Plan
JSOTF	joint special operations task force
JTF	joint task force
kHz	kilohertz
kmph	kilometers per hour
kt	knot
kW	kilowatt

Glossary

LAN	local area network
LBE	load-bearing equipment
LD	line of departure
LFM	low-frequency module
LN	local nationals
LNO	liaison officer
LOGSTAT	logistics status
LOP	line of persuasion
LSS	loudspeaker systems
LZ	landing zone
MAJ	major
MBITR	Multiband Intra-Team Radio
MDMP	military decision-making process
MEB	Marine expeditionary brigade
MEDCAP	medical civic action program
MEDEVAC	medical evacuation
MEF	Marine expeditionary force
METT-TC	mission, enemy, terrain and weather, troops and support available, time available, civil considerations
MHz	megahertz
MI	military intelligence
mm	millimeter
MOC	media operations complex
MOE	measure of effectiveness
MOOTW	military operations other than war
MOS	military occupational specialty
MP	military police
MPAD	mobile public affairs detachment
mpg	miles per gallon
mph	miles per hour
MPLS	man-portable loudspeaker
MSC	major support command
MSR	main support route
MTOE	modified table of organization and equipment
MTW	major theater war
NATO	North Atlantic Treaty Organization
NBC	nuclear, biological, and chemical
NCO	noncommissioned officer
NCOIC	noncommissioned officer in charge
NEO	noncombatant evacuation operation
NGO	nongovernmental organization

NIPRNET	Nonsecure Internet Protocol Router Network
NLT	not later than
NM	nautical mile
NSN	National Stock Number
NTSC	National Television Systems Committee
NVG	night vision goggle
OAKOC	observation and fields of fire, avenues of approach, key terrain, obstacles, and cover and concealment
OCONUS	outside the continental United States
OD	other detainee
ODA	operational detachment A
OGA	other government agency
OIC	officer in charge
OPCON	operational control
OPLAN	operation plan
OPORD	operation order
OPSEC	operations security
ORP	objective rallying point
PAL	phase alternation line
PAMT	Portable Amplitude Module Transmitter
PAO	Public Affairs Office
PAW	product/action work sheet
PDB	Psychological Operations dissemination battalion
PDC	Psychological Operations development center
PDD	Psychological Operations development detachment
PDS	product distribution system
PDT	Psychological Operations development team
PDW	Product Development Workstation
PDW-L	Product Development Workstation-Light
PERSTAT	personnel status
PFC	private first class
PFMT	Portable Frequency Module Transmitter
PIR	priority intelligence requirements
PMCS	preventive maintenance checks and services
PO	Psychological Operations objective
POAS	Psychological Operations automated system
POAT	Psychological Operations assessment team
POB	Psychological Operations battalion
POC	point of contact
POG	Psychological Operations group
POL	petroleum, oils, and lubricants

POMR	postoperations maintenance and recovery
POTF	Psychological Operations task force
POV	privately owned vehicle
PPD	plans and programs detachment
PPT	plans and programs team
PSE	Psychological Operations support element
PSYACT	Psychological Operations action
PSYOP	Psychological Operations
PTA	potential target audience
PTAL	potential target audience list
PTM	Psychological Operations transmission matrix
PZ	pickup zone
QRF	quick-reaction force
R	Reinforcing
RC	Reserve Component
RFI	request for information
ROE	rules of engagement
ROI	rules of interaction
RP	retained person
RTO	radio/telephone operator
S-1	personnel staff officer
S-2	intelligence staff officer
S-3	operations staff officer
S-4	logistics staff officer
S-6	command, control, communications, and computer operations (C4 Ops) officer
S-7	information operations staff officer
S-9	civil-military operations staff officer
S&RO	stability and reconstruction operations
SCAME	source, content, audience, media, and effects
SCW	series concept work sheet
SDW	series dissemination work sheet
SecDef	Secretary of Defense
SEM	series execution matrix
SES	series executive summary
SF	Special Forces
SFC	sergeant first class
SFODA	Special Forces operational detachment A
SGT	Sergeant
SINCGARS	single-channel ground and airborne radio system
SIPRNET	SECRET Internet Protocol Router Network

Glossary

SITREP	situation report
SJA	Staff Judge Advocate
SO	special operations
SOC	special operations command
SOF	special operations forces
SOMS–B	Special Operations Media System–Broadcast
SOP	standing operating procedure
SOR	statement of requirement
SOSB	special operations support battalion
SOSCOM	special operations support command
SOTSE	special operations theater support element
SP	start point
SPC	Specialist
SPO	supporting Psychological Operations objective
SPOTREP	spot report
SPP	supporting Psychological Operations program
sq	Square
SROE	standing rules of engagement
SSD	strategic studies detachment
SSG	staff sergeant
STANAG	standardization agreement
SWO	staff weather officer
TA	target audience
TAA	target audience analysis
TAAD	target audience analysis detachment
TAAP	target audience analysis process
TAAT	target audience analysis team
TAAW	target audience analysis work sheet
TACON	tactical control
TACP	tactical air control party
TACSOP	tactical standing operating procedure
TALO	theater airlift liaison officer
T-ASA	Television Audio Support Activity
TCP	traffic control point
TDA	Table of Distribution and Allowance
TED	testing and evaluation detachment
TF	task force
TLP	troop-leading procedures
TM	technical manual
TOC	tactical operations center

TOE	table of organization and equipment
TPC	tactical Psychological Operations company
TPD	tactical Psychological Operations detachment
TPDD	tactical Psychological Operations development detachment
TPFDD	time-phased force and deployment data
TPT	tactical Psychological Operations team
TSC	Theater Support Command
TS/SCI	Top Secret/sensitive compartmented information
TV	television
UEx	unit of employment (division)
UEy	unit of employment (corps)
UIC	unit identification code
ULLS	Unit-Level Logistics System
U.S.	United States
USACAPOC	United States Army Civil Affairs and Psychological Operations Command
USAF	United States Air Force
USAJFKSWCS	United States Army John F. Kennedy Special Warfare Center and School
USASOC	United States Army Special Operations Command
USSOCOM	United States Special Operations Command
UTM	universal transverse mercator
UW	unconventional warfare
UXO	unexploded explosive ordnance
VIP	very important person
WARNO	warning order
WMD	weapons of mass destruction
WSADS	wind supported aerial delivery system
XO	executive officer

SECTION II – TERMS

adversary

Anyone who contends with, opposes, or acts against one's interest. An adversary is not necessarily an enemy.

area of responsibility

The geographical area associated with a combatant command within which a combatant commander has authority to plan and conduct operations. (JP 1-02)

asset (intelligence)

Any resource—person, group, relationship, instrument, installation, or supply—at the disposition of an intelligence organization for use in an operational or support role. Often used with a qualifying term such as agent asset or propaganda asset. (JP 1-02)

assign

To detail individuals to specific duties or functions where such duties or functions are primary and/or relatively permanent. (JP 1-02)

attach

The detailing of individuals to specific functions where such functions are secondary or relatively temporary, e.g., attached for quarters and rations; attached for flying duty. (JP 1-02, definition 2)

campaign

A series of related military operations aimed at accomplishing a strategic or operational objective within a given time and space. (JP 1-02)

chain of command

The succession of commanding officers from a superior to a subordinate through which command is exercised. Also called command channel. (JP 1-02)

Civil Affairs

Designated Active and Reserve component forces and units organized, trained, and equipped specifically to conduct civil affairs activities and to support civil-military operations. (JP 1-02)

coalition

An ad hoc arrangement between two or more nations for common action. (JP 1-02)

combatant command

A unified or specified command with a broad continuing mission under a single commander established and so designated by the President, through the Secretary of Defense and with the advice and assistance of the Chairman of the Joint Chiefs of Staff. Combatant commands typically have geographic or functional responsibilities. (JP 1-02)

concept of operations

A verbal or graphic statement, in broad outline, of a commander's assumptions or intent in regard to an operation or series of operations. The concept of operations frequently is embodied in campaign plans and operation plans; in the latter case, particularly when the plans cover a series of connected operations to be carried out simultaneously or in succession. The concept is designed to give an overall picture of the operation. It is included primarily for additional clarity of purpose. (JP 1-02)

conditions

Those external elements that affect a target audience but over which they have little or no control.

Glossary

contingency

An emergency involving military forces caused by natural disasters, terrorists, subversives, or by required military operations. Due to the uncertainty of the situation, contingencies require plans, rapid response, and special procedures to ensure the safety and readiness of personnel, installations, and equipment. (JP 1-02)

conventional forces

1. Those forces capable of conducting operations using nonnuclear weapons. 2. Those forces other than designated special operations forces. (JP 1-02)

counterpropaganda

Series designed to nullify propaganda or mitigate its effects.

crisis

An incident or situation involving a threat to the United States, its territories, citizens, military forces, possessions, or vital interests that develops rapidly and creates a condition of such diplomatic, economic, political, or military importance that commitment of U.S. military forces and resources is contemplated in order to achieve national objectives. (JP 1-02)

critical information

Specific facts about friendly intentions, capabilities, and activities vitally needed by adversaries for them to plan and act effectively so as to guarantee failure or unacceptable consequences for friendly mission accomplishment. (JP 1-02)

data

Representation of facts, concepts, or instructions in a formalized manner suitable for communication, interpretation, or processing by humans or by automatic means. Any representations such as characters or analog quantities to which meaning is or might be assigned. (JP 1-02)

deception

Those measures designed to mislead the enemy by manipulation, distortion, or falsification of evidence to induce the enemy to react in a manner prejudicial to the enemy's interests. (JP 1-02)

dissemination

The delivery of PSYOP series directly to the target audience.

distribution

The movement of completed products from the production source to the point of dissemination. This task may include the temporary physical or electronic storage of PSYOP products at intermediate locations.

force multiplier

A capability that, when added to and employed by a combat force, significantly increases the combat potential of that force and thus enhances the probability of successful mission accomplishment. (JP 1-02)

force protection

Actions taken to prevent or mitigate hostile actions against Department of Defense personnel (to include family members), resources, facilities, and critical information. These actions conserve the force's fighting potential so it can be applied at the decisive time and place and incorporate the coordinated and synchronized offensive and defensive measures to enable the effective employment of the joint force while degrading opportunities for the enemy. Force protection does not include actions to defeat the enemy or protect against accidents, weather, or disease. (JP 1-02)

foreign internal defense

Participation by civilian and military agencies of a government in any of the action programs taken by another government or designated organization to free and protect its society from subversion, lawlessness, and insurgency. (JP 1-02)

Glossary

functional component command

A command normally, but not necessarily, composed of forces of two or more Military Departments which may be established across the range of military operations to perform particular operational missions that may be of short duration or may extend over a period of time. (JP 1-02)

human intelligence

A category of intelligence derived from information collected and provided by human sources. (JP 1-02)

impact indicators

Observable events of intelligence related to the PSYOP effort that aid in determining the degree to which SPOs are being achieved. All impact indicators are either positive or negative and contain a direct or indirect association.

insurgency

An organized movement aimed at the overthrow of a constituted government through use of subversion and armed conflict. (JP 1-02)

joint

Connotes activities, operations, organizations, etc., in which elements of two or more Military Departments participate. (JP 1-02)

joint force

A general term applied to a force composed of significant elements, assigned or attached, of two or more Military Departments operating under a single joint force commander. (JP 1-02)

joint operations

A general term to describe military actions conducted by joint forces or by Service forces in relationships (e.g., support, coordinating authority) which, of themselves, do not create joint forces. (JP 1-02)

joint Psychological Operations task force

A joint special operations task force composed of headquarters and operational assets. It assists the joint force commander in developing strategic, operational, and tactical psychological operations plans for a theater campaign or other operations. Mission requirements will determine its composition and assigned or attached units to support the joint task force commander. (JP 1-02)

joint task force

A joint force that is constituted and so designated by the Secretary of Defense, a combatant commander, a subunified commander, or an existing joint task force commander. (JP 1-02)

line of persuasion

An argument used to obtain a desired behavior or attitude from the TA.

local nationals

These include town and city dwellers, farmers and other rural dwellers, and nomads in the AO.

measure of effectiveness

Tools used to measure results achieved in the overall mission and execution of assigned tasks. Measures of effectiveness are a prerequisite to the performance of combat assessment. (JP 1-02)

media

Transmitters of information and Psychological Operations products. (FM 3-05.30)

multinational operations

A collective term to describe military actions conducted by forces of two or more nations, usually undertaken within the structure of a coalition or alliance. (JP 1-02)

Glossary

national objectives

The aims, derived from national goals and interests, toward which a national policy or strategy is directed and efforts and resources of the nation are applied. (JP 1-02)

nongovernmental organizations

Transnational organizations of private citizens that maintain a consultative status with the Economic and Social Council of the United Nations. Nongovernmental organizations may be professional associations, foundations, multinational businesses, or simply groups with a common interest in humanitarian assistance activities (development and relief). (JP 1-02)

operational control

Command authority that may be exercised by commanders at any at any echelon at or below the level of combatant command. Operational control is inherent in combatant command (command authority) and may be delegated within the command. When forces are transferred between combatant commands, the command relationship the gaining commander will exercise (and the losing commander will relinquish) over these forces must be specified by the Secretary of Defense. Operational control is the authority to perform those functions of command over subordinate forces involving organizing and employing commands and forces, assigning tasks, designating objectives, and giving authoritative direction necessary to accomplish the mission. Operational control includes authoritative direction over all aspects of military operations and joint training necessary to accomplish missions assigned to the command. Operational control should be exercised through the commanders of subordinate organizations. Normally this authority is exercised through subordinate joint force commanders and Service and/or functional component commanders. Operational control normally provides full authority to organize commands and forces and to employ those forces as the commander in operational control considers necessary to accomplish assigned missions; it does not, in and of itself, include authoritative direction for logistics or matters of administration, discipline, internal organization, or unit training. (JP 1-02)

operations security

A process of identifying critical information and subsequently analyzing friendly actions attendant to military operations and other activities to: a. identify those actions that can be observed by adversary intelligence systems; b. determine indicators that hostile intelligence systems might obtain that could be interpreted or pieced together to derive critical information in time to be useful to adversaries; and c. select and execute measures that eliminate or reduce to an acceptable level the vulnerabilities of friendly actions to adversary exploitation. (JP 1-02)

opponent

An antagonistic force or organization that counters mission accomplishment by military means.

peace operations

A broad term that encompasses peacekeeping operations and peace enforcement operations conducted in support of diplomatic efforts to establish and maintain peace. (JP 1-02)

priority intelligence requirements

Those intelligence requirements for which a commander has an anticipated and stated priority in the task of planning and decision making. (JP 1-02)

production

The transformation of approved PSYOP product prototypes into various media forms that are compatible.

propaganda

Any form of communication in support of national objectives designed to influence the opinions, emotions, attitudes, or behavior of any group in order to benefit the sponsor, either directly or indirectly. (JP 1-02) By policy and practice, PSYOP forces use the term to indicate PSYOP, or information activities, conducted by enemy or hostile forces, elements, or groups against U.S. or coalition forces.

Glossary

Psychological Operations

Planned operations to convey selected information and indicators to foreign audiences to influence their emotions, motives, objective reasoning, and ultimately the behavior of foreign governments, organizations, groups, and individuals. The purpose of psychological operations is to induce or reinforce foreign attitudes and behavior favorable to the originator's objectives. (JP 1-02)

Psychological Operations action

An action conducted by non-PSYOP personnel that is planned primarily to affect the behavior of a TA.

Psychological Operations assessment team

A small, tailored team (approximately 4 to 12 personnel) that consists of psychological operations planners and product distribution/dissemination and logistic specialists. The team is deployed to theater at the request of the combatant commander to assess the situation, develop psychological operations objectives, and recommend the appropriate level of support to accomplish the mission. (JP 1-02)

Psychological Operations development center

The PDC is the central core of a POTF and mainly responsible for conducting the PSYOP process. The PDC consists of a target audience analysis detachment, a test and evaluation detachment, a plans and programs detachment, and a product development detachment.

Psychological Operations objective

A statement of measurable response that reflects the desired behavioral change of foreign target audiences (TAs) as a result of Psychological Operations (PSYOP).

Psychological Operations support element

A tailored element that can provide limited psychological operations support. Psychological operations support elements do not contain organic command and control capability; therefore, command relationships must be clearly defined. The size, composition and capability of the psychological operations support element are determined by the requirements of the supported commander. A psychological operations support element is not designed to provide full-spectrum psychological operations capability; reachback is critical for its mission success. (JP 1-02)

Psychological Operations task force

A task force composed of PSYOP units formed to carry out a specific psychological operation or to prosecute PSYOP in support of a theater campaign or other operations. The Psychological Operations task force may have conventional non-psychological operations units assigned or attached to support the conduct of specific missions. The Psychological Operations task force commander is usually a joint task force component commander.

PSYOP annex/tab

Consists of PSYOP objectives, supporting PSYOP objectives, PTAL, and MOE developed to aid the supported commander accomplish his mission.

PSYOP enabling action

Action required of non-PSYOP units or non-DOD agencies in order to facilitate or enable execution of a PSYOP plan developed to support a commander, joint task force, a commander in chief, or other non-DOD agency.

PSYOP OPLAN/OPORD

The POTF/PSE OPLAN/OPORD articulates how the PSYOP objectives are going to be accomplished by all the subordinate elements (even those detached from the POTF/PSE and attached to a maneuver unit). This OPLAN/OPORD is more complete than the annex or tab written as part of the supported unit's OPLAN/OPORD. This plan must be centrally controlled and promulgated to all PSYOP units involved in the operation in order to ensure that the plan is being executed at all levels.

PSYOP process

A seven-phase that must be completed to conduct PSYOP. It consists of planning, target audience analysis, series development, product development and design, approval, production, distribution, dissemination, and evaluation.

PSYOP product

Any audio, visual, or audiovisual communication intended to change the behavior of foreign target audiences.

PSYOP program

All the supporting PSYOP programs and their subordinate series (PSYOP products and actions) that support the accomplishment of one PSYOP objective. The term "PSYOP program" has also been used to refer to SecDef-approved themes and objectives.

refugee

A person who, by reason of real or imagined danger, has left their home country or country of their nationality and is unwilling or unable to return. (JP 1-02)

request for information

Any specific time-sensitive ad hoc requirement for intelligence information or products to support an ongoing crisis or operation not necessarily related to standing requirements or scheduled intelligence production. A request for information can be initiated to respond to operational requirements and will be validated in accordance with the theater command's procedures. (JP 1-02, definition 1)

rules of interaction

Rules that articulate with whom, under what circumstances, and to what extent soldiers may interact with other forces and the civilian populace.

SCAME

The acronym used to remember the steps in analyzing propaganda. The letters stand for **s**ource, **c**ontent, **a**udience, **m**edia, and **e**ffects.

series

All Psychological Operations (PSYOP) products and actions directed at a single target audience (TA) in support of a specific supporting Psychological Operations objective (SPO).

supported commander

The commander having primary responsibility for all aspects of a task assigned by the Joint Strategic Capabilities Plan or other joint operation planning authority. In the context of joint operation planning, this term refers to the commander who prepares operation plans or operation orders in response to requirements of the Chairman of the Joint Chiefs of Staff. (JP 1-02, definition 1)

supporting PSYOP program

All actions and products developed in support of a single supporting PSYOP objective.

symbol

A visual, audio, or audiovisual means, having cultural or contextual significance to the target audience, used to convey a line of persuasion.

tactical control

Command authority over assigned or attached forces or commands, or military capability or forces made available for tasking, that is limited to the detailed direction and control of movements or maneuvers within the operational area necessary to accomplish missions or tasks assigned. Tactical control is inherent in operational control. Tactical control may be delegated to, and exercised at any level at or below, the level of combatant command. When forces are transferred between combatant commands, the command relationship the gaining commander will exercise (and the losing commander will relinquish) over these forces must be specified by the Secretary of Defense. Tactical control provides sufficient authority for controlling and directing the application of force or tactical use of combat support assets within the assigned mission or task. (JP 1-02)

tactical Psychological Operations company

PSYOP unit that normally provides Psychological Operations (PSYOP) support to a division (high intensity conflict) or can support a brigade-sized element (S&RO).

tactical Psychological Operations team

Psychological Operations (PSYOP) unit that normally provides PSYOP support to a battalion (combat operations) or can support a company or Special Forces operational detachment A team-sized unit (S&RO).

target audience analysis

A detailed, systematic examination of Psychological Operations (PSYOP)-relevant information to select target audiences (TAs) that can accomplish a given supporting Psychological Operations objective (SPO).

theme

An overarching subject, topic, or idea. Is often from policy makers and establishes the parameters for the conduct of Psychological Operations (PSYOP).

threat

The ability of an enemy or potential enemy to limit, neutralize, or destroy the effectiveness of a current or projected mission, organization, or item of equipment. (TRADOC Regulation 381-1)

unconventional warfare

A broad spectrum of military and paramilitary operations, normally of long duration, predominantly conducted through, with, or by indigenous or surrogate forces who are organized, trained, equipped, supported, and directed in varying degrees by an external source. It includes, but is not limited to, guerrilla warfare, subversion, sabotage, intelligence activities, and unconventional assisted recovery. (JP 1-02)

References

AR 190-8. *Enemy Prisoners of War, Retained Personnel, Civilian Internees and Other Detainees.* 1 October 1997.

CJCSI 3110.05C. *Joint Psychological Operations Supplement to the Joint Strategic Capabilities Plan.* FY 2002. 18 July 2003.

CJCSI 3121.01A. *Standing Rules of Engagement for U.S. Forces.* 15 January 2000.

DA Form 1594. *Daily Staff Journal or Duty Officer's Log.*

DA Form 2404. *Equipment Inspection and Maintenance Worksheet.*

DA Form 5988-E. *Equipment Inspection Maintenance Worksheet (EGA).*

DOD Directive 5111.10. *Assistant Secretary of Defense for Special Operations and Low-Intensity Conflict (ASD[SO/LIC]).* 22 March 1995.

FM 1. *The Army.* 14 June 2005.

FM 2-0. *Intelligence.* 17 May 2004.

FM 3-0. *Operations.* 14 June 2001.

FM 3-05.30. *Psychological Operations.* 15 April 2005.

FM 3-05.102. *Army Special Operations Forces Intelligence.* 31 August 2001.

FM 3-05.201. *Special Forces Unconventional Warfare Operations.* 30 April 2003.

FM 3-05.301. *Psychological Operations Tactics, Techniques, and Procedures.* 31 December 2003.

FM 3-07. *Stability Operations and Support Operations.* 20 February 2003.

FM 3-13. *Information Operations: Doctrine, Tactics, Techniques, and Procedures.* 28 November 2003.

FM 3-19.40. *Military Police Internment/Resettlement Operations.* 1 August 2001.

FM 3-25.26. *Map Reading and Land Navigation.* 18 January 2005.

FM 4-0. *Combat Service Support.* 29 August 2003.

FM 5-0. *Army Planning and Orders Production.* 20 January 2005.

FM 6-0. *Mission Command: Command and Control of Army Forces.* 11 August 2003.

FM 20-3. *Camouflage, Concealment, and Decoys.* 30 August 1999.

FM 27-10. *The Law of Land Warfare.* 18 July 1956, with Change 1, 15 July 1976.

FM 34-2. *Collection Management and Synchronization Planning.* 8 March 1994.

FM 34-130. *Intelligence Preparation of the Battlefield.* 8 July 1994.

FM 100-7. *Decisive Force: The Army in Theater Operations.* 31 May 1995.

FM 100-25. *Doctrine for Army Special Operations Forces.* 1 August 1999.

Geneva Convention, Paragraph 1, Article 3: The Hague Conventions. 12 August 1949.

JP 0-2. *Unified Action Armed Forces (UNAAF).* 10 July 2001.

JP 1-02. *Department of Defense Dictionary of Military and Associated Terms.* 12 April 2001 (Amended through 30 November 2004).

JP 3-0. *Doctrine for Joint Operations.* 10 September 2001.

JP 3-05. *Doctrine for Joint Special Operations.* 17 December 2003.

JP 3-07.1. *Joint Tactics, Techniques, and Procedures for Foreign Internal Defense (FID).* 30 April 2004.

JP 3-08. *Interagency Coordination During Joint Operations, Volumes I and II.* 9 October 1996.

JP 3-13. *Joint Doctrine for Information Operations.* 9 October 1998.

JP 3-53. *Doctrine for Joint Psychological Operations.* 5 September 2003.

References

JP 5-0. *Doctrine for Planning Joint Operations.* 13 April 1995.

JP 5-00.2. *Joint Task Force Planning Guidance and Procedures.* 13 January 1999.

NSDD 77. *Management of Public Diplomacy Relative to National Security.* 14 January 1983.

NSDD 130. *U.S. International Information Policy.* 6 March 1984.

PDD 68. *U. S. International Public Information (IPI).* 30 April 1999.

Psychological Operations Handbook: Equipment Types, Specifications, and Capabilities. February 2005.

TC 9-21-01. *Soldiers Improvised Explosive Device (IED) Awareness Guide: Iraq and Afghanistan Theaters of Operation.* 28 May 2004.

Index

A

access to the supported commander, 4-10, 7-1, 9-3 A-3, A-7

accessibility, 2-8, 6-5, 6-7, 6-12, 6-42, 7-16, B-4

advanced echelon (ADVON), 5-8, 7-7

after-action report/review (AAR), 9-5, J-4

Air Mobility Command (AMC), 6-41

Air Service component Command (ASCC), 3-3, 3-4, 9-3, 9-4

ammunition supply point (ASP), 9-3, A-3

Annex, PSYOP, 2-4

appeal, 6-6, 6-20, 6-38, 7-5, 7-14, 7-15, B-4, C-1, C-5, J-4

appendix, 2-4, 3-6, 4-2, 4-4, 4-5, 4-8, 5-6, 6-1, 6-3, 6-4, 6-18, 6-20, 6-33 through 6-37, 6-41, 7-3, E-1 through E-5, F-2

approval, 1-1, 1-4, 4-4, 4-5, 4-7, 4-11, 4-13, 4-14, 6-1, 6-2, 6-4, 6-18, 6-31 through 6-33, 6-36, 6-37, 7-2, A-2, C-4, E-2, E-4, F-2

approval authority, PSYOP, 1-4, A-2

argument, 6-6, 6-12, 6-14, 6-18, 6-20, 6-24, 6-26, 6-30, 6-48

authority, coordinating, 3-3, 3-4, 5-1, A-2

B

balance, 5-4, 6-24 through 6-26, K-1

board
  product review, 6-32
  series review, 6-11, 6-18

brief
  backbrief, 4-19
  confirmation, 4-19

briefing
  capabilities, F-1 through F-3
  commander's decision, 4-7, 4-11

C

change, 1-1, 1-4, 2-1, 4-10, 6-1, 6-2, 6-5 through 6-7, 6-11, 6-12, 6-14, 6-33, 6-44, 7-6, 7-16, 8-5, 8-7, D-4, D-5

civilian on the battlefield (COB), 7-4 through 7-6

civil-military operations (CMO), 7-6, 7-7, A-3

combatant command (COCOM), 1-4, 3-1, 3-2

command, and control (C2), 1-3, 2-1, 4-17, 4-18, 5-1, 5-4, 8-4, 8-8, C-2

command authority, 1-3, 3-2, 3-4

command relationships, 3-1, 3-2, 3-3, 3-6, 5-4, 6-33, 6-37, 7-2, F-2

commander's critical information requirements (CCIR), 4-4, 4-13, 8-3, 8-4, 8-7, A-5

commander's intent, vi, 4-1, 4-2, 4-5, 4-6, 4-13 through 4-15, 4-19, 5-3, 6-1, 7-2, 7-3, 7-21, 8-5, 8-6, A-1, A-5, A-7, H-8

COMMANDO SOLO, 6-40, 8-3, E-1

communications, 2-1, 2-2, 2-8, 3-1, 5-2, 5-6, 5-8, 7-11, 7-16, 7-20, 8-7, 9-5, 9-6, A-1 through A-7, C-2, C-5

conditions, 1-3, 2-3, 2-8, 4-19, 4-20, 5-5 through 5-7, 6-5, 6-6, 6-7, 6-24, 7-4 through 7-6, 7-9, 7-10, 7-17, 7-21, 8-5 through 8-7, 9-4, A-5, B-2 through B-4, C-4, I-1, I-10, I-14, J-1

coordination chain, 3-3 through 3-6, A-2, F-2

coordination, PSYOP, 3-3 through 3-6, 5-2, 9-2, A-2, F-2

core task, PSYOP, 1-1

counterpropaganda, 1-1, 7-7, 8-2, D-1, D-3, D-6

course of action (COA), 4-1, 4-2, 4-5 through 4-18, 5-6, 8-1, 8-2, 8-5, 8-6

D

deception, support, 4-6, 5-2, 6-2, 7-4 through 7-8, E-2

decision point (DP), 4-6, 6-12

Deployable Print Production Center (DPPC), 2-2, 5-3 through 5-5

development, product, 1-1, 2-2, 2-4, 2-5, 2-7, 5-6, 5-8, 6-18, 6-19, 6-32, C-5 through C-7

Digital Video Distribution System (DVDS), 5-1

dissemination, 1-1, 2-1, 2-2, 2-4, 5-4, 5-9, 5-10, 6-11 through 6-14, 6-18, 6-26, 6-33, 6-37, 6-40 through 6-43, 6-47, 7-2, 7-4, 7-5, 7-7, 7-9, 7-11 through 7-13, 7-16, 8-2 through 8-5, 8-7, A-2, A-3, C-2, D-2, D-3, D-5, D-7, E-1, E-5, G-1, H-1, H-9, H-10, K-2

dissemination PSYOP battalion, 2-1, 2-2, 5-1, 5-3, 5-4, 6-33, 8-3, 9-2

distribution, 1-1, 2-1, 2-4, 5-1, 5-3, 5-9, 6-18, 6-33, 6-37, 6-40, 6-41, 7-2, 9-2, B-4, E-1, E-2

E

electronic warfare, 6-35, 6-42

enemy prisoner of war (EPW), 7-10, 7-18, 8-6, A-3, A-5, C-1, G-3

essential elements of friendly information (EEFI), 8-4

Index

evaluation, 1-1, 2-1, 2-4, 4-6, 4-7, 4-11, 6-3, 6-43, 6-44, 6-46, 6-47, 8-1, 8-2, 8-7, 9-5, D-5, J-2

events, spontaneous, 6-18, 6-43, 6-44, 6-47, 8-7

eye direction, 6-24, 6-25

F

face-to-face encounter outline (FFEO), 6-22, 6-26 through 6-29, 7-16

facts and assumptions, 4-2, 4-4, 4-5, 7-20

fire support coordinator (FSCOORD), 7-10

Flyaway Broadcast System (FABS), 2-2

focus groups, 6-23, 6-24, 6-32, 6-43, D-6

foreign humanitarian assistance (FHA), 1-1

foreign internal defense (FID), 5-5, 7-7

force protection, 1-4, 2-7, 4-5, 6-42, 7-12, A-3, E-2, I-4, I-17, J-4, K-1

fragmentary order (FRAGO), 3-3, 3-4, 4-9, 4-11, 4-13, 4-14, 6-2, 6-33, 6-37, 7-3, A-5

friendly forces information requirement (FFIR), 8-3

functions, PSYOP, 2-1, 3-6, 5-3, 5-5 through 5-8, 8-1, 8-5, C-3

G

geographic combatant commander (GCC), 1-4, 2-1, 3-2, 3-4, A-2, C-1

I

impact indicators, 1-1, 5-7, 5-10, 6-3, 6-5, 6-8, 6-18, 6-43, 6-44, 6-46, 6-47, 7-1, 7-9, 7-20, 8-2, 8-7, B-3, D-5, D-7, E-5, G-1

improvised explosive device (IED), 7-7, I-18, I-19

index, PAW, 6-33, 6-36

information operations (IO), 1-3, 2-4, 3-4, 3-6, 4-2, 4-4, 5-2, 6-1, 6-35, A-3, D-1, E-1, E-4

information requirement (IR), 4-4, 4-18, 5-6, 5-7, 6-3, 6-14, 8-1 through 8-4, 8-8, A-5

intelligence preparation of the battlefield (IPB), 4-2, 4-4, 4-7, 4-9, 4-10, 4-18, 5-8, 8-1, 8-2, 8-4, 8-5

interagency coordination, A-4

internment/resettlement (I/R), 2-1 through 2-3, 2-5, 2-7, 7-18, C-1 through C-4, C-6, C-7, F-1

interpreter, 5-10, 7-2, 7-15, 7-17, 7-20, A-6, J-1 through J-6

J

Joint Chiefs of Staff (JCS), 1-4, 5-9

joint combined exercise for training (JCET), 5-9

joint force land component commander (JFLCC), 3-4, 3-5

joint Psychological Operations task force (JPOTF), vi, 3-4, 3-5, 5-4, A-2

joint special operations task force (JSOTF), 3-4, 3-5, 5-4, E-1

joint task force (JTF), 1-4, 3-1, 3-2, 3-4, 5-1, 5-4, 6-2, C-1, E-1

K

key communicator, 5-10, 7-1, 7-6, 7-13, 7-16, 7-20, 7-21, 8-6, B-1, B-3, B-8, C-6, H-1

L

layout, 5-8, 6-24 through 6-26, 9-6, C-2, C-3

level of PSYOP, 1-1, 1-3, 1-4, 2-1, 2-2, 2-4, 2-6, 2-8, 3-4 through 3-6, 4-1, 4-2, 4-20, 5-1, 5-3, 5-5, 5-6, 6-1 through 6-3, 6-35, 7-1, 7-3, 7-4, 8-5, 9-3, A-2, A-4, E-1, F-2

liaison officer (LNO), 3-6, A-4 through A-6

line of persuasion (LOP), 5-6, 5-7, 6-4 through 6-7, 6-11, 6-12, 6-14, 6-18, 6-20, 6-26, 6-43, 7-7, 7-18, 7-21, 8-6, D-6

logistics, 3-1 through 3-3, 5-2, 5-3, 5-5, 5-9, 7-1 through 7-3, 7-15, 8-1, 8-5, 8-6, 9-2 through 9-4, A-3, A-5, A-7, C-2, D-4, E-2, E-5, G-1, I-1, I-8

loudspeakers, 1-3, 2-4, 2-5, 2-7, 2-8, 3-3, 4-15, 4-16, 5-4, 5-6, 5-7, 5-9, 5-10, 6-2, 6-26, 6-42, 7-2, 7-4 through 7-11, 7-16, 7-20, 8-5, 9-4, 9-6, C-4, C-6, E-2, E-5, I-3

M

maintenance, 2-7, 5-2, 5-3, 5-8 through 5-10, 7-2, 7-19, 8-6, 9-1 through 9-7, E-5, G-1, I-1

measure of effectiveness (MOE), 1-1, 4-2, 5-6, 5-7, 6-1, 6-3, 6-8, 6-43, 6-44, 6-46, 6-47, 7-2, 8-2, 8-7, A-2, E-2, E-3, E-5, F-3, G-1

military decision-making process (MDMP), 2-3, 4-1 through 4-4, 4-8 through 4-10, 4-12, 4-13, 4-15, 4-20, 5-5, 5-6, 5-8, 5-9, 6-1, 7-2, 7-3, 8-1, 8-4

military operations other than war (MOOTW), 1-2, K-1

mission analysis, 4-2, 4-4 through 4-6, 4-10, 4-13, 4-15 through 4-18, 5-6, 5-8, 5-9

receipt of, 4-3, 4-10, 4-14

missions, principal PSYOP, 1-1

N

nongovernmental organization (NGO), 4-16, 6-41, 7-20, B-9, B-11, B-12

O

operational control (OPCON), 1-1, 3-1, 3-2, 5-3, A-5

operation order (OPORD), 2-4, 3-3, 3-4, 4-4, 4-8, 4-12, 4-14, 4-15, 4-18, 5-6, 6-1, 6-14, 7-3, 7-10, A-5, F-2

operation plan (OPLAN), 2-4, 3-3, 3-4, 6-14, A-5

orders preparation, 4-7, 4-8, 4-11, 4-16, 4-18

other government agency (OGA), 6-1, 6-39, 6-41

P

panel
  of experts, 6-23, 6-24
  of target audience, 6-23, 6-24
  of representatives, 6-23, 6-24, 6-34

peace operations, 7-1

personnel recovery, 9-5

planning, deliberate, 5-5

plans and programs team (PPT), 2-3, 5-5, 5-6

potential target audience (PTA), 4-2, 4-4, 4-5, 5-6, 5-9, 6-1 through 6-5, 7-4, 8-1, 8-2, 8-6, A-2, E-2, E-3

product/action work sheet (PAW), 6-18 through 6-24, 6-26, 6-28, 6-29, 6-32, 6-33, 6-36 through 6-39, 6-42, 7-16, 7-18

product
  design, 6-19, 6-26, 6-32
  development, 1-1, 2-2, 2-5, 2-7, 5-6, 5-8, 6-18, 6-19, 6-32, C-5, C-7
  numbers, 6-4, 6-36

product distribution system (PDS), 5-1, 6-41

propaganda, 1-1, 1-2, 2-3, 2-4, 5-6, 7-2, 7-7, 7-15 through 7-17, 8-2, 8-3, 8-7, B-3, C-1, C-7, D-1 through D-7, E-1, E-2, F-2

Psychological Operations assessment team (POAT), 3-6

Psychological Operations automated system (POAS), 6-41

Psychological Operations development team (PDT), 2-3, 2-4, 5-5, 5-7, 5-8

Psychological Operations transmission matrix (PTM), 6-33, 6-35

PSYOP action (PSYACT), 6-26, 6-32

PSYOP detachment, C-2

PSYOP development center (PDC), 2-3, 5-5, 5-6, 5-8

PSYOP group (POG), A-3

PSYOP objective (PO), 1-1, 4-5, 6-1, 6-2, 6-5, 6-20, 6-36

PSYOP support element (PSE), 2-3, 2-6, 3-6, 4-2, 5-1 through 5-6, 5-8 through 5-10, 6-1 through 6-5, 6-43, 8-2, G-1, H-1

PSYOP task force (POTF), vi, 1-3, 1-4, 2-1 through 2-4, 2-6, 3-4 through 3-6, 4-4, 5-1 through 5-10, 6-1 through 6-5, 8-2, 8-4, 9-3, 9-4, A-2 through A-4, C-1, C-4 through C-6, E-1, E-2, G-1

Q

questionnaires
  pretest, 6-18, 6-19, 6-29, 6-30, 6-33
  posttest, 6-18, 6-19, 6-29, 6-30, 6-33

R

reachback, 5-2, 5-4, C-4, E-1

recovery, 9-4 through 9-6

regional PSYOP battalion, 5-4

rehearsal, 4-7, 4-13, 4-14, 4-19, 6-27, 7-17, 7-21, F-1, I-9

request for information (RFI), 6-6, 6-35, 6-42, 8-4

risk, 3-6, 4-2, 4-4, 4-6, 4-7 through 4-9, 4-13, 7-13, H-9, H-10, I-18, J-3

roles, traditional, 1-2

rules of engagement (ROE), 4-5, 7-2, 7-7, 7-20, 7-21, 8-5, A-2, E-2, K-1, K-2

S

Secretary of Defense (SecDef), 1-4, 3-2, 4-4, 6-1, 6-3, E-1

security, 2-2, 2-7, 4-13, 4-16, 4-18, 5-2, 6-6, 6-37 through 6-39, 7-6 through 7-13, 7-16 through 7-21, 9-5, A-1, A-3, A-5 through A-8, B-1 through B-3, C-5, G-3, I-3, I-4, I-17 through I-19, J-2, J-3

series, 1-1, 1-4, 2-3 through 2-7, 3-4, 4-5, 4-6, 4-10, 4-14, 5-1, 5-4 through 5-10, 6-4 through 6-6, 6-8, 6-11, 6-12, 6-14, 6-17, 6-18, 6-20, 6-21, 6-30, 6-32, 6-33, 6-35 through 6-37, 6-39, 6-41 through 6-47, 7-1, 7-2, 7-4 through 7-7, 7-10, 7-18, 7-19, 7-21, 8-2, 8-7, 8-8, C-1, C-2, E-1, E-2, E-4, F-2, F-3, G-1, I-7

series concept work sheet (SCW), 6-11 through 6-14, 6-18, 6-20, 6-33

series dissemination work sheet (SDW), 6-11, 6-14 through 6-18, 6-20, 6-33, 6-37, 6-40, 6-41

series evaluation grid, 6-46, 6-47

series execution matrix (SEM), 4-6, 4-11, 6-17 through 6-21, 6-33, 6-34, 6-37, 6-39, 6-41, 6-43, E-2

series executive summary (SES), 6-33, 6-35, 6-36

situation report (SITREP), 5-1, 5-2, 5-7 through 5-9, 6-14, 7-20, 8-8, 9-2, A-2, A-3, E-2, E-5, G-1

source, content, audience, media, and effects (SCAME), 2-3, 5-6, 7-17, D-2 through D-7

Special Operations Media System–Broadcast (SOMS–B), 2-2, 8-3

special operations support battalion (SOSB), 9-3

special operations support command (SOSCOM), 9-3, 9-4

special operations theater support element (SOTSE), 1-3, 9-3, 9-4, E-2

stability and reconstruction operations (S&RO), 1-2, 2-1, 2-2, 2-4 through 2-6, 3-6, 5-1, 5-3, 5-10, 7-1, 7-6, 7-7, 7-19, 8-6, C-4, K-2

statement of requirement (SOR), 7-2, 9-3, 9-4, A-3

storyboard, 6-22, 6-26, 6-32, 6-39, 6-40

support
close, 3-1, 3-2
direct (DS), 2-2, 3-1 through 3-3, 7-1, 7-6, 9-1, 9-3
general (GS), 3-1 through 3-3, 9-1
mutual, 3-1, 3-2, 5-6, A-4, I-13

supply, classes, 9-2, E-2

supporting Psychological Operations objective (SPO), 1-1, 4-2, 4-5, 4-6, 6-1 through 6-5, 6-7, 6-8, 6-11, 6-12, 6-20, 6-29, 6-30, 6-33, 6-36, 6-43, 6-44, 6-47, 7-6, 8-2, 8-6, 8-7, A-3, E-2 through E-4, F-2

supporting PSYOP program, 5-8, 6-44, 6-47, C-4, E-2

susceptibility, 6-5, 6-7, 6-12

symbol, 5-6, 5-7, 6-4, 6-5, 6-7, 6-12, 6-20, 6-21, 6-43, 7-18, 8-6, 8-8, B-3, B-4, D-2, D-3

T

table of organization and equipment (TOE), 2-1, 2-7, A-5

tab, PSYOP, 2-4, 6-3, 6-4

tactical air control party (TACP), 7-10

tactical control (TACON), 1-1, 3-1 through 3-3

tactical Psychological Operations battalion, 2-1, 2-2, 5-1, 9-4

tactical Psychological Operations company (TPC), 2-1 through 2-3, 2-5, 2-8, 3-6, 5-1, 5-3, 5-4, 6-33, 7-5, C-2, C-5, E-1, E-2, F-2

tactical Psychological Operations detachment (TPD), 1-2, 2-2 through 2-7, 4-1, 4-13 through 4-15, 4-18, 5-1 through 5-10, 6-33, 7-1, 7-3, 7-17, 7-18, 9-2, A-2, C-2 through C-4, C-6, C-7, E-1, E-2, E-5, F-2, G-1

tactical Psychological Operations development detachment (TPDD), 1-2, 2-3 through 2-6, 5-1 through 5-8, 6-17, 6-18, 6-33, 6-40, 6-43, 7-6, 8-1, C-2, C-6, E-1, E-2, E-4

tactical Psychological Operations team (TPT), 1-2, 2-3 through 2-8, 4-1, 4-12 through 4-20, 5-1, 5-3, 5-6, 5-8 through 5-10, 6-2, 6-14, 6-33, 6-42, 7-1 through 7-21, 8-4, 8-6 through 8-8, 9-2, 9-5, A-2, A-3, B-1, C-4 through C-6, F-2, G-1, I-1 through I-5, I-12, I-14 through I-18

target audience analysis (TAA), 1-1, 2-3, 4-5, 4-6, 4-10, 5-6, 5-7, 6-4, 6-5, 6-43, 7-2, 7-4, 8-2, 8-6, 8-8, A-3, C-1, C-4, H-1

target audience analysis process (TAAP), 6-4, 6-5, 6-41

target audience analysis team (TAAT), 2-3, 2-4, 5-5 through 5-7, 6-5, 6-7, 8-2

target audience analysis work sheet (TAAW), 6-4 through 6-12, 6-18, 6-20, 6-21, 6-24, 6-30, 6-32, 6-33, 6-35

targeting, 1-1, 4-6, 5-6, 6-7, 6-14, 7-2, 8-2, A-2, D-3

tasks, specified and implied, 2-4, 4-2, 4-4, 4-15, 4-17, 7-21

Team, Country, 1-4, 5-9, 6-1

Television Audio Support Activity (T-ASA), 9-1

testing and evaluation, 2-1 pretesting and posttesting, 1-1, 5-6, 5-7, 5-10, 6-18 through 6-20, 6-23, 6-24, 6-29 through 6-33, 6-37 through 6-39, 6-42, 6-43, 6-47, 7-1, 7-6, 7-16, 7-18, 8-6, 8-8, C-1, C-5, C-7, D-6, E-5, G-1
spontaneous events, 6-18, 6-43, 6-44, 6-47, 8-7

theater airlift liaison officer (TALO), 7-10

theme, 1-4, 5-6, 6-1, 6-3, A-2, C-6, D-3, E-1, E-2

translation, 2-4, 5-7, 6-18, 6-37, 6-38, 7-17, 7-18, J-5, J-6

translator, 5-7, 5-8, 6-37, 6-38, 6-40, 7-11, 7-16, 7-21, C-4, C-7

troop-leading procedure (TLP), 4-1, 4-12 through 4-15, 4-18, 4-19

U

unconventional warfare (UW), 5-5, 7-6, 7-7

United States Army Civil Affairs and Psychological Operations Command (USACAPOC), 9-3

United States Army Special Operations Command (USASOC), 9-3, 9-4

United States Special Operations Command (USSOCOM), 3-2

V

vulnerabilities, 5-6, 6-5 through 6-7, 7-9, 8-5, 8-7, B-4, C-5, D-6

W

warning order (WARNO), 4-3 through 4-5, 4-7, 4-9 through 4-15

www.ingramcontent.com/pod-product-compliance
Lightning Source LLC
Chambersburg PA
CBHW081719100526
44591CB00016B/2426